Leviticus

Continental Commentaries

Old Testament

Genesis 1–11, Genesis 12–36, Genesis 37–50
Claus Westermann

1 and 2 Kings
Volkmar Fritz

Psalms 1–59, Psalms 60–150
Hans-Joachim Kraus

Theology of the Psalms
Hans-Joachim Kraus

Qoheleth
Norbert Lohfink

The Song of Songs
Othmar Keel

Isaiah 1–12, Isaiah 13–27, Isaiah 28–39
Hans Wildberger

Obadiah and Jonah
Hans Walter Wolff

Micah
Hans Walter Wolff

Haggai
Hans Walter Wolff

* * * *

New Testament

Matthew 1–7
Ulrich Luz

Galatians
Dieter Lührmann

Revelation
Jürgen Roloff

JACOB MILGROM

LEVITICUS

A BOOK OF RITUAL
AND ETHICS

A Continental Commentary

FORTRESS PRESS
MINNEAPOLIS

Cynthia Milgrom Corngold

in memoriam

LEVITICUS
A Book of Ritual and Ethics

Library of Congress Cataloging-in-Publication Data

Milgrom, Jacob, 1923-
  Leviticus : a book of ritual and ethics / Jacob Milgrom.
    p. cm. — (Continental commentaries)
  Includes bibliographical references and index.
  ISBN 0-8006-9514-3 (alk. paper)
  1. Bible. O.T. Leviticus—Commentaries. I. Title. II. Series.
BS1255.53.M55 2004
222'.1307--dc22
                            2004006956

The paper used in this publication meets the minimum requirements of American National Standard for Information Sciences—Permanence of Paper for Printed Library Materials, ANSI Z329.48-1984.

Manufactured in the U.S.A.

Contents

Contents

Contents

Preface

Fifty years ago, when I began to research the book of Leviticus, I discovered to my great surprise that it had hardly been the subject of critical examination. Indeed, during the past century, until the 1990s, only one comprehensive commentary on Leviticus appeared—in German. I stumbled on the reason accidentally in conversation with the chancellor of a Protestant seminary.

When I received my doctorate—not on Leviticus but on the prophets—I was invited by the same chancellor to join his faculty. "What book will you teach," asked the chancellor. With trepidation I replied, "Exilic Isaiah (chapters 40–66)." I knew that these chapters were quoted in the New Testament more than any other part of the Hebrew Bible. (The nerve of a rabbi who would teach Christians the very sources of their faith!) The chancellor replied unhesitatingly, "Fine. But no sermons, ONLY THE TRUTH." He just wanted the plain, unadorned, undoctrinaire meaning of the text—the truth! I knew then that this was the beginning of a beautiful relationship.

My intuition about the chancellor was enforced when I invited him and other faculty members to my home to partake of the Passover service and meal. The moment they saw the bottles of wine on the table they froze. I had forgotten they were tea-totaling Baptists. I should have set out grape juice for them. All eyes were on the chancellor. Calmly, he picked up a bottle, slowly read the label, and then announced: "It's OK boys. It's sacramental." Obviously, he had compromised his principles so as not to embarrass me.

There were similar incidents during the entire semester. I shall cite only the last one. The school baccalaureate took place in the campus church. Its climax was the Eucharist. The congregation partook of the bread and wine symbolic of Jesus' body and blood. When the plate came down my row it was my turn to freeze. The chancellor, who sat at my side, passed it on and whispered, "It's not for you. It's only grape juice."

I had to tell you of my extraordinary relationship with the chancellor, because without it you would never have understood why I was shocked at our next encounter. During that year I had experienced a breakthrough in understanding the enigmatic dietary laws in the book of Leviticus. I could hardly wait to share my insights with my seminary students. Thus, when my friend, the chancellor, asked me what book I intended to teach, I replied without hesitation "Leviticus." His face darkened, and he burst out, "No!" Later, when I recovered from my shock, I began to comprehend his reactions. After all, Leviticus would be useless to seminary students in preparing their sermons. But why the anger? Why the outburst? Apparently, the chancellor had internalized the Christian teaching that the laws of the Torah, concentrated mainly in Leviticus, are null and void. For Christians, like the chancellor, Leviticus might not only be irrelevant but repugnant. In that moment I grasped why there were no Christian commentaries on the book of Leviticus.

The reason for the absence of Leviticus commentaries among Jews stems from other grounds. Ask a Jewish scholar to interpret a verse in Leviticus; he or she will pinpoint where it occurs in the Talmud, and what are its halakic (legal) implications. Others, less learned, might cite the interpretation of the medieval commentator Rashi (eleventh century), studied in Jewish elementary schools. Tellingly, in Israel today, Leviticus is not in the school curriculum. Even in advanced schools of Torah studies, the yeshivot, Leviticus is not studied in its entirety, but only in a verse here, a verse there.

However, one cannot understand the trees without encompassing the forest. All the sacrifices (chapters 1–7) are part of a system; all the impurities (chapters 11–16) form their own system. Each system is comprised of symbols, many of ethical import. The bottom line is that, in contrast with the wealth of commentaries on every book of the Bible published in the last century, Leviticus was singularly barren, an interpretive tabula rasa.

Thus, when I started to research Leviticus, I found myself on the ground floor. Early on I discovered that rituals are meaningless in themselves. Only when seen as a set of symbols do their inherent values come to light. I shall cite an example from the same dietary laws. Quadrupeds that qualify for the table must chew the cud and show split hoofs (11:3). These criteria sound absurd. But consider: they effectively eliminate the entire animal kingdom from human consumption, except for three domestic herbivores: cattle, sheep, and goats. Moreover, these are the same three animals permitted on the sacrificial altar (17:3). The implications are clear. All life is sacred and inviolable. Only these three stipulated quadrupeds are eligible for the human table because they are eligible for God's altar/table. The dining table symbolically becomes an altar, and all the diners are symbolically priests. (In Judaism, the equivalence of table and altar is carried further: just as the priest must wash [Exod 30:17-21] and salt the meat before offering the sacrifice [Lev 2:13], so must the diners ritually wash their hands and salt the table's bread, which represents the sacrifice.) Above all, the table is transformed into a sacred altar and the meal must be treated as sacred—a time for thanking God for the repast (cf. Lev 7:11-13), requesting a blessing for the future (Num 6:22-26), and engaging in conversation befitting the sanctified meal.

Three years after I published my article on Leviticus 11 (1963), Mary Douglas published her seminal book *Purity and Danger* (1966), in which she also devoted a chapter on Leviticus 11, but from a purely anthropological perspective. Since then, her anthropological school has taught me, among other things, that when a "primitive" community wished to preserve and teach its basic values, it did not rely on words but ensconced them in rituals. Accordingly, I have discovered that the rituals in Leviticus contain fundamental values that in aggregate prescribe a holy and ethical life.

A suggestion to the reader: have an open Bible before you as you read this book. Any modern translation will do. First, read the SELECTED THEME(S) to get an idea of some of the chapter's important values. Then, read the translation with the help of the SELECTED TEXTS. Greater detail can be found in my three-volume comprehensive commentary published in the Anchor Bible series. The book of Leviticus, so long thought to be esoteric and irrelevant, will turn out to be an old-new guide toward achieving quality life.

In conclusion, I offer profound thanks to my granddaughter Talia Milgrom-Elcott who, in the midst of a busy law practice, employed her artful editorial skills to "translate" my formal academic style into a smooth, lucid, and, I trust, appealing work. I also wish to thank Adi Savran for her assistance with proofreading.

Abbreviations

AAA	*Annals of Archaeology and Anthropology*
AB	Anchor Bible
ABD	*Anchor Bible Dictionary*
ᶜAbod. Zar.	*ᶜAbodah Zarah*
Abot R. Nat.	*Abot de Rabbi Nathan*
AfO	*Archiv für Orientforschung*
AnBib	Analecta biblica
ANET	*Ancient Near Eastern Texts Relating to the Old Testament,* edited by James B. Pritchard. 3d ed. Princeton: Princeton Univ. Press, 1969
AnOr	*Analecta orientalia*
AOAT	Alter Orient und Altes Testament
AOS	American Oriental Series
ᶜArak.	*ᶜArakin*
b.	Babylonian Talmud *(Babli)*
BA	*Biblical Archaeologist*
bar.	baraita
BAR	*Biblical Archaeology Review*
BASOR	*Bulletin of the American Schools of Oriental Research*
BBR	Heinrich Zimmern, *Beiträge zur Kenntnis der babylonischen Religion.* Leipzig: Hinrich, 1901
ʙᴄᴇ	Before the Common Era; corresponds to ʙᴄ
Ber.	*Berakot*
Bik.	*Bikkurim*
BJS	Brown Judaic Studies
BM	*Beth Mikra*
BO	*Bibliotheca orientalis*
B. Qam.	*Babba Qamma*
BR	*Bible Review*
c.	circa
CAD	*The Assyrian Dictionary of the Oriental Institute of the University of Chicago,* 1956–
CBC	Cambridge Bible Commentary

Abbreviations

CBQ	*Catholic Biblical Quarterly*
CD	Damascus Document
CE	Common Era; corresponds to AD
cf.	compared to
CH	Code of Hammurabi
CTA	*Corpus des tablettes en cunéiforms alphabétiques découvertes à Ras Shamra-Ugarit de 1929 à 1939,* edited by A. Herdner. Paris: Geuthner, 1963
D	Deuteronomic source
diss.	dissertation
EA	Tell el-Amarna letter
EM	*Encyclopaedia Miqraʾit*
EncJud	*Encyclopedia Judaica*
ErIsr	*Eretz-Israel*
ʿErub.	*ʿErubin*
ExpTim	*Expository Times*
Fest.	Festschrift
FRLANT	Forschungen zur Religion und Literatur des Alten und Neuen Testaments
Gen. Rab.	*Genesis Rabbah*
H	Holiness source
Ḥag.	*Ḥagigah*
HAR	*Hebrew Annual Review*
HAT	Handbuch zum Alten Testament
HL	Hittite Laws
Hor.	*Horayot*
HSM	Harvard Semitic Monographs
HUCA	*Hebrew Union College Annual*
Ḥul.	*Ḥullin*
ICC	International Critical Commentary
IDB	*Interpreter's Dictionary of the Bible*
IDBSup	*Interpreter's Dictionary of the Bible, Supplementary Volume*
JAAR	*Journal of the American Academy of Religion*
JAOS	*Journal of the American Oriental Society*
JBL	*Journal of Biblical Literature*
JCS	*Journal of Cuneiform Studies*
JQR	*Jewish Quarterly Review*
JNES	*Journal of Near Eastern Studies*
Josephus	Josephus (LCL editions)
Ant.	*Antiquities of the Jews*
Ag. Ap.	*Against Apion*
War	*The Jewish War*

JPSTC	Jewish Publication Society Torah Commentary
JSOT	*Journal for the Study of the Old Testament*
JSOTSup	Journal for the Study of the Old Testament Supplement Series
JTS	*Journal of Theological Studies*
Jub.	*Jubilees*
KAI	Herbert Donner and Wolfgang Röllig, *Kanaanäische und aramäiche Inschriften.* 3 vols. Wiesbaden: Harrassowitz, 1968–71
KAR	*Keilschrifttexte aus Boghazköy*
Ker.	*Keritot*
Ket.	*Ketubot*
KJV	King James Version
LCL	Loeb Classical Library
Let. Aris.	*Letter of Aristeas*
Lev. Rab.	*Leviticus Rabbah*
LXX	Septuagint
m.	*Mishna*
Mak.	*Makkot*
MAL	Middle Assyrian Laws
Meg.	*Megilla/Megillat* (e.g., *Megillat Taʿanit*)
Mek.	*Mekilta*
Menaḥ.	*Menaḥot*
Mid.	*Middot*
Midr.	*Midrash*
MT	Masoretic text
NAB	New American Bible
NCBC	New Century Bible Commentary
NEB	New English Bible
Ned.	*Nedarim*
Neg.	*Negaʾim*
NICOT	New International Commentary on the Old Testament
NJPS	New Jewish Publication Society Bible
NRSV	New Revised Standard Version
Num. Rab.	*Numbers Rabbah*
ʾOhol.	*ʾOholot*
Or	*Orientalia*
OTL	Old Testament Library
OTS	*Oudtestamentische Studiën*
P	Priestly source
PAAJR	*Proceedings of the American Academy of Jewish Research*
PEQ	*Palestine Exploration Quarterly*
Pesaḥ.	*Pesaḥim*
Pesiq. Rab Kah.	*Pesiqta de Rab Kahana*

Abbreviations

Philo	Philo (LCL editions)
Prob.	*That Every Good Man Is Free (Quod omnis probus liber sit)*
Spec. Laws	*On the Special Laws (De specialibus legibus)*
Virt.	*On the Virtues (De virtutibus)*
Pol.	Aristotle, *Politica* (Politics)
1QS	Qumran, Cave 1, *Rule of the Congregation (Serek ha-Yaḥad)*
1QSᵃ	Appendix A to 1QS
4Q252	Qumran, Cave 4, Commentary on Genesis A
4Q274	Qumran, Cave 4, Tohoroth A
4QDeut	Qumran, Cave 4, Deuteronomy
11QT	Qumran, Cave 11, Temple Scroll
Qid.	*Qiddušin*
RA	*Revue d'assyriologie et d'archéologie orientale*
RB	*Revue biblique*
RIDA	*Revue internationale des droits de l'antiquité*
RLA	*Reallexikon für Assyriologie*
Roš Haš.	*Roš Haššanah*
RS	Ras Shamra document
Šabb.	*Šabbat*
Sam.	Samaritan version
Sanh.	*Sanhedrin*
SANT	Studien zum Alten und Neuen Testament
SBLDS	Society of Biblical Literature Dissertation Series
SBLSP	*Society of Biblical Literature Seminar Papers*
Šebi.	*Šebiʿot*
Šebu.	*Šebuʿot*
SHANE	Studies in the History of the Ancient Near East
SJLA	Studies in Judaism in Late Antiquity
Soṭ.	*Soṭah*
Suk.	*Sukkot*
SWBA	Social World of Biblical Antiquity
t.	*Tosefta*
Taʿan.	*Taʿanit*
TCS	Texts from Cuneiform Sources
TDOT	*Theological Dictionary of the Old Testament*
Tem.	*Temurah*
Tg. Neof.	*Targum Neofiti*
Tg. Onq.	*Targum Onqelos*
Tg. Ps.-J.	*Targum Pseudo-Jonathan*
Tg. Yer.	*Targum Yerushalmi*
T. Levi	*Testament of Levi*

UF	*Ugarit-Forschungen*
VT	*Vetus Testamentum*
VTE	D. J. Wiseman, *The Vassal-Treaties of Esarhaddon. Iraq* 20, Part 1. London: British School of Archaeology in Iraq, 1958
VTSup	Vetus Testamentum, Supplements
WBC	Word Biblical Commentary
WMANT	Wissenschaftliche Monographien zum Alten und Neuen Testament
y.	Jerusalem Talmud *(Yerushalmi)*
Yal.	*Yalquṭ*
Yeb.	*Yebamot*
ZAW	*Zeitschrift für die alttestamentliche Wissenschaft*
Zebaḥ.	*Zebaḥim*

List of Illustrations

Introduction

Can Critical Scholarship Believe
in the Mosaic Origins of the Torah?

Values are what Leviticus is all about. They pervade every chapter and almost every verse. Many may be surprised to read this, since the dominant view of Leviticus is that it consists only of rituals, such as sacrifices and impurities. This, too, is true: Leviticus *does* discuss rituals. However, underlying the rituals, the careful reader will find an intricate web of values that purports to model how we should relate to God and to one another.

Anthropology has taught us that when a society wishes to express and preserve its basic values, it ensconces them in rituals.[1] How logical! Words fall from our lips like the dead leaves of autumn, but rituals endure with repetition. They are visual and participatory. They embed themselves in memory at a young age, reinforced with each enactment.

To be sure, when rituals fail to concretize our theological commitment they become physical oddities, superstitions, or small idolatries. Ritual is the poetry of religion that leads us to a moment of transcendence. When a ritual fails because it either lacks content or is misleading, it loses its efficacy and its purpose. A ritual must signify something beyond itself, whose attainment enhances the meaning and value of life. This, I submit, is the quintessence and achievement of Leviticus.

According to Leviticus, the rituals derive their legitimacy directly from YHWH. As the text oft recites, "YHWH spoke to Moses." Can this be taken literally? What does the claim of the divine origin of the rituals mean to the rational reader of Leviticus? And how does the claim of divine authorship mesh with the internal inconsistencies and contradictions found in the Torah?

For example, the tithe laws are revealed to Moses three times. In Leviticus, the farmer gives his tithes to God (27:30); in Numbers, to the Levites (18:21); and in Deuteronomy, to himself (14:23). Moreover, Numbers and Deuteronomy limit the

---

[1] So the Durkheimian school of cultural anthropology; see Durkheim 1965; Douglas 1966; Turner 1967; 1969; Shaughnessy 1973.

1

tithe to grain (barley and wheat), must (fresh wine), and oil (olive), whereas Leviticus imposes the tithe on all produce and animals. How can these flatly contradictory tithe laws be ascribed to one author, Moses? I turn to a rabbinic story:

> Moses (in heaven) requested of God to visit R. Akiba's academy. Permission was granted. He sat down in the back and listened to R. Akiba exposit a law purportedly based on the Torah. Moses didn't understand a word; "his energy flagged." At the end of R. Akiba's discourse, the students challenged him: "What is your source?" R. Akiba replied, "*halakah lemošeh missinay*" '(It is) an oral law from Moses at Sinai.' The story concludes that Moses was reinvigorated, "his mind was put to rest."[2]

The obvious deduction from this story is that between the time of Moses and Akiba, the laws of the Torah had undergone vast changes, so much so that Moses was incapable of even following their exposition. But the story conveys a deeper meaning. Why was Moses relieved when Akiba announced that the law originated with Moses at Sinai? It could not be true. Moses knows that he never said the words Akiba ascribes to him—he cannot even follow the argument! The answer, however, lies on a different plane. After Akiba announced that it was an oral law from Moses at Sinai, Moses recognized that it was based on Mosaic foundations. Akiba was not creating a new Torah, but was applying Moses' Torah to problems faced by Akiba's generation. Moses transmitted *principles and rules;* successive generations transmuted them into laws.

What are the Mosaic principles that lie behind the tradition of the Torah? What, according to the tale, did Moses hear in Akiba's classroom that reassured him that his ideals were continuing to manifest themselves? In Akiba's teaching, Moses may have heard the principles of the Ten Commandments.

The book of Leviticus and many of its sometimes contradictory laws can be understood as the various manifestations of the principles of the Ten Commandments, or Decalogue. The kernel of the Decalogue is terse. Without penalties, it reads more like directions or *principles* than laws: "Do not murder. Honor your father and your mother. Do not steal." On the other hand, the quotidian details about how life should be lived—like many laws that fill the book of Leviticus—are nowhere found in the commandments at Sinai. They must be derived from the broad principles of the Decalogue, but delicately, so that the core of the Ten Commandments is respected even as new laws emerge. This is implied by R. Ishmael: "*Generalizations* were stated in Sinai, details were stated in the Tent of Meeting."[3] Indeed, a case can be mounted that all of the Torah's codes are compilations of traditions comprising interpretations and applications of Mosaic principles.[4] No wonder, then, that the rules stemming from different authors and at different times might vary from one another in form and content.

---

[2] *b. Menaḥ.* 29b.

[3] *b. Zebaḥ.* 115b.

[4] But see some reservations at 25:6.

2

The second commandment orders: "You shall not make for yourself a sculptured image" (Exod 20:7). Does this mean that images are forbidden in our homes and synagogues? The earliest opinion is found in the appendix to the Decalogue, which prohibits gold or silver images of the Lord, who should be worshiped on imageless altars of wood or unhewn stone (Exod 20:19-23). Other interpretations are found in the Torah: this prohibition includes imageless pillars (Lev 26:1; Deut 16:22). Yet the absence of pillars from the second commandment indicates that they were tolerated in Israel's early worship—thus they are connected to Jacob (Gen 28:18, 22; 31:52-53; 35:14), Moses (Exod 24:4), and the Israelite sanctuary unearthed at Arad.[5] Indeed, they were situated in the temple itself until destroyed in the eighth century by Hezekiah (2 Kgs 18:4) and in the following century by Josiah (2 Kgs 23:14).

Thus the second commandment was limited in one interpretation (Exodus 20) and expanded in another (Leviticus 26), showing that various traditions were at work, applying the Decalogue to questions that arose in their age (see also Deut 4:19-20). Each tradition could rightfully claim that it is "an oral law from Moses at Sinai." This is specifically the case for some of the priestly and Deuteronomic traditions. No wonder, then, that these traditions stemming from different authors might differ in form and content.

Instead of understanding the Torah's "YHWH spoke to Moses" as a claim that the laws that follow came from the mouth of Moses, we can understand the Torah as signaling that the principles underlying the laws are Mosaic principles, emanating from Moses himself. Writing in the Talmud, the rabbis employed a similar device. Thousands of years after the Torah's compilation, the rabbis would explain the origins of a new law by connecting it to Moses as "an oral law from Moses at Sinai." If the rabbis believed that some of their laws were traceable to Moses, all the more is it true a millennium earlier for the anonymous authors of the Torah's legislation. The claim that "YHWH spoke to Moses" expressed their certainty that the laws they proposed were not of their invention, but were derivable from Mosaic principles and, as such, connected up to the Bible's core values.

To put it another way, as does David Weiss Halivni,[6] an authority on rabbinic thought, the story of Moses and Akiba expresses the minimalist position, averring that only general principles were revealed at Sinai. This way of understanding the voice of God in the Bible stands in sharp contrast to the maximalist position, which dogmatically asserts that the entire oral, as well as written, Torah, including "whatever novelum an earnest scholar will someday teach[,] has already been declared to Moses at Sinai."[7]

Americans can fully appreciate this distinction. All our laws theoretically

---

[5] Manor and Herion 1992:331–36.

[6] 1989:30.

[7] *y. Pe'ah* 17a.

derive from the Constitution. However, the Constitution is a fixed document, speaking to a particular political and social moment in history. When new problems arise, new laws must be made to address them. Because all laws must comport with the Constitution, we turn to judges and, ultimately, the Supreme Court to help us determine whether the new laws comply. Like the rabbis of the Talmud and the authors of the Torah, the judges have an obligation to connect their rulings with the Constitution. How the judges approach this task, however, depends mightily on whether they are maximalists or minimalists, otherwise known as conservatives or liberals. The maximalist position gives great authority to the specific words of the Constitution and therefore demands that new laws uphold the specific intention of the founding fathers. Judges who ascribe to this view often spend time poring over the notes of the Constitution's authors, trying to determine whether they had in mind a law such as the one before the Court. The minimalist position, on the other hand, looks to the core values of the Constitution and seeks to apply them to the new situation. Minimalists have a broader view of the directives of this founding document, asking questions about underlying principles and new applications more than specific intent.

Those who look to the Torah for guiding principles for today will find that maximalists will read the Torah literally. They will study it for its precise meaning. Their ultimate and exclusive criterion is the written text. Minimalists will also study it for its precise meaning. They do so, however, with two other purposes in mind. First, they will extrapolate the basic principles behind the Torah's laws (and rituals). Then they will ask: If the composers of the Torah were living today, how would *they* apply these principles to the issues of our day?

As will be shown, all of Leviticus's laws (and rituals) contain or imply rationales that address many relevant issues facing us today. In other words, properly unpacked, Leviticus reveals a series of values that can help us resolve the vexing moral and social issues confronting humanity in our time.

The minimalist view allows us to see divine origins in the Bible even as we acknowledge that the specific words used do not emanate from God at Sinai. Akin to the way new laws can be constitutional even if they do not appear in the founding document itself, the laws of Leviticus can be divine because they are interpretations of Mosaic principles. Internal contradictions do not undermine this belief: contradictory ideas can derive from the same source.

Contradiction is built into our belief system in yet another way. Halivni cites an ancillary minimalist opinion that also tries to wrestle with the conflict between divine origins and human interpretation. The tension is illustrated by the following rabbinic midrash, in which we find Moses once again sitting in on a class many centuries after his death: "R. Yannai said, 'The words of the Torah were not given as clear-cut decisions. . . . When Moses asked, "Master of the Universe, in what way shall we know the true sense of the law?" God replied, "The majority is to be followed"[8]—when a

---

[8] A play on Exod 23:2bβ.

4

majority declares it is impure, it is impure; when a majority says it is pure, it is pure.'"[9] As Halivni perceptively concludes: "Contradictions are thus built into revelation. Revelation was formulated within the framework of contradiction in the form of argumentation pro and con. No legitimate argument or solution can be in conflict with the divine opinion, for all such arguments and solutions constitute part of God's opinion."[10]

These two minimalist stories about Moses and the origins of biblical law portray the human role in the revelatory process. Revelation was not a one-time event at Mount Sinai. It behooves human beings—indeed, it compels them—to be active partners of God in determining and implementing the divine will.

What Halivni has discovered in rabbinic tradition applies to the written Torah. If it can be maintained that insights of, or disagreements among, the rabbis are traceable to Sinai, all the more so is it true for innovations or discrepancies ensconced within the biblical text itself. Legal formulations may presume earlier, reputedly Sinaitic precedents (Moses in R. Akiba's academy), and conflicting laws may justifiably claim Sinaitic origin (Moses in R. Yannai's midrash).

Both positions are frequently attested in Leviticus itself. One tradition (P) holds that holiness inheres only in the sanctuary and its priests. The other (H) differs from it radically by extending holiness to the entire land and its Israelite occupants. (This will be dealt with in detail in chap. 19.)

Thus it was possible for all three tithe laws to maintain that they stemmed from a Mosaic principle. This principle never made it into the Torah canon. Its possible wording, however, may be suggested by examining the oldest Torah law code, Exodus 21–23. It contains no specific tithe, but it may hold its earliest formulation: *me'le'atka wedim'aka lo' te'aḥer,* "You shall not delay the first (processed) produce of your vat and granary" (Exod 22:28a [Eng. 29a]). Perhaps this law refers to the processed firstfruits, mainly the grain, wine, and olive oil (Num 18:12). However, we do not know when, where, what, and to whom. I suggest that the original tithe law, if not this one, was similarly worded: "You shall not delay tithing your produce." Israel's neighbors, who regularly tithed their crops for the sanctuary or the king, show that the obligation of the tithe can be presumed.

Each derived tradition that contributed to the composition of the Torah, even if internally inconsistent, believed itself to be based on principles traceable to Mosaic origins. The compilers of the Torah were theologically pluralistic. They were willing to include variant traditions into the master text that became our Bible, trusting that each of these traditions emanated from the Mosaic core, although they may have chosen different ways of interpreting it. The text itself does not make a truth claim among the traditions, nor does it try to reconcile them blithely. Instead, the text happily

---

[9] *Midr. Tehillim* 12:4; cf. fuller version in *b. Ḥag.* 3b; Greenberg 1996.
[10] Halivni 1989:30.

transmits the various, oftentimes conflicting, traditions to its readers. None proclaimed exclusive access to the divine word. None labeled the other "false" (as the prophets later labeled their rivals).[11] To explain their divergences, their students might have answered in words similar to those coined by a later generation of rabbis concerning the different schools of Rabbis Hillel and Shammai: "Both are the words of the living God."[12]

In Leviticus there are two priestly traditions, P and H; P is found in chapters 1–16 and H falls mostly in chapters 17–27. P is a repository of rituals; H also contains rituals but is mainly a repository of behavioral commandments. Both traditions, as will be shown, are replete with ethics. These ethical values are buried in recondite rituals and in misunderstood (and mistranslated) commandments. Understanding the rituals and letting them infuse our lives are the means of achieving the life of holiness that Israel's priests imparted to their people and to us.

The Structure of Leviticus

The integrity and unity of the book of Leviticus can be demonstrated. It is visibly distinct from Numbers. Whereas Leviticus is static, Numbers is dynamic. Throughout Leviticus, Israel is encamped at Sinai; in Numbers, Israel is preparing for, undertaking, and completing its journey through the wilderness. Leviticus's boundary with Exodus, however, is not sharp. To be sure, there is a break in the content: Exodus closes with the construction and erection of the tabernacle (Exodus 35–40), and Leviticus begins with the laws of sacrifices (Leviticus 1–7). But the transition point is blurred: Lev 1:1 is an incomplete verse; it is semantically and grammatically bound with Exod 40:34-35. Nonetheless, disjoining Leviticus from Exodus can be substantiated. Exodus 40:36-38, briefly describing the role of the divine fire-cloud in leading Israel through the wilderness, has been inserted as a prolepsis of the detailed account in Num 9:15-23. Frankel has demonstrated that these closing, but intrusive, verses are a late priestly stratum, which I identify as H_R, the exilic redactor.[13] That is, Exod 40:36-38 is an advance notice of the book of Numbers, and it represents the view of the redactor who has inserted it in the interstice between Exodus and Leviticus.

However, is Leviticus itself a unity? Is there a comprehensive design for the entire book? The most commendable attempt to account for the organization of Leviticus has been proposed by Mary Douglas. Using as a model the ring structure attested in contemporary Greek poetry,[14] she arranges the chapters of Leviticus in the form of a ring.[15]

---

[11] e.g., Jer 5:31; 28:15.
[12] *y. Ber.* 1:7.
[13] 1998.
[14] E.g., Hesiod in the 8th century BCE.
[15] Douglas 1995:247–55.

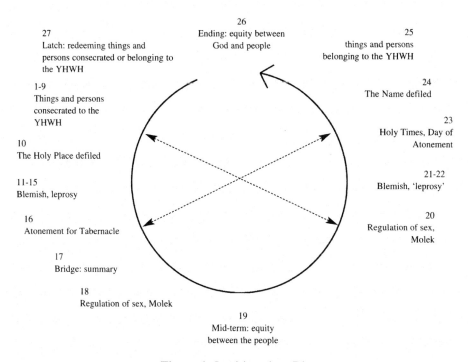

Figure 1. Leviticus in a Ring

The virtues of the ring construction (overlooking its terminological impreci-sion) are, moving upward, as follows:

1. The central turning point (chap. 19) is flanked by two chapters of equivalent content (18 and 20) in chiastic relation.

2. The beginning of the central turning point (19:1-4) is matched in content (the Decalogue) by the beginning of the closing turning point (26:1-2) and offers a reason why the latter was inserted as the prefix to the chapter on blessings and curses (26:3-46). The two chapters share a theme: the holy righteousness of Israel (19) and God (26).

3. Chapter 17 is not a summary but a bridge between the two parts of Leviticus, chapters 1–16 and 18–27.

4. Chapters 11–16 and 21–23 form a giant introversion in the center of the ring. Carcasses are innately "blemished" (chap. 11),[16] as are certain sacrificial animals (22:17-25) and certain priests (21:16-23). Carcasses of common animals also create "blemishes" (lit. "impurity") on persons (11:24-38),

---

[16] Milgrom 1992a.

especially priests (22:3a-9). Impure issues and scale disease in laity (chaps. 12–15) and priests (22:3-9) are identical in diagnosis and treatment; these form the center of the chiasm. The holiest day (chap. 16) corresponds chiastically with the holy (festival) days (chap. 23).

5. The two narratives in Leviticus (10:1-4; 24:10-23) face each other in the ring; they share a theme: defilement of the tabernacle (10) and of God's name (24). Chapter 24 was placed in its present spot for the sake of this ring structure, even though its subject matter is alien to its context.

6. Holy things, sacrifices (chaps. 1–9), are complemented by holy land and its sabbatical and Jubilee regulations (chap. 25).

7. The latch (chap. 27), which links it to chaps. 1–7, thereby completing the circle, was appended after the logical ending (blessings and curses, chap. 26) in order to lock with the opening topic (chaps. 1–9). Both deal with sanctifications of sacrifices (chaps. 1–9) and of persons, animals, houses, and land (chap. 27).

The common denominator of this material (chaps. 17–27 [H]) is the theme of holiness. Its source and rationale is chap. 19. Logically, this chapter would have introduced this holiness material, were it not for the redactor's desire to underscore its centrality for the entire book of Leviticus by flanking it with two similar collections of sexual prohibitions (chaps. 18 and 20) in chiastic relation. This is followed by holiness precautions for priests and Israelites (chaps. 21-22), the holiness of time (chap. 23), YHWH's name (chap. 24), land (chap. 25), the covenant (chap. 26), and consecrations (chap. 27). The root "holy" appears throughout, except, notably, in the beginning (chaps. 17–18). "Holy" appears in sixteen of the twenty divine speeches. The anomalous chapter 17 was needed by HR because of its associations with and allusions to P's closing chapter 16 and thus could form a needed bridge between P and H. The theme of holiness thus accounts for the choice of these H chapters.

The Priestly Theology of Chapters 1–16 (P): A Survey

The basic premises of pagan religion are (1) that its deities are themselves dependent on and influenced by a metadivine realm, (2) that this realm spawns a multitude of malevolent and benevolent entities, and (3) that if humans can tap into this realm they can acquire the magical power to coerce the gods to do their will.[17] The eminent Assyriologist W. G. Lambert has stated, "The impression is gained that everyday religion [in Mesopotamia] was dominated by fear of evil powers and black magic rather than a positive worship of the gods . . . the world was conceived to be full of evil demons who might cause trouble in any sphere of life. If they had

---

[17] Kaufmann 1937–56:1.297–350; 1960:21–59.

attacked, the right ritual should effect the cure. . . . Humans, as well as devils, might work evil against a person by the black arts, and here too the appropriate ritual was required."[18]

The Priestly theology negates these premises. It posits the existence of one supreme God who contends neither with a higher realm nor with competing peers. The world of demons is abolished; there is no struggle with autonomous foes, because there are none. With the demise of the demons, only one creature remains with "demonic" power—the human being. Endowed with free will, human power is greater than any attributed to humans by pagan society. Not only can one defy God but, in Priestly imagery, one can drive God out of his sanctuary. In this respect, humans have replaced demons.

The pagans secured the perpetual aid of a benevolent deity by building him/her a temple-residence in which the deity was housed, fed, and worshiped in exchange for protective care. Above all, the temple had to be inoculated by apotropaic rites—utilizing magic drawn from the metadivine realm—against incursions by malevolent forces from the supernal and infernal worlds. The Priestly theologians make use of the same imagery, except that the demons are replaced by humans. Humans can drive God out of the sanctuary by polluting it with their moral and ritual sins. All that the priests can do is periodically purge the sanctuary of its impurities and influence the people to atone for their wrongs.

This thoroughgoing evisceration of the demonic also transformed the concept of impurity. In Israel, impurity was harmless. It retained potency only with regard to sanctums. Laypersons—but not priests—might contract impurity with impunity; they must not, however, delay their purificatory rites lest their impurity affect the sanctuary. The retention of impurity's dynamic (but not demonic) power in regard to sanctums served a theological function. The sanctuary symbolized the presence of God; impurity represented the wrongdoing of persons. If persons unremittingly polluted the sanctuary, they forced God out of his sanctuary and out of their lives.

The Priestly texts on scale disease (chaps. 13–14) and chronic genital flows (chap. 15) give ample witness to the Priestly polemic against the idea that physical impurity arises from the activity of demons who must be either exorcised or appeased. Purification is neither healing nor theurgy. The afflicted person undergoes purification only after being cured. Ablutions are wordless rites; they are unaccompanied by incantation or gesticulation—the quintessential ingredients in pagan healing rites. The adjective used is "purified," not "cured"; the verb "cure" never appears in the ritual. A moldy garment or a fungous house (13:47-58; 14:33-53) does not reflect on the character of its owner, for the owner brings no sacrifice and performs no rite that might indicate culpability. Even though the scale-diseased person does bring sacrifices for possible wrongdoing, the only determinable "wrong" is that the

---

[18] Lambert 1959:194.

owner's impurity has polluted the sanctuary. Especially noteworthy is the bird rite at the beginning of this purification process, which, in spite of its clear exorcistic origins, has solely a symbolic function in Israel. Above all, it seems likely that most, if not all, of the varieties of scale disease described in chapter 13 are not even contagious, which supports my conclusion that scale disease is only one part of a larger symbolic system.

Another example of the way the Priestly legists excised the demonic from impurity is the case of the person afflicted with chronic genital flux (15:1-15, 25-30). It is the discharge that contaminates, not the person. Hence, objects that are underneath such a person—bed, seat, saddle—but no others are considered impure. In Mesopotamia, however, one's table and cup transmit impurity. The difference is that in Israel, the afflicted man does not contaminate by touch as long as he washes his hands. As a result, he was not banished or isolated but was allowed to remain at home. The same concessions were extended to the menstruant, who was otherwise universally ostracized (chap. 15). She, too, defiled only that which was beneath her. Touching such objects, however, incurred greater impurity than touching her directly (15:19, 21-22). As illogical as it seems, it makes perfect sense when viewed from the larger perspective of the primary Priestly objective to root out the prevalent notion that the menstruant was possessed by demonic powers.

The parade example of the evisceration of the demonic from Israel's cult is provided by Azazel (16:10). Although Azazel seems to have been the name of a demon, the goat sent to him is not a sacrifice requiring slaughter and blood manipulation; nor does it have the effect of a sacrifice in providing purification, expiation, and the like. The goat is simply the symbolic vehicle for dispatching Israel's sins to the wilderness (16:21-22). The analogous elimination rites in the pagan world stand in sharp contrast (see chap. 16). The purification of the corpse-contaminated person with the lustral ashes of the red cow (Numbers 19) can also claim pride of place among Israel's victories over pagan beliefs. The hitherto demonic impurity of the corpse has been devitalized, first by denying its autonomous power to pollute the sanctuary and then by denying that the corpse-contaminated person must be banished from his community during his purificatory period (see chap. 4, Theme A).

Israel's battle against demonic beliefs was not won in one stroke. Scripture indicates that it was a gradual process. The cultic sphere attests a progressive reduction of contagious impurity in three primary human sources: scale disease, pathological flux, and corpse contamination. The earliest Priestly tradition calls for their banishment (Num 5:2-4) because the presence of God is coextensive with the entire camp, but later strata show that banishment is prescribed only for scale disease (Lev 13:46). The fact that genital flux and corpse contamination permit their bearers to remain at home indicates that the divine presence is not viewed as confined to the sanctuary. Henceforth in P, the only fear evoked by impurity is its potential impact on the sanctuary. H, which extends God's presence over the entire land of Israel, also innovates a nonritual and nonexpiable impurity (chap. 18). The driving force behind this impurity reduction is Israel's monotheism. The baneful still inheres in things, but it spreads only under special conditions, for example, carrion when consumed and genital discharges when contacted. But note that impurity springs to life, resuming its virulent character, only in regard to the sphere of the sacred (5:1-13), and that these impurities are not to be confused with evils.

A similar gradation in the contagion of holiness is also exhibited in Scripture, but for different reasons. In the earliest traditions of the Bible, the sanctums communicate holiness to persons, the sanctuary's inner sanctums more powerfully so—directly by sight (if uncovered) and indirectly by touch (if covered), even when the contact is accidental. According to the early narratives, this power can be deadly; note the stories about the ark (1 Sam 6:19; 2 Sam 6:6-7), Mount Sinai (Exod 19:12-13), and the divine fire (Lev 10:1-2). In P a major change has occurred. This fatal power is restricted to the rare moment in which the tabernacle is dismantled (Num 4:15, 20), but otherwise the sanctums can no longer infect persons, even if touched (chap. 7). Clearly, this drastic reduction in the contagious power of the sanctums was not accepted by all Priestly schools. Ezekiel holds out for the older view that sanctums (in his example, the priestly clothing, 44:19; 46:20) are contagious to persons (contrary to P; see Lev 10:5).

The texts are silent concerning the motivation behind this priestly reform. Undoubtedly, the priests were disturbed by the superstitious fears of the fatal power of the sanctums that might keep the masses away from the sanctuary (Num 17:27-28). To the contrary, they taught the people that God's holiness stood for the forces of life (see below) and that only when approached in an unauthorized way (Lev 10:1-2; cf. Num 4:15, 20) would it bring death. Contact with the sanctums would be fatal to the encroacher, that is, the nonpriest who dared officiate with the sanctums (Num 16:35; 18:3), but not to the Israelites who worshiped God in their midst. There is also a more realistic motivation—the anarchic institution of altar asylum. Precisely because the altar sanctified those who touched it, it thereby automatically gave them asylum regardless of whether they were murderers, bandits, or other assorted criminals. By taking the radical step of declaring that the sanctums, in particular the altar, were no longer contagious to persons, the priests ended, once and for all, the institution of altar asylum. In this matter they were undoubtedly abetted by the king and his bureaucracy, who earnestly wanted to terminate the veto power of the sanctuary over their jurisdiction (details in chap. 6, Theme A).

One can see from the preceding discussion that the ritual complexes of Leviticus 1–16 make sense only as aspects of a symbolic system. As noted, only a few types of scale disease (many clearly noncontagious) were declared impure. Yet, to judge by the plethora of Mesopotamian texts dealing with the diagnosis and treatment of virulent diseases, it is fair to assume that Israel knew them as well (chap. 13) but did not classify them as impure. The same situation obtains with genital discharges. Why are secretions from other orifices of the body not impure: mucus, perspiration, and above all, urine and feces? This leads to a larger question: Why are there only these three sources of impurity—corpse/carcass, scale disease, and genital discharges? There must be a comprehensive theory that can explain all of the cases. Moreover, because the phenomena declared impure are the precipitates of a filtering process initiated by the priests, the "filter" must be their invention. In other words, the impurity laws form a system governed by a priestly rationale.

This rationale comes to light once it is perceived that there is a common denominator to the three above-mentioned sources of impurity—death. Genital discharge from the male is semen, and from the female, blood. They represent the life force; their loss represents death (chap. 12). The case of scale disease also becomes comprehensible with the realization that the Priestly legists have not focused on disease per se but only on the *appearance* of disease. Moldy fabrics and fungous houses (13:47-58; 14:35-53) are singled out not because they are struck with scale disease but because they give that appearance. So too the few varieties of scale disease afflicting the human body: their appearance is that of approaching death. When Miriam is stricken with scale disease, Moses prays, "Let her not be like a corpse" (Num 12:12). The wasting of the body, the common characteristic of the highly visible, biblically impure scale disease, symbolizes the death process as much as the loss of vaginal blood and semen.

It is of no small significance that the dietary laws (Leviticus 11), which are contiguous to and form a continuum with the bodily impurities (chaps. 12–15), are also governed by criteria such as cud chewing and split hoofs, which are equally arbitrary and meaningless in themselves but serve a larger, extrinsic purpose. This purpose can be deduced from the explicit assumption of relevant texts (Gen 9:4; Lev 17:3-5, 10-14), to wit: animal life is inviolable except for a few edible animals, provided they are slaughtered properly (i.e., painlessly, chap. 11) and their blood (i.e., their life) is drained and thereby returned to God. To be sure, the rationale of holiness and the equation of blood and life are first articulated in H (Lev 11:43-45; 17:10-14), but they are already adumbrated in P (Gen 9:4).

Because impurity and holiness are antonyms, the identification of impurity with death must mean that holiness stands for life. No wonder that reddish substances, the surrogates of blood, are among the ingredients of the purificatory rites for scale-diseased and corpse-contaminated persons (Lev 14:4; Num 19:6). They symbolize the victory of the forces of life over death. A further example: the blood of the purification offering symbolically purges the sanctuary by symbolically absorbing its impurities (see below)—another victory of life over death. Moreover, the priest is commanded to eat the flesh of the purification offering (6:19, 22 [Eng. 26, 29]; 10:17), and the high priest dispatches the sanctuary's impurities together with the people's sins (16:21). In neither case is the priest affected. Again, holiness-life has triumphed over impurity-death. Impurity does not pollute the priest as long as he serves God in his sanctuary. Israel, too, as long as it serves God by obeying his commandments, can overcome the forces of impurity-death.

Because the quintessential source of holiness resides with God, Israel is enjoined to control the occurrence of impurity lest it impinge on his realm (see below). The forces pitted against each other in a cosmic struggle are no longer the benevolent and the demonic deities who populate the mythologies of Israel's neighbors, but the forces of life and death set loose by persons themselves through their obedience to or defiance of God's commandments. Despite all of the changes that are manifested in the evolution of Israel's impurity laws, the objective remains the same: to sever impurity from the demonic and to reinterpret it as a symbolic system reminding Israel of the divine imperative to reject death and choose life.

It will be shown that the distinction between animals that are abominable and those that are impure is, according to Genesis 1 (P), that the former were created from the sea and the latter from the land. That Leviticus 11 is rooted in Genesis 1 is of deeper theological import. It signifies that, from the Priestly point of view, God's revelation is twofold: to Israel via Sinai and the tabernacle and to humankind via nature. The refrain of P's account of creation is: "God saw that it was good." In common with Israel's contemporaries, P holds that God punishes humankind through flood (Gen 6:19-22), plague (Exod 7:8-13; 8:12-15; 9:8-12), sickness (Leviticus 13), and death. It is, however, P's distinctive teaching that nature maintains a balance between the forces of life and death, and it is incumbent on the human being, by dint of one's intelligence, to discern the difference between them and to act accordingly. Israel, moreover, is charged with the additional obligation to distinguish between pure and impure, thereby providing it with a larger database for distinguishing between the forces of life and death. With P, therefore, we can detect the earliest groupings toward an ecological position.

It would do well to point out that the blood prohibition is an index of P's concern for the welfare of humanity. In Leviticus, to be sure, all of P is directed toward Israel. But one need only to turn to the P stratum in Genesis to realize that it has not neglected the rest of humankind. P's blood prohibition in Genesis appears in the bipartite Noachide law, which states that human society is viable only if it desists from the shedding of human blood and the ingestion of animal blood (Gen 9:4-6). Thus it declares its fundamental premise that human beings can curb their violent nature through ritual means, specifically, a dietary discipline that will necessarily drive home the point that all life, shared also by animals, is inviolable, except—in the case of meat—when conceded by God (see further Leviticus 11).

The P strand in Genesis also indicts the human race for its violence (Gen 6:11). Because the Noachide law of Genesis 9 is the legal remedy for violence,[19] it probably denotes murder (as in Ezek 7:23), though in subsequent usage, especially under

---

[19] Frymer-Kensky 1977.

prophetic influence, it takes on a wide range of ethical violations.[20] Thus the blood prohibition proves that P is of the opinion that a universal God imposed a basic ritual code upon humanity in general. Israel, nonetheless—bound by its covenantal relationship with the Deity—is enjoined to follow a stricter code of conduct.

One would expect a sharp cleavage separating the Priestly theology from the non-Priestly strands of the Pentateuch. Still, it may come as a shock to realize that even the two Priestly sources, P and H, sharply diverge on many theological fundamentals (see introduction to chap. 17). Here let it suffice to present my provisional conclusions in summary form.

The sacrificial system is intimately connected with the impurity system. Nonetheless, it possesses a distinctive theology (rather, theologies) of its own. No single theory embraces the entire complex of sacrifices. All that can be said by way of generalization is that the sacrifices cover the gamut of the psychological, emotional, and religious needs of the people. I therefore adopt the more promising approach of seeking the specific rationale that underlies each kind of sacrifice. Even with this limited aim in mind, the texts are not always helpful. Nevertheless, hints gleaned from the terminology and the descriptions of the rites themselves will occasionally illumine our path. As of now, the comprehensive rationales for two sacrifices, the burnt and cereal offerings, still elude us, whereas the three remaining sacrifices—the well-being, purification, and reparation offerings—can be satisfactorily explained.

The burnt offering (chap. 1) is intended for the individual who desires to present a sacrificial animal in its entirety to God either as an expression of loyalty or as a request for expiation (1:4). The cereal offering that follows (chap. 2) is probably intended for the same purposes as the burnt offering on behalf of the poor who cannot afford entire animal offerings.

The well-being offering (chap. 3) is connected with the blood prohibition. This connection, however, was not present from the beginning. In the P stratum, the well-being offering is brought solely out of joyous motivations: thanksgiving, vow fulfillment, or spontaneous free will (7:11-17). The meat of the offering is shared by the offerer with his family and invited guests (1 Sam 1:4; 9:21-24). The advent of H brought another dimension to this sacrifice. H's ban on nonsacrificial slaughter meant that all meat for the table had initially to be sanctified on the altar as a well-being offering (Lev 17:3-7). To be sure, the prohibition to ingest blood had existed before (Gen 9:4; cf. 1 Sam 14:32-35), implying that although humans were conceded meat, its blood, which belongs to God, had to be drained (see chap. 11, Themes A and B). Now that the blood had to be dashed on the altar (3:2, 8, 13), however, it served an additional function—to ransom the life of the offerer for animal (17:11). Thus the principle of the inviolability of life was sharpened by this new provision: killing an animal is equivalent to murder (17:3-4) unless expiated by the well-being offering.

---

[20] Haag 1980.

14

The rationale for the purification offering (4:1—5:13) has been alluded to above. The violation of a prohibitive commandment generates impurity and, if severe enough, pollutes the sanctuary from afar. This imagery portrays the Priestly theodicy that I have called the priestly *Picture of Dorian Gray*. It declares that while sin may not scar the face of the sinner, it does scar the face of the sanctuary. This image graphically illustrates the Priestly version of the old doctrine of collective responsibility: When the evildoers are punished, they bring down the righteous with them. Those who perish with the wicked are not entirely blameless, however. They are inadvertent sinners who, by having allowed the wicked to flourish, have also contributed to the pollution of the sanctuary. In particular, the high priest and the tribal chieftain, the leaders of the people, bring special sacrifices (4:9, 23), for their errors cause harm to their people (4:3 and 10:6). Thus, in the Priestly scheme, the sanctuary is polluted (read: society is corrupted) by brazen sins (read: the rapacity of the leaders) and also by inadvertent sins (read: the acquiescence of the "silent majority"), with the result that God is driven out of his sanctuary (read: the nation is destroyed). In the theology of the purification offering, Israel is so close to the beliefs of its neighbors and yet so far from them. Both hold that the sanctuary stands in need of constant purification lest it be abandoned by its resident god. But whereas the pagans hold that the source of impurity is demonic, Israel, having expunged the demons from its beliefs, attributes impurity to the rebellious and inadvertent sins of humans instead.

The reparation offering (5:14-26) seems at first glance to be restricted to offenses against the property of God, either his sanctums or his name. It reflects, however, wider theological implications. The Hebrew noun translated "reparation, reparation offering" is related to the Hebrew verb translated "feel guilt," which predominates in this offering (5:17, 23, 26) and in the purification offering as well (4:13, 22, 27; 5:4, 5). This fact bears ethical consequences. Expiation by sacrifice depends on two factors: the remorse of the worshiper and the reparation he brings to both humans and God to rectify his wrong. This sacrifice, however, strikes even deeper ethical roots. If someone falsely denies under oath having defrauded his fellow, subsequently feels guilt and restores the embezzled property and pays a 20 percent fine, he is then eligible to request of his Deity that his reparation offering serve to expiate his false oath (5:20-26). Here we see the Priestly legists in action, bending the sacrificial rules in order to foster the growth of individual conscience. They permit sacrificial expiation for a deliberate crime against God (knowingly taking a false oath) provided the person repents before he is apprehended. Thus they ordain that repentance converts an intentional sin into an unintentional one, thereby making it eligible for sacrificial expiation.

It should already be clear that the Priestly polemic against pagan practice was also informed by ethical postulates. The impurity system pits the forces of life against the forces of death, reaching an ethical summit in the blood prohibition. Not only is blood identified with life; it is also declared inviolable. If the unauthorized taking of animal life is equated with murder, how much more so is the illegal taking of human life? And if the long list of prohibited animals has as its aim the restriction of meat to three domestic quadrupeds, whose blood (according to H) must be offered up on the altar of the central sanctuary, what else could the compliant Israelite derive from this arduous discipline except that all life must be treated with reverence?

The reduction of sanctum contagion may have been motivated by the desire to wean Israel from the universally attested morbid fear of approaching the sanctums. But, as indicated earlier, there coexisted the more practical goal of breaking the equally current belief that the sanctuary gave asylum even to the criminal. As also noted, the ethical current also ran strong in the rationale for the sacrifices. The purification offering taught the ecology of morality, that the sins of the individual adversely affect one's society even when committed inadvertently, and the reparation offering became the vehicle for an incipient doctrine of repentance. The ethical thrust of these two expiatory sacrifices can be shown to be evident in other respects as well. The Priestly legists did not prescribe the purification offering just for cultic violations but extended the meaning of the term "communal" to embrace the broader area of ethical violations (4:2). And the texts on the reparation offering make absolutely clear that in matters of expiation persons take precedence over God; only after rectification has been made with the person can it be sought with God (5:24b-25).

A leitmotif of the sacrificial texts is their concern for the poor: everyone, regardless of means, should be able to bring an acceptable offering to the Lord. Thus birds were added to the roster of burnt offerings (see 1:14-17), and the pericope on the cereal offering (chap. 2) was deliberately inserted after the burnt offering, implying that if a person could not afford birds he could bring a cereal offering. Indeed, this compassion for the poor is responsible for the prescribed sequence of the graduated purification offering: flock animal, bird, cereal (5:6-13). This concession of a cereal offering, however, was not allowed for severe impurity cases (12:8; 14:21-32; 15:14) because of the need for sacrificial blood to purge the contaminated altar (12:8).

The ethical impulse attains its zenith in the great Day of Purgation, Yom Kippur. What originally was only a rite to purge the sanctuary has been expanded to include a rite to purge the people. To begin with, as mentioned above, the pagan notion of demonic impurity was eviscerated by insisting that the accumulated pollution of the sanctuary was caused by human sin. Moreover, another dimension was introduced that represented a more radical alteration. The scapegoat, which initially eliminated the sanctuary's impurities, now became the vehicle of purging their source—the human heart. Provided that the people purge themselves through rites of penitence (16:29; 23:27, 29; Num 29:7), the high priest would confess their released sins upon the head of the scapegoat and then dispatch it and its load of sins into the wilderness. Thus an initial widely attested purgation rite of the temple was broadened and transformed into an annual day for the collective catharsis of Israel. God would continue to reside with Israel because his temple and people were once again pure.

The ethical contents of each chapter are detailed in the discussion below.

Leviticus 1–7

The Sacrificial System

The book of Leviticus opens with a description of the sacrifices that the Israelites are commanded to bring to the sanctuary. At first glance, nothing could seem more distant from our modern lives than a system of animal sacrifice. However, behind the specific laws of sacrifice is a profound design for creating a sense of spiritual connectedness. In sacrificing, people felt a direct line of communication with God; the sight of smoke ascending heavenward could be seen as a physical symbol of personal prayers and wishes rising to God. By allowing laypersons to make their own sacrifices, under the auspices of the priests, the sacrificial laws gave people a degree of control over their spiritual lives. By inviting people into the sanctuary for the sacrifice, people felt themselves personally invited into God's earthly home.

In essence, the system of sacrifice provided a metaphor, a method, for the Israelites to reach God, responding to the deep psychological, emotional, and religious needs of the people. Indeed, this is the meaning of the Hebrew word for "sacrifice"; it comes from a verb meaning "to bring near." Thus a sacrifice is that kind of an offering that enables us to approach God. The word "sacrifice" comes from a Latin word meaning "to make sacred." The quintessential act of sacrifice is the transference of property from the common to the sacred realm, so making it a gift for God. As a gift, the sacrifice is sometimes intended to solicit divine aid: (1) external aid to secure fertility or victory or blessing; (2) internal aid to ward off or forgive sin and impurity, in other words, for expiation. Both meanings, for example, are ensconced in the burnt and cereal offerings (chaps. 1 and 2). They are gifts to God to obtain blessing or forgiveness. The Judeo-Christian tradition and practice has long followed the words of the prophet Hosea, "Instead of bulls we will pay [the offering] of our lips" (14:3). Nonetheless, we should recognize that the system underlying the sacrifices provides insight into the human need to feel personally connected to God and spiritually fulfilled.

Why did the Israelites eagerly bring their animals to the sanctuary to be offered on the altar to God? Early in the history of the ancient Near East the belief prevailed that the sacrifice was food for the worshiped god. This premise is imprinted on the architecture of the tabernacle, Israel's earliest sanctuary (fig. 2). The outer shrine was God's private dining room. The candelabrum (menorah) provided light; the incense altar, aroma; the bread loaves on the display table, the laden dining table. The innermost (most holy) room was God's resting place. It contained the ark (God's footstool) flanked by two winged seraphim (God's steeds) representing God's flying throne. The throne, however, was unoccupied by an image. The tabernacle represented the people's belief that the sacrifices might bring God to visit his earthly home to respond to the prayers of his people.

According to P, the Priestly source (mainly Exodus 25–40; Numbers 1–10), the tabernacle tent could only be entered by priests and officiated in by the high priest. Laypersons were excluded from the tent. They had access to God at the outer altar in the tabernacle court. Their sacrifices turned into smoke and rose to God's heavenly throne. Again, the descriptive language is highly anthropomorphic: the sacrifice is called "my bread, my food-gift, my sweet odor" (Num 28:2), and the altar is called "my table" (Ezek 48:16). Though these terms are linguistic fossils and should not be taken literally, they reflect the viewpoint of the people at large. For them, God was personally accessible, not in his tent domicile, the province of the consecrated priests, but in his heavenly residence, by means of their sacrifice on the outer altar.

Why then were the Israelites drawn to the sanctuary and its sacrificial service? First, the sanctuary was God's earthly home; they felt his presence there. Then, they could reach God by their sacrifice. The officiating priest would choose the appropriate sacrifice that corresponded to the emotional needs of the offerers. And when the latter saw the aromatic smoke rising from the altar, they felt that their prayers/requests were also ascending.

Modern animal rights advocates might protest, Why wasn't God satisfied with prayer, without animal killing? And weren't there sensitive Israelite souls who were reviled by heaps of burning flesh and rivers of blood on God's altar? I would argue that ancient Israel would have been unruffled by these questions. First, according to the Bible, the life of the animal was its blood (Gen 9:4). Out of respect for that life force, all biblical sources agree that it was forbidden to imbibe blood. While the Israelites were allowed to sacrifice, therefore, they had to return the blood to God, its divine creator, by offering the blood of sacrificial animals on an altar. If they neglected to do so, thereby flouting the sanctity of the animal life, they would be considered murderers (see chap. 17). Because the source of the animal's life was its blood, there was no need to harbor guilt for slaughtering an animal for its meat so long as its blood was drained and returned to God via the altar. According to the Priestly source, the prohibition to imbibe blood is incumbent on all humanity; only the flesh of the animal is permitted to human appetite, a concession by God to satisfy humanity's hunger (9:4; see chap. 11).

In what may seem like an ironic twist, then, these and other dietary rules are founded on the sanctity and inviolability of life. In this way, the sacrificial laws exemplify one of the most exciting characteristics of the book of Leviticus: behind the seemingly arcane rituals lies a system of meaning that we can draw into our own, modern lives.

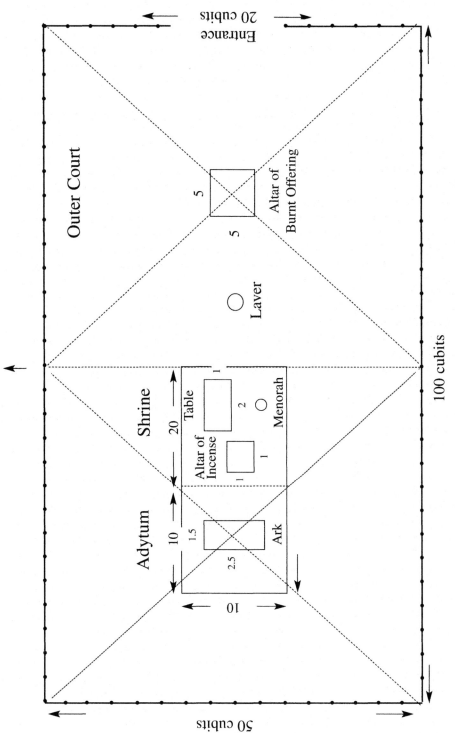

Figure 2. Ground Plan of the Tabernacle

19

Leviticus 1–7: The Sacrificial System

No single theory embraces the entire complex of sacrifices. All that can be said by way of generalization is that the sacrifices cover the gamut of the psychological, emotional, and religious needs of the people. We therefore adopt the more promising approach of seeking the specific rationale that underlies each kind of sacrifice. Even with this limited aim in mind, the texts are not always helpful. Nevertheless, hints gleaned from the terminology and the descriptions of the rites themselves will occasionally illumine our path.

In chapters 1–5, the sacrifices are listed from the point of view of the donor: chapters 1–3, the spontaneously motivated sacrifices (burnt, cereal, and well-being), and chapters 4–5, the sacrifices required for expiation (purification and reparation). Their common denominator is that they arise from an unpredictable religious or emotional need and are thereby set off from the sacrifices of public feasts and fasts that are fixed by the calendar. Chapters 6 and 7 also deal with the same sacrifices, albeit in a different order, from the point of view of the priests. The sacrificial instructions of chapters 1–7 constitute the first divine pronouncement from the newly erected sanctuary (Exodus 40), a fact that underscores the paramount importance of the sacrifices and the priestly cult that performed them. From a more practical view, however, these prescriptive sacrificial procedures had to come first in order to make sense of the descriptive sacrificial procedures of the consecrations that follow: that of the sanctuary, the priesthood, and the inauguration of the public cult (chaps. 8–9).

The Burnt Offering

This first chapter of Leviticus ostensibly discusses the burnt offering. However, the current that runs beneath the technical description of the offering reveals much about the emerging Israelites' efforts to distinguish their religion from the pagan religions that existed at the same time.

The ritual procedure with the burnt offering can be reconstructed as follows: After the offerer has performed the hand-leaning rite and slaughtered his animal, the officiating priest dashes the animal's blood—collected by his fellow priest(s)—upon all the sides of the altar, while the offerer skins and quarters the animal and washes its entrails and skins. Once the priests have stoked the altar fire, laid new wood upon it, and then laid the animal parts, the officiating priest supervises the incineration of the sacrifice.

Selected Themes
A. Contrast with Pagans

A. L. Oppenheim succinctly characterized Mesopotamian religion as "the care and feeding of the god."[1] We owe Israel's priesthood for eviscerating every trace of this notion from the sacrificial system. Pagans regularly set food and drink on their god's table, but the Priestly legists banned all food rites inside the shrine. All sacrifices were to be offered on the outer altar in the open courtyard (see fig. 2), visible to all worshipers and removed from the tent, YHWH's purported domicile. The text specifically prohibited the burnt offering (flesh), the cereal offering (bread), and all libations (drink) on the inner altar (Exod 30:9). Further, the frankincense, a precious spice, offered with the bread of the Presence, is not placed on the bread, as is the case with other cereal offerings (Lev 2:1, 15; 6:8) but is uniquely set apart from it, so that the bread can be eaten in its entirety by the priests (Lev 24:9), while the frankincense alone is burned on the inner altar (Exod 30:7-8). Thus all food gifts brought as sacrifices are conspicuously removed from the tent, YHWH's purported domicile, thereby erasing any suspicion that Israel's God consumed the sacrifices (see Psalm 50).

---

[1] 1964:183–97; for Egypt see Sauneron 1960:80–90.

Leviticus 1–7: The Sacrificial System

The rules governing the worship service further served to differentiate the Israelite tradition from the pagan religions. The entire sacrificial ritual of the tabernacle, aptly labeled "the sanctuary of silence" by Y. Kaufmann,[2] was conducted in silence. The lack of speech can be best explained as the concerted attempt of the priestly legists to distance the rites of Israel's priest from the magical incantations that necessarily accompanied and, indeed, empowered the ritual acts of his pagan counterpart. Kaufmann's insight can be supplemented and confirmed by the parallel phenomenon of Moses, the putative father of Israelite prophecy, who is also constrained to silence during his performance of a miracle.[3] In the instance of the plagues, Moses not only acts without speech, but on four occasions, when he accedes to Pharaoh's plea to request their cessation, he leaves Pharaoh's presence and prays to God in private—so that he should not be taken for a heathen magician.[4] Likewise, Moses' intercessory prayers for Israel are always in private, again in order to dissociate himself from his pagan counterpart.[5] Thus all of the biblical narratives on Moses and Aaron agree that, in the initial stages of the formation of Israelite cult and prophecy, the actions of the divine representative, whether in sacrifice or in miracle, were performed in total silence[6] (see also INTRODUCTION, C).

B. Partnership with the Laity

The rules governing the burnt offering carve out a large area of control for the ordinary Israelite who was offering an animal for sacrifice. All the preliminary rites with the sacrificial animal are performed by the offerer: hand-leaning, slaughtering, flaying, quartering, and washing. The priest takes over at the altar and continues the sacrificial ritual in silence. The rule of thumb for all sacrifices is that the altar is the province of the priest; all other rituals are the province of the offerer. This means that the offerer is directly engaged in this interaction with God.

Once the sacrifice reaches the area of the altar, however, the priest takes over. The offerer commissions the priest to be his or her agent at the altar. In other words, the priest, by virtue of his sacred status, acts as the offerer's (silent) intermediary before God. He is more than a mere technician. In effect, he is the cultic counterpart of the prophet. Both represent the Israelites before God. Both intercede on their behalf, one through ritual, the other through prayer (though silence also plays a role in the prophetic office,[7] and prayer is not absent from the priestly ministrations).

---

[2] 1937–56:2.476–77; 1960:303–4.
[3] Milgrom 1990:448–55.
[4] Exod 8:8, 25-26; 9:29, 33; 10:18—all JE.
[5] E.g., Exod 5:22; 32:11-13, 30-31; 37:7-11—again, all JE.
[6] Details in Milgrom 1983c:258–61.
[7] Milgrom 1983c:258–62.

There is one other elitist aspect of Israel's priesthood (as represented by the priestly sources) that cannot be gainsaid: its strict hereditary character. Even non-priestly sources indicate that everywhere in Israel a member of the tribe of Levi, one of the sons of Jacob, was the preferred priest.[8] It is also possible that the hereditary model was less a result of elitism than it was an antidote to the excesses that occurred in religions that depended on laypeople to act as priests. Egypt provides a telling example: "Because of its lay character and the ever recurring 'rotation' in the life of the priest, the Egyptian clergy was open to committing abuses of every sort."[9] To be sure, Israel's priests were on occasion guilty of corruption, venality, and assorted human failings.[10] Still, a consecrated class of individuals who from childhood could be trained according to the high standards demanded by the Priestly texts stood the best chance of resisting abuses that flourished outside the sanctuary.

In the middle of the discussion of the burnt animal offering, a strange side-note about bird sacrifice is inserted. Because the introduction (vv. 1-2) deals only with sacrifices from four-legged animals, it is reasonably clear that the pericope on birds (vv. 14-17) must have been added subsequently. Another reason for considering this pericope an addition is that the introduction (vv. 1-2) is also the heading for the offering of well-being (chap. 3), and the latter contains no provisions for birds.

Why was the bird pericope added? Its purpose is to provide the poor with the means to sacrifice the burnt offering. Such, indeed, is the explicit purpose of special allowances for birds in other sacrifices: the scaled purification offering (5:7-10) and the offerings of the parturient (12:8) and the healed "leper" (14:21-22). The same motivation applies to the cereal offering (chap. 2; 5:11-13). Built into the Israelite system of sacrifices is a mechanism to ensure that all Israelites, regardless of wealth, could communicate directly with God and participate in the spiritual life of their people.

Selected Texts

[1:1] According to the Priestly source, here is where Moses enters the holy of holies (adytum) to stand before the ark. Other traditions in the Torah talk about Moses speaking to God "face to face" (Exod 33:11) or "mouth to mouth" (Num 12:8), but the Priestly source takes great pains to deny that Moses ever saw God's Presence in the holy of holies. Moses' only distinction is that he sees visions of the *kavod* (the fire-cloud that envelopes God) in the tent and listens to the voice of God as he stands in front of the veil that conceals the ark. He needs to be alone to listen to God. In the Priestly source, visual theophany is public (Lev 9:23-24; Num 9:15-16), but listening to God is private.

---

[8] Cf. Judg 17:7—18:20.
[9] Sauneron 1960:23.
[10] E.g., 1 Sam 2:22; Ezek 22:26; Hos 4:6-8.

Leviticus 1–7: The Sacrificial System

[1:4] There are two leading explanations for this hand-leaning: *transference* of sin to the animal[11] or of possession to God,[12] and *ownership*,[13] signifying that the animal belongs to the offerer. The key to understanding this rite is that only one hand is employed. So Ibn Ezra, who reasons as follows: "That two hands are explicitly stipulated for the scapegoat (16:21), a transference rite, clearly implies that the scapegoat differs from all other hand-leanings on animals, which, therefore, must only involve one hand." This insight automatically eliminates the transference theory, which invariably requires two hands.[14] The one-handed hand-leaning signifies that the benefits of the sacrifice redound to the offerer.

If the offering is unblemished it will be acceptable on the offerer's behalf, but "if you present a lame or sick one—it does not matter! Just offer it to your governor: will he accept you?" (Mal 1:13).[15] From this citation we can derive two things. First, to be acceptable to God (or the governor), the sacrifice must be unblemished. Just as a king expects perfection in his gifts, so does the divine King of kings. Second, the function of the burnt offering here is to elicit the favor of the Deity.

A Brief History. That the burnt offering answers every conceivable emotional and psychological need leads to the inference that it may originally have been the only sacrifice offered except for the well-being offering, which provided meat for the table (see chap. 3). With the advent of a tabernacle/temple, however, it became imperative to design specific sacrifices to purge the sacred house and its sanctums of their contamination and desecration. Thus the purification and reparation offerings, respectively (chaps. 4 and 5), were devised. These two sacrifices, once introduced into the sacrificial system, became the expiatory sacrifices par excellence and ultimately usurped the expiatory function of the burnt offering for the individual. That these two sacrifices are later than the burnt, cereal, and well-being offerings is shown by the fact that the latter offerings are provided with no cases. The motivations for bringing them are taken for granted. Not so for the purification and reparation offerings: their cases are spelled out in detail precisely because knowledge of them is not widespread.[16] Thus the reference to expiation in the exposition of the burnt-offering procedure (1:4) may reflect an early stage on the history of this offering.[17]

---

[11] Shadal; Volz 1901.

[12] Dillmann and Ryssel 1897.

[13] Pedersen 1940:366; Robinson 1942; Lohse 1951; Eichrodt 1961–67:1.164–66; de Vaux 1964:28; Ringgren 1966:169; Wright and Jones 1986.

[14] Péter 1977; cf. Sansom 1982–83.

[15] See also Lev 22:19-20 and *Sipra Nedabah* par. 3:13.

[16] Dillmann and Ryssel 1897.

[17] Job 1:5; 42:8.

The Cereal Offering

For the poor, offering up an animal sacrifice could be very costly. To allow all Israelites access to God through the sacrificial system, the priestly legist created an alternative sacrifice for the poor: the cereal offering.[1] Support for this position is the attested practice in the nearby Mesopotamian cult, which explicitly labels cereal as the offering of the poor: "The widow makes her offering to you [plural] with cheap flour, the rich man with a lamb."[2]

Selected Theme
The Poor Person's Sacrifice

In the Mesopotamian cult, cereal offerings were offered up to the gods by totally burning them on improvised altars. In the biblical version, however, it is forbidden to burn the cereal offering except for a token portion (v. 2). Indeed, the injunction to turn over the cereal offering to the priests except for a token portion is mentioned twice (vv. 3, 10). Based on the difference between the Mesopotamian and the Israelite practice, the biblical command that the cereal offering go to the priest may spring from a polemic against contemporaneous pagan practice. The text of the cereal offering, therefore, inserts into its prescriptions a caveat that, irrespective of what the pagans do and, indeed, what might be expected of the cereal offering as a surrogate burnt offering, Israel should not offer up the cereal offering—even though it belongs to God—but award it to the priests as their perquisite.

The placement of the text on the cereal offering right after that of the burnt offering would also tend to support the view that the two are related. Their relationship would then be comparable to the graduated purification offerings, where too the cereal offering follows that of birds (5:7-10, 11-13) and where the reason for allowing both of them is explicitly stated: "if his means do not suffice (for an animal)" (vv. 7, 11). The juxtaposition of the cereal-offering prescriptions (chap. 2) after the burnt offering of birds (1:14-17) can be explained by the same rationale. The cereal

---

[1] *Lev. Rab.* 8:4; Philo, *Spec. Laws* 1.271.
[2] *CAD,* 10.331, s.v., *mašatu.*

25

offering must be viewed as a discrete, independent sacrifice that functions to duplicate the manifold purposes of the burnt offering for the benefit of those who cannot afford a burnt offering of quadruped or bird.

The most likely definition for the cereal offering is "a present made to secure or retain good will."[3] The emphasis, then, is clearly conciliatory. The cereal offering in Scripture is of two types. First, it is an accompaniment to animal sacrifices, the required auxiliary of the burnt offering and the well-being offering. "When the Hebrew ate flesh, he ate bread with it and drank wine, and when he offered flesh on the table of his God, it was natural that he should add to it the same concomitants which were necessary to make up a comfortable and generous meal."[4]

The cereal offering could also be offered by itself, in which case, according to the priestly rules, it would be accompanied by oil and, if uncooked, by frankincense (2:1-3, 14-16). If it was cooked, the requirement of frankincense was waived (see at vv. 4-10) as a special concession to the poor, for whom even a few grains of this precious spice would have strained their means.

Selected Texts

[2:1] Frankincense is a fragrant gum-resin tapped from three species of the *Boswellia* tree native only to southern Arabia and Somaliland. The best information on its costliness is found in classical authors such as Pliny; its price in the year 1960 would vary between $87.50 and $175 per pound, depending on its quality.[5] As a result, southern Arabia became very prosperous during the first millennium BCE.

[2:3] In none of the sacrificial prescriptions (chaps. 1–5) are priestly perquisites mentioned; the latter are the subject of the next section (chaps. 6–7). Why then are they mentioned here (and again in v. 10)? The answer can only be that, contrary to expectations, the cereal offering is not burned on the altar in its entirety. The cereal offering is the poor man's surrogate for the burnt offering, which is entirely consumed (except for its skin) on the altar. Lest one think that the cereal offering is treated similarly, the text makes clear that only a token portion is burned and the remainder is given to the priests.

[2:11] Leaven is the arch-symbol of fermentation, deterioration, and death, and hence taboo on the altar of blessing and life. Wine, the epitome of fermentation, is never burned on the altar hearth, but is poured on the altar base, and so the prohibition against "turning into smoke" any fermented substance has not been transgressed.

---

[3] Driver 1900:587.

[4] W. Robertson Smith 1927:222, anticipated much earlier by Abravenel (on Numbers 15).

[5] Van Beek 1960.

The honey mentioned here is fruit honey (see 2 Chr 31:5; cf. Neh 10:36). The stereotyped metaphor for Canaan, "a land flowing with milk and honey," must intend fruit honey, because Canaan from time immemorial was known for its abundant fruits, especially dates, figs, and grapes.

[2:13] Salt was the preservative par excellence in antiquity.[6] Moreover, its preservative qualities made it the ideal symbol of the perdurability of a covenant.[7] The apostles are called "the salt of the earth" (Matt 5:17). In other words, they are said to be the preservers, the guardians, of God's word and the teachers who protect and preserve the world against moral decay.

[2:14] What precisely is the first-ripe cereal offering: barley, wheat, or both? To this day Arab peasants roast barley precisely as described in this verse, but not wheat because of the latter's flat taste.[8] Moreover, that barley is intended here is confirmed by the structure of this chapter. The previously mentioned cereal offerings are of wheat groats; but that section (vv. 1-10) is separated from the first-ripe cereal offering (vv. 11-13). Thus this chapter's structure makes it likely that the first-ripe cereal offering was deliberately severed from the other cereal offerings because it was a different grain—not wheat but barley.

---

[6] See Philo, *Spec. Laws* 1.289.

[7] *Tg. Ps.-J.*

[8] J. Feliks, oral communication; and cf. Dalman 1928:1.457.

The Well-Being Offering

The well-being offering is, at its core, an offering of thankfulness. Although it takes on three unique forms, discussed below, its overarching purpose is to provide a ritual by which the Israelites could acknowledge the miracles of their lives and express gratitude for them.

Selected Theme

The Joyous Offering

The "well-being offering" falls into three categories: "freewill," "vow" and "thanksgiving." The common denominator of all three categories is joy. "You shall sacrifice the well-being offering and eat them, *rejoicing* before the Lord your God" (Deut 27:7). The freewill offering is the spontaneous byproduct of one's happiness, whatsoever its cause: "with a whole heart they made freewill offerings to YHWH" (1 Chr 29:9). Rabbi Eleazar wrote, "One who is not commanded and fulfills is greater than on who is commanded and fulfills."[1] After all, of what value is a gift brought under duress of being commanded? If the emotion is lacking, the offering brought is a sterile gift at best.

The votive offering is brought following the successful fulfillment of a vow. "Jacob then made a vow, saying, 'If I return safe to my father's house—the Lord shall be my God'" (Gen 28:20-22).

Finally, there is the thanksgiving offering. The rabbis derive from Psalm 107 that four occasions require a thanksgiving offering: safe return from a desert journey (vv. 4-8), release from prison (vv. 10-16), recovery from illness (vv. 17-22), and safe return form a sea voyage (vv. 23-25).[2]

The main function of all the well-being offerings is to provide meat for the table. Except for kings and aristocrats, meat was eaten only on rare occasions, usually surrounding a celebration. Because a whole animal was probably too much for the

---

[1] *y. Šebi.* 6:1.
[2] *b. Ber.* 54b.

nuclear family, it had to be a household or clan celebration. All joyous celebrations would have been marked by a well-being offering, the joyous sacrifice par excellence.

The well-being meal was probably preceded by a table blessing, as the book of Samuel describes: "for he [Samuel] must first bless the sacrifice, and only then will the guests eat" (1 Sam 9:13). Thus the freewill sacrifice makes a link between individual/communal joy and thanksgiving: in our moments of greatest happiness, the sacrificial system teaches us, we pause to appreciate the blessings in our lives and say thanks. This practice is still followed by Christians, Jews, and others.

Selected Texts

[3:3] "Suet" refers to the layers of fat beneath the surface of the animal's skin and around its organs that can be peeled off, in contrast to the fat that is inextricably entwined in the musculature. It was the exclusive reserve for the Deity and was forbidden for private use. That it was considered the choicest of the animal's portions is demonstrated by its metaphoric use; for example, "the *suet* [erroneously 'fat'] of the land" (Gen 45:18), "the *suet* of wheat" (Deut 32:14), where it denotes "the best."

[3:4] Kidneys are frequently associated with the heart as the seat of thoughts, emotions, and life;[3] like the blood, the proverbial life force, they must be returned to their creator.

The caudate lobe is a fingerlike projection from the liver. It was used extensively in the ancient Near East for divination, as was the entire liver (hepatoscopy). Possibly, its consignment to the altar also disqualified the entire liver for divinatory purposes.

[3:9] The tail part of the suet is known as the broad tail. As early as Herodotus, it was observed that the sheep of Palestine had broad tails. Their average weight was 15 pounds, but some weighed as much as 50 pounds.

[3:17] This verse along with 16b bans common slaughter and insists that all meat must initially be a well-being offering and its suet must be offered upon the altar (see further chap. 17, THEME A).

---

[3] Jer 11:20; 17:10; 20:12; Ps 7:10 (Eng. 9); 16:7; 139:13.

The Purification Offering

This chapter and the next concern themselves with the two expiatory sacrifices: the purification offering (4:1—5:13) and the separation offering (5:14-26). These sacrifices, in contrast to the preceding ones (chaps. 1–3), are mandatory. They expiate for sin: the violation of prohibitive commandments or the violation of sanctums.

The violation of a prohibitive commandment pollutes the sanctuary, and unless the sanctuary is purged by a purification offering the community is in danger that their God will be forced to abandon the sanctuary. The deeper ethical implications underlying this specification are discussed in THEME A. How the postulate of the purification offering resolves the paradox of the red cow ritual is reserved for THEME B, and examples of genital discharges are cited in THEME C.

Selected Themes
A. The Priestly Picture of Dorian Gray

In the introduction I stated that biblical rituals are symbolic acts that, in the main, contain within them ethical values. This axiom is nowhere better illustrated than in the purification offering (often wrongly translated as "sin offering"). To make this point I will focus on one rite, with one ingredient, of one sacrifice: the daubing of blood on the horns of the altar (vv. 7, 25).

According to Leviticus, the purification offering is prescribed as a response to moral impurity—defined as an unintended breach of prohibitions (4:2)—and to severe cases of physical impurity. Physical impurity in this context applies to either gender and has to do only with ritual, not with one's character or morality. Two examples of such physical impurity are the genital flow from a new mother and from a gonnorhean (chaps. 12 and 15).

The first question to ask is naturally: Who or what is being purified? Surprisingly, it is not the person with the moral or physical impurity. According to Leviticus, if his or her impurity is physical, only bathing is required to purify the body; if the impurity is moral (the unintended breach of a prohibition), a remorseful conscience clears the impurity. In neither case does the offering purify the person bringing the offering.

If the bringer of the sacrifice is not affected, who then is being purified? The telling clue is the destination of the blood of the sacrifice. It is not smeared on the offerer; it is smeared, rather, on the altar. The act is described by the word *kippur*, "purge" (as in Yom Kippur: the Day of Purgation). In commanding that the blood be daubed on the horns of the altar, the text is indicating that the altar is contaminated and must be purified. Since the offerer must bring the sacrifice, the offerer must in some way be implicated in the contamination of the altar.

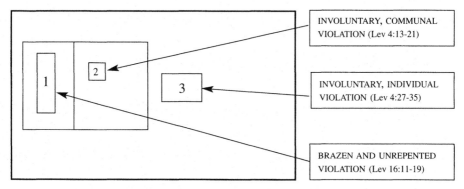

1 = The ark. 2 = Incense altar. 3 = Sacrificial altar

Figure 3. Purification and the Altars

Thus the first principle: Blood is the ritual cleanser that purges the altar of impurities inflicted on it by the offerer.

If an individual has accidentally violated a prohibition, the priest purges the outer (sacrificial) altar with the blood of the offerer's purification offering (4:27-35). If the entire community has accidentally violated a prohibition, the priest purges the inner (incense) altar and the shrine, the outer room of the tent, with the blood of the purification offering brought by the community's representatives (4:13-21). If, however, individuals have brazenly violated prohibitions, then, once a year, on Yom Kippur, the high priest purges the entire sanctuary, beginning with the inner and holiest area containing the ark. In this case, the purification offering is not brought by the culprits—deliberate sinners are barred from the sanctuary—but by the high priest himself (see fig. 2).

This graded impurity of the sanctuary and its purgation leads to the second principle: A sin committed anywhere will generate impurity that, becoming airborne, penetrates the sanctuary in proportion to its magnitude. Israel's neighbors also believed that impurity polluted the sanctuary. For them, however, the source of impurity was demonic. Therefore, their priests devised rituals and incantations to immunize their temples against demonic penetration. Israel, however, in the wake of its monotheistic revolution, abolished the world of demonic divinities. Only a single being capable of demonic acts remained—the human being. The humans were even more powerful than their pagan counterparts: they could drive God out of God's sanctuary.

Thus the third principle: God will not abide in a polluted sanctuary. To be sure, the Merciful One would tolerate a modicum of pollution. But there is a point of no return. If the pollution levels continue to rise, the end is inexorable. God abandons the sanctuary and leaves the people to their doom.

What are Israel's priests trying to convey through this ritual? I submit it is their answer to the question of questions, as voiced by Jeremiah, "Why does the way of the wicked prosper?" No intellectual circle within ancient Israel evaded the challenge of theodicy (justifying the ways of God), but none found an adequate explanation. The prophets agonized over it but came up with no immediate solutions—they only prophesied that answers would be provided by a future messianic king. The wisdom teachers gave their superficial answers: for example, the wicked will ultimately receive their comeuppance—and an entire book (Job) was written to refute them. We should expect a priestly answer, but we search in vain. Is it possible that Israel's priests, whose prime function was "to teach the Israelites" (10:11), had nothing to say regarding God's providence?

We know now where to find their answer—not in words but in rituals, not in legal statutes but in cultic procedure—specifically, in the rite with the blood of the purification offering. I call their response "the priestly *Picture of Dorian Gray*." In the novel by Oscar Wilde, when virtuous Dorian was granted eternal youth, he embarked on a career of increasing evil. Oddly, his evil acts did not affect his young, handsome appearance. His portrait, however, hidden away, became ever uglier and more grotesque. Like this Wilde character, the priestly writers would claim that sin may not blotch the face of the sinner, but it is certain to blotch the face of the sanctuary, and, unless quickly expunged, God's presence will depart.

Thus the fourth and final principle: the priestly doctrine of collective responsibility. Sinners may go about apparently unmarred by their evil, but the sanctuary bears the wounds, and with its destruction, all the sinners will meet their doom.

What of the innocents who will suffer along with the sinners? The priestly doctrine of collective responsibility yields a corollary. The "good" people who perish with the evildoers are not innocent. For allowing brazen sinners to flourish, they share the blame. Indeed, they, the involuntary sinners, have contributed to the pollution of the sanctuary (fig. 2). What of the "silent majority" of every generation—the Germans who tolerated the Nazi rise to power and territorial aggression, and the peoples of the free world who acquiesced in silence?

A column by Michael D. Hausfeld in the *Houston Tribune* dated Friday, February 27, 2001, revealed that IBM "inadvertently" aided Nazi Germany *even during the war years* by selling it advanced technological equipment that compiled, sorted, and classified information. He concluded: "Crimes against humanity are not limited to perpetrators who define or sign the orders of extermination, pull the triggers, drop the pellets, or crack the whips. Those who aid, abet, or unconsciously participate in the furtherance of those crimes have their own responsibility for which they must be held legally accountable."

In the Holocaust Museum in Washington, D.C., there is an enlarged photograph, covering an entire wall, of Allied planes over Auschwitz flying on to other destinations. It is estimated that the Auschwitz crematorium was gassing two thousand Jews and other "undesirables" each day. Imagine, had these planes released but one bomb, they could have stopped that killing machine for months!

How would Israel's priests see our world today? Without hesitation they would spot the growing physical pollution of the earth: oil spills, acid rain, strip mining, ozone depletion, nuclear waste. They would be aghast at the unending moral pollution of the earth: the murder of thousands in Bosnia, Somalia, Sudan, East Timor, Armenia, Angola, Rwanda, Chechnya . . . the millions dying of hunger or AIDS, while again the free world, involuntary moral sinners, silently observe the carnage on TV and—flip the channel. How long, the priests would cry out, before God abandons God's earthly sanctuary?

I have limited myself to one rite, of one ingredient, of one sacrifice. If only this ritual were fully understood and implemented, it could transform the world.

B. The Paradox of the Red Cow

A heathen questioned Rabban Yohanan ben Zakkai, saying: "The things you Jews do appear to be a kind of sorcery. A cow is brought, it is burned, it is pounded into ash, and its ash is gathered up. Then when one of you gets defiled by contact with a corpse, two or three drops of the ash mixed with water are sprinkled upon him, and he is told, 'You are cleansed!'"

Rabban Yohanan then asked the heathen if he had ever seen an exorcism, which he had. The ritual of exorcism, which the man believed in, was quite akin to the ritual of the red cow.

Rabban Yohanan then said: "Do not your ears hear what your mouth is saying? It is the same with a man who is defiled by contact with a corpse—he, too, is possessed by a spirit, the spirit of uncleanness, and Scripture says, 'I will cause [false] prophets as well as the spirit of uncleanness to flee the land'" (Zech 13:2).

Now when the heathen left, Rabban Yohanan's disciples said: "Our master, you put off that heathen with a mere reed of an answer [lit. "you shoved aside the heathen with a reed"], but what answer will you give us?"

Rabban Yohanan answered: "By your lives, I swear: the corpse does not have the power by itself to defile, nor does the mixture of ash and water have the power by itself to cleanse. The truth is that the purifying power of the red cow is a decree of the Holy

Leviticus 1–7: The Sacrificial System

> One. The Holy One said: 'I have set down as a statute, I have issued it as a decree. You are not permitted to transgress my decree. This is the statute of the Torah (Num 19:1).'"[1]

Essentially, Rabban Yohanan, one of the great scholars of the rabbinic period, was telling his students that there was no logic behind the ritual of the red cow. "You should do it because God said so" is the best he can come up with. The story itself—the discrepancy between the explanation given to the heathen and to the students, the rabbi's inability to explain the practice—reveals the great bewilderment among early Jewish scholars concerning the working and meaning of this ritual. Although the ritual is parallel to a pagan exorcism, Rabban Yohanan flatly denies their similarity. At the same time, he is at a loss to find a rationale. His perplexity is aggravated not just by the form of the rite, but by its paradoxical effect. Whereas the ashes of the red cow purify those whom they sprinkle, they defile those who do the sprinkling (vv. 19, 21) and, indeed, anyone who handles them (v. 21) or is involved in preparing them (vv. 6-10). This paradox is neatly captured in the rabbinic apothegm: They purify the defiled and defile the pure.[2]

The key to unlock the paradox of the red cow is that it is a purification offering. Though it is so stated unambiguously by the text: "it is a purification offering" (v. 9), no commentator, past or present, ever realized its significance in resolving the paradox. The function of the purification offering, as has been demonstrated, is to remove contamination. As the red cow is labeled a "burnt purification offering" (v. 17), it falls into the category of the purification offering brought for severe impurities whose flesh may not be eaten but is burned outside the camp (Lev 4:6-7, 11-12; cf. 6:23 [Eng. 30]; 10:18).

Yet the difference in the ritual procedure is glaring: the blood of the red cow is not offered up on the altar as is the blood of every purification offering and, indeed, of every other sacrifice; but the whole cow, together with its blood, is incinerated outside the camp (v. 5). As such, at first glance it does not appear to be a sacrifice at all. After all, nothing is given to God via the altar. How could the ritual of the red cow be a purification offering if nothing is offered to God?

This discrepancy is a serious one, but it can be resolved. The blood of the red cow is not offered on the altar for the simple reason that it is needed. By keeping the blood with the ashes of the sacrifice, the ashes become a continuing purification offering. It has been shown (in chap. 4) that the element of the purification offering that does the decontaminating is the blood. Its placement on the horns of the altars (4:4, 7, 18, 25, 30, 34), in the shrine (4:6, 17), or in the adytum (16:14) is what purges these sacred areas of their accumulated impurities. True, other traditional purgatives are contained in the ashes—cedar, hyssop, and crimson yarn—but these elements are

---

[1] *Pesiq. Rab Kah.* 4:7.
[2] Cf. *Pesiq. Rab Kah.* 4:6; *m. Para* 4:4; *Midr. Num. Rab.* 19:1, 5.

clearly secondary to the blood. It is the blood that infuses the ashes with their lustral power.

By thinking of the red cow as a purification offering, we can unlock the paradox of the sacrifice that purifies the defiled and defiles the pure. The unique characteristic of all purification offerings is that they defile their handlers. Thus the one who burns the purification offering outside the camp "shall launder his clothes and bathe his body in water; and after that he may reenter the camp" (16:28). With the ritual of the red cow, we have a precise parallel: The one who burns the red cow outside the camp is defiled and must undergo a similar purification (Num 19:8). Furthermore, like the purification offering blood, which bears the impurity it has absorbed, the remnants of the red cow, which contain the same blood, contaminate anything they touch (Lev 6:20b [Eng. 27b]). Hence, the laws of impurities prevail in regard to the objects touched by the purification offering: Earthenware must be broken (cf. 6:21a [Eng. 28a] with 11:33, 35; 15:12a) and metalware scoured (cf. 6:21b [Eng. 28b] with Num 31:22-23).

In this manner, the ashes of the red cow are a burnt purification offering and, as such, they defile their handlers and purify their recipients. As scientific method teaches us, the simplest and most economical theory should be adopted to explain any set of data (parsimony). The one postulate of the purification offering does exactly that: if we think of the red cow as a purification offering, the seeming paradoxes of the red cow cease to exist.

Still, there is one detail that the purification offering postulate does not explain, a detail that occurs not in the preparation of the ashes but in their use. The ashes of the red cow are sprinkled not only on impure objects but also, and primarily, on impure persons. This constitutes a break with the rule that the purification offering blood is applied solely to objects that have been polluted by the physical impurity or the inadvertent wrong of the one who offers the purification offering. In the case of all other purification offerings, the offerer is cleansed of physical impurity by ablutions and cleansed of wrongdoings by remorse, but never by the purification offering blood (see above).

Why uniquely with the red cow do we sprinkle the purification offering ashes on the body of the corpse-contaminated person? This aspersion constitutes a vestige of the ritual's pre-Israelite antecedents. In Mesopotamia, for example, an impure person might be purified by changing or laundering his garments, bathing with pure water, being aspersed with tamarisk and *tullal*-plant or fumigated with censer and torch, and, above all, being wiped with specially prepared detergents. In Mesopotamia purification rituals are performed on the body of the afflicted. No wonder that Rabban Yohanan could put off the heathen with his rationale: exorcisms continued to be performed by aspersing the victim with magical substances, not only in ages gone by, but in his time as well.

Leviticus 1–7: The Sacrificial System

The question needs to be asked: Why did the authors of the red cow ritual maintain a pagan custom? Why did not the Priestly legislators eliminate this "sore thumb" from the purification ritual that cleansed corpse contamination? The answer must surely be that corpse contamination evoked an obsessive, irrational fear in individuals. In a Mesopotamian Namburbi ritual, the victim is in mortal fear that the evil he has seen has infected him with lethal impurity. He requires an exorcistic incantation in addition to sacrificing, bathing, changing his clothing, and remaining shut up in his house for *seven days*.[3] That the fear of corpse contamination prevailed into rabbinic times is seen from the report of Josephus that King Herod had to use force to settle Jews in newly constructed Tiberias and, to appease them, even built them homes and gave them tracts of land—all because he had built Tiberias over a graveyard.[4]

Thus it stands to reason that the one who has been contaminated by contact with a corpse would demand an exorcism, the application of powerful countervailing forces to his body that would expunge the dreaded impurity. Even had the Priestly legislators desired to eliminate the use of the ashes (a doubtful supposition), it is hard to believe that the people at large would have let them.

In truth, a rite of exorcism has been preserved in nearly pristine form in the Bible: the first-day purification of the healed "leper" and fungous house (Lev 14:4-8, 49-53). As noted above, the same elements that comprise the ashes of the red cow are prescribed for the "leper's" purification: cedar, hyssop, crimson yarn, and above all blood. Once again, it is the blood that constitutes the chief detergent, because each element must be dipped into it (vv. 6, 51). Even the decisive verb "decontaminate" is used (vv. 49, 52), thereby indicating that an exorcism is called for—to remove the impurity from the stricken person or home. Yet the slain bird that has supplied the blood is not called a purification offering. Nor should we expect it, for the blood is not sprinkled in the direction of the tabernacle as is the blood of the red cow. The aspersion of the "leper," then, must represent the more original rite, and the red cow, transformed into a purification offering, constitutes a later, Israelite stage.

That the red cow rite represents a later stage than does the "leper" is also shown by the fact that it is the priest who performs the latter's aspersion rite (Lev 14:4-7; cf. vv. 48-53). This is what we would expect on the basis of exorcistic practices in the ancient Near East, which were always performed by a cultic specialist. In Israel, however, the purification of the corpse-contaminated person breaks with the pattern: "A person who is pure shall . . . sprinkle . . . the pure person shall sprinkle. . . . Further, he who sprinkled . . ." (Num 19:18, 19, 21). Clearly, the text reflects a deliberate attempt to declare that the aspersion is to be performed by anyone—not a priest, not a specialist, but by any layperson. The nexus between exorcism and purification is severed.

---

[3] Ebeling 1954:178–81.
[4] *Ant.* 18.36-38.

One additional requirement in the rite of the "leper" points to its antiquity: a live bird must be dipped into the blood of the slain bird and then dispatched to the open country (Lev 14:6-7, 51-53). Thus it is not enough to exorcise the "leper's" impurity; the impurity must be sent off to an uninhabited area where it can no longer do harm. There is no comparable requirement in the purification performed with the ashes of the red cow.

This double requirement of removing and dispatching the impurity is also found in the ritual for the Day of Purgation: the impurity of the sanctuary is purged (Lev 16:16, 17, 18, 20) by the blood of a slain goat and bull. The impurity is then loaded upon the head of a live goat, which thereafter is dispatched to an inaccessible place in the wilderness (vv. 21-22). Here too the complete ritual, including exorcism and elimination, has been preserved for the reason that its locus is the sanctuary. The impurity of the sanctuary not only is purged but must be banished to an inaccessible place whence it can harm the sanctuary no more. Yet despite the retention of the dispatch ritual, the Israelite transformation has been thorough: not only is the blood detergent taken from the purification offering (vv. 11, 15), but the dispatched goat is also called a purification offering (vv. 5, 9), even though it is not sacrificed at all.

The ritual of the red cow falls between the two rituals of the "leper" and of the Day of Purgation. Like the latter, the red cow is called a purification offering and follows, in nearly all respects, the procedure of a purification offering. Like the former, the blood and the same accompanying ingredients are used to asperse persons. Yet unlike either, the dispatch element is missing; there is no live animal to carry off the impurity. Thus the Israelite transformation of the presumed original ritual of exorcising and dispatching impurity is more thoroughgoing for corpse contamination than for scale disease or the sanctuary. Except for the use of the ashes, the red cow ritual conforms completely to the Israelite sacrificial system.

The metamorphosis of the red cow ritual is evident in yet another vital area: the power of corpse contamination has been vastly reduced. First, unlike the "leper," no ablutions are required of the corpse-contaminated person on the first day. The reason, I submit, is clear. Whereas the "leper" is required to bathe before entering the camp (Lev 14:8), the corpse-contaminated person need not bathe because he or she does not leave the community. True, another and probably older law requires the corpse-contaminated person to leave the camp (Num 5:2), but Numbers 19 implies otherwise: (1) Nowhere does it state that the corpse-contaminated person leaves the camp. (2) The clause "and then he may return to the camp" found in the prescription for the priest who prepares the ashes (v. 7) and for other bearers of impurity who are outside the camp (e.g., Lev 14:8; 16:26, 28) is conspicuously absent from the otherwise detailed purification procedure of Numbers 19. (3) The ashes deposited outside the camp (Num 19:9) are brought to the corpse-contaminated person (vv. 17-18a), not the other way around, implying that this person remains inside the camp. (4) Failure to undergo the water lustration "defiles the Lord's tabernacle/sacred precincts" (vv. 13,

20), a consequence that is possible only as long as he or she remains inside the camp. That the corpse-contaminated person, unlike the "leper," is not required to bathe on the first day or be banished from the camp during the week of purification is a clear indication that the priestly legislators eventually downgraded the degree of his impurity.

Further evidence for the diminution of an originally more powerful corpse contamination arises from another vantage point: the corpse-contaminated person brings no sacrifice at the end of the purification. Unlike the parturient, the "leper," and the chronic genital discharger, who bring a purification offering no sooner than the eighth day of the purificatory period (Lev 12:6-8; 14:10, 21-23; 15:14, 29), the corpse-contaminated person completes purification in seven days and brings no purification offering. This means that the impurity *ab initio* is not severe enough to pollute the sanctuary, as are the other impurities requiring a purification offering. Only if he or she delays purification does the impurity, so to speak, gather force to impinge on the sanctuary, subjecting the corpse-contaminated person to the excision penalty if the negligence is deliberate (Num 15:30-31) or to a purification offering if he or she has inadvertently forgotten (cf. Lev 5:2-3). Lastly, that Numbers 19 reflects a reduction in the potency of corpse contamination is shown by the contrasting and more conservative view held by the priest-prophet Ezekiel that a corpse-contaminated priest must bring a purification offering at the end of the purificatory period (Ezek 44:27). The older taboos are still evident in the command to the high priest not to leave the sanctuary to follow a funeral bier (Lev 21:12), in other words, he may not even gaze upon a corpse. In effect, the Priestly legislators have reduced the degree of corpse contamination from the most severe impurities to the least of them. That is, the severe impurities requiring a minimum of eight days of purification actually rank higher than corpse contamination, which requires seven days of purification and no sacrifice. The corpse-contaminated person is placed on a par with the menstruant, who also requires a seven-day purification without sacrifice. Just as she remains in the camp, so, it follows, does the corpse-contaminated person. There is, however, historical evidence that the menstruant was quarantined in the city during the Second Temple times.[5]

In sum, the lustral ashes of the red cow are the only vestige of a pre-Israelite rite of exorcism for the corpse-contaminated person. Otherwise the rite has been transformed by the Israelite values inherent in its sacrificial procedures. Above all, the hitherto demonic impurity of corpses has been devitalized, first by denying it the automatic power to contaminate the sanctuary (requiring a purification offering) and then by denying that the corpse-contaminated person need leave the camp or city during his purificatory period. Finally, the procedure for preparing the ashes has been restructured to conform to the purification offering requirements and integrated into Israel's sacrificial system. That the purification offering system was artificially imposed upon this ritual is betrayed by the fact that those who prepare the ashes

---

[5] Cf. Josephus, *Ant.* 3.261; *m. Mid.* 7:4; 11QT 48:16-17.

become unclean even though the ashes have not been used. Because of these changes, the ritual of the red cow, as presently constituted in Numbers 19, is relatively later than the rituals for the severe impurities of Leviticus 12–15, which betray more primitive traces; and that, in the long run, is perhaps what accounts for its insertion in Numbers rather than Leviticus. Thus Rabban Yohanan's answer to the heathen reflects the probable origin of the red cow ritual. But neither the rabbi nor his students believed it. For them, and for Judaism, it was inconceivable that any rite was inherently efficacious. In the absence of rational explanation there was, solely and sufficiently, the inscrutable will of God. The break with paganism was complete, but it was not the achievement of their age. More than half a millennium earlier the Priestly legislators of this ritual severed its pagan roots and remodeled it to accord with their norms and praxis.

Excursus: Numbers 19

The purification offering postulate for the ritual of the corpse-contaminated person commends itself for the additional reason that all by itself it can explain the main details in the preparation of the red cow ashes (Numbers 19), as follows:

1. At first sight, the requirement of a cow clashes with the purification offering postulate, for everywhere else the purification offering for the individual is either a bull or a female of the flock. The discrepancy is chimerical. A bovine is required in order to provide the maximum quantity of ashes; the bull cannot be chosen because it represents the purification offering either of the high priest (4:1-12; 16:11) or of the community (4:13-21). Thus, because the red cow must theoretically supply the purificatory needs of the entire population, the largest female animal is selected—a cow. Moreover, the Tannaim (rabbis of the first to third centuries CE) had a tradition that only very few red cows had been slaughtered even at the end of the Second Temple period, thus indicating that the ashes of a single cow had to last for a long time.[6]

2. "Red" (Num 19:2). The association of red with blood is widely attested in primitive cultures. Thus the red hide of the cow symbolically adds to the quantity of blood in the ash mixture, as do the crimson yarn and the (red) cedar (v. 7), and enhances its potency. The same phenomenon is attested in other cultures. For example, among the Ndembu, the celebrant reddens the river not only with the blood of a fowl but also other red coloring matter such as powdered red clay and powdered red gum.[7] The purpose of the remaining ingredient, the hyssop, is to provide ample ashes.[8]

3. "Without blemish" (Num 19:2), the basic requirement for sacrificial animals (Lev 22:17-20).

4. "In his presence . . . in his sight" (Num 19:3-5). The cow is slaughtered and burned with Eleazar in attendance. The need for continuous priestly supervision betrays

---

[6] *m. Parah* 3:5.
[7] Turner 1967:62.
[8] *t. Parah* 4:10.

the inherent danger that the ritual may slip back into its pagan moorings (see above, THEME B). Incorporating the ritual into the sacrificial regime effectively places it under priestly control.

5. "Eleazar the priest shall take some of the blood with his finger and sprinkle it seven times toward the front of the tent of meeting" (Num 19:4). Sprinkling the blood toward the tabernacle proves, in my opinion, that the rite is a sacrifice. Instead of sprinkling the blood on the altar—precluded by the need to add the blood to the ashes (see above)—the blood is sprinkled toward the altar. The effect is the same: the blood becomes consecrated. In a similar manner the priest sprinkles oil seven times "before the Lord" prior to the purification of the "leper" (14:16). That is, he must consecrate the blood before he can use it.

An equally cogent parallel is provided by the purification offering blood on the Day of Purgation. It is daubed on the outer altar's horns and then sprinkled on the altar seven times. The purpose of this double manipulation is supplied by the text: "purify it [the altar] of the pollution of the Israelites and consecrate it" (16:19). After the altar is cleansed it needs to be reconsecrated, an act accomplished by the sevenfold aspersion with the purification offering blood. By the same token, the sevenfold aspersion of the red cow's blood also consecrates the blood that it may always act as a purgative when, in the form of ashes, it is sprinkled upon the impure.

6. "The cow shall be burned in his sight—its hide, flesh, and blood shall be burned, its dung included" (Num 19:5). The parts of the cow that are burned duplicate those of the purification offering animal that are burned (Lev 4:11), with the notable exception of the blood. Indeed, it is the blood in the ashes that endows them with purificatory powers. According to the Tannaim, the red cow was slaughtered in the very pit in which it was burned.[9] Thus all its blood, except for the few drops used for sprinkling, was consumed in the fire. Moreover, after performing the sprinkling, the high priest would wipe his hands on the carcass so that not a single drop of blood would go to waste.[10]

7. "Cedar wood, hyssop, and crimson yarn" (Num 19:6). These ingredients, together with the blood, are added to the "leper's" lustral waters (Lev 14:6, 49-50). Thus the mixtures that purify the corpse contaminated and the "leper" are of the same composition. Yet their effect on their manipulators is not the same: the waters for corpse contamination defile, but the waters for scale disease do not. The obvious explanation is that the blood used for the scale-disease ritual is not a purification offering. In other words, the first-day ritual for purifying the "leper" was not incorporated into the purification offering system, and it still retains its pre-Israelite form (see further below).

8. The priest who throws the cedar, hyssop, and crimson yarn into the fire (Num 19:6) is impure as well as the person who sets the cow in the fire (vv. 5, 8) and the one who collects the ashes (v. 10). But neither the slaughterer of the cow (v. 3) nor the priest who consecrated its blood (v. 4) is said to have become impure. The difference is one of

---

[9] *m. Parah* 3:9; *Sipre Zuṭa* to Num 19:9.
[10] *m. Parah* 3:9; *Sipre* Numbers 124.

time: only those who make contact with the red cow after the consecration of its blood become impure. This proves that the blood consecration transforms the red cow into a purification offering, for anyone handling the purification offering becomes impure (16:28).

9. "It is a purification offering" (Num 19:9). This is the attested formula by which a given sacrifice is declared a purification offering (cf. Lev 4:24; 5:9, 11, 12; Exod 29:14). Yet this formula's use here bears greater significance. It follows up the sentence stating that the ashes of the red cow are to be "preserved by the Israelite community for waters of lustration." "It" is masculine and refers not to the cow but to the ashes. Thus the ashes of the red cow continue to operate as a purification offering.

C. Genital Discharges

Not all ritually impure persons bring a purification offering, only those whose impurity lasts more than seven days. The parturient "new mother" and one with an abnormal genital discharge each brings a bird (Lev 12:6; 15:14-15, 29-30), one with scale disease brings a female sheep or, if poor, a bird. Whoever brings a bird (turtledove or pigeon) brings another of the same kind as a burnt offering to provide an adequate gift to the altar.[11] The purification offering for impurity, like the one for inadvertences, purges sanctuary pollution.[12] But it is not required for impurities that endure less than seven days. Thus the person who experiences a nocturnal emission or engages in sex need only bathe the following day, and by evening the state of impurity is over (15:16-18).

The menstruant is a good case in point. If her periodic flow stops in a few days, as expected, her impurity lasts for seven days. On the seventh day she bathes and is pure in the evening (see 15:19). But "when a woman has a discharge of blood for many days, not at the time of her menstrual impurity, or when she has a discharge beyond the time of her menstrual impurity" (15:25), she requires a weeklong period of purification after her flow stops followed by a sacrificial rite on the eighth day (15:28-30). Her prolonged impurity is considered to have developed enough power not just to contaminate by contact but to pollute the sanctuary from afar. Hence a purification offering is mandatory. Indeed, the prolongation of impurity is considered so dangerous that even a person who has contracted impurity secondarily—by coming into contact with an impure person or animal—will incur capital punishment if one wittingly neglects to purify oneself as commanded to do (Num 19:13, 20; and see at Lev 17:15-16); if the neglect to purify oneself is not intentional, one must bring a graduated purification offering (5:1-13). The implication here is clear: the contracted impurity, be it even so slight at the outset, will grow in force until it has the power to

---

[11] Ibn Ezra on 5:7.
[12] *b. Ker.* 26a.

41

pollute the sanctuary from afar (5:1-13). Let electromagnetism serve as an illustrative analogy. The minus charge of impurity is attracted to the plus charge of the sanctuary, and if the former builds up enough force to spark the gap, then, lightning-like, it will strike the sanctuary. The subject of impurity prolongation is discussed in 5:1-13 below.

Selected Texts

[4:2] Inadvertence is a key criterion in all expiatory sacrifice. There is a consequence to a misdeed even performed in error. It leaves a mark that must be confronted and eventually wiped clean. The damage is done irrespective of intention. A deliberate, brazen sinner, however, is barred from the sanctuary (Num 15:30-31). Presumptuous sins are not expiable but are punished with *karet*—excision. Unconsciousness of the sin and consciousness of the act are always presumed,[13] as recognized by the rabbis: "Scripture says *inadvertently* implying the existence of consciousness."[14] By contrast, an unconscious wrong, when the offender is unaware of both the act and the sin, when one only suspects that one has done wrong, is expiated by a different sacrifice (see Lev 5:17-19).

God's commandments can be divided into two categories: performative and prohibitive ("dos" and "don'ts"). The performative commandments are violated by refraining from them or neglecting to do them. The omission of a religious duty is a personal failing, but the sinner alone is affected. Because no act was performed, the sin carries no impact on the environment. The violation of prohibitive commandments, by contrast, involves an act. It sets up reverberations that upset the divine ecology. Specifically, in the Priestly conceptual scheme, an act forbidden by God generates rays of impurity, which impinge upon God's sanctuary. For example, Molek worship and corpse contamination pollute the sanctuary[15] and can be lethal to the community of Israel unless it is purified—by the purification offering.

The term "commandments" applies only to the religious commandments (*fas*), not to civil ones (*jus*), to those enforceable solely by God, not by human beings. The limitation of the purification offering to laws punishable by God but not by people assumes central importance in evaluating the import of this superscription. It extends beyond the bounds of ritual law to include ethics, an area that is also unenforceable in human courts. Thus it should occasion no surprise when later in Leviticus ethical and ritual prescriptions are intertwined, and both are stamped with the divine imprimatur, "I YHWH."[16]

---

[13] Contra Kiuchi 1987:25–31.
[14] *b. B. Qam.* 26b.
[15] 18:27-28; Num 35:34-35.
[16] 19:3, 4, 10, 12, 14, 16, 18, etc.

The fusion of ethics and ritual is not an innovation of Israelite law. It is to be found in the earliest documents of the ancient Near East.[17] Hence in pagan cultures too the violation of ethical as well as ritual norms can enrage the gods. But it is in Israel alone that both norms are tied to the purification offering and its central message: that the violation of ethics and/or ritual leads to the pollution of the sanctuary and its national consequence, the abandonment of the entire community of Israel by its God. Israel's neighbors also held to, indeed were obsessed by, a fear that their temples would be defiled and the concomitant need to purify them. But the source of this defilement, in their system, was not human beings but demons and the plethora of incantations, unctions, and rituals, for the purification of the temple was directed toward eliminating or warding off this supernal evil. It was the genius of Israel's priesthood, as reflected in this sacrificial ritual, to give a national dimension to ethics, to make ethical behavior an indispensable factor in determining Israel's destiny.

[4:7] The altar's horns are right-angle tetrahedra projecting from the four corners. They are not added onto the altar but are of one piece with it.[18] In the ancient Near East, the horns on the altar are emblems of the gods.[19] They are found on top of shrines[20] and on the headdresses of the gods.[21] They signify the horns of a powerful animal (e.g., a bull or a ram) and are symbols of strength and force. Indeed, horns in the Bible are invested with the same symbolism.[22] In Israel the altar horns were clearly essential; to cut them off was to desecrate the altar.[23] Their daubing with the purification blood meant the purgation of the entire altar, by the principle of *pars pro toto*.

Like the sacrificial altar (see v. 25), the altar of fragrant incense contained rings and staves for carrying and was made of acacia wood. It differed, however, in being plated with gold, not with bronze. Also, the plating extended over the top, for it was solid and had a roof, in contrast to the sacrificial altar, which was hollow. Its place was directly in front of the veil, flanked by the two other golden cult objects, the candelabrum[24] and the display table (see fig. 1).[25] Incense was burned on it twice daily at

---

[17] For example, from Egypt, "The Protestation of Guiltlessness," *ANET*, 34–36; from Mesopotamia, Šurpu II (Reiner 1958:13–15); or from Hattia, Mastiggas (*ANET*, 350–51; cf. Moyer 1969:143; Wright 1987:262).

[18] Exod 27:2; 30:2.

[19] Galling 1925.

[20] Obbink 1937.

[21] Boehmer 1975.

[22] 1 Sam 2:1, 10; 2 Sam 22:3; Jer 48:25; Zech 2:4; Ps 75:5-6, 11 (Eng. 4-5, 10); 89:18, 25 (Eng. 17, 24); etc.

[23] Amos 3:14.

[24] Exod 25:31-40.

[25] Exod 25:23-30.

the time of the daily offering, but no offering other than the prescribed incense was permitted. The ascent of the smoke of incense became the visible manifestation of prayer: "Let my prayer be counted as incense before you, and the lifting up of my hands as an evening sacrifice."[26]

[4:13-21] The purification offering of the high priest and the community comprise a single case.[27] The high priest has erred in judgment, causing him to "harm the people" (v. 3) whereby, in following the high priest's ruling, the people also err. Because both their errors comprise inadvertent violations of prohibitive commandments (vv. 2, 13) which pollute the tabernacle shrine, each party is responsible for purging the shrine with the blood of a similar sacrifice—a purification-offering bull.

How is it possible for the entire people to err simultaneously? The thesis that vv. 1-21 form a single case, propounded above, whereby the high priest's erroneous decision causes the whole community to err, makes this eventuality highly plausible. For example, if the high priest declares the new moon on the wrong day, festivals falling in the ensuing month will be observed by everyone on the wrong day.

[4:20] The offender who brings the purification offering does so because he knows that his wrong, though committed inadvertently, has polluted the altar and hence has alienated him from God. By his sacrifice he hopes to repair the broken relationship. He therefore seeks more than forgiveness. If God will accept his sacrifice he will be once again restored to grace, at one with his Deity.

[4:22] Each tribe was composed of clans, each with a chieftain. Eleazar's title was literally "chief of the Levite chieftains" (Num 3:32).

[4:25] The altar of the burnt offering takes its name from its most frequent sacrifice, required twice daily[28] and at every festival.[29] It was the only sacrifice entirely consumed on the altar. Because this altar was part of a portable sanctuary, it was fitted with four rings and two staves. Moreover, it was hollow and hence not burdensome. The altar was only a portable frame because, in contrast to the incense altar,[30] there is no mention of a roof, and at each encampment it would therefore be filled with earth and rocks.[31] It is an assumption common to biblical tradition that a sanctuary is not fully consecrated—or is not divinely sanctioned—unless it has a tradition of theo-

---

[26] Ps 141:2.
[27] Abravenel.
[28] Exod 29:38-43.
[29] Numbers 28–29.
[30] Exod 30:3.
[31] In conformity with Exod 20:24.

phany upon its altar[32] or its altar is built on the site of a theophany.[33] The sanctity of the altar is evidenced by the asylum it provided to anyone who "seized its horns."[34] An early law, however, stipulated that this privilege was not to be extended to murderers.[35] In order to prevent the pollution of the altar by criminals, the priestly legists nullified its sacred contagion to persons and, in order to provide justifiable asylum, specifically in the case of unintentional homicide, invented the scheme of asylum cities distributed throughout the land.[36]

Israel's altar may not bring God to earth but it enables people, through their worship, to reach heaven. This is nowhere more evident than in the dedicatory prayer for the temple, attributed to Solomon, that even in a foreign land Israel's armies or exiles need but turn to the temple and their prayer will travel to God along a trajectory that passes through their land, city, temple, and then, at the altar, turns heavenward.[37] The altar, then, is the earthly terminus of a divine funnel for human communion with God. It is significant that later Judaism carries the tradition that the air space above the altar is an extension of its sanctity.

[4:31] This is the only place in all the expiatory sacrifices where the phrase "a pleasing aroma to YHWH" appears (contrast the other sacrifices, e.g., 1:9, 13, 17; 2:2, 12, 19; 3:5, 16). The studied absence of this phrase from the expiatory sacrifices indicates a conscious effort to distance Israel from the notion that these expiatory sacrifices possess the inherent power to appease God.

---

[32] 1 Kgs 18:38; 2 Chr 7:1.
[33] Gen 28:16-19.
[34] E.g., 1 Kgs 1:50-51.
[35] Exod 21:14.
[36] Milgrom 1981.
[37] 1 Kgs 8:44, 48; cf. vv. 31, 38.

Offerings, Sacrilege, Repentance

5:1-13: The Graduated Purification Offering

Immediately following the discussion of the purification offering in chapter 4 is a description of four cases in which a ritual akin to the purification offering is required. Why the repetition of two nearly identical discussions? A closer examination of the two sets of purification offerings reveals a number of distinctions. The most obvious is that in 5:1-13 the sacrifice is scaled according to the financial means of the offender.

Selected Themes

A. The Protean Verb ʾašam

The verb ʾašam describes the syndrome of sin, guilt, and punishment. It has a psychological dimension. Wrongdoing creates guilt and fear of punishment, and conversely suffering reinforces the feelings of guilt. Thus we find one word bridging all expiatory offerings: ʾašam.

For involuntary sin ʾašam, "remorse," is sufficient. For a deliberate sin, the remorse must be verbalized, the sin articulated, and responsibility assumed. Before transgressors may approach God for expiation, they must first make restitution to the people they wronged. In civil justice matters people take priority over God—a startling innovation.

The repentance of sinners, through remorse (ʾašam) and confession, reduces intentional sin to an inadvertence, which is then eligible for sacrificial expiation. Confession is then the legal device fashioned by Israel's priesthood to transform deliberate sins into inadvertencies, thereby qualifying them for sacrificial expiation. The priestly legists have postulated a new category of jurisprudence: verbalized repentance as a factor in the mitigation of divine retribution (see further on the priestly contribution to the doctrine of repentance, 5:20-26, THEME A).

In vv. 1-4 the confession is made to God because the offense is to God alone. If the tangible damage is done to a person, it is likely that the confession was made to the injured party.

B. The Delay to Purify Oneself

Why has the purification offering been mitigated in these cases? My hypothesis is that the graduated purification sacrifice is a distinct sacrificial category, enjoined for the failure or inability to cleanse impurity as soon as it occurs. Thus the wrong that has been committed is not the original wrongdoing that first caused the impurity but instead is its *prolongation*.

Modern critics tend to regard 5:1-13 as the "poor man's" purification offering, giving the option to the commoners of 4:27-35 who cannot afford the prescribed flock animal to bring less expensive sacrifices to expiate their sins.[1] This interpretation, however, is beset with stylistic and contextual difficulties and should not satisfy us; something else differentiates the four cases of chapter 5 and explains why a simpler offering is tolerated.[2]

The differences are three. The *Keter Torah,* a fourteenth-century commentary on the Bible, summarizes them neatly for us. In chapter 4 the offenders are distinguished by their *social status,* and their offenses are *inadvertent* violations of *prohibitions*; in 5:1-13 the offenders are distinguished by their *economic status,* and their offenses consist of *deliberate* violations of *performative commandments.*

An analysis of the cases of vv. 2-4 confirms my claim that the graduated purification sacrifice remedies the prolongation of an earlier wrongdoing. In verses 2-3 someone has contracted impurity knowingly, even deliberately, by violating a commandment to do something but has forgotten to purify him- or herself within the prescribed time limit. In verse 4 someone has sworn an oath knowingly, even deliberately, and has forgotten to fulfill it. If he or she subsequently remembers and feels guilt, that person must confess the wrong and expiate it by a purification offering (v. 5).

Unlike the general purification offering scenario, the wrongdoers have not violated any prohibitions. They have simply neglected to do something that they should have done, either a general commandment applicable to everyone or a personal obligation taken onto themselves. These types of wrongdoing generally remain with the individual and do not spread throughout the community, since inaction is seen as a lesser contaminant than wrongful action. In general, if a person has not violated a prohibition, no purification offering is required. So why is a purification offering look-alike necessary in these scenarios?

The wrongdoers are being called to task for not acting quickly to right the wrong. The reason for the offering, therefore, is not the original sin but the delay in remedying it. By bringing the offering, the wrongdoers are cleansing the sanctuary of the pollution caused by the procrastination. Yet because they have not violated a

---

[1] E.g., de Vaux 1961:419–21; 1964:92; Snaith 1967; Noth 1977; Elliger 1966; Rendtorff 1967:207–10.

[2] See Milgrom 1991:308.

prohibitive commandment, the sine qua non of the purification offering, the stringent rules that generally govern the purification offerings are relaxed and the sacrifices that purify the temple of procrastination are scaled according to the economic circumstances of the bearer.

The graduated offerings of chapter 5 offer an important reminder for the busy citizen of the modern age. There are many ways of defiling our community and our relationships. One is to act badly. Another way, also potent, is to neglect to do something we are committed to do. Finally, to delay apologizing for the hurt inflicted on others may lead inevitably to serious reprisals. Every additional moment that someone feels hurt by us allows that hurt to fester and grow.

This is precisely what Leviticus has in mind: "You shall not hate your brother in your heart. Reprove your fellow openly so that you will not bear punishment because of him" (Lev 19:17). That is, the one who lashes out criminally against another will be punished.

We are all familiar with the domestic crime of wife bashing that begins with a quarrel and terminates in violence. The Bible records the more serious case of Absalom, who hated his half brother Amnon for raping Tamar, Absalom's sister and Amnon's half sister. "Absalom did not utter a word to Amnon good or bad" (2 Sam 13:22). Two years later Absolom's repressed but mounting anger caused him to have Amnon murdered (vv. 28-29). In all these instances, anger is the (minor) impurity that needs to be dissipated (purified). Otherwise it turns into violence (major impurity) requiring societal intervention (or divine intervention unless conciliated with sacrifice).

Perhaps, in our busy lives, it is all too easy to put off making amends for ways we have hurt others. After all, it takes time—to say nothing of courage—to make things right, and the apology itself can be so difficult. But Leviticus demands of us, in these four esoteric cases (5:1-4), to act quickly to remedy our hurts and to fulfill our obligations. To do otherwise is to contaminate not just the people we love but also the society we inhabit.

Selected Texts

[5:1] The first case is more of a crux than the others. First, it does not follow the structure of the subsequent cases (vv. 2-4). Instead, we have a case stating that a witness who defies an imprecation (of the court) to testify will suffer its consequences. Thus, in contrast to the following cases, there is no lapse of memory or any other ameliorating factor. Moreover, there is no subsequent feeling of guilt. Hence there can be no question that the witness has acted deliberately, brazenly. How then can the offense be expiated by sacrifice?

I would suggest that this first case was originally an independent law stating that whoever defies a public imprecation by refusing to testify will be punished by the Deity. This law was amended by the priestly legists, who incorporated it into the graduated purification-offering cases, which provided that if the offender subsequently felt remorseful and confessed to the wrong, the offender could qualify for sacrificial expiation (v. 5). The ability of the priests to ameliorate a divine penalty is fully exemplified in the discussion of 5:20-26 below.

The proclamation is enforced by a contingent curse. Take, for example, the case of the suspected adulteress: "May YHWH make you a curse and imprecation among your people, as YHWH curses your thigh to sag and your belly to distend" (Num 5:21).

Once again, P shows its awareness of the sins of the "silent majority" (chap. 4, THEME A). Here the silent witnesses, in spite of the public imprecation to testify, withhold their testimony. Why don't they testify? There are any number of reasons, such as (a) complicity;[3] (b) "influenced by friendship or shame or fear";[4] (c) indifference: "Why should we bother with this mess?"[5] Indeed, the wisdom teachings of the ancient Near East are unanimous in actually advising witnesses *not* to testify: "Do not frequent a law court, /Do not loiter where there is a dispute, /For in the dispute they will have you as a *testifier*. . . . When confronted with a dispute, go your own way; pay no attention to it."[6] Meandering through the Egyptian records reveals a similar passage: "If there is a quarrel in the street. . . . If you stand there and watch, you will be required to give witness before the court."[7] Implicit in all of these counsels is that the witness stand should be avoided even after hearing a public imprecation! With this widespread sapiential background, it is no wonder that the Priestly legist felt it necessary to warn the reluctant witness that the imprecation is bound to take effect.

In any event, the witness's defiance of the imprecation is deliberate and so constitutes a brazen misdemeanor. But the subsequent remorse, the feeling of guilt, converts a deliberate sin into an inadvertence expiable by sacrifice (see 5:20-26, THEME A).

[5:2] The case here and in the next verse is that of impurity contracted secondarily, by contact with the source of the impurity. The sin rests only in the neglect to purify oneself of the impurity[8] within the prescribed one-day time limit (11:28, 31-40), thereby increasing the possibility that one will pollute the sanctuary and its sanctums (see above). This limitation of impurity is significant. In Israel an impure animal can transmit impurity only when it is dead, and this impurity is harmless and of no consequence unless the affected person does not purify him- or herself in time or, in the case of severe impurity, neglects to bring the prescribed purification offering.

---

[3] Prov 29:24 and *Midr. Lev. Rab.* 6:2.

[4] Philo, *Spec. Laws* 2.26-28.

[5] *m. Sanh.* 4:5.

[6] Lambert 1960:101, lines 31-36.

[7] Audet 1952:65, line 20.

[8] Dillmann and Ryssel 1897.

[5:4] The implication here is that the oath was taken heedlessly. But it is the articulation of the oath, expressed with lips, that is the decisive factor. The exchange between Jephthah and his daughter is most instructive: "'I have opened my mouth to YHWH [i.e., uttered a vow] and I cannot retract.' 'Father,' said she, 'you have opened your mouth to YHWH: Do to me according to what came forth from your mouth.'"[9] Intention is only binding when it is expressed.[10]

Isaac's intention was to bless Esau. When he discovered the trickery and how he actually conferred the blessing on Jacob, the Torah reports: "Isaac was seized with very violent trembling. Who was it then, he demanded, that hunted game and brought it to me? Moreover, I ate of it before you came, and I blessed him; now he must remain blessed" (Gen 27:33-35).

What is true for blessing holds true for oaths. Both are recited in the name of YHWH and cannot be revoked. The oath in this verse from Leviticus is a promissory oath that imposes an obligation on the oath taker. A vow is slightly different than an oath. It is also promissory, but it is conditional. It takes effect only if the condition is fulfilled. In this case, the oath has a time limit in which it is to be kept. However, the oath taker inadvertently forgot to fulfill the oath within the set time limit.

[5:5] Confession must be verbalized because it is the act that counts, not just its intention. Confession in thought would therefore be inadequate. By the same token, neither can mere thought bear evil consequences (see further 5:20-26).

[5:7] Because the meat of the purification offering belongs to the officiating priest (6:19), there is very little that remains for God (i.e., the altar). Hence a burnt offering is added so there will be a respectable offering on the altar.

[5:8] The reason for the priority of the purification offering is best explained by the rabbis: "[Because it is] like an intercessor who enters [to appease the king]: When the intercessor has appeased [him], the gift [i.e., the burnt offering] follows."[11]

[5:13] How can semolina effect purgation when it contains no blood, the ritual detergent of the purification offering? This constitutes another concession to the poor.

5:14-26 (Eng. 5:14—6:7): The Reparation Offering

The reparation offering seems at first glance to be restricted to offenses against the property of God, either God's sanctums or God's name. It reflects, however, wider theological implications, revealed by looking at the linguistic roots of the word

---

[9] Judg 11:35-36.
[10] Num 30:3.
[11] b. Zebah. 7b.

ᵓašam, "reparation offering." The noun *ᵓašam*, "reparation/reparation offering," is related to the verb *ᵓašam*, "feel guilt." Feeling guilt dominates the description of the reparation offering (vv. 17, 23 [Eng. 6:4], 26 [Eng. 6:7]) and the purification offering (4:13, 22, 27; 5:4, 5). As I explain below, the compilers of Leviticus use the reparation offering to help develop a moral conscience in the young Israelite nation by allowing intentional sins, usually unremediable, to be expiated through sacrifice so long as the sinner feels guilt for his or her actions.

As a general matter, expiation by sacrifice depends on three factors: the unintentionality of the sin, the remorse of the worshiper, and the reparation the worshiper brings to rectify the wrong. Intentional crimes cannot be remedied by sacrifice. This sacrifice, however, breaks the mold. If someone falsely denies under oath having defrauded his fellow—an intentional crime—and subsequently feels guilt, restores the embezzled property, and pays a twenty percent fine, he may then bring a reparation offering to expiate his false oath (5:20-26 [Eng. 6:1-7]). Here we see the Priestly legists in action, bending the sacrificial rules in order to foster the growth of individual conscience. They permit sacrificial expiation for a deliberate crime against God (in this case, knowingly taking a false oath), provided the person repents without being apprehended. Thus they ordain that repentance converts an intentional sin into an unintentional one, thereby making it eligible for sacrificial expiation.

Both the purification and reparation offerings are exclusive expiatory sacrifices, but they differ totally in their effect. The former expiates the pollution of sanctums, the latter their desecration. What is the difference between pollution and desecration? The difference may seem semantic, but its roots are deep. Desecration is noncontagious, affecting only its committer, and is expiated by a reparation offering; pollution, on the other hand, is contagious and can drive Israel out of its land and even God out of the sanctuary unless it is expiated by a purification offering.

5:14-16: Sacrilege

Selected Theme
Sacrilege against Sanctums
"Sacrilege" is the legal term for the wrong that is redressed by the reparation offering.[12] Its antonym is "sanctify," as in "you committed sacrilege against me . . . you did not sanctify me" (Deut 32:51).

The common denominator of all instances of sacrilege is sin against God. It falls into two major categories: the sacrilege against sacred space and the violation of the sacred oath. Although the two types of sacrilege may seem quite distinct, they are

---

12 Lev 5:15, 21; Num 5:6; cf. Ezra 10:10, 19.

integrally related. When a sacred oath is broken, the violated sanctum is none other than the Deity himself. YHWH's name, by which an oath is taken, is called a sanctum, God's "holy name."[13] Moreover, desecration of sanctums is simultaneously desecration of the covenant, because reverence for such sanctums is presumed in the covenantal relationship. Thus the two categories of sacrilege are really one. Both are acts against the Deity. Although the rules regarding oath violation are clearly laid out in the text, there is much less information to help us understand the sin of sacrilege against the sanctum.

A Hittite text actually pinpoints both kinds of sacrilege as responsible for the plague that befalls the Hittite kingdom. The key passages follow:

> Now a plague has been rampant in the Hatti land since the days of my father, and we have never performed the offerings to the river Mala. . . .
>
> The Hattians as well as the Egyptians were under oath to the Hattian Storm-god, the Hattians ignored their obligations; the Hattians promptly broke the oath of the gods . . . has this perhaps become the cause of the anger of the Hattian Storm-god, my lord? And (so) it was established.[14]

Thus the oracle reveals that the gods have sent a plague upon the Hittites for two reasons: they have violated their sanctums and they have broken their treaty oath. It is no accident that in the Bible both sins fall under the category of sacrilege (see further on 5:15 below); the practice seems to have been commonplace throughout the region.

In the area of cult, for example, Israel had no compunctions about imitating forms of architecture and administration, even modes of worship, because any alien religious content could be replaced by the norms and values of Israel's faith. Similarly, Israel's concern regarding sacrilege was certainly shared with its neighbors, for all ancient Near Eastern peoples believed that sacrilege against sanctums threatened the general welfare. We may therefore be able to find, from among Israel's neighbors, parallel laws, customs, and concepts that also deal with the issue of sacrilege.

One such source of insight is the Hittite "Instructions for Temple Officials," an Anatolian document that precedes the creation of the people of Israel; it covers the full range of biblical sacrilege regarding the misappropriation of sanctums. These include keeping, eating, using, selling, gifting, delaying, or exchanging the temple's animals, fields, or grain; by appropriating and using or wearing the temple's implements or garments; or by changing the time fixed for rites. However, it is not the enumeration of the various forms of sacrilege, but the range of penalties for such sacrilege, that proves most insightful.

The punishments are as follows: (1) death by the gods (collective—the family) if the sinner goes unapprehended for sins against the gods, expropriates sacrificial

---

[13] E.g., Lev 20:3; Isa 57:15; Ezek 36:20-22; Amos 2:7; Ps 119:9.

[14] *ANET*, 395.

animals, or changes the time of a rite; (2) death by humans (collective) if the sinner is convicted by ordeal for expropriating firstlings or sacrificial animals or is apprehended for igniting destructive fire from an unquenched hearth; and (3) death by humans (criminal only) if the sinner is apprehended for dividing sacrificial portions, encroachment, approaching the gods' sacrificial loaves and libation bowl in an unclean condition, or expropriating a plow ox, firstling, or sacrificial animal.

The Hittite gods punish not only the offender but also his or her household. The prologue to the "Instructions" confirms this: "If . . . anyone arouses the anger of the god, does the god take revenge on him alone? Does he not take revenge on his wife, his children, his descendants, his slaves, and slave-girls, his cattle (and) sheep together with his crop and will utterly destroy him?"[15] However, if the juridical authorities convict the offender, they will execute the criminal alone and will not include the family. In some instances, the authorities may execute an offender together with his family, but only if the culprit has been *convicted* by the gods (by ordeal or by oracle).

The environment surrounding ancient Israel provides an obvious resource for clarifying the idea behind biblical sacrilege. Forms and ideas were freely exchanged among cultures of the ancient Near East, unless they happened to clash with the particular value system of the borrowing culture. Israel's concern regarding sacrilege was shared with its neighbors, for all ancient Near Eastern peoples believed that sacrilege against sanctums threatened the general welfare. If we look to neighboring civilizations, we find parallel laws, customs, and concepts that deal with the issue of sacrilege.

The Hittite text "Instructions for Temple Officials" deals exclusively with the subject of sanctum desecration. In the Hittite tradition, deliberate sacrilege against sanctums is punishable by the human court or the heavenly court. If the Hittite gods are doing the punishing, then not only the offender but also his or her household are killed. If, however, the juridical authorities convict the offender, they will execute the criminal alone and will not include the family. In some instances, the authorities may execute an offender together with his family, but only if the culprit has been *convicted* by the gods (by ordeal or by oracle). This corresponds with a basic postulate of Israel's law (see below).

While deliberate sacrilege against sanctums is not explicitly handled in the biblical law-codes, a number of biblical narratives describe an Israelite committing sacrilege against God's sacred space and the punishment that ensues. The Priestly tradition itself adduces the examples of Nadab and Abihu[16] and Korah and the chieftains.[17] The sin of deliberate sacrilege is held by the Chronicler to be the cause of

---

[15] *ANET*, 208, lines 34-37.
[16] Lev 10:1-2.
[17] Num 16:16-40.

Uzziah's leprosy[18] and the destruction of Judah.[19] For the desecration of proscriptions—the worst sacrilege of all—the wrath of God consumes the nation.[20] In all of these cases the penalty is explicit: the trespasser is struck down by God.

Ostensibly, the case of Achan, who is killed by human court for sacrilege together with his family, contradicts this principle, because this execution is performed by human beings (Josh 7:24-25). Yet the exception proves illusory. Achan's guilt is discovered by lot, which means that God himself designates the culprit, and it is by God's expressed command that collective punishment is carried out (v. 15). Similarly, in a direct Hittite precedent, the temple herdsmen who are convicted by oracle—that is, by the gods—are also put to death together with their families. Thus both in Hattia and in Israel, convictions by oracle result in collective executions by the court.

Every unapprehended act of sacrilege against God, whether against the sanctums or against the name of God, leads to the destruction of the community as well as the offender. In the Bible, sacrilege against "the Name" is clear: it refers to breaking sacred oaths and is amply attested. By contrast, sanctum desecration in the Bible is neither defined nor clearly illustrated. The contrast between the few biblical examples offered us and Hittite tradition helps to clarify Israel's understanding of the sin of desecrating the sanctuary. Israelite law operates with two postulates: (1) sins against God are not punishable by human beings; and (2) collective punishment is a divine right that may not be usurped by humans.[21]

Thus we see that Israel and Hattia held a common legal principle (which may have been violated in practice). One might refer to it as an embryonic religious pluralism. One could not be arrested for violating the state religion. It was an egregious sin, but its punishment resided with the offended deity, not with human authorities. This principle comes into play in a notorious biblical case (see 24:15-16).

Selected Texts

[5:15] The reparation offering is the only one in the entire roster of sacrifices that is commutable to currency.[22] The commutability of the reparation offering also speaks to its antiquity. It appears only twice in the early biblical narratives, and in both places it is not an animal sacrifice but a monetary payment. The first refers to the golden mice and tumors for the plague that beset the Philistines because they possessed the holy ark.[23] The other mention of the reparation offering is in connection with King

---

[18] 2 Chr 16:16-18.

[19] 2 Chr 30:10.

[20] Achan, Joshua 7; 22:20; 1 Chr 2:7; Amalek, 1 Sam 15:3-31; Ben-hadad, 1 Kgs 20:42.

[21] For details see Milgrom 1976a:16–35.

[22] Lev 5:15, 18, 25; and 1 Sam 6:3-17.

[23] 1 Sam 5:6; 6:3-17.

Joash's temple repairs.[24] This latter account speaks of "reparation silver," testifying that in First Temple days, offerers had the option of donating its monetary equivalent.

[5:16] "one-fifth of its value." That the Priestly legists imposed such a small fine of one-fifth for sacrilege is nothing short of astounding. Their leniency can only be appreciated by comparing this case with other kinds of theft found in the legal statutes of the Bible.[25] The answer was correctly noted by Greenberg: Eliminating penalties for self-confessed theft encouraged "voluntary surrender in these cases, where, owing to lack of evidence, or to the impotence of the victims—the victims of robbery are almost invariably poor and defenseless (Ps 35:6; Isa 3:14; Jer 7:6; Amos 4:1)—legal means of recovery were of little avail."[26] There is a tendency in all ancient jurisprudence to encourage the voluntary surrender of illegally acquired goods by reducing the usual penalties.

As will be developed below (on 5:25 [Eng. 6:6]), a basic legal and theological postulate of the Priestly legists is that persons can seek reconciliation with God only after they have made the required restitution to the desecrated sanctuary or to the defrauded person.

5:17-19: The Suspected Desecration of Sanctums

Concern over unconscious sin permeates the Bible.[27] Picture it: A person is experiencing psychological (and perhaps even physical) suffering whose cause he does not understand. Because he cannot attribute his suffering to any sin he knows he committed, he attributes it to an unwitting offense against God, confirming the psychological truth that one who does not know the exact cause of his suffering imagines the worst. This section speaks to the unwitting sinners who, without knowing what sin they have committed to cause such grief, believe they have affronted the Deity, committed sacrilege against the sanctums, and "incurred liability to YHWH" (v. 19). The law of 5:17-19 responds to this psychological phenomenon by offering the suffering individual a way to repair the unknown wrong and, it is hoped, thereby ease his or her suffering. One of the most significant contributions of Israel's expiatory sacrifices, therefore, is that all accidental sins are expiable by sacrifice. Intention does play a role in the divine judgment. This constitutes a major break with the theology of the ancient Near East and of old Israel.

It is reasonable to assume that this concern had greater theological significance for Israel than for any of its neighbors. The polytheist, acknowledging evil as an

---

[24] 2 Kgs 12:17.
[25] See Milgrom 1991:328–29.
[26] 1962:741b.
[27] E.g., Deut 29:28 (Eng. 29); 1 Sam 26:19; Ps 19:13 (Eng. 12); Job 1:5.

autonomous, supernatural force, could posit that evil could be requisitioned by any person—through the agency of a sorcerer—and used to inflict harm upon another. This is why in many conjuration rituals the evil is not only exorcised from the victim but is also hurled back upon his enemy, the sorcerer originator. Israel's monotheism, conversely, having vitiated the premise of autonomous, supernatural evil, had no choice but to attribute its existence to the one God. Natural evil, then, could be understood by the pagan as emanating from a supernatural force, but to the Israelite it was a scandal, a blatant contradiction of God's goodness and justice.[28]

Selected Theme
Unwitting Violations

The increased importance of the reparation offering at the end of Second Temple period bespeaks a development whose significance cannot be underestimated. Heretofore, people tended to dichotomize the world into the sacred and the profane, the discrete realms of the gods and humanity. People believed that as long as they did not infringe on the sacred, the gods would not molest them; people might even thrive under their gods' beneficence if people regularly rendered them their due. With the promulgation of Lev 5:17-19, whereby the unwitting violation of any "of YHWH's commandments" requires expiation for sanctum desecration, the boundaries between the sacred and the profane are obliterated forever. Henceforth, the sacred is unbounded; it is coextensive with the will of God. It embraces ethics as well as ritual, the relations between people and not just those between people and God. In short, the violation of any of the Torah's prohibitions constitutes sacrilege, the expiation of which is essential if Israel is to remain in divine grace.[29]

Selected Texts

[5:17] The key phrase in this case, "without knowing it," is pinpointed by Rabbi Jose the Galilean: "The text punishes one who does not know (his sin)."[30] Thus this inadvertence was unwitting.

[5:19] In the Hebrew, the key verb translated "incur liability" appears twice in succession (infinitive absolute plus perfect), possibly for emphasis. The sense would be: "He surely has incurred liability to YHWH." If so, then the meaning would be that even if a person merely suspects that he has desecrated a sanctum, he should take no

---

[28] Indeed, a case can be made that Job's polemic against his friends rests on their disagreement over unconscious sin in theodicy: Job's friends champion the traditional view of Israel and its environment that Job is suffering for his unconscious sin; Job, by contrast, emphatically denies this doctrine and insists that his suffering is unjustified until he knows wherein he has sinned: "Let Shaddai answer me. Let my opponent write a document" (Job 31:35).

[29] Details in Milgrom 1976a:74–84.

[30] *Sipra Ḥobah* par. 12:7.

chances but promptly bring a reparation offering to avert the wrath of the Lord in case he actually committed sacrilege. Because there is no certainty that sacrilege was committed, no restitution is required.

5:20-26 (Eng. 6:1-7): Sacrilege against Oaths; Repentance

(20) YHWH spoke to Moses, saying: (21) When a person sins by committing a sacrilege against YHWH in that he has dissembled to his fellow in the matter of a deposit or investment or robbery; or having withheld from his fellow (22) or having found a lost object he has dissembled about it; and he swears falsely about any one of the things that a person may do and sin thereby—(23) when one has thus sinned, and feeling guilt, he shall return that which he robbed or that which he withheld, or the deposit that was entrusted to him, or the lost object he found, (24) or anything else about which he swore falsely; he shall restore it in its entirety and add one-fifth to it. He shall pay it to its owner as soon as he feels guilt. (25) Then he shall bring to the priest, as his reparation to YHWH, an unblemished ram from the flock, or its assessment, as a reparation offering. (26) The priest shall effect expiation on his behalf before YHWH so that he may be forgiven for whatever he has done to feel guilty thereby.

Selected Themes
A. The Paradox and Its Corollary
The justification for the translation of 5:20-26 (Eng. 6:1-7), which differs from all extant ones, depends on answering the paradox raised by this pericope. As rendered, it flies in the face of the fundamental premise of P, that there can be no sacrificial expiation for the presumptuous sinner; he is barred from the sanctuary because "he acts defiantly . . . reviles YHWH . . . has spurned the word of YHWH and violated the commandment" (Num 15:31). Indeed, the reparation offering cases thus far presume that their respective offenses were committed unintentionally. This reparation offering passage, however, confronts us with the one who defrauds both God and his fellow willfully and yet is forgiven if he brings the proper sacrifice.

To resolve this paradox we must identify the two basic postulates informing this legislation. The first postulate: The reparation offering, which in vv. 14-19 was enjoined for real or suspected desecration of God's property, is now imposed in vv. 20-26 (Eng. 6:1-7) for the desecration of God's name.

A corollary of this passage should not be overlooked: the priority of restitution. In this passage, only after the rectification has been made with one's fellows can it be sought with God. This is the explicit stipulation of 5:24b-25 (Eng. 6:5b-6): "He shall pay it [the restitution] to its owner as soon as he feels guilt. Then he shall bring to the priest. . . ." This inference is corroborated by the practice of the Second Temple, as reflected in both tannaitic law and the New Testament. For example, the Day of Purgation atones for sins between persons and God. But the Day of Purgation does not atone for the sins between people and their fellows until they have made restitution to each other;[31] "He who robs his fellow a penny's worth and swears (falsely and then confesses) must bring it to him even in the land of the Medes."[32] "If when you bring your gift to the altar, you suddenly remember that your brother has a grievance against you, leave your gift where it is before the altar. First go make peace with your brother, and only then come back and offer your gift."[33] It marks a startling innovation in jurisprudence: in matters of justice, people take priority over God. That this postulate constitutes a radical change can be best appreciated from the vantage point of the sacrificial system, which postulates the reverse: God must receive God's due from the altar before persons receive theirs. The violation of this axiom constitutes the sacrilege of Eli and his sons: "You honor your sons above me by fattening yourselves upon the choicest parts of every offering of Israel ahead of me" (1 Sam 2:29 LXX); "ahead of me" (LXX) is preferable to "to my people" (MT).

B. The Priestly Doctrine of Repentance

Leviticus 5:20-26 (Eng. 6:1-7) states that each case of fraud was aggravated by a false oath, thus compounding a civil crime against humanity with a capital crime against God. Yet from the prescribed punishment one is forced to deduce that a death sentence has been commuted to sacrificial expiation! Rephrasing the paradox exposes its audacity to the full. By what right did the Priestly legists presume to mitigate God's penalty? That they could reduce the fine paid to the injured owner is readily explicable: the crime was a civil one, falling under the jurisdiction of the human court. But when they legislate that a false oath is expiable not by death but by sacrifice, they, the priests, "my intimates" (10:3), have encroached upon the divine sphere. They have arrogated to themselves the power to alter God's decree. The paradox, then, is not the reduction of the monetary fine, for which ample precedent is available, but the unprecedented right of humans to commute the death sentence imposed by the heavenly court. Indeed, the crime of desecrating God's name, instead of being expiated by sacrifice, would seem to be aggravated by it—humans have overruled the will of God![34]

A resolution of this question is now possible. I submit that the repentance of sinners, through their remorse and confession, reduces their intentional sin to an inadvertence, thereby rendering it eligible for sacrificial expiation.

What is it about the confession that endows it with such power? Is it only a legal fiction invented by the Priestly legists to ameliorate the crime, or does it possess

---

[31] *m. Yoma* 8:9.

[32] *m. B. Qam.* 9:5; cf. *Abot R. Nat.* B 21 and its modification in the baraita, *b. B. Qam.* 103b; cf. also *m. B. Qam.* 9:12; *t. Pesaḥ.* 3:1.

[33] Matt 5:23-24 (NEB), and cf. *t. Pesaḥ.* 3:1.

[34] For details see Milgrom 1976a: 84–117.

some innate force that, as the Priestly legists intuited, can generate a behavioral change? The answer lies in the psychological realm. It can be elucidated by an analogous phenomenon in the contemporary world. I cite from "The Twelve Steps of Alcoholics Anonymous":

1. We admitted that we were powerless over alcohol—that our lives had become unmanageable.

2. Came to believe that a Power greater than ourselves could restore us to sanity.

3. Made a decision to turn our will and our lives over to God as we understood Him.

4. Made a searching and fearless moral inventory of ourselves.

5. Admitted to God, to ourselves and to another human being the exact nature of our wrongs.

6. Were entirely ready to have God remove all these defects of character.

7. Humbly asked Him to remove our shortcomings.

8. Made a list of all persons we had harmed, and became willing to make amends to them all.

9. Made direct amends to such people wherever possible, except when to do so would injure them or others.

At first glance, the anthem of Alcoholics Anonymous seems unbridgeably distant from Leviticus. Ostensibly the alcoholics have sinned only against themselves, hurting neither God nor fellow. Yet the cure, according to the Twelve Steps, lies precisely in the alcoholics' recognition that they in fact offended God and fellow and, until rectification is made to both, the alcoholics cannot be cured. First the alcoholics must experience remorse before God: "feel guilt" (nos. 1-4). Then the alcoholics must confess their wrongs to God and to other human beings (nos. 5-7). Finally, the alcoholics must make full restitution to those they have wronged (nos. 8-9). Thus their chance of regaining control over their lives depends on being reconciled with God and humanity. Only when they are at peace with the external world can they attain peace in their inner world.

And the confession plays a critical role. It assumes that it takes greater courage to verbalize one's faults to others than just to understand them oneself and that, correspondingly, the ability to confess bespeaks a more resolute desire to alter the status quo. Furthermore, the act of confession assumes the response of forgiveness, human and divine. Thereby the erstwhile (self-imposed) isolation of the alcoholics is by the single stroke of confession converted to a supportive relationship; the universe, which has ostracized them (or so they may have felt), now takes them into its embrace. By the same token, Leviticus also presumes that the greater effort to articulate one's contrition and, if necessary, to make proper amends will affect one's reconciliation with God and persons "so that he may be forgiven" (5:26 [Eng. 6:7]).

P postulates a new category of jurisprudence: repentance as a factor in the mitigation of divine retribution. The Priestly authors took a postulate of their own tradition, that God mitigates punishment for unintentional sins, and empowered it with a new doctrine, that the voluntary repentance of a deliberate crime transforms the crime itself into an involuntary act. True, P could go only as far as its theological premises would allow: repentance reduces the penalty but cannot nullify it. But it stands as a major step in the development of the prophetic doctrine of repentance. For the first time in history, perhaps, humans are assured that their repentance is both desired and required by God. In truth, how far is this doctrine from the prophetic teaching that repentance leads to the remission of all sin? The difference is one of degree, but in substance the principle is the same: a person's repentance is a prerequisite for divine forgiveness.

The root purpose underlying the expiatory sacrifices is now seen in its true significance. Often the Priestly system of sacrificial expiation was construed as a legalized witch hunt, hounding the person's conscience and damning them with guilt for their every accidental, presumed, or unapprehended crime. Now it is clear that the reverse is true. All of the cases stipulated or implied by the expiatory sacrifices present us with the existential situation of people in torment, racked by conscience over their actual or suspected sin. No one can help them, for their pain is known only to themselves. Not even God can come to their aid, for they will not disclose their burden to heaven. It is to these silent sufferers that the Priestly law brings its therapeutic balm: If the prescribed restitution is inspired by their repentance, their sin can be absolved. They need suffer no more.[35]

Selected Texts

[5:21 (Eng. 6:2)] Tannaitic law distinguishes clearly between robbery and theft, the difference being that robbery is committed openly by force[36] whereas theft is by stealth.[37] Although robbery is included in this list, theft is conspicuously missing. Why is the thief omitted? Surely, one may argue, the thief may also be subject to the acts that characterize the cases of vv. 20-26, to wit: suspicion, denial, false oath. The common denominator in all of the cases in vv. 20-26 (Eng. 6:1-7) is that the claimant feels certain that he can identify the possessor of his object. Because the claimant cannot produce witnesses or documents, however, the possessor needs but to assert his ownership under oath in order to retain the contested object. Thus it should be clear that ordinary theft has no place in this series. Theft, by definition, means that the

---

[35] Details in Milgrom 1976a:114–24.

[36] "Openly and forcibly," Ibn Ezra on 19:13.

[37] See *t. B. Qam.* 7:2; *Mek.* on Exod 22:6; *b. B. Qam.* 7a, b; *Midr. Gen. Rab.* 54:3.

object has been separated from its owner without his knowledge; hence, he has not seen the thief.

In sum, the understanding of the cases of vv. 20-26 (Eng. 6:1-7) is based on the realization that they concern religious and not civil law, *fas* and not *jus*. All that matters to the Priestly legist is to enumerate those situations wherein the defrauding of human beings leads, by false oath, to the defrauding of God. The general category of theft in which the thief remains unidentifiable is therefore irrelevant to the Priestly legislator's purpose.

[5:22 (Eng. 6:3)] The false oath does not apply to a discrete wrong. Rather, it applies to all the preceding cases: not only have the offenders defrauded their fellows but they have denied it under oath. The "sacrilege against YHWH" (v. 21 [Eng. 6:2]) is, therefore, fully clarified: YHWH has been made an accomplice to the defrauding of humanity.

The Priestly Sacrificial Duties

Chapter 6 marks a change in audience for the book of Leviticus. Whereas the first five chapters address the people, setting out a system of sacrificial observance, chapters 6 and 7 address the priesthood, delineating their role in the sacrificial system. Indeed, even the order of the discussion of the sacrifices reflects the very different view that the Bible has of the ordinary Israelite and the priest. For the layperson, the sacrifices are divided mundanely into those which are voluntary (chaps. 1–3) and those which are mandatory (chaps. 4–5), reflecting the average individual's day-to-day interaction with the sacrificial rituals. For the priests, on the other hand, the sacrifices are divided between most holy (6:1-7, 10 [Eng. 8-14, 17]) and holy (7:11-36), attention to holiness being the domain of the priests.

These two chapters deal with two seemingly unconnected concepts: sanctum contagion, and *karet:* excision and/or afterlife. Sanctum contagion describes the ultra-sacred objects whose own sanctity is so powerful that it can sanctify others; when misused, it can cause their downfall. *Karet* describes the specific punishment that ensues. In both cases, the biblical legalists struggle to make sense of older traditions that do not find an easy resting place in the ordered system of Leviticus. For sanctum contagion, the priests choose to reduce the contagious power of the sanctum in order to rid the sanctuary of criminals who flocked there for protection from civil authorities. In the instance of *karet*, the priests assert their conviction that criminals may escape conviction by a civil court, but they cannot escape divine retribution: the destruction of their family line and, possibly, their assurance of an afterlife.

Selected Themes

A. Sanctum Contagion

Sanctum contagion describes the set of things that sanctify all that touch them. In the words of Leviticus: "who-/whatever [lit. 'all that/who'] touches . . . will be sanctified." The formula for sanctum contagion is used four times in P, each time connected to the tabernacle. Of the four instances in which the formula for sanctum contagion is used, twice it is in connection with sacred furniture of the tabernacle (Exod 29:37; 30:26-29), and twice with sacred offerings (Lev 6:11, 20 [Eng. 18, 27]).

While it may be unusual for us to imagine that merely being exposed to an object could be cleansing, in the scheme of Leviticus it is not surprising that a sacred object could sanctify that which touches it. What is unusual about the formula for sanctum contagion is the ambiguous use of the simple particle "all." Does "all" include persons, or is it restricted to inanimate objects? In other words, shall it be rendered "whoever" or "whatever"? The difference transcends mere semantics. If people as well as things can be sanctified, then any criminal who wishes to escape apprehension by civil authorities need only flee to the sanctuary, seize hold of the altar horns—thereby becoming himself sanctified—and he would be off-limits to the nonsacred, profane world. This is attested in Scripture; however, premeditated murder is made an exception (see Exod 21:4; 1 Kgs 1:51; 2:2-3). Indeed, by the law of the medieval church, a fugitive from justice or a debtor would be entitled to immunity to arrest. Is it any wonder that one of today's meanings of the word "sanctuary" is a reserved area whose birds and animals were protected from hunting or molestation? As will be shown, the answer to this question will open a new chapter in Israel's cultic history.

The question as to whether people are susceptible to the contagious sanctum is hotly contested in ancient texts. The rabbis are unanimous in eliminating the human factor completely. Indeed, they even reduce the compass of "whatever" to relatively few objects.

Poles apart from the restricted contagion posited by the rabbis stands the cultic system of Ezekiel, who holds that most holy offerings consecrate persons and not just inanimate objects (Ezek 46:20). Not only does Ezekiel allow humans to be consecrated by sanctum contagion, he adds a category of contagious sanctum not included in the rabbis' system (or in the Pentateuch), namely, the priestly garments (Ezek 44:19; cf. 42:14).

It is germane to inquire whether Ezekiel's ruling is his own innovation or reflects an older law. An answer is at hand if we examine P's position on this matter. To be sure, P contains no explicit law concerning the contagion of the priestly garments; but its very omission from P's prescription on the contagion of sanctums in Exod 30:26-30 betrays P's position in a striking way. These verses warrant close examination: "With it [the sacred anointing oil] anoint the tent of meeting, the ark of the pact, the table and all its utensils, the lampstand and all its fittings, the altar of incense, the altar of the burnt offering and all its utensils, and the laver and its stand. Thus you shall consecrate them so that they may be most sacred; whatever touches them shall be sanctified. You shall anoint Aaron and his sons, consecrating them to serve me as priests." Our formula comes not at the pericope's end but in its penultimate verse, after the roster of cult objects and before the anointing of the priests (v. 29b). Thus the conclusion is unavoidable that the legislator intentionally excluded the priestly garments from the application of the formula because, in his system, the priestly garments do not communicate holiness. P is engaged in a polemic; it is deliberately opposing a variant tradition that is found in the book of Ezekiel.

Leviticus 6–7: The Priestly Sacrificial Duties

Holiness is lethal to all but the priests. That is, only the consecrated priests, who themselves have become holy, have the right to approach and handle the sanctums. The early narratives corroborate this assumption: the most sacred sanctums are lethally contagious to unauthorized persons even when their contact with them is respectful, for example, Uzzah's touching the ark (2 Sam 6:6-7) and the Beth-shemeshites' viewing it (1 Sam 6:19). The theophany at Sinai provides a particularly illuminating example. Whoever trespasses on the mountain must be slain, but his slayers must heed that "no hand shall touch him, he shall be either stoned or pierced through" (Exod 19:13, JE). The implication is clear: the holiness communicated to the offender is of such power that it can be transmitted through a medium. Hence the instrument of death must not allow contact between the offender and his executioner. P also provides a telling example: the death of Nadab and Abihu (Lev 10:1-5). The divine fire has executed them for their cultic offense, but their bodies may not be touched directly; they must be wrapped in other garments before being removed from the sanctuary (v. 5). Again, the holiness contracted by persons can be imparted by touch to a third party with fatal results. This second-degree holiness is attributed to the sanctum associated with the very presence of God (e.g., the ark, Mount Sinai, the divine fire).

The high voltage of the supersanctums is also evidenced by their power to communicate not only by contact but by sight. This has already been noted in the story of the ark at Beth-shemesh (1 Sam 6:19). But even in P—which, as will be shown, strives for a reduction in the contagious power of the sanctum—the sanctums still possess the power to kill their viewers when they are being dismantled (Num 4:20). Thus even in the early sources a gradation may be detected in the most sacred sanctum; the supersanctums—those considered to be earthly manifestations of the Deity—are fatally contagious to those who view them directly and to those who contact them through a medium. As the Ezekiel text (above) exposes, the original range of sanctum contagion formula was unrestricted: even persons were included and intention was not a factor. Indeed, that "all" was chosen for the formula probably indicates that initially no exceptions were intended. The narrative of Nadab and Abihu's death (Lev 10:1-5) is a remnant of this tradition: they have encountered the sanctums illegitimately and the divine fire has executed them for their cultic offense. It would seem that P preserves a *narrative* tradition that ascribed contagious power to the tabernacle sanctum, but this contagion was severely restricted in P's *legal* pronouncements.

What was the motivating force behind the Priestly obsession to reduce the contagious power of the sanctums? In ordaining that the formula "all that touches [the sanctums] becomes sanctified" (6:11, 20; Exod 29:37; 30:26-29) applies to objects but not persons, the priests had the altar chiefly in mind. They were probably deeply disturbed by the stream of murderers, thieves, and assorted criminals who flocked to the altar and resided on the sanctuary grounds on the basis of hoary, venerable traditions that the altar "sanctifies"; so they declared that those who entered the sacred precincts were not under divine protection. The priests therefore took the radical step of declaring that the altar was no longer contagious to persons; those who touched it were no longer "sanctified," so they might be wrested from the altar by the authorities with impunity. In this cultic reform the priests would have won the support of the king and his bureaucracy, who would have earnestly wished to terminate the sanctuary's veto power over their jurisdiction.

Because the only attested case of altar asylum in the Bible—but surely not the first—is David's tent-shrine in Jerusalem (1 Kgs 1:51; 2:2-3), it is highly probable that this reform was enacted under Solomon, who used his royal power to introduce many administrative and cultic changes. The new altar in the new temple was declared off-limits to every nonpriest, and it never afforded asylum.

B. Karet: *Excision and Deprival of Afterlife*

There are eighteen cases of *karet* in the Torah, all in Priestly texts. They can be subsumed under the following categories: sacred time, sacred substance, purification rituals, illicit worship, and illicit sex.

A. Sacred time
1. Neglecting the Passover sacrifice (Num 9:13)
2. Eating leaven during the Unleavened Bread Festival (Exod 12:15, 19)
3. Working on the Sabbath (Exod 31:14)
4. Working or not fasting on Yom Kippur (Lev 23:29, 30)

B. Sacred substance
5. Imbibing blood (Lev 7:27; 17:10, 14)
6. Eating sacrificial suet (Lev 7:25)
7. Duplicating or misusing sanctuary incense (Exod 30:38)
8. Duplicating or misusing sanctuary anointing oil (Exod 30:33)
9. Eating a sacrifice beyond the permitted period (Lev 7:18; 19:8)
10. Eating a sacrifice in a state of impurity (Lev 7:20-21)
11. Blaspheming (flauntingly violating a prohibitive commandment, Num 15:30-31; cf. Lev 24:15)

C. Purification rituals
12. Neglecting circumcision (Gen 17:14; the purification is figurative, Josh 5:9)
13. Neglecting purification after contact with the dead (Num 19:13, 20)

D. Illicit worship
14. Molek and other forms of idolatry (Lev 20:2-5; Ezek 14:8)
15. Consulting the dead (Lev 20:6)

16. Slaughtering animals outside the authorized sanctuary (Lev 17:4)
17. Sacrificing animals outside the authorized sanctuary (Lev 17:9)
E. Illicit sex
18. Effecting forbidden consanguineous and affinal marriages (Lev 18:27-29)

As for the exact nature of *karet,* two opinions command attention. The first is that *karet* means extirpation,[1] meaning that the offender's line is terminated. He may live a full life or an aborted one. His death need not be immediate, as would be the case if his execution were the responsibility of a human court, because divine power is ensuring that, no matter how long he lives, he will leave no offspring on this earth.

The other possible meaning of *karet* is that the punishment is indeed executed upon the sinner but only after his death; he is not permitted to rejoin his ancestors in the afterlife. This meaning for *karet* is supported by the idiom that is its antonym: "be gathered to one's [kin, fathers]" (e.g., Num 20:24, 27:13; 31:2; Gen 15:15; 47:30; Judg 2:10). Particularly in regard to the patriarchs, the language of the Bible presumes three stages concerning their death: they die, they are gathered to their kin, and they are buried (cf. Gen 25:8; 35:29; 49:33). "It [the term 'gathered'] designates something that succeeds death and precedes sepulture, the kind of thing that may hardly be considered as other than reunion with the ancestors in Sheol."[2] *Karet* implies that ordinarily after death we are gathered into our family, not into God but into the company of those who more directly gave us life and identity. Our family mediates our identity in this world and receives us in the next. The implication is that we retain our own individual identity in the next world. We are not engulfed by God, in whom we would have shed ourselves. To shed one's identity after death is not immortality. Only if there is some continuity of identity after death is there meaningful immortality. The idea that we have a spark of God in us that returns to God is of no comfort unless the spark carries our individual identity. It also makes the punishment *karet* that much more frightening. It is not some impersonal, neutral soul that is cut off, but my very being, my identity, and for eternity.

This biblical term has its counterpart in the contiguous river civilizations of Egypt (e.g., "going to one's Ka") and of Mesopotamia (e.g., "joining the ghosts of one's ancestors"),[3] all of which is evidence for a belief in the afterlife that permeated the ancient world and the concomitant fear that a wrathful deity might deprive a person of this boon. This interpretation would be in keeping with *karet* as an individual, not a collective, retribution. Finally, that a person is cut off from one's "kin" implies the existence of a family sepulcher in which one's kin have been gathered. That allusions to the afterlife are all that exist in Scripture is evidence that the concept of an

---

[1] Ibn Ezra; cf. also Tosafot on *b. Šabb.* 25a.
[2] Alfrink 1948:128.
[3] Wold 1978.

afterlife was deliberately suppressed. The reason, I submit, is that it was associated with ancestor worship (see the discussion in chap. 20, THEMES A and C).

It is difficult to determine which of these meanings is correct. Because they are not mutually exclusive, it is possible that *karet* implies both of them; in other words, there are no descendants in this world and no life in the next.[4]

Selected Texts

Chapters 6–7 can be subdivided into nine sections: the burnt offering (6:1-6 [Eng. 8-13]), the cereal offering (6:7-11 [Eng. 14-18]), the high priest's daily cereal offering (6:12-16 [Eng. 19-23]), the purification offering (6:17-23 [Eng. 24-30]), the reparation offering and the priestly prebends from the most holy offerings (7:1-10), the well-being offering (7:11-21), the prohibition against eating suet or blood (7:22-27), the priestly prebends from the well-being offering (7:28-36), and the summary (7:37-38). Each section begins with "YHWH spoke to Moses" (6:12 [Eng. 19]; 7:22, 28) or "This is the ritual for" (6:7 [Eng. 14]; 7:1, 11, 37); in two instances both opening formulas occur together (6:1-2, 17-18 [Eng. 8-9, 24-25]).

The book of Leviticus contains ten *torot*, comprising a decalogue of ritual life,[5] as follows: five *torot* of sacrifice—6:2 [Eng. 9] (the burnt offering); 6:7 (Eng. 14) (the cereal offering); 6:18 (Eng. 25) (the purification offering); 7:1 (the reparation offering); and 7:11 (the well-being offering)—and five *torot* of impurity—11:46 (animals); 12:7 (the parturient); 13:59 and 14:54-57 (scale disease); 14:2, 32 (the purification of the scale diseased); and 15:32 (genital discharges). These *torot* were documents probably stored in the sanctuary archives. They were the special lore of the priesthood. The word *torot* itself means rituals or instructions.

The Altar Fire (6:1-6 [Eng. 8-13])

The elimination of the altar ashes takes place in two stages, their removal to the side of the altar and, afterward, their removal outside the camp. The two-stage removal stems not from ritualistic considerations but from more pragmatic ones. All acts involving the altar are *eo ipso* rituals and require the priests to wear their sacred vestments. Conversely, all acts taking place outside the sanctuary are profane and hence bar the wearing of the sacred vestments. Thus it is simply the priest's need to change his clothes that has resulted in separating the ash removal into two parts, its removal from the altar and its removal outside the camp.

Among Israel's neighbors (e.g., Hittites, Mesopotamians), substances that absorb impurity are themselves lethally dangerous and must be "taken out to the plain, the pure place."[6] Yet the similarity to Israel's praxis ends here. In Israel only the

---

[4] For proof texts that validate each position, see Milgrom 1991:458–60.
[5] Hoffmann 1953:297.
[6] Reiner 1958:7.63.

blood of the purification offering acts as a ritual detergent, and even in the instance of this sacrifice, the flesh is normally eaten by the priest (6:19, 22 [Eng. 26, 29]), and only purification offerings brought for severe impurities are incinerated "in a pure place" outside the camp.[7] All other sacrifices, such as the burnt offering, discussed here, are incinerated on the altar, and their ashes are simply disposed of. They have no inherent powers; their holiness is not contagious.

An offering of wood for the altar (6:5 [Eng. 12]) is well-attested in various sources pertaining to the Second Temple period. The earliest reference is in Nehemiah (10:35; 13:31), which relates that lots were drawn to determine which families would supply wood for the temple at various times during the year. The rabbis assign nine dates for the wood offering, eight of them reserved for specific families and the ninth (the fifteenth of Av) for the public at large.[8] They claim that all woods except the grapevine and olive wood were valid for the offering.[9] This rule is explained as a sign of respect for the trees whose fruit (grapes and olives) are used for libations on the altar.[10] The more probable reason, however, is that both of the aforementioned woods do not burn well and produce too much smoke.[11] Another tradition is preserved in the pseudepigraphical literature that restricts the types of offerable wood to twelve.[12]

The wood was brought to the temple with great ceremony. Bearers of the wood were forbidden to work on that day and were required to spend the night in Jerusalem, returning to their homes the following morning. Haggadic tradition tells of the courage and perseverance of those bringing the wood even in the face of danger to their lives.[13]

The requirement for a "perpetual fire" (v. 6) stresses the importance of maintaining the fire even if the sacrifices are totally consumed. This prescription, found in other cultures as well (e.g., the ancient Greeks), may stem from the mundane necessity of keeping the fire burning during days on which kindling one was difficult.[14] But a more likely explanation is indigenous to Israel's priestly circles. The sacrifices offered up at the inauguration of the public cult were consumed miraculously by a divine fire (9:24), and it is *this* fire that is not allowed to die out so that all subsequent sacrifices might claim divine acceptance.[15]

---

[7] 4:12; see chap. 4, THEME B.

[8] *m. Ta'an.* 4:5; cf. Josephus, *War* 2.430; additionally, preferred manuscripts of the Mishna (e.g., Kaufmann, Parma, Geniza fragments) as well as other tannaitic sources (e.g., *t. Bik.* 2:9) include a tenth occasion—also for the public offering (the ninth of Av; see Safrai 1965:221–22).

[9] *m. Tamid* 2:3.

[10] *Midr. Lev. Rab.* 7:6; *Midr. Haggadah* and *Leqah Tov* on 1:8.

[11] *b. Ta'an.* 29b.

[12] *T. Levi* 9:12; *Jub.* 21:12-14.

[13] *t. Ta'an.* 4:7-8.

[14] Yerkes 1952:158.

[15] See Philo, *Spec. Laws* 1.286, and the discussion of 9:24 below.

The Cereal Offering (6:7-16 [Eng. 14-23])

Clearly, the "holy place" (6:9 [Eng. 16]) is here identified as the tabernacle court.[16] That is, because theoretically the entire tent-shrine as "a holy place" would also qualify as the priests' dining room, the text delimits the dining area to the court.

There is even stronger scriptural evidence for this identification. The place in which the priestly consecrands are to cook their sacrificial meat is called in Exod 29:31 "a holy place," but in Lev 8:31 is described as "the entrance to the tent of meeting." Thus the priestly dining area must be located in the tabernacle court. The cereal offering is eaten by the priests "beside the altar" (10:12). Because the sacrificial altar is situated in the very center of the court (see fig. 1), the expression "beside the altar" must designate the area within the altar's circumference, that is, anywhere inside the court. At the same time, there is good reason to believe that *in practice* the priests actually dined on their prebends in the inner court, called by the rabbis by the biblical expression "between the porch [of the temple] and the altar."[17]

Mention should also be made of the archaeological findings in Arad that the courtyard of its sanctuary (datable to the First Temple period) was clearly divided into two parts on either side of the sacrificial altar, thus suggesting the possibility that the bipartite division of the sanctuary court extends back into biblical times. Hence this adduced evidence may indicate the existence of two priestly traditions: the theory, which allowed them to dine anywhere within the sacred precinct, and their practice, which confined their eating and, indeed, all of their private activities, to the inner part of the court.

The Purification Offering (6:17-23 [Eng. 24-30])

[6:19 (Eng. 26)] "The priest who offers it as a purification offering" (lit. "the priest who performs the decontamination rite," i.e., removes the impurity of the altar by means of the blood). Presumed is that more than one priest officiates at each sacrifice. To be sure, at early, simple sanctuaries, a single priest would see the sacrifice through form beginning to end, and even in larger sanctuaries no more than a single priestly family would suffice to administer and perform the entire cult. It was only the temple of Jerusalem that employed a large priestly cadre, which ultimately had to be broken into "divisions" and "fathers' houses."[18]

[6:21 (Eng. 28)] Scripture was forced to tolerate the contradictory notion that the technique of purging the sanctuary of its impurities—the purification offering—could simultaneously be a most sacred offering and a source of impurity. In the manner of objects contacted by the flesh of the purification offering, the subject of this pericope,

---

[16] Rashi.
[17] Joel 2:17.
[18] 1 Chronicles 24.

a similar paradox ensued: although the objects that came into contact with the purification offering were treated as if they were impure, they were nonetheless considered to be holy. That is, these objects became or remained the property of the sanctuary because they were rendered holy but were dealt with as impurities: bespattered garments were washed, copper vessels were scoured and rinsed, and earthen vessels smashed and discarded (or buried).

[6:22 (Eng. 29)] "Any male among the priests may eat of it." Ostensibly, this statement contradicts the previous one that only the officiating priest shall eat it (v. 19 [Eng. 26]). The contradiction evaporates as soon as one realizes that although the officiating priest, who manipulates the blood, does indeed receive the prebend, he may, if he so desires, distribute it among his fellow priests.[19]

[6:23 (Eng. 30)] These purification offerings are the bull of the high priest (4:1-12), the bull of the community (4:13-21), and the bull of the high priest and the he-goat of the community on Yom Kippur (16:27).

The Priestly Prebends (7:7-10)

[7:8] The hide was a handsome prebend, considering the great number of private burnt offerings that were sacrificed each day.[20]

[7:9] This statement that the cooked cereal offering belongs to the officiating priest constitutes an innovation and an ostensible contradiction to 2:10, which assigns the cooked cereal offering to all of the priests. As already noted, a similar contradiction prevails in the purification-offering pericope: the meat of the sacrifice is eaten by both the officiant and the entire priestly cadre (6:19a, 22 [Eng. 26a, 29]). All it means, however, is that the officiant has the right to distribute his prebend among his fellow priests. A similar problem and solution will again prevail in the pericope on the well-being offering: its right thigh is awarded to both the officiant and to all of the priests (vv. 33-34). A practical consideration may be involved: "It was in the interests of priests to share their prebends, since in that way they would reduce the extremes in which some might get a lot and others a little, or some better portions and others worse portions . . . comparable to arrangements among waiters to share their tips."[21]

The Well-Being Offering (7:11-36)

[7:11] Three kinds of well-being offering are herewith prescribed. But why were they not cited in chapter 3, which deals exclusively with the well-being offering? An obvi-

---

[19] See Shadal on 7:10
[20] Philo, *Spec. Laws* 1.151.
[21] D. N. Freedman, written communication.

ous answer is that the priestly prebends from this sacrifice are detailed here (vv. 14, 31-35) in like manner as the other sacrifices (6:9-11, 19, 22 [Eng. 16-18, 26, 29]; 7:6-10). Another reason may be the constant need for priestly supervision. For example, one type of bread accompanying the thank offering is leavened (v. 13). Heaven forbid that it become mixed with the unleavened bread and offered upon the altar (see 2:11)! Furthermore, this is the only sacrifice whose meat is eaten by laypersons, and their negligence may lead to its desecration or contamination (7:15-21). Hence the priests must keep a watchful eye over the proceedings. But this pericope tacitly (vv. 11-21) and the following ones expressly (vv. 22-23, 28-29) are addressed to the laity, not to the priests, an indication that the supervisory responsibility has shifted from the priests to the laity.

"that one may offer to YHWH." This phrase is an admission that it is permitted to eat the meat of pure, nonsacrificial animals, for example, blemished animals (22:21-25) and game (17:13-14), as well as sacrificial animals slaughtered profanely for their meat.

[7:12] The sacrifice of thanksgiving is the original name of this sacrifice before it was subsumed in P under the well-being offering. Yet the tradition that the thank offering is an independent offering that must be distinguished from the well-being offering is firmly anchored in all sources but P,[22] including even rabbinic sources.[23]

[7:13] Though not permitted on the altar, cakes of leavened bread are still considered an offering.[24]

P alone has subsumed the thank offering under well-being, resulting in this artificial and awkward construction.

[7:14] The function of the "gift" is to transfer the object from its owner to the Deity. In this respect it is similar to the "elevation" (v. 30), but with this crucial distinction: the "elevation" is performed "before YHWH," whereas the "gift" is never "before" but always "to YHWH." Thus the "elevation" and "gift" comprise two means of dedication to God: the former by a ritual in the sanctuary, and the latter by a ritualless dedication outside the sanctuary, either by the offerer's oral declaration (Judg 17:3), after which he brings the "gift" to the sanctuary (Exod 35:24; Num 18:13), or by physically handing the gift directly to the priest.

The centrality of the blood ritual is indicated here by its being the rite that determines the recipient of the priestly prebends. The more basic question needs to be

---

[22] E.g., 22:21, 29 (H, not P); Jer 17:26; 2 Chr 29:31-33; 33:16.

[23] *m. Zebaḥ.* 5:6-7; cf. 1 Macc 4:54-56.

[24] Cf. v. 14a; 23:17-20; Amos 4:5.

asked: Why is the blood rite so essential to the well-being offering? It will be addressed in 17:11.

[7:16] The votive offering is brought following the successful fulfillment of a vow. That is, a well-being offering is vowed to God if a prayer is answered.

The common denominator of all motivations in bringing a well-being offering is rejoicing. Therefore, on purely logical grounds, the freewill offering would be the most frequently sacrificed, for it is the spontaneous by-product of one's happiness whatever its cause.

[7:18] How is it possible that the sacrifice is not acceptable, when it has already been offered?[25] The equivalent law in 19:8 provides the answer: "for he has desecrated the sanctum of YHWH." Implied is that the meat—and indeed all parts—of the sacrifice retains its holiness until the time of its elimination. Thus by desecrating the sacrifice, in allowing it to remain beyond its prescribed time limit, the offerer has invalidated the entire sacrifice retroactively. A classic case of retroactivity in cultic law is the reparation offering brought for embezzlement, which is founded on the principle that voluntary repentance of a deliberate crime retroactively transforms the crime into an involuntary act (see 5:14-26).

The rabbis, however, were reluctant to allow for the principle of retroactivity in the sacrificial system. They claim that if the offerers permitted the sacrifice to become desecrated by eating it beyond its time limit, they must surely have intended to do so from the beginning. Thus the rabbis introduce a new principle, intentionality.[26] It is assumed that the intentionality of the beginning of the act was also flawed, and therefore the sacrifice was never a proper one. So, for example, if a convert (to whatever religion) abandons the accepted religion, one could argue that the conversion process itself was done without the proper intention, and the entire process was flawed from the beginning. Statements of intention aside, actions and deeds reveal intentionality. The true test of what one believes is the actions one takes.

How do I prove the content of my thoughts? I begin a process of action that initiates goodness. But toward the end of the process I cease doing good and do something that is not good. The rabbis argue that I never did have a clear grasp of goodness. The misdeed, or misaction, shows that I chose wrongly and therefore the process is invalidated. My intentionality was initially flawed.

[7:20] "while impure." The person is the source of the impurity;[27] for instance, he has gonorrhea or a nocturnal emission (15:1-17). The case of one who is secondarily infected is taken up in the next verse.

---

[25] Asked by Rabbi Eliezer in *b. Zebaḥ.* 29a.

[26] *m. Zebaḥ.* 2:2-3; 3–6.

[27] *Sipra Ṣaw* 14:4.

72

"YHWH's" (lit. "[flesh from the sacrifice of well-being] that is YHWH's"). Why this ostensibly superfluous clause? The implication is clear: Meat that is not "YHWH's" is also permitted. That is, it is not brought to the altar as a sacrifice but is slaughtered profanely or consists of game (17:13-14) and blemished animals (22:21-24).

The phrase "that person shall be cut off from his kin" (17:20) is a penalty formula for *karet*, which as explained above, declares that the person's line will be terminated by God and, possibly, that he will be denied life in the hereafter. The question needs to be addressed here whether such a drastic punishment is inflicted even if the wrongdoing proved accidental, for example, if he is unaware that he is impure or that the meat is sacred. The principle of intention is nowhere expressed in this pericope. Nonetheless, a sound deduction can be made from the sacrificial system in general, and the case of the impure priest in particular. The laws of the purification and reparation offerings make clear that sacrificial expiation is possible when a violation of a prohibitive commandment is committed inadvertently or unwillingly (4:2; 5:14, 17). Brazen sins against God are punished by God with *karet* (Num 15:30-31). As mentioned above, the parallel pericope dealing with the priest who eats sacred food is introduced by the generalization: "If any man among your [Aaron's] offspring, while in a state of impurity, *intentionally contacts* any sacred gift that the Israelite people may consecrate to YHWH, that person shall be cut off from before me: I YHWH (have spoken)" (22:3). Thus excision by divine agency is imposed on the impure priest only when he presumptuously comes into contact with holiness. The same must hold here, and we must assume, in consonance with the sacrificial system, which clearly recognizes the principle of intention (chaps. 4–5), that if any persons inadvertently eat sacred food, their wrong will be expiated by a purification offering (4:22-35). It must also be predicated that the advertent, presumptuous consumer of sacred food (or violator of any other prohibition) can avert the *karet* penalty if such a person feels remorse and voluntarily confesses the crime, thereby converting the advertent act into an inadvertent one (see 5:20-26).

[7:21] Assumed is that the impurity is contagious to people, a situation that can only occur if the human source bears a severe impurity lasting nominally for seven days, such as the gonorrhean or menstruant (chap. 15), the parturient (chap. 12), or the corpse-contaminated person (Numbers 19). But if the impurity is of one-day duration, for instance, resulting from sex or ejaculation (Lev 15:16-18), touching a severely impure person (15:19; Num 19:22), or entering a fungous house (Lev 14:46), then it cannot contaminate a person (for details, see chap. 15).

Verses 19-21 deal with contact between impurity and sacrifice. It is important to note, however, that no penalty exists for eating an impure sacrifice; there is only a warning that it should be burned and not eaten (v. 19). The reason is stated succinctly by the rabbis: "because one is culpable only on account of personal impurity."[28] The implication is fundamental. Contrary to the rule in the pagan world, Israel holds that impure animals—even if they are brought into contact with sanctums (e.g., by being sacrificed)—offer no threat to society. Danger resides in impurity only if it emanates from the human being.[29] This will be fully developed in chapters 11–15.

[7:23] The introduction "Speak to the Israelites thus" differs from all those of the previous pericopes in chapters 6 and 7 in that it explicitly addresses the laity and not the priests (contrast 6:2, 13, 18 [Eng. 9, 20, 25]). The reason is clear. Because the offerer is responsible for bringing the suet to the altar (7:29-30), he may neglect to bring all of it and instead leave some behind to be eaten with the flesh, thereby incurring the *karet* penalty (v. 25).

[7:24] "An animal that died" refers to the carcass of an animal that dies a natural death. Presumed is that the carcasses of these wild animals do not defile upon contact; else how could their suet be handled with impunity?

There is no prohibition (in any priestly source) against eating the meat of a carcass or mauled animal (but only a warning to cleanse oneself of the resultant impurity, 17:15-16), for if it were eligible for sacrifice as a well-being offering, it would be eaten by its owner. Without exception, however, the suet of such a sacrificial animal belongs to God; for this reason, if anyone eats the suet, even if the animal died naturally and can no longer be offered on the altar, it is as if that person had encroached upon divine property and is subject to divine sanctions.

[7:25] The first half of this verse is a circumlocution for sacrificial animals. Therefore, the suet of nonsacrificial animals—namely, game—may be eaten.

[7:26] "Blood, from any source, even from game, and in any place, even your settlements." This prohibition has already been given in 3:17. Why is it repeated here? The contrast with suet provides the answer. In 3:17 the two were equated because the context was that of sacrifice. Here they are differentiated because the focus has shifted to nonsacrificial animals: nonsacrificial suet may be eaten, but nonsacrficial blood is forbidden—hence, the addition of the word "bird," that is, game.

[7:30] Because the elevation rite transfers the object from the offerer to the Deity (represented by the priest), the hands of both the offerer and the priest are placed under the offering to perform this rite.

---

[28] *m. Zebaḥ.* 13:1.
[29] See chap. 4, THEME A.

[7:32] The right thigh is of the hind legs, not the shoulder of the forelegs. It was choice meat, to judge by the fact that it was put aside by Samuel for Saul (1 Sam 9:24).

[7:34] "The thigh of the gift" is the stock expression for this prebend.[30] The word "gift" indicates that it was set aside, in other words, dedicated to God outside the sanctuary, an act by which God symbolically acquires it.

[7:37-38a] This is a summary and subscript to chapters 6–7.

[7:37] The ordination offering is prescribed in Exodus 29 and described in Leviticus 8. So why is it mentioned here? One must seriously reckon with the possibility that a special *torah* for the ordination offering originally stood before the pericope on the well-being offering (vv. 11-21.). If this conjecture be allowed, the *torah* would have enumerated the prebends from this offering and their disposition (corresponding in content to 8:26-29, 31-33) but it was subsequently omitted when chapters 1–7 were inserted between Exodus 40 and Leviticus 8 because of the repetition of these same provisions in the latter.[31]

[7:38] According to P, Moses received the laws concerning the construction of the tabernacle and its sanctums on Mount Sinai.[32] Moreover, there are other laws also attributed to the Sinaitic revelation (chaps. 25–26 [H]). The terms "Mount Sinai" and "wilderness of Sinai" (below) are not identical. The former literally refers to the peak itself and—in the cited instances above—to its summit, where Moses spoke with God. The latter refers to Israel's encampment in the vicinity of Sinai,[33] where God spoke to Moses only inside the tent of meeting.[34]

The wilderness of Sinai is the specific area at the foot of Mount Sinai where Israel was encamped from the third month of the first year of the exodus (Exod 19:1) until the twentieth day of the second month of the second year (Num 10:11-12). Lev 7:37-38 distinguish between the *torah* instructions imparted to Moses on Mount Sinai (chaps. 6–7) and the commands given *to the Israelites* (not the priests, 6:2 [Eng. 9]) concerning *their* sacrificial duties—an unmistakable reference to chapters 1–5, the sacrificial laws directed to the Israelites (1:2; 4:2).

---

[30] Exod 29:27; Lev 7:34; 10:14, 15; Num 6:20; 18:18.
[31] For evidence that chap. 8 originally followed Exodus 40, see Milgrom 1991:545–49.
[32] Exod 31:18; 34:32.
[33] Exod 19:1, 2; Num 10:12.
[34] Lev 1:1; cf. Exod 25:22; 29:42; Num 7:89.

Leviticus 8–10

The Inauguration of the
Tabernacle Service

These chapters continue the narrative in Exodus, which has been interrupted by Leviticus 1–7. Specifically, God commands Moses to build a tabernacle (Exodus 25–31). After an interruption caused by the apostasy of the golden calf (Exodus 32–34), we learn of the construction of the tabernacle (Exodus 35–40). But before it can be dedicated and operated, Moses must be instructed about the sacrifices, their function and use (Leviticus 1–7). Chapter 8 now tells us of the consecration of the priests; chapter 9 of how Aaron successfully conducted the inaugural; and chapter 10 of how he meets with a personal tragedy.

The Consecration of the Priests

The eighth chapter of Leviticus provides the fulfillment of the command at Exodus 29 to "consecrate Aaron and Aaron's sons to the priesthood." Why is the realization of the command so far from the initial decree? The answer is clarified by the context. Moses is commanded to consecrate Aaron and his sons into the priesthood by means of a series of sacrifices. Thus Moses must learn the sacrificial procedures (Leviticus 1–7) before he can proceed with the priestly consecration. He will also need to consecrate the tabernacle (8:10-11) before he can consecrate the priests, for when the tabernacle and its sanctums were assembled (Exod 40:17-33) they had not been consecrated.

Why, after such a long hiatus, is it important that the Bible records that Moses anoints Aaron and his sons? It is not only because it represents the fulfillment of a prior obligation; it is also a lesson to the reader about the importance of ritual markers. The Bible is reminding us not to let important moments slide by unnoticed, but instead to mark occasions with rituals that establish the significance of the moment and emblazon them on our collective memory.

Selected Themes

A. Consecration: A Rite of Passage

Our lives are filled with important passages of time. We are born. We start school. We go to college. We get married. We have children. We watch our children have children. We die. If we are lucky, these moments are marked by rituals or rites of passage that help us to contextualize and understand the relevance of the shift that is taking place—from childhood to adulthood, from bachelorhood to marriage, from life to death. We are baptized/circumcised. We go to graduation ceremonies at elementary school, high school, college. We undergo consecration or bar/bat mitzvah. We enter marriage under oath. We take last rites on our deathbed.

Most of the time, though, in the rush of everyday existence, transitions of great import go unmarked: we start new jobs without taking the time to reflect on why we left in the first place; we have children without welcoming them into our family and community; we die alone. The Bible teaches a powerful lesson on the value of rites in marking the important passages of our lives. A. van Gennep has defined rites of passage as "rites which accompany every change of place, state, social position and age."[1] In the priestly period, one of the most significant rites of passage occurred at the consecration of the priests and the high priest. Like other rites of passage, the ceremony marking the transition from layperson to priest is marked by three phases: rite of separation from the previous state, margin (or *limen,* signifying "threshold" in Latin), and rite of aggregation of new powers and obligations.[2] As we analyze the rite of passage that the priests-elect undergo, there is much that is instructive for us in our choices about how we mark significant moments in our own development.

"During the liminal period, the characteristics of the subject (the passenger) are ambiguous: He passes through a cultural realm that has few or none of the attributes of the past or coming state . . . as liminal beings, they have no status, property, insignia, secular clothing indicating rank or rule, position in a kinship system—in short, nothing that may distinguish them from their fellow neophytes or initiands. Their behavior is normally passive or humble; they must obey instructions implicitly, and accept arbitrary punishment without complaint."[3]

This description of the liminal state bears many similarities to the biblical rite of priestly consecration, described in detail below. Before jumping into a discussion of priestly consecration, however, a specific comparison will throw these similarities into sharper relief. During the installation rites of the Kanongesh (senior chief) of the Ndembu, the chief-elect is isolated in a special hut.[4] He is clad in nothing but a ragged waist-cloth and sits crouched in a posture of shame or modesty. The officiant conducts the rite of *Kumukindyila,* which literally means "to speak evil or insulting words against him." His homily begins with these words: "Be silent! You are a mean and selfish fool, one who is bad-tempered! You do not love your fellows, you are only angry with them! Meanness and theft are all you have! Yet we have called you and we say that you must succeed to the chieftainship." After this harangue, any person who considers that he has been wronged by the chief-elect in the past is entitled to revile him, while the latter has to sit silently with his head downcast. In the meantime, the officiant strikes his buttocks insultingly. The night before the rite, the chief-elect is prevented from sleeping, partly as an ordeal, and partly because he may doze off and have bad dreams about the shades of dead chiefs. For the duration of the rite, he is submissive, silent, and sexually continent.[5]

The similarities to the biblical rite of priestly consecration are quickly recognizable: the seclusion of the consecrands (in the sanctuary court), their silence and

---

[1] 1960.

[2] Leach 1976:78.

[3] Turner 1969:94–95.

[4] Ndembu *kafwi,* a term derived from *ku-fwa,* "to die," where he dies from his commoner state.

[5] Turner 1969:100–109.

79

submissiveness (they are commanded but do not respond), their sexual continence (they are isolated within the sacred premises), and their mortal fear lest they break any of the taboos. Regarding the last point, the biblical text is frustratingly brief. It specifies only one taboo, that of leaving the sanctuary. Clearly there were others. For example, because their status was still that of laymen, they were forbidden to officiate on the altar or enter the shrine (cf. v. 35; Num 18:3); they cooked and ate the sacrificial portions reserved for the laity in the area reserved for the laity (v. 31) instead of eating the priestly prebends (vv. 26-29) in the inner court (see 10:4)—the exclusive preserve of the priests (see 10:12). Moreover, being in the sanctuary, they would have taken precautions against the occurrence of ritual impurity. The chief-elect of the Ndembu was prevented from sleeping the night before his installation because of the fear of a polluting dream. Likewise, the high priest of Israel was kept awake on Yom Kippur night for fear of a polluting emission. "If he sought to slumber, young members of the priesthood would snap their middle finger before him and say to him, 'My lord, high priest, get up and drive away [sleep] this once [by walking] on the [cold] pavement.' And they used to divert him until the time of slaughtering drew near."[6] One must suppose that equally effective measures were enjoined for priestly consecration lest a nocturnal emission pollute the sanctuary.

It is the Babylonian New Year Festival that provides the most illuminating parallels to the cases cited above. For the Babylonians, New Year was a momentous rite of passage. The fate of the nation was decreed during this period: "He [the *šešgallu*-priest] shall strike the king's cheek. If, when [he strikes] the king's cheek, the tears flow, (it means that) the god Bel is friendly: if no tears appear, the god Bel is angry: the enemy will rise up and bring about his downfall."[7] Moreover, the studied humiliation of the king is a prominent feature of the festival: "When he (that is, the king) reaches [the presence of the god Bel], the *šešgallu*-priest shall leave (the sanctuary) and take away the scepter, the circle, and the sword [from the king]. He shall bring them [before the god Bel] and place them [on] a chair. He shall leave (the sanctuary) and strike the king's cheek. . . . He shall accompany him (the king) into the presence of the god Bel . . . he shall drag (him by) the ears and make him bow to the ground."[8]

Thus anthropology helps illuminate the priestly consecration ceremony. The virtual quarantining of the consecrands within the sanctuary court and the admonition that they must observe the restrictions placed upon them (as laymen) give the unshakable impression that we have here a rite of passage wherein the priestly consecrands and their ordination offering share a transitional, liminal status. The priestly consecration, therefore, begs further anthropological analysis.

---

[6] *m. Yoma* 1:7.
[7] *ANET*, 334.
[8] *ANET*, 334.

Why the liminal state is always a perilous one is difficult to answer. Perhaps the establishment, entrenched outside, regards the anarchical, amorphous status of the consecrands as a danger to societal law and order.[9] Mary Douglas's investigation would, rather, point to the anomalous position of the consecrands, which is feared as dangerous, by the very fact that it defies classification.[10] In either case, there would be complete agreement that Aaron and his sons underwent a transformation during their rite of passage. Henceforth they are priests; however, their acquired privileges and prestige are matched by greater responsibilities and restrictions.

B. The Purpose of Anointing

The main role of symbolic anointment in the ancient Near East, aside from its cosmetic, therapeutic, and magical functions, was to ceremonialize an elevation in legal status: the freeing of a slave woman, the transfer of property, the betrothal of a bride, and the deputation of a vassal; and—in Israel—the inauguration of a king, the ordination of a priest, and the rehabilitation of a "leper." These cases indicate that, in Israel as opposed to other parts of the Near East, symbolic unction took place in the cult but not in legal proceedings. The implication of anointing as a sacred rite is that the anointed one receives divine sanction and that his person is inviolable.[11]

In Israel anointment conferred upon the king the "spirit" of YHWH, that is, his support,[12] strength,[13] and wisdom.[14] The anointment of the high priest, however, served an entirely different function. It conferred neither YHWH's spirit nor any other divine attribute. Moses, for example, transferred his powers (by hand-leaning) to a spirit-endowed Joshua (Num 7:18-20), but when he transferred the high priest's authority from Aaron to his son Eleazar, these spiritual features are conspicuously absent (Num 20:25-29). In the story of Joshua's investiture—told by P—Eleazar is declared the indispensable medium to ascertain the divine will, though, tellingly, not by virtue of any innate spiritual powers but rather by his authority to work the oracle (Num 27:21). This instance is a vivid illustration of the function of the high priest's anointment, which is otherwise designated by the verb "sanctify." Indeed, the anointment "sanctifies" the high priest by removing him from the realm of the profane and empowering him to operate in the realm of the sacred, namely, to handle the sanctums.

According to P, the sons of Aaron were anointed with him. The respective ceremonies differ sharply: The sons were sprinkled after the sacrifice (8:30; Exod 29:21), whereas Aaron's head was doused separately, before the entire service (8:12;

---

[9] Turner 1969:108–9.
[10] 1966:39–40, 54–57.
[11] 1 Sam 24:7, 8; 26:9, 11, 16, 23; 2 Sam 1:14, 16; 19:22.
[12] 1 Sam 16:13-14; 18:12.
[13] Ps 89:21-25 (Eng. 20-24).
[14] Isa 11:1-4.

Exod 29:7). Furthermore, whereas each succeeding high priest was anointed (6:15 [Eng. 22]), the anointing of the first priests was never repeated; it was to be valid for their posterity (Exod 29:9; 40:15b). This concept has proved to be ancient, for it is found in the Tell el-Amarna letters, in which a vassal stakes his authority on his grandfather's anointment.[15] The difference between the status of the high priest and that of the ordinary priest explains the difference in the consecratory rites. The ordinary priest was born a priest, a status that is inherited and requires no special sanctification. The high priest, however, requires a special inaugural rite to elevate him to this position.

Selected Texts

[8:2] The priestly vestments are listed first as the priests will be dressed in them (vv. 7-9, 13) before the sacrificial service begins (vv. 14-29). The text is here concerned with the procedural order. Even the sacrificial items are listed in the order of their use: purification offering (vv. 14-17), the burnt offering and ordination rams (vv. 18-25), and the basket of unleavened bread (v. 26). This trait is not peculiar to the Priestly writer, but is standard scribal style in the ancient Near East.

[8:4] The expression "As YHWH commanded him" appears seven times in the chapter (vv. 4, 9, 13, 17, 21, 29, 36) and seven times in the accounts that describe the manufacture of the priestly vestments (Exod 39:1-31) and the assembling of the tabernacle (Exod 40:17-38). This refrain subdivides the chapter into seven coherent sections and constitutes the scaffolding upon which Leviticus 8 is constructed. The significance of this refrain derives from the belief that "unless YHWH builds the house, its builders labor in vain on it" (Ps 127:1).

[8:7] The priestly vestments total eight in all, four undergarments worn by all of the priests and four outer garments worn by Aaron, the high priest, alone. They are described in Exodus 28 and 39. Aaron's four outer garments are the ephod, the breastpiece, the robe, and the gold plate. Whereas the robe is fashioned out of one material, dyed wool, the ephod and the breastpiece are of fine linen, dyed wool, and gold. The mixture of linen and wool was prohibited in nonsacred garments because it was considered holy (on the sash see v. 13). The four undergarments are a tunic (the high priest's was more elaborate; see below), a sash, a headdress (the high priest's again more elaborate; see below), and breeches. The breeches are omitted from the list of vestments donned by either Aaron or his sons (vv. 7, 13) and appear only in an appendix to the inventory of the priestly vestments in Exod 28:42-43, which suggests that they were not considered sacred. Sandals were forbidden on sacred ground.

The "ephod" is made primarily of gold with blue-purple, red-purple, and red woolen threads and fine linen skillfully woven into it. It is shaped like an apron that

---

[15] EA 51:4-9.

covers the loins (waist to thigh?) and is suspended from two shoulder pieces (Exod 28:6-14). It must be distinguished from the linen ephod attributed, in sources other than P, to the ordinary priest,[16] and from the oracular ephod,[17] though the same basic garment may be intended.[18]

[8:8] Breastpieces or pectorals were a common royal accoutrement in the ancient Near East. They were generally made of gold frames with precious stones set in them. These pectorals were suspended by twisted gold cords or chains strung through gold rings on the edges or backs of the pectoral.

The breastpiece served two purposes as part of the high priest's vestments. First, it served as a continual reminder of the twelve tribes before God. The names of the twelve tribes were engraved, each on a stone (Exod 28:21). Aaron bore these names upon his heart (hence we know that the breastpiece was worn on the upper chest and not at the waist). Because the high priest officiated in silence,[19] the engravings on the stones spoke to God. Second, the breastpiece—also called "the breastpiece of decision"—served an oracular purpose; it became the receptacle for the Urim and Thummim.

The Urim and Thummim were a form of oracle placed inside a pocket of the breastpiece, worn by the high priest on his chest. According to the Priestly tradition they were used exclusively by the high priest inside the tabernacle. Their shape and operation are unknown. The proposed theories can at best be considered only attractive speculations. The riddle of the Urim and Thummim still awaits resolution.

[8:9] The plate was suspended from the high priest's turban by a blue cord. Because of its inscription "holy to YHWH" (Exod 28:36), it had the power "to remove the sin of the holy things that the Israelites consecrate, from any of their sacred donations" (Exod 28:38). In other words, any inadvertent impurity or imperfection in the offerings to the sanctuary would be expiated by the plate.

However, just as the plate, whatever its original meaning, became identified with the object that bore it on the high priest's head, so did the diadem. Although it originally referred to some emblem that projected from the object that fastened it to the head, it eventually became identified with the object itself. Hence I have adopted the rendering "diadem" here.

[8:10] The term "tabernacle" here means not the entire tabernacle complex but its more restricted and more precise sense, the inner curtains of the tent.[20]

---

[16] E.g., 1 Sam 2:18; 22:18; 2 Sam 6:14.
[17] 1 Sam 23:6, 9; Hos 3:4.
[18] Haran 1955.
[19] Kaufmann 1960:303, 384.
[20] Cf. Exod 26:7; 36:14.

Leviticus 8–10: The Inauguration of the Tabernacle Service

[8:11] The altar, standing exposed in the tabernacle court, is the most vulnerable of all the sanctums. It might have been considered advisable to inoculate the altar with additional sprinklings of consecrating oil to buttress it against incursions of impurity. The prophylactic power of oil was acknowledged in the ancient Near East. It was believed to possess the intrinsic power to impart vitality to and repel evil from the statues of the gods: for example, "Oil, oil . . . you are on Horus's forehead. . . . You give him power over his body. You impose his fear on all who look at him and hear his name."[21] Anointing oil was an important component of magical formularies. Thus the anointing of vassals was not mere ceremonial trapping: "As oil penetrates your flesh, so may they [the gods] make this curse enter your flesh."[22] The magical power of oil was rejected by Israel (Judg 9:9). Still, the sevenfold sprinkling of the altar with anointing oil may betray an original apotropaic function (for the function of anointment in Israel, see THEME B).

Another attractive explanation for the altar's sevenfold sprinkling stems from the work of A. Hurowitz.[23] In Israel the altar was always independent of the temple. Before the centralization of the cult under Josiah, private altars abounded. Indeed the prevalent "high place" probably designates an open cult area dominated by its altar.[24] Even when the temple was destroyed, sacrifices continued to be offered at its site on an improvised altar (Jer 41:5). The returning exiles built, consecrated, and sacrificed on an altar long before they constructed the temple (Ezra 3:1-3). Thus the autonomous existence of the altar allows for the possibility that it developed its own consecration ceremonial wholly independent of the consecratory rites performed in the tabernacle/temple, consisting of a sevenfold sprinkling with the anointing oil.

[8:12] As the oil is inherently holy (Exod 30:32), it can be applied directly; contrast the sacrificial blood, which must first be made holy by its contact with the altar (v. 30). It is important to emphasize that the purpose of the priestly investiture is sanctification (vv. 12, 30), in contrast to the purpose of Levitical investiture, which is purification (Num 8:6, 7, 21). Indeed, the Priestly texts never use the terms "consecrate" or "holy" in connection with the Levites; in matters of holiness they rank no higher than the laity.[25]

[8:13] The requirement that a priest wear a sash of *šaʾatnez*, a mixture of wool and linen, completes the picture of graded holiness within the ranks of Israel. The high priest alone wears outer garments of *šaʾatnez*, which match the inner tabernacle curtains. Thus the high priest is sartorially of the same degree of holiness ("most holy")

---

[21] Otto 1960:122, scene 95, line 11.

[22] Cf. Wiseman 1958:78, lines 622-24.

[23] Hurowitz 1974:115–6.

[24] Haran 1978:48–57.

[25] Milgrom 1970:29 n. 103.

as the area—inside the tent—in which he officiates. The ordinary priest is of lesser holiness than the high priest. He may not officiate inside the tent but only on the altar; he is not "most holy" but "holy," and the symbol of his reduced holiness is his *ša'atnez* sash. Finally, the Israelite who may not officiate at all is neither "most holy" nor "holy." Nonetheless, he is enjoined to wear *ša'atnez* on the fringes of his outer garment as a reminder that he should aspire to a life of holiness (for details, see 19:19).

[8:15] The basic postulate of the purification offering is that it is required of the one who inadvertently violates a prohibition (4:2), and it is he or she who must perform the hand-leaning rite (4:4, 15, 24, 29, 33); the sole exception is the presumptuous sinner, who is banned from the sanctuary, for whom the high priest on the Day of Purgation performs the hand-leaning (16:11). Thus, as it is Aaron and his sons who perform the hand-leaning on the purification offering (8:14) and on the two subsequently sacrificed animals (vv. 18, 22), the only possible inference is that they themselves are at fault. Living day and night for an entire week in the proximity of the altar, it is not difficult to contemplate the incidence of unavoidable physical impurities (e.g., a nocturnal emission, 15:16-17), which, because of their occurrence within the sacred precincts, would necessitate a purification offering.

"To effect atonement," that is, in the future. It is totally unrelated to the purification offering just sacrificed. Rather, it refers to the permanent function of the newly consecrated altar; its effect is forevermore. Its use is not limited just to the purification offering and its exclusive purgative function but embraces all of the sacrifices in their expiatory roles: the burnt offering, the cereal offering, the reparation offering (chaps. 1, 2, 5:14-26) and even the well-being offering (chap. 17). Hence the general, comprehensive rendering "atonement" is employed here.

[8:22] Literally *millu'im* means "filling" or, more precisely, "[hand-]filling," from the expression "fill the hand of" (discussed in detail in v. 33).

[8:23] There is abundant attestation of ritual daubing in the ancient Near East. The incantations recited during the ritual smearing of persons, the statues of gods, and buildings testify that their purpose is purificatory and apotropaic: to wipe off and ward off the incursions of menacing demonic forces. Always it is the *vulnerable* parts of bodies (extremities) and structures (corners, entrances) that are smeared with magical substances.[26] Thus it can be seen that the blood daubing of the altar's extremities—its horns—closely resembles the blood daubing of the extremities of the priests. But it is the dedicatory rite of Ezekiel's altar that most closely corresponds to the daubing of the priests, for the purificatory blood is daubed not only on the altar's

---

[26] E.g., *ANET*, 338; Wright 1987:34–36.

horns but also on the corners of its two gutters, located at its middle and bottom (Ezek 43:20). These points correspond to a person's earlobe, thumb, and big toe. It is safe then to conclude that these two congruent rites share the same purpose, which in the case of Ezekiel's altar is made explicit: "And you shall decontaminate it and thus purge it" (Ezek 43:20); "they shall purge the altar and thus purify it" (Ezek 43:26). Therefore, the daubing of the priest at points of his body and the daubing of comparable points on the altar must possess a similar goal: purging. Thus the function of the blood daubing of the priests is also purgative.

[8:29] According to P, Moses should have received nothing: he is not a priest. Indeed, he gets nothing from the offerers. The right thigh, which normally would have been given directly to the officiant by the offerers, is instead given over to God and burned on the altar (vv. 25, 28). Moreover, Moses receives a prebend not from the offerers but from God: the breast is subject to the elevation rite, that is, it is transferred to the authority of the divine so that God might award it to him.

[8:30] That the anointing oil consecrated the priests and their clothing is obvious; such is the exclusive power of the anointing oil (Exod 30:22-30). But how is it possible for the blood to possess consecratory power? Its expiatory role in the sacrificial system is emphasized over and over again. Indeed, the very daubing of the priests with the blood of the ordination ram (vv. 23-24) is for expiation (see v. 23). How then can the same blood—from the ordination ram—suddenly have a consecratory role? The answer is provided by the text itself; it informs us that, as opposed to the daubing of the priests wherein the blood was applied directly from the animal to the priests, the aspersion of the priests must be done with blood taken from the altar. Thus in keeping with the basic Priestly rule "whatever touches the altar is sanctified" (Exod 29:37b), as soon as the blood impinges upon the altar it partakes of its holiness and is then able to impart holiness to others.[27] A confirmatory ritual is the consecration of the outer altar on Yom Kippur (16:19). The purificatory blood had first impinged on the outer altar before it was applied a second time to the outer altar. The initial application sanctified the remainder of the blood.

[8:33] It is likely that Aaron and his sons did not budge from the sanctuary at all during the week of their consecration—perhaps not even to relieve themselves. There is a possibility that somewhere *within* the courtyard enclosure there was a space reserved for toilet facilities.

If the first-day rites were to be repeated each day, their purpose could well have been that of reinforcement.[28] But the text is silent concerning purpose and confines

---

[27] Hazzequni on Exod 29:21.
[28] Baentsch 1903.

itself to prohibitions: the consecrands are forbidden to leave the sanctuary for seven days on pain of death (v. 35). We are dealing here with a rite of passage, such as the seven days after birth (circumcision on the eighth day marks the first day of the child's life, Gen 17:12), the seven days of marriage celebration (Gen 29:27), and the seven days of mourning (Gen 50:10). "All these are 'passage times' when a person moved from one house of life to another, dangerous occasions when demons were most active."[29] Thus the fact that Aaron and his sons are constrained to remain in the sanctuary for seven days can only mean that rites are being performed on them during this period by which they can pass from the house of commoners to the house of priests. They are consecrated as priests only at the end of the week, and during the liminal period they are highly vulnerable, not to demonic assault—the world of demons has been expunged from priestly notions—but to human sin and impurity. The peril that attends all liminal periods is attested in cultures throughout the world, discussion of which is reserved in THEME A. Here let it further be noted that the status of the ordination sacrifice is a perfect match for the consecrands. The sacrifice is itself transitional and anomalous. It ranks lower than the most holy offerings and higher than the lesser holy offering (7:38), and shares the characteristics of both. So too with Aaron and his sons: they participate in the sacrificial services as offerers, not as priests; at the same time they are consecrated with holy oil. Theirs is a seven-day passage. It is inconceivable that after the first day they merely wait out the week at the tabernacle door. Each day's rites will remove them farther from their former profane state and advance them to the ranks of the sacred, until they emerge as full-fledged priests.

---

[29] Snaith 1967 on 4:6.

The Inaugural Service

The eighth day marks the inauguration of the regular public cult. During the previous week, the tabernacle was consecrated and the priests were invested, all in preparation for this day. The eighth day is thus the climax of the foregoing seven, as in so many other rituals and events (see on v. 1). Aaron is the exclusive officiant (assisted by his sons), and he offers up every kind of sacrifice with the exception of the reparation offering, the only sacrifice that is wholly private and never incorporated into the public cult. The provision for well-being offerings guarantees the festive nature of this day (see v. 4). Indeed, the promised theophany (vv. 4b, 6b) is a happy prognostication that the consecration of the sanctuary and its priesthood will merit divine acceptance. The TEXTS lay the foundations for the THEME, and therefore are presented first.

Selected Texts

[9:1] The eighth day is not like the previous seven. The first seven serve as the investiture of the priesthood (chap. 8), and the consecration of the sanctuary (8:10-12), whereas the eighth day serves an entirely different purpose—the inauguration of the public cult conducted by its newly invested priesthood. The technical name for this inauguration is *hanukkah*, "initiation," or, more precisely, "the initiation of the altar" (this is elucidated in the THEME). The concentration of the entire chapter is upon the altar, as demonstrated by the curtailed description of the sacrificial procedure, which omits nearly every rite that is unrelated to the altar (e.g., the hand-leaning) but includes every rite involving the altar, even the most minute (e.g., the disposition of the suet pieces, vv. 19-20), climaxed by the unique theophany upon the altar (vv. 3-24). The etymology of this term *hanukkah*, its relationship with the gifts of the chieftains (Numbers 7), and the paradigm of this eight-day celebration for subsequent temple initiations are discussed in the THEME below.

[9:2] Koch wonders why Aaron must now bring a purification offering and a burnt offering after having already done so for the seven previous days.[1] The answer lies in

---

[1] 1959:70.

the contrasting function of the two periods. The week-long ceremonies focused on the investiture of the priests, but the eighth-day service marks the inauguration of the public cult in which all sacrifices play a role. That is, all sacrifices but the reparation offering are prescribed for the eighth day, and its absence proves the case: the reparation offering is always a private offering; it is never required in the public cult. A comparable situation prevails when the chieftains bring their gifts for the newly consecrated altar: again, all sacrifices are accounted for but the reparation offering (Num 7:12-17; see the THEME below). Thus the sole absence of the reparation offering from the prescribed sacrifices for the eighth day implies the inauguration of the public cult.

[9:4] The importance of the theophany in the newly consecrated tabernacle cannot be exaggerated. It renders the tabernacle the equivalent of Mount Sinai: God's presence was made manifest at both places. But whereas the people experienced God's voice at Sinai (Exod 20:18), only an elite saw God (Exod 24:10-11). In contrast, all of the people were privileged to see God sanction the inauguration of the regular cult in the tabernacle. Thus P, in effect, regards the theophany at the tabernacle as more important than the theophany at Sinai. Nonetheless, P has equalized the two theophanies in its supplement to the Sinaitic account, which relates that YHWH's *kavod*—fire encased in a cloud—made itself visible at Sinai (Exod 24:17) just as it subsequently did at the tabernacle inauguration (Lev 9:6b, 23b, 24a). Still, according to this P verse it is not YHWH's *kavod* but YHWH who will be seen by all of Israel. Therefore, the possibility must be entertained—presuming the accuracy of the MT—that P deliberately allowed this description of the theophany in this verse to be unqualified by YHWH's *kavod*, or any other metonym, though YHWH's *kavod* is what they actually saw (vv. 6b, 23b). In this way the absolute equivalence of the tabernacle theophany with that of Sinai is stressed. The equivalence of the tabernacle to Sinai is an essential, indeed indispensable, axiom of P. The tabernacle, in effect, becomes a portable Sinai, an assurance of the permanent presence of the Deity in Israel's midst.

In Israel, the ark, the symbolic seat of the Godhead, is installed—the first among all of the sanctums (Exod 40:20-21)—before God's presence in the fire-cloud descends on the tabernacle (Exod 40:34-35). In the Solomonic temple, although the ark is the last of the sanctums to be installed (1 Kgs 8:3-5), it still precedes—following the tabernacle model—the divine fire-cloud (1 Kgs 8:10-11). Israel's experience of the theophany is also precisely the opposite of Mesopotamia's. Whereas in the latter the people behold their deity as his or her image *enters* the temple, the Israelites behold their God emerging *from* the tabernacle in the form of fire (Lev 9:23-24). Thus in Israel, according to P, the severance of God from the ark is unambiguous: even if the fire-cloud emerges from the ark room, it has arrived there separately from and subsequent to the ark's installation.

The *kavod*, in the encased fire-cloud, presumably brightens in intensity as a signal to Moses whenever God desires an audience with him (Num 17:7-8) or when

Leviticus 8–10: The Inauguration of the Tabernacle Service

Moses (with Aaron) seeks divine counsel (Num 20:6-7) before it condenses between the outspread wings of the cherubim in the adytum. Otherwise the *kavod,* encased in cloud, remains suspended above the tabernacle so that it is visible to all of Israel at night (Exod 40:38; Num 9:15). Here, uniquely at the inauguration of the public cult in the tabernacle, the *kavod* separates itself from its nebulous encasement in order to consume the sacrifices in the sight of all of Israel (see further v. 23).

[9:6] The earthly manifestation of God is termed *kavod,* and it takes the form of fire.

[9:7] This is the only occasion on which Aaron is commanded to come forward. The reason is obvious: he officiates for the first time.

[9:11] Only this purification offering and that of the priestly consecration were burned outside the camp, though their blood did not enter the tent (see 6:23 [Eng. 30]). In this case the reason is obvious: priests do not benefit from their own expiatory sacrifices;[2] hence the only resort is to incinerate them.

[9:22] Aaron "came down," from where? Theoretically, he need not have ascended the altar, for its top could have been reached standing on the ground; it was only three cubits (approx. 4½ ft.) high. But its length and width were five by five cubits (approx. 7½ x 7½ ft.). Thus the priest would have no choice but to ascend it in order to reach every part of its upper surface. Either steps or a ramp would be required.[3]

[9:23] Why did they enter the tent? The reason only can be conjectured: to pray for the emergence of the *kavod* from the adytum.[4] Despite Moses' promise of the forthcoming theophany (vv. 4b, 6b), he had no guarantee that it would take place—hence his prayer.

[9:24] Whence the fire? The silence of the text allows for ample speculation. The most probable answer is that it came from the adytum. The fire passed through the shrine, where it kindled the incense on the inner altar, incinerated Nadab and Abihu (10:2), and then exited into the court and consumed the sacrifices on the altar (see fig. 1).[5]

Anthropologists see the altar fire as a gateway to the other world through which offerings are transmitted to God and through which the power of God is directly manifested to humanity.[6] The correctness of this observation is accentuated by a Priestly

---

[2] *Sefer Hamivhar.*

[3] The prohibition of Exod 20:26 mandates the latter, and a ramp was built into the altar of the Second Temple (e.g., *m. Mid.* 3:4), but probably not Ahaz's altar of the First Temple (2 Kgs 16:10-13).

[4] Ibn Ezra, Rashbam, Hazzequni, *Keter Torah.*

[5] Rashbam; cf. *Sifre Zuṭa* on Num. 11:1.

[6] E.g., Leach 1976:88.

rule concerning the altar fire: it must never be allowed to die out. This admonition is given twice in two consecutive verses (6:5-6 [Eng. 12-13]). The reason is now apparent. Because the fire is of divine origin it must be perpetuated.[7] The fire is symbolic, representing God's presence; if the fire goes out God will have left. Furthermore, a more pragmatic purpose underlies this injunction. Just as the initial appearance of the divine fire signified God's approval, so every sacrifice offered on the same altar will, with God's grace, also merit God's acceptance.

Selected Theme

Hanukkah: Eight Days of Initiation

Chapter 8 opens with the words, "On the eighth day." The account of the rites that celebrate the completion of Solomon's temple supplies us with the technical name for this day. Solomon offers a series of sacrifices: burnt, cereal, and well-being offerings (1 Kgs 8:64). This last sacrifice is described in detail (1 Kgs 8:62-63) in which the verb *hanak* is generally mistranslated as "dedicate." The proper translation is "initiate." Rashi (on Gen 14:14) must be credited as the first to have provided the correct meaning: "The word *hanak* signifies introducing a person or thing, for the first time, to some particular occupation in which it is intended that he (or it) should remain; similarly Prov 22:6; Num 7:84; and Ps 30:1; in French *enseigner*."

This new rendering for *hanak* enables us to understand the purpose of the special contributions made by the Israelite chieftains to the tabernacle altar (Numbers 7). The twelve tribal chieftains jointly contribute expensive gifts to the consecrated tabernacle consisting of six draught carts and twelve bulls so that the Gershonite and Merarite Levites can haul the dismantled tabernacle. Then, individually and on successive days, each chieftain contributes to the consecrated altar the identical gift, as follows: one silver bowl and one silver basin, each filled with choice flour and oil for cereal offerings, one gold ladle filled with incense, and the same number and species of sacrificial animals. These altar gifts now can be rendered "initiation offerings for the altar" (Num 7:10, 11, 84, 88). What the chieftains did was to contribute an initial supply of vessels and animals so that the altar could begin to function for the requisite ceremonies of the public cult. Thus it was not enough to purify and consecrate the altar by appropriate sacrifices and anointings during the week of priestly investiture, and it was not enough for Aaron and the people to contribute the necessary flour and animals for the eighth day's initiation rites. The chieftains continue the altar's initiation rite for an additional twelve days, thereby extending its dedicatory period to twenty days—a fitting inauguration for the tabernacle. Nevertheless, it was the eight-day celebration of the inauguration of the tabernacle that became a paradigm for subsequent temple inaugurations.[8]

---

[7] *Sipra Nedabah* 5:10.
[8] See Milgrom 1991:593–94.

Leviticus 8–10: The Inauguration of the Tabernacle Service

A final word is needed on the Festival of Hanukkah initiated by the Hasmoneans (165/164 BCE). That it was ordained for eight days may rest ultimately upon the tabernacle tradition. Undoubtedly, its earliest name "The Days of Tabernacles in the Month of Kislev" (2 Macc 1:9), which may indicate that it celebrated a postponed Feast of Tabernacles,[9] also provided an impetus for the eight-day observance. In either case, the true meaning of its name, *hanukkah*, is preserved: "They celebrated the dedication of the altar for eight days, joyfully bringing burnt offerings and sacrificing well-being offerings and thank offerings" (1 Macc 4:56). How does this preserve the meaning "initiate"? It seems to confirm the mistranslation "dedicate." But the altar was "dedicated" through its use. Indeed, when Josephus describes the festival he "nowhere uses the Greek word 'dedicate.' Even in his paraphrases of our passage, he uses only Greek words connoting resumption or restoration or renewal, and he speaks not of the consecration of the new altar but of the resumption of the temple cult and the restoration of the Temple. . . . It would appear that his abstention from the word 'dedication' here is deliberate, whatever the reason for it."[10] The reason is not too difficult to discern. "Consecration" would be altogether wrong, for the rite of anointing was never reintroduced in the Second Temple, and "dedication" would be wrong because *hanukkah* means "initiation [of the altar]," precisely that which happened in Maccabean times and on all of the preceding occasions.

---

[9] Goldstein 1976:273–84.
[10] Goldstein 1976:282.

The Tragic Aftermath

It was still the eighth day. The sacrifices had been offered (9:8-21) but had not yet been eaten by the priests (10:12-20). Nadab and Abihu were Aaron's eldest sons who, according to the Epic (JE) tradition (Exod 24:1, 9-11), were next in importance after Moses and Aaron, ranking even higher than the seventy elders. In their eagerness to officiate for the first time, they wish to offer incense but make a fatal mistake. They are struck down on the spot. The same divine fire that consumes Israel's sacrifice (9:24), authenticating Aaron's role as high priest, strikes down Aaron's sons, in the same day, during he same ceremony. The TEXTS lay the foundation for the THEME and are presented first.

Selected Texts

[10:1] Pans for incense offering are mentioned in the Priestly account (see below), but in the case of Nadab and Abihu, the text also specifies "each his pan," in other words, it was their private possession and not that of the sanctuary. Still, one should not conclude that an incense offering on a pan was unacceptable in the official cult. There must have been pans for this purpose, as can be inferred from the command to Aaron on two occasions to burn incense on "the pan" (16:12; Num 17:11). Moreover, a number of other (non-P) verses clearly imply a discrete incense offering,[1] apart from the incense burned twice daily on the inner altar.

The nature of Nadab and Abihu's sin is contained in the words "unauthorized coals." The adjective "unauthorized" provides the clue. "Unauthorized coals" implies that they were not the right kind. This can only mean that instead of deriving from the outer altar (e.g., 16:12; Num 17:11), the coals came from a source that was "profane"[2] or "outside,"[3] such as an oven.[4] The possibility must also be recognized that the coals were invalidated because they may have been placed on the personal pans of Nadab and Abihu instead of on those of the sanctuary; still, that the sin is specified as

---

[1] Cf. Deut. 33:10; 1 Sam 2:28; Isa 1:13.

[2] *Tg. Onq.* on 16:1.

[3] *Tg. Yer.* on 10:1.

[4] *Sipra Milluʾim Shemini* 32; *Tg. Ps.-J.*; cf. *b. ʿErub.* 63a; *b. Yoma* 53a; *Midr. Num. Rab.* 2:23.

93

"unauthorized coals" and not "unauthorized pans" makes this alternative less likely. The nature of the violation and the possible polemic that lurks behind it are explored in the THEME below.

[10:2] A measure-for-measure principle, attested often enough in divine punishments, is present here: those who sinned by fire are punished by fire.[5] Note the nuance of change: whereas the sinner's fire was impure, God's fire was pure.[6]

The fire could not have been lightning or its heavenly origin would have been mentioned. Neither could it have originated from the inner altar, which had no fire except for the brief incense offering burned twice daily, nor the outer altar, for which the verb "came forth," that is, "exited," would have been inappropriate. The only remaining answer is that the fire stemmed from the adytum, in keeping with the Priestly *kavod* theology, that the divine fire-cloud rests on the ark whence it emerged twice on the same day, to consume the sacrifices and to incinerate Nadab and Abihu.

The deaths of God's intimate priests, Nadab and Abihu, perform the function of sanctifying God—providing awe and respect for God's power to all who witness the incident or who will subsequently learn of it.

[10:3b] The implication of the first half of this statement was fully comprehended by the medieval exegetes: "Those who serve God endanger themselves more. Just as those who are closest to the battlefront are more likely to die so those closest in the service of the sanctuary are more prone to err."[7]

"By sanctifying myself through my intimates I thereby glorify myself before all of the people." "So by a single action, YHWH affirms his total sanctity . . . and also establishes his glory among the onlookers."[8] The implication of the second half of this statement was not overlooked by the medieval exegetes, for instance, "They [the people] will apply *a fortiori* reasoning to themselves: If such [things happen] to his intimates, others will all the more so have cause to fear."[9]

Aaron's silence contrasts starkly with the people's shouting, only a few moments earlier (9:24).[10]

[10:7] The anointing oil is the rationale for the prohibition against mourning. It can justify either of two explanations: (1) Because the oil has anointed your priestly garments, you may not interrupt your duties while you are wearing them; or (2) because you yourselves are anointed you are subject to the same restrictions as the high priest,

---

[5] Hazzequni, *Sefer Hamivḥar, Keter Torah.*
[6] *Sipra Milluʾim Shemini* 22.
[7] Abravenel.
[8] D. N. Freedman, written communication.
[9] Bekhor Shor; cf. *b. Zebaḥ* 115b.
[10] Wenham 1979.

who may not mourn—thus defiling himself by contact with a corpse—under any circumstance. As the wording here states explicitly that the oil is "upon you"—not "upon your vestments"—the second explanation is preferable.

[10:10] The making of distinctions is the essence of the priestly function. Ezekiel scores the priests of his time precisely on this point: "Her priests have *violated* my teaching: They have *desecrated* what is sacred to me, they have not distinguished between the sacred and the common, they have not taught the difference between the unclean and the clean . . . *I am desecrated* in their midst" (Ezek 22:26). The failure of the priests to distinguish between the sacred and the common has resulted in the desecration of God's name. It constitutes "violence," the very sin for which God brought a flood on humankind (Gen 6:11, 13) and for which Ezekiel's compatriots face destruction.[11]

The relations among the four categories mentioned here can be better understood by examining Figure 4.

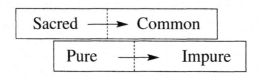

Figure 4. Priestly Distinctions

Persons and objects are subject to four possible states: sacred, common, pure, and impure, two of which exist simultaneously—either sacred or common and either pure or impure. Nevertheless, one combination is excluded in the priestly system: whereas the common may be either pure or impure, the sacred may not be impure. For example, the layperson (common) is in a state of purity unless polluted by some impurity, such as forbidden meat (chap. 11), a sexual flow (chap. 15), or a corpse (Numbers 19), for which purification procedures are prescribed. Still, there is neither danger nor liability for the layperson to contract impurity as long as he or she does not allow it to be prolonged (see 5:1-14). Not so for the sacred. The sanctuary, for example, must at all times remain pure; impurity befalling it must immediately be purged, lest the whole community be blighted (chap. 4, THEME A).

These relationships are depicted in the diagram. The common is contiguous with the realms of the pure and the impure, but the sacred is contiguous only with the pure; it must not contact the impure. The broken line separating each of the two polarities indicates that these relationships are not static. In particular, it is incumbent upon the priests, through their constant instruction (v. 11), to enlarge the realms of the

---

[11] Ezek 7:23; 9:9.

sacred and the pure by reducing the areas of the common and the impure. Israel is to be instructed by the priests on how to reduce the incidence of impurity by purifying (and avoiding) it. Hence the goal is that the categories of common and impure shall largely disappear by their respective conversion into the sacred and the pure. The priestly task is, therefore, a dynamic one. It is to make all of Israel into "a royalty of priests and a holy nation" (Exod 19:6). This objective is the hallmark of H, a fact that raises the possibility that vv. 10-11 stem from the hand of H.

[10:11] The teaching of God's commandments is one of the main functions of the priesthood (Deut 24:8). In one statement it is mentioned exclusively: "For the lips of a priest guard knowledge, and rulings are sought from his mouth" (Mal 2:7a). In another it is mentioned first, ahead of the priests' cultic duties: "They shall teach your norms to Jacob and your instructions to Israel. They shall offer you incense to savor and whole offerings on your altar" (Deut 33:10).[12]

The priests are not the recipients of the divine teachings. These teachings are imparted to Israel through Moses. The priests, then, carry no new instruction; they transmit the old. In this respect, Israel broke sharply with its environment, where the divine instruction was, jealously and zealously, the guarded secret of the priesthood. It is no wonder, then, that the corpus of laws in Leviticus exclusively concerned with priestly duties is, nearly in its entirety, to be taught to Israel and, with one exception (vv. 8-9), mediated to the priests through Moses. The sacrificial rituals (chaps. 1–5) are commanded to the Israelites (1:2). Those sacrificial laws that are the exclusive concern of the priests (chaps. 6–7) nonetheless conclude with "[these are the rituals . . .] when he commanded the Israelites to present their offerings to YHWH, in the wilderness of Sinai" (7:38). The section on impurities (chaps. 11–15), many of which require sacrificial remedies, ends with the injunction, "You shall set apart the Israelites from their impurity" (15:31). The service of the Day of Purgation, though the sole prerogative of the high priest (16:1-28), is nevertheless followed by directions to the Israelites (vv. 29-31). The discussion of priestly impurities and blemishes is, to be sure, addressed to the priests (21:1), yet it concludes with the comment, "thus Moses spoke to Aaron and his sons and to all of the Israelites" (21:24). There can be no esoteric doctrine hidden away in the priestly archives: "The Torah commanded us by Moses is the heritage of the congregation of Jacob" (Deut 33:4).

[10:17] The purification offering whose blood is daubed on the horns of the outer altar (4:25, 30, 34) but not brought inside the tent (6:23 [Eng. 30]) must be eaten by the officiating priest (6:19 [Eng. 26]), in this case Aaron. What he cannot finish must be eaten by the rest of the priestly cadre (6:22 [Eng. 24]), his sons. The reasons for such stringency in the case of the eaten purification offering are explored in the THEME.

---

[12] Cf. Deut 17:8-13; 21:5; 24:8.

It is clear that the function of the priest is to remove Israel's iniquity. The only doubt that remains concerns his method. What is his modus operandi? Is it purging the sanctuary with the blood of the purification offering, in reward for which he receives its meat, or ingesting the purification offering, which has symbolically absorbed the purged impurity?

The latter answer, at face value, seems more logical. Once the blood has removed the impurities they are symbolically transferred to the carcass, which must now be disposed of. Because a carcass bearing severe impurities is burned (4:12; 16:27), it must therefore follow that the carcass bearing lesser impurities is eliminated by ingestion. Indeed, the text confirms this thesis, providing an unambiguous response: Israel's impurity is removed by eating the purification offering. As succinctly stated by the rabbinic aphorism, "When the priests eat [the purification offering] the offerers are expiated."[13]

Ingestion of impurity as a means of eliminating it is not unknown in other cultures. In some forms of Hinduism, "when mechanistic transfer is unavoidable, recourse is made to the Brahmin who in a literal sense is believed to digest the impurity without himself becoming impure."[14] In more recent times, one can cite the old English custom of hiring a "sin-eater" at funerals, who was given sixpence together with a loaf of bread and a bowl of beer to consume over the corpse, "in consideration whereof he tooke upon himself (ipso facto) all the Sinnes of the Defunct."[15]

If ingestion proves to be the modus operandi of the priest for eliminating impurity, a larger question surfaces in its place: If the impurity-laden carcass must be eliminated, why cannot the purification offerings for severer impurities be eaten instead of being burned; and, conversely, what is so terribly wrong about eliminating the lesser impurities by burning the purification offering, as did Aaron and his sons, instead of eating it? This larger question is discussed in the THEME.

[10:18] The rule that purification offerings whose blood was brought into the tent are burned and not eaten is found in 6:23 (Eng. 30).

[10:19] Aaron omits any mention of himself in order to emphasize the dimensions of the tragedy: his four newly consecrated sons had ministered for the first time, and two had died in the effort.

[10:20] This entire pericope ends as mysteriously as it began. Moses' ire is aroused because the priests alter the procedure with one of the sacrifices, the purification offering. One suspects that more is involved than just a slight deviation in sacrificial

---

[13] *Sipra Shemini* 2:4.
[14] Hayley 1980:123.
[15] Aubrey 1881:35.

ritual; the deeper possibilities are explored in the THEME. Equally enigmatic is the ultimate approval of this deviation by both Moses and, by implication, God. This problem is also explored and a solution offered in the THEME.

There is, however, one deduction from this pericope that can be made at once. Although Aaron gets the better of Moses on a legal point, the fact that the ministration of Aaron and his sons required the approval not only of God but of Moses is striking proof that the superiority of the prophet (Moses) over the priest (Aaron) is acknowledged by the Priestly source (P)!

Selected Theme
What Lies behind the Nadab and Abihu Incident

The Nadab and Abihu incident must be understood exactly as it reads. Its background is not political but religious. It is based not on some single event but on an ongoing rite. To be sure, the story's motivation is to protect the vested interests of its Priestly authors and tradents. They saw only too well that offering incense was an easily accomplished ritual, requiring no sanctuary, no elaborate apparatus, and above all, no priests. But we would sell the priests short by attributing to them this one, selfish motive. They also saw that offering incense was a widespread idolatrous practice[16] and that in times of despair Israel, especially its women (Jer 44:15-19), might be seduced by other gods. If my understanding of the Nadab and Abihu incident is correct, then the priests are to be added to the historic company of Israel's other spiritual leaders—the Deuteronomists, civil authorities, prophets, and rabbis—who disapproved of and remonstrated against private incense offering, but to no avail. Against the backdrop of the wilderness narratives, the story of Nadab and Abihu is the Priestly counterpart to the episode of the golden calf. Just as the latter followed upon the theophany of God at Sinai, so the former took place upon the aftermath of the divine theophany at the tabernacle. Clearly, Nadab and Abihu's heresy (and hence the heresy of those who followed their example) was deliberately equated in the mind of the Priestly writer with the heresy of Israel at Sinai.

That Aaron and his sons deviated from the prescribed rite by refraining from eating the purification offering is certified by Moses' accusation (v. 18; cf. 6:23). Yet nothing is said or implied concerning the priests' motivation for altering the rite. It is apparent from Aaron's enigmatic response (v. 19) that he did not change the rite inadvertently. He acted deliberately, but his reasons remain hidden.

Thus the answer must reside in the specific and exclusive nature of the purification offering. There is something inherent in its function that made it *mandatory* for the priests to eat it, and, correspondingly, that made Aaron absolutely certain that he and his sons were unqualified to eat it.

---

[16] For details see Milgrom 1991:628–30.

It is precisely because the purification offering is associated with impurity that its ingestion by the priest becomes so crucial. The priest is the personification of holiness; the purification offering is the embodiment of impurity. In the Priestly symbolic system (fully developed in H), holiness stands for life, whereas impurity stands for death (see the THEMES in chaps. 11, 12, and 15). When the priest consumes the purification offering he is making a profound theological statement: holiness has swallowed impurity; life can defeat death. This symbolism carries through all of the rites with the purification offering. The priest is unaffected by daubing blood on the altar, though the blood is absorbing impurity (4:13-21, 22-35; chap. 4, THEME A). The trepidation the high priest feels when entering the adytum on Yom Kippur is not because of the virulent impurity that has been implanted there, but on the contrary, because of the virulent holiness of the ark (16:2, 13). Indeed, not only does the high priest effect the removal of all of the sanctuary's impurities, he also transfers them (together with Israel's sins) onto the head of a live goat by means of a hand-leaning ritual—yet he emerges unscathed (see 16:21, 24).

The priest's immunity stands in stark contrast to the sanctuary's vulnerability. As demonstrated (chap. 4, THEME A), the sanctuary is polluted by every physical and moral aberration, even those inadvertently committed. But within that same sanctuary the priest is impervious to impurity. Once he leaves it his immunity is canceled; hence not his brothers, also priests, but his Levite cousins remove the corpses of Nadab and Abihu (10:4). Also, the priest who prepares the ashes of the red cow *outside the sanctuary* is rendered impure (Num 19:6-7). Herein lies an ancillary teaching of the Priestly impurity system. Impurity pollutes the sanctuary, but it does not pollute the priest *as long as he serves God in the sanctuary.* H applies this teaching to the people at large. As long as they live a life of holiness and serve God by obeying God's commandments, they can overcome the forces of impurity-death. "You shall heed my statutes and my rules, which if one does them, he shall live by them" (Lev 18:5).

Finally, it is hardly an accident that the story of Nadab and Abihu is followed by the laws of impurity (chaps. 11–15). To be sure, this story adds the impurity of corpse contamination to those in the subsequent impurity collection that must be purged on Yom Kippur (see 16:1). But its significance lies deeper. Through their uninterrupted service, the remaining priests exemplify the principle that holiness is more powerful than impurity, that life can conquer death. The Holiness school carries the meaning further: the priest must teach this truth to the people (10:10-11 [H]) so that they too will aspire to a life of holiness.[17]

If this theory proves correct, it answers all of the questions posed above with a single stroke. Aaron and his remaining sons would eat the sacrificial prebends of the cereal and well-being offerings because they were forbidden to mourn the death of

---

[17] 11:43-45; 19:2; 20:7-8, 26, etc.—all H.

Nadab and Abihu. Yet they refrained from eating the purification offering because they apparently felt that the deaths of Nadab and Abihu in the very midst of the sacred precinct had polluted the entire sanctuary, and, though the purification offering blood had been applied only to the outer altar, its carcass was too laden with impurity to be safely ingested. Moses, by contrast, became enraged when he learned that Aaron and his sons had burned an ordinary purification offering—its blood had not been brought into the shrine (6:23 [Eng. 30])—instead of eating it. He was afraid that the priests would thereby engender the suspicion that they were indeed afraid of the harm that might befall them if they ate the impurity-laden meat of the purification offering, a belief that was current in Israel's contemporary world but that P assiduously attempted to eradicate. Aaron, however, answered Moses that after "such things have befallen me" (v. 19), he could not be expected to eat the purification offering. And subsequent events, according to the Priestly redactor (16:1), prove him correct. This incident is followed by the complete purgation of the sanctuary with two *burnt* purification offerings, one on behalf of the priests and one on behalf of the people (16:1-28).

In sum, we are dealing with a borderline case. As the purification blood was offered on the outer altar, the meat should have been eaten, according to Moses. But because Nadab and Abihu died before the purification meat was eaten, their corpses contaminated the sacrifice. In Aaron's view, the impurities absorbed by the purification offering by dint of its blood manipulation were now increased by corpse contamination, thereby making it subject to the law of the burnt purification offering and not the eaten purification offering. Thus their disagreement turned on a point of cultic law. But behind it, as shown above, lurked the fear of magical, pagan beliefs that Israel's priests assiduously fought to extirpate. After all, it is not surprising that it is the Priestly school that preserves the tradition that it was their founder, Aaron, who taught Moses a lesson in cultic law.

Leviticus 11–16

The Impurity System

The only permitted four-legged animals that may be eaten must have cloven hoofs and chew their cud. Some benign skin diseases are diagnosed and quarantined, passing by the spate of known contagious diseases. Genital discharges are declared impure but not issues from other orifices. These are the subjects of the impurity laws of animals and humans. They sound bizarre. But as symbols they reveal deeper, basically ethical values that remain relevant to this day.

Impurity is the realm of death, and only life can be its antidote. Life purges the sanctuary by nullifying, overpowering, and absorbing the Israelites' impurities that adhere to it, allowing the divine presence to remain and Israel to survive.

The Dietary Laws

The animal kingdom is classified in terms of what is permitted as human food. Animals like humans possess a *nefesh*, usually rendered "soul." Hence their blood must be buried. Animals are responsible under the law. If they kill a human being they must die; their meat may not be eaten nor their carcass sold (Exod 21:28). Bestiality incurs the death penalty for the animal as well as for the human participant (Lev 20:15). Animals were part of God's covenant (Gen 9:9-10); if they belong to an Israelite, they must keep the Sabbath (Exod 20:10; Deut 5:14). The firstborn males of both humans and animals are God's property. In the messianic age they will renew their covenant with God (Hos 2:20 [Eng. 18]) and will no longer be predators (Isa 11:3).

In the Priestly source (P), the classification of the animal world mirrors the classification of the human society and its values. The correspondences between the animal and human worlds come into clearer focus once it is noticed that each compiles three identical divisions that can be represented by concentric circles, as depicted in Figure 5.

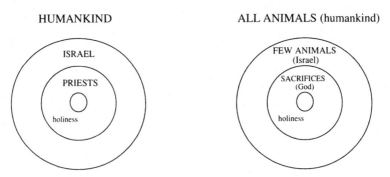

Figure 5. Classification in P

Humankind is divided into three parts, corresponding to three of its covenants with God. The three classifications are: (1) the priesthood (Num 25:12-15); (2) Israel in particular (with the patriarchs, Gen 17:2; Lev 26:42); and (3) humankind in general

(Gen 9:1-11, including the animals). These three human divisions are matched by three animal divisions: (1) the priest is permitted to sacrifice only the domesticated and unblemished from among the edible animals; (2) Israel, a subdivision of humanity, is permitted to eat only a few animals as detailed in this chapter of Leviticus and in Deuteronomy 14; and finally (3) humankind in general is entitled to use all animals (except their blood).

According to the Holiness source (H), although priests are inherently holy, all of Israel is enjoined to achieve holiness. By scrupulously observing God's commandments, moral and ritual alike, Israel can achieve holiness. This is represented by the Holiness arrows. Israel can achieve the status of a "priestly nation" (Exod 19:6); part of its requirement is that all meat for the table is sacrificed at the altar (for details see Lev 17:3-5). Holiness is the goal. The implications are discussed in THEMES A–H.

Selected Themes

A. The Dietary Laws as an Ethical System

Humans will have meat for their food and will kill to get it. The Bible has therefore worked out a system of restrictions whereby humans may satiate their lust for animal flesh and yet not be dehumanized in the process. The basic rules are these:

1. The choice of animal food is severely limited. Considering the variety of fauna that roam the earth, it is startling to realize how few, comparatively, are for the table, and that these are of the domesticated-herbivorous species only. There is no restriction whatsoever on the vegetable and fruit kingdom.

2. Even the few permitted animals may not be killed by just anyone but only by those who can qualify by their skill and piety: skill in employing a hallowed technique of slaughtering that renders death painless, and piety in being aware of the divine sanction that has permitted such slaughter. These qualifications ensure that these few slaughterers themselves do not become brutalized though incessant killing.

3. Even the few permitted animals, though ritually slaughtered, are still not fit for consumption until their blood is drained. "You shall not partake of the blood of any flesh, for the life of all flesh is its blood. Anyone who partakes of it shall be cut off" (Lev 17:14b). Humans have a right to nourishment, not to the life of others. Hence the blood, which is the symbol of life, must be drained and returned to the universe, to God.

By now it should be apparent that the Bible's method of taming the killer instinct in humans is none other than its system of dietary laws. If readers are startled by this identification, they can be forgiven. Every reason but this one has been given for the observance of the dietary laws, or, more often, for their abandonment. The most popular explanation is that it is a series of health measures dictated by the primitive hygienic conditions of the ancient world. This comment is usually followed by the clincher: "Today we have government inspection, sanitary handling, large-scale refrigeration. Why then should we keep these laws?"

Yet this widely prevalent notion of the hygienic origin of the dietary laws flies squarely in the face of all the basic rules enumerated above. The theory of protective sanitation cannot explain the limitation of the animal world to only three domesticated-herbivorous quadrupeds, the abstention from blood, or the requirement for a ritually and spiritually qualified slaughterer.

Does a theory that can explain all these factors exist? I submit it does: the dietary laws serve as an ethical guide—a system whereby people will not be brutalized by killing animals for their flesh.

The obvious point of departure in discussing the dietary laws is the biblical assumption that humans were originally vegetarians. To those unaware of this premise, a rereading of the first pages of Genesis will prove a revelation. Adam and Eve are told to "rule the fish of the sea, the birds of the sky, and all the living things that creep on the earth." To "rule," as rabbinic commentators note, includes the right to domesticate the animal world but not to use it as provender. Where shall the humans get their food? "God said, 'See, I give you every seed-bearing plant . . . and every tree . . . ; they shall be yours for food'" (Gen 1:28-29). These verses may be an accurate reflection of the commonly held anthropological theory that humans went through a herbivorous stage before they began eating meat. But for the Bible the significance of these verses lies in the fact that they are part of the story of humanity's rebellion. Adam and Eve are not satisfied with their role as the stewards of paradise. They want to be the active agents of their own destiny. They eat the forbidden fruit, for which they are punished with mortality and labor. And these new humans are also carnivorously inclined. No longer Adam, the ideal, but Noah, the real, he and his spouse insist on bringing death to living things to gratify their appetite and their need. The sons of Noah are permitted flesh: "Every creature that lives shall be yours to eat; as with the green grasses, I give you all these" (Gen 9:3). This concession is granted to them, but not without reservation: "You must not, however, eat flesh with its lifeblood in it" (9:4). The human beings' craving for meat is to be indulged, but they are to abstain from consuming the blood.

B. Blood Is Life: Part I

The importance of this blood prohibition, enjoined upon all humans and not only on Israel, is clearly disclosed by contrasting it with the idolatrous practices of Israel's environment. None of Israel's neighbors possessed this absolute and universally binding blood prohibition. Blood is everywhere partaken of as food. If a blood taboo was observed, it was applied only to sacrificial animals and not to ordinary flesh. In such instances, it was reserved for the gods only, and hence offered up at the altar. One may recall the psalm where God taunts the would-be imitator of the surrounding

Canaanites: "If I were hungry, I would not tell you; for the world is mine, and the full-ness thereof. Do I eat the flesh of bulls, or drink the blood of goats?" (Ps 50:12-13).

Since Israel alone among its neighbors enjoined a universal blood prohibition that was for both Israelite and non-Israelite, for both sacrificial animals and the ordi-nary kind, we may conclude that this blood prohibition was the result of a rational, deliberate opposition to the prevalent practice of the environment. Why did Israel choose to stand alone in its absolute prohibition of blood? The reason for this oppo-sition becomes clear when we recall that the blood prohibition is unveiled when the concession to eat meat is given for the first time (Gen 9:3-4, quoted above). Humans have no right to put an animal to death except by God's sanction. Blood is the essence of life and belongs not to humans but to God. Hence they must eschew the blood, drain it, and return it, as it were, to the Creator. Blood taboos may have existed else-where. But for the first time they are ethicized and extended to all animal life. The pagan fear of expropriating the *food* that is divine now becomes transmuted into Israel's innovation—the fear of expropriating *life* that is divine. The abstention from blood is a constant reminder to humans that, though they may satisfy their appetite for food, they must curb their hunger for power. Because life is inviolable it may not be tampered with indiscriminately.

That the blood prohibition runs as a leitmotif through all of Israel's ancient leg-islation is an indication of its antiquity. That, as already noted, it is projected back to the days of Noah—the first negatively phrased commandment in the Bible—shows that even the editors of the Torah accepted it as being of primordial origin.

It is clear, then, that in ancient times slaughtering an animal involved not only spilling its blood but also consecrating it to God. And there was more: directives for matters of place, person, and performance. These clues are sparse, but they suggest a discernible picture. We review them briefly.

C. The Slaughter and the Slaughterer

What is probably the oldest sacrificial law in the Bible is contained in Leviticus 17. It designates the proper place and person for animal slaughtering as the local sanctuary and its priest, respectively. One of the later Judean kings, however, centralized the cult in Jerusalem and abolished the local sanctuaries, making it necessary to permit the laity to slaughter their meat at home.

Such permission is reflected in the code of Deuteronomy. Its very language is instructive: "If the place where YHWH your God has chosen to establish his name is too far for you, you may slaughter any of the cattle or sheep that YHWH gives you, *as I have instructed you*" (Deut 12:21). This verse clearly implies that there was already established not only a proper place for slaughtering but a proper method as well. Although they are released from the requirement as to place, the people are still bound to the method. What is the proper method? The Bible gives us no answer. Rather, it takes the answer for granted. The Talmud provides the solution, and with many details. All of these clearly demonstrate the perfection of a slaughtering technique whose purpose is to render the animal immediately unconscious with a minimum of suffering. The plethora of regulations cannot be entered into here. Let the example of the slaughtering knife suffice: it must be razor-keen and must regularly be inspected for imperfections, lest the slightest notch cause unnecessarily prolonged pain. Could this concern for humaneness be the invention of the rabbis rather than the legacy of the past? Hardly so. The rabbis themselves are ignorant of the humane origin of their method and point to the verse quoted above from Deuteronomy as proving that the same technique was employed by the biblical priest. And in keeping with the originally sacral nature of the rite of slaughtering, they insist that he who would perform the slaughtering, though not a priest, shall act as a priest. He shall recite an appropriate blessing, thus dedicating his slaughter to God. Moreover, by virtue of his training and piety, his soul shall never be torpefied by his incessant butchery but kept ever sensitive to the magnitude of the divine concession in allowing him to bring death to living things.

Thus from a brief tracing of the history of the blood prohibition and the established slaughtering method, we have seen that the dietary system rests on foundations that are essentially ethical, and ethical in the highest sense. They teach the inviolability of all life, that animal life is conceded to humanity's lust and need, only on the condition that a qualified few (priest/ritual slaughterer) will actually do the killing, and that death must be effected in such a way (by painless slaughter and spilling of the blood) that the slaughterer's sense of reverence for life may never be blunted.

Only now are we prepared to deal with the final area of the dietary laws of the Bible—the prohibited foods. In truth, the need for such laws could now be logically deduced: if the blood is to be abjured, the slaughtering confined to one humane method, and the number of slaughterers effectively reduced, then one should expect restrictions in the choice of animal food as well. This is exactly what we find. The Israelites are asked to go beyond the abstention from blood, which is enjoined upon all people. They are to discipline their appetites further by narrowing down the permitted animals to a few. In this way they may aspire to a higher level of life, which the Bible calls qadosh, or holy.

D. On Being Holy: Part I

To the casual reader of the Bible it comes as a great surprise that the exalted concept of holiness is given as the reason for the restrictions in all four sources where the prohibited foods are enumerated (Exod 22:30 [Eng. 31]; Lev 11:44-45; 20:22-26; Deut 14:21). Moreover, one whose ear is sensitive to repetition will react to these verses as a Geiger counter to a load of uranium. Listen to Lev 11:44: ". . . make yourselves holy . . . that you be holy . . . for I am holy." Of the six Hebrew words here, three contain the root qdš, "holy." And twice more it occurs in the succeeding verse. Relatively few individual statutes of the Bible are coupled with the demand for holiness. Of these, none has the demand with the same staccato emphasis and repetition as do the food prohibitions.

Thus the Bible takes greater pains to offer a rationale for these laws than for any other commandment. Yet because the rationale, holiness, has been so variously interpreted, we are at a loss to understand its exact meaning. Since both the blood prohibition and the ritual slaughtering are invested with the same ethical principle, as we have seen, we might surmise that the food prohibitions, as part of the same dietary system, would be similarly rooted in ethics. But our surmises and guesswork are not sufficient; an investigation of the biblical concept of holiness, however brief, must be essayed.

Again we must resort to the heathen environment of ancient Israel to understand both its common cultural legacy as well as the distinctiveness of Israel's religion. An examination of Semitic polytheism (and indeed of any primitive religion) shows that the realm of the gods is never wholly separate from or transcendent to the world of humans. Natural objects such as specific trees, rivers, and stones are invested with supernal force. But this earthbound power is independent of the gods and can be an unpredictable danger to them as well as to humans. "Holy" is thus aptly defined, in any context, as "that which is unapproachable except through divinely imposed restrictions," or "that which is withdrawn from common use."

In opposition to this widespread animism we notice that there is no animism in the Bible. Holiness is not innate. The source of holiness is assigned to God alone. Holiness is the extension of God's nature; it is the agency of God's will. If certain things are termed holy—such as the land (Canaan), person (priest), place (sanctuary), or time (holy day)—they are so by virtue of divine dispensation. Moreover, this designation is always subject to recall. Israel is also commanded to distinguish between the holy and the common, as well as between the pure and the impure. The former antonymous set has a totally different rootage in Scripture. There is no holiness in creation except for the Sabbath. But this holiness rests in time, not in space. However, whenever Scripture designates space as holy—especially the sanctuary and its sanctums—this holiness does not inhere in creation but stems from divine revelation, God's unfathomable will and wisdom.

Thus the Bible exorcises the demonic from nature; it makes all supernatural forces coextensive with God. True, just as in the idolatrous religions, the sanctums of the Bible can cause death to the unwary and the impure who approach them without regard for the regulations that govern their usage. But for Israel the holy is the extension of God's will. It becomes a positive concept, an inspiration, and a goal associated with God's nature and desire for humanity. "You shall be holy, for I am holy" (Lev 19:2). That which humanity is *not*, nor can ever fully be, but that which humanity is commanded to emulate and approximate, is what the Bible calls *qadosh*, "holy." Holiness means *imitatio Dei*—the life of godliness.

107

In general the emulation of God's holiness demands following the ethics associated with God's nature. The food prohibitions are the Torah's personal recommendation as the best way of achieving this higher ethical life. Together the food prohibitions, the blood prohibition, and ritual slaughter reveal an intricate ethical web of dietary restrictions that teaches the Israelites to have reverence for life by (1) reducing their choice of flesh to a few animals, (2) limiting the slaughter of even these few permitted animals to the most humane way and by the few who can qualify, and (3) prohibiting the consumption of the blood, as acknowledgment that bringing death to living things is a concession of God's grace and not a privilege of humanity's whim.

The dietary system, then, is the Torah's prerequisite for the ethical life. Only through a daily regimen of disciplines that remind humans that life is sacred can humans aspire to a way of life fully informed by other ethical virtues. The dietary laws are rungs on the ladder of holiness, leading to a life of pure thought and deed, characteristic of the nature of God (see further the THEMES in chap. 19).

That the dietary laws are anchored in an ethical foundation was not unknown to the rabbis of the talmudic age. For them, not only these but most of the commandments were ethically oriented. Hence their well-known generalization: "The commandments were given only to refine humanity." Often overlooked, however, is that this frequently cited statement appears most often in one context—as the rationale for the dietary laws. Let one citation serve as an example of the others: "What does God care whether a man kills an animal in the proper way and eats it, or whether he strangles it and eats it? . . . Or what does God care whether a man eats unclean animals or clean animals? . . . Hence, the commandments were given only to refine humanity." Here, with sheer aplomb, the rabbis deny the rituals and institutions of Judaism as ends in themselves, understanding them only as vehicles to the higher ethical life. That they derive this far-reaching principle from the dietary system shows that for them, as well as for the Bible, it is the ethical discipline par excellence.

E. Separation from Idolators

Now we can turn to the problem posed by the seeming arbitrariness of the specific food prohibitions: Why some animals and not others? Why particularly the hare, the camel, and the pig among quadrupeds, and the crustaceans among fish? Here we tread on uneasy ground. Until now we have inquired into the dietary system as a whole, as canonized in the Bible. Now we are asked to get behind the biblical sources and trace back each food interdiction to its separate origin. Frankly, this sleuthing assignment cannot be fulfilled. The tracks lose themselves in the sands of unrecorded time. Even if some origins can be detected in some primitive taboo, our findings may be more misleading than helpful. The reasons that give rise to a specific food interdiction may not account for its later inclusion in the dietary system; by then, they may have been reinterpreted in order to fit the ethical scheme. Yet it is possible to speak with some certainty about one of these original factors. Further research may even prove it to be the most important factor of all; that is, the determination to set apart the Israelites from the idolatrous practices of their neighbors. That this factor can be isolated and identified is thanks to the perfection of the scientific discipline of comparative linguistics as applied to biblical research.

We recall that Hebrew *qdš* has more than the positive meaning of supernal power permeating the natural world; in the cognate languages it also has the obverse meaning noted earlier—to withdraw from profane use. This negative connotation of holiness is already adumbrated in the Bible. In Lev 20:26 the basic formula of holiness is tellingly lengthened: "You shall be holy to me; for I YHWH am holy, and I have set you apart from other peoples to be mine." Holiness, then, means separation from the heathen. (For greater detail, see chap. 20, THEMES B and D.) Furthermore, when we scan the pentateuchal codes for all other instances in which Israel is enjoined to holiness, we find them clustered in the dietary laws, as we have already seen, and in just two other places: the priesthood and idolatry. As to the former, we notice, for example, that seven times in three verses (Lev 21:6-8) the root *qdš* is used. From the biblical viewpoint, the priesthood, Israel, and humanity, respectively, form three concentric rings of decreasing holiness about the center, God. The biblical ideal, however, is that all Israel shall be "a kingdom of priests and a holy [*qadoš*] people" (Exod 19:6). If Israel is to move to a higher sphere of holiness, then it is bound to a more rigid code of behavior. And just as the priest lives by more stringent standards than his fellow Israelite, so Israelites shall be expected to follow different standards from their fellow human beings. Here again, holiness implies separation. As for idolatry, since the very seat of immorality was imputed to the cult of idolators, it is not startling to find the third grouping of *qdš* words in the context of a stern admonition to Israel to separate itself from idolatry (Lev 20:1-7; Deut 7:4-6; 14:1-6).

Thus, from an examination of the word *qadoš* in the Bible and in cognate languages, we can feel certain that many of the specific food prohibitions within the dietary system were included as preventative measures. Their purpose was to keep Israel undefiled by the idolatrous customs of the environment, and thus to move the nation closer to the Mosaic ideal of becoming "a kingdom of priests and a holy people."

Some of the food prohibitions were probably motivated in part by entirely different factors. Aesthetics may have played a part. Some creatures were downright disgusting to the Israelites; it was unthinkable that humans would allow their bodies to incorporate the flesh of an animal whose sight revolted them. Even the hygienic element played its role: an ancillary attribute of the holy is cleanliness, and the filthy animal would most likely be entered into the forbidden lists. Finally, it is entirely possible that some animals were renounced because of ancient taboos. Their primitive origins may have been forgotten, but their hold on society lingered. Because of these taboos, some animals may have held place in the forbidden lists without reinterpretation.

Whereas the hypotheses enumerated here may not have been the decisive ones, they may account for the survival of some individual prohibitions. Even in these individual cases, as we have seen, greater credence should be given to the factor of intentional separation from the practices of idolatrous nations. But in no manner can they begin to account for the biblical dietary system *in its entirety,* whose main tenets are deliberate deviations from the practices of the idolatrous world. Of all the theories, the ethical one best fits the facts: to teach reverence for life through restricted access to animal life as food.

F. The Four Anomalous Quadrupeds

Were the animals first tabooed and criteria later devised to justify the taboos, or were the criteria drawn up first, then used to classify the animals? We are back to the contest between the hygienist and the anthropologist. Who is correct?

I submit that the four anomalous quadrupeds—the camel, the hare, the rock badger, and the pig—can serve as a decisive test. Let us first set the terms. If the hygienic theory holds, then these animals were tabooed because they were injurious to health. Only much later a classification was devised to justify their exclusion: chewing the cud and having split hoofs. That there were just four anomalous quadrupeds bearing one of the two qualifying criteria can only mean that ancient Israel had a negative culinary experience only with those four anomalies. Indeed, goes the hygienist's theory, the chances are that Israel's environment possessed other such anomalies, but they were not entered into the list of prohibited animals either because, being wild, they were unattainable or because they were indigestible. If the anthropological argument is correct, and the criteria came first, then it would have fallen upon Israelite zoologists to scour their environment to find all anomalous creatures possessing one of the two qualifying criteria.

This then is the test: if the four anomalies were listed because they were unfit for the table (the hygienist's theory), then Israel's zoological ambience probably numbers other quadrupeds with the same anomaly. But if they are listed because, as the text states, they do not fit the criteria, then the list is complete: there should be no other such quadrupeds in Israel's environs. Thus if it turns out that even one more animal known to Israel is akin to the specified four, bearing one criterion but not the other, then it is a fatal blow to the anthropologist.

The results are in. As the hygienist would hope, there are six animals that bear this anomaly: the biblical four plus the llama and the hippopotamus. The llama is indeed a ruminant whose hoofs are not cloven. The hippopotamus, conversely, is cloven-hoofed, herbivorous, and nonruminant. However, the case is more complicated than it first appears. The llama and its relatives (the alpaca, the guanaco, etc.)

are indigenous to South America and clearly were unknown to ancient Israel. They, therefore, do not lend credibility to the hygienic theory. The hippopotamus, on the other hand, did exist in the marshy (Philistine) coastal areas[1] and probably was eaten.[2] What can the anthropologist say to this finding?

The cleft in the hoofs of the hippopotamus is so slight that it was missed by the ancients and even omitted by Aristotle in his *Historia animalis* (for other mistakes made by biblical zoologists, see the rock badger and the hare, vv. 5-6). Thus, despite the seeming victory for those who would argue that the standards followed the diet, the verdict cuts the other way: it appears that the criteria came first and only afterward four anomalies were found. Had the ancient Israelites correctly classified the hippopotamus, it too would have been classified as impure.

The Bible itself corroborates our findings. It is significant that the Deuteronomist is not satisfied merely to cite the criteria for quadrupeds; he takes pains to enumerate all of the permitted animals (Deut 14:4-5): three domestic and seven wild, mostly unidentifiable. This list is then followed by the criteria, as follows: "And any *other* quadruped that has hoofs . . ." (Deut 14:6). Therefore, this passage is saying that these ten quadrupeds are permitted plus all others that fit these criteria but as yet have not been found. The Deuteronomist lists the domestic animals because they need no longer be brought to the altar as a sacrifice but may be slaughtered profanely, that is, they are treated as game. He is induced, however, to include the seven wild species, only for the reason that the criteria were before him and impelled him to sponsor an investigation of all the fauna of the land, even in wild, inaccessible places, in order to find all the quadrupeds that matched the criteria.

G. The Enigma of the Unnamed Fish

Ancient Israel had little acquaintance with marine life. This is proved not only by the fact that Adam names the whole animal kingdom with the exception of the fish (Gen 2:19-20), but also by the fact that in the entire Hebrew Bible not a single fish is named except the *tanninim* (Gen 1:21; Isa 51:9; Ps 74:13) and the *livyatan* (Ps 74:14; 104:26; Job 3:8; 40:25)—and both are mythical! To be sure, the city of Jerusalem could be entered via "the Fish Gate" (Neh 3:3; 12:39; 2 Chr 33:14), implying a fish market nearby, but it is no accident that the fish trade in Jerusalem was controlled by Tyrian merchants (Neh 13:16). Israelites simply were not fishermen—at least, not until the end of Second Temple times (e.g., Matt 4:18, 21; Mark 1:16; Luke 5:1-10). Finally, it should not be overlooked that when the other Priestly source, called H, summarizes the forbidden foods, it lists all of the generic categories of chapter 11—beasts, birds, and swarmers—but omits the fish (Lev 20:25).

---

[1] Hass 1953; perhaps alluded to in Job 40:15-24.
[2] Davis 1985.

Leviticus 11–16: The Impurity System

The exigencies of geography are responsible. There were few fresh streams under the control of ancient Israel. The largest body of fresh water, the Sea of Galilee, was for most of the time the contested border between Aram and Israel and, subsequently, annexed by Assyria during the collapse of northern Israel. Even then, to judge by the small variety present today in its waters—and this, after the artificial breeding of new species—ancient Israel would, at best, have known only a few species of freshwater fish. The Israelite access to the Mediterranean was also blocked during many periods of its history and, to judge by the silence of the Bible on this matter, there were no Israelites who earned their livelihood by fishing the sea. Yet would not the rich variety of fish contained in their waters have been known to Israel—if not by their own fishermen, at least through the agency of foreign merchants (e.g., Neh 13:16)? The answer to this question hangs on a personal tale.

On July 11, 1973, I chanced upon a lecture on the Berkeley campus given by Eugene C. Haderlie of the Naval Post-graduate School at Monterey, California, on ecological changes in the marine life of the Suez Canal, the substance of which was soon afterward published (1973). It was fascinating to hear that with the opening of the Suez Canal in 1869 the rich marine life of the Red Sea began to migrate successfully to the Mediterranean. He explained that the eastern Mediterranean had a very low nutritive capacity due to the fact that the rich silt of the Nile flowed counterclockwise along the coasts of Israel and Lebanon but in currents that were too deep for most fauna to reach until it surfaced in the Aegean Sea. The import of his statement did not strike me until I left the lecture hall. This means, I realized, that before the canal, before the Red Sea fauna had penetrated the Mediterranean, the eastern Mediterranean littoral was an impoverished area for marine life. The scientific studies on this phenomenon, subsequently supplied me by Dr. Haderlie, fully confirmed his point. "It can be said that the Eastern Mediterranean is a zoogeographical 'cul de sac,' a tropical sea, undersaturated with an Atlantic-temperature fauna. By reopening artificially the contact with the Red Sea—a typical tropical sea—Lesseps helped unknowingly to reestablish a zoogeographical equilibrium and to fill this particular ecological vacuum in the Eastern Mediterranean."[3] The success of the Red Sea migration can be measured by the fact that of the twenty-four species of immigrant fish along the Levant coast, thirteen are extremely common and eleven are of commercial value.[4]

The implications of this scientific finding for the present pericope are unambiguous and decisive. The Israelites were unacquainted with fish not because they had no contact with the sea but, to the contrary, the sea with which they had contact was virtually devoid of fish. The fish brought to Jerusalem by Tyrians (Neh 13:16) came

---

[3] Por 1971:156.
[4] Ben-Tuvia 1966.

from fishing fleets that plied the far-off waters of the Aegean but were beyond the reach of the Israelites. Hence it is this piscatorial dearth in the immediate vicinity of ancient Israel that accounts for the fact that denominations for the fish are lacking.

There is a concomitant conclusion that is germane to the subject. The fact that fish species are few to begin with means that imposing the fins-scales criterion severely restricts the edible varieties. Surely only a few species passed muster. The criterion, however, also excludes crustaceans and other burrowers that thrived on the coast, just to judge by the heaps of murex shells along the Lebanese coast.[5] It therefore seems reasonable to conclude that the very purpose of the criteria for fish, just like the criteria for quadrupeds (THEME F, above) was to limit Israel's access to the animal world.

H. The Seminal Distinction between šeqeṣ and ṭameʾ

It can hardly be an accident that the very species that are *šeqeṣ,* and do not contaminate by contact have, according to the Priestly creation story, their origin in water: "God said, 'Let the waters bring forth swarms of living creatures, and birds that fly above the earth across the expanse of the sky" (Gen 1:20). Thus both fish and birds were created from (and by) the waters, and therefore like the waters (Lev 11:36a), they do not contaminate by touch. Yet reptiles, which are creatures of both water (Gen 1:20) and land (Gen 1:25, 26), do not contaminate in the main (*šeqeṣ,* Lev 11:41-43), but some do (*ṭameʾ,* vv. 29-38). Thus reptiles occupy an ambivalent state.

This distinction between animal carcasses that do and do not contaminate stems from the creation story, and this story may have been known to the rabbis. "In that which was created on the first day there is impurity; on the second (day) there is no impurity; on the third (day) there is impurity; on the fourth and fifth (days) there is no impurity. . . . All that was created on the sixth is impure."[6] Thus fish and birds, the total creations of the fifth day, are declared pure, so they do not contaminate by touch. It was the rabbis' way of grounding the distinctions between animals that do and do not contaminate by touch on the principle of whether they were created on land or in water. On the first day the earth was created (out of which stems earthenware—the most vulnerable of all materials to impurity, Lev 11:33, 35). On the third day, trees (i.e., wooden vessels, also permeable to impurity, v. 32) were created. And all that was created on the sixth day, quadrupeds, reptiles, and humans—all of the defiling creatures—were created on the land. Conversely, on the second, fourth, and fifth days the heavenly bodies and the sea creatures were created—and these, according to the rabbis, do not impart impurity by touch.

---

[5] Milgrom 1983a.
[6] *m. Kelim* 17:14.

Leviticus 11–16: The Impurity System

Thus the Priestly distinction between animal carcasses that are *ṭameʾ* and those that are *šeqeṣ*—traces of which are detectable in the tannaitic sources—is rooted in the Priestly scheme of creation. But what are its presuppositions?

On what basis did the Priestly legists decide that creatures from the sea are pure whereas those from the land are impure, and that the sources of water are pure but those detached from their source are impure? It appears to me that the Priestly school derived this distinction from existential reality. From experience they knew that water both defiles and vivifies. If all water sources were declared susceptible to impurity—including cisterns, springs, rivers, and seas—human existence would be endangered. If this conjecture be proven correct it would correlate with my assumption concerning the fundamental rationale behind the concept of impurity: it symbolizes death.[7] Therefore Israel is commanded to distinguish between the impure and the pure in order that it may learn to distance itself from relationships and behavior that lead to death and to embrace those that bestow life. Hence water, which is essential to life, is pure at its source (Lev 11:36). In contrast, the earth symbolizes death, since the word "land" also can denote the underworld,[8] and the word "dust" also can denote the grave or the underworld.[9] Therefore, creatures stemming from the earth are susceptible to impurity because they symbolize death.

The Priestly source maintains that God's will was revealed not only on Mount Sinai but also in creation. Natural law reflects the divine will as much as God's revelations to Moses and the prophets. Thus if the Israelites are commanded to study Scripture, so must they occupy themselves with the study of nature. According to the Priestly source, human beings order their lives according to natural phenomena: the heavenly bodies determine their days, years, and seasons (Gen 1:14), vegetation provides their food and animals, their needs (1:24, 29), and the rainbow assures them of God's eternal covenantal grace (9:14). The reverse also holds: When the cycles of nature are violently upset, as happened during the time of the flood (6:9-22) and the Egyptian plagues (Exod 7:8-13; 8:12-15; 9:8-12), human beings learn of the consequences of their failings and wrongdoing.

The statement "And God saw that it was good" is not only an aesthetic evaluation of each day but a purposeful dictum: the world was created for the welfare of the summit of creation, the human race. Thus the Priestly distinction between pure and impure is not an arbitrary divine fiat but a rational decision that is derived from the laws of nature. However, the refrain "it was good" ostensibly contradicts human experience. The world is not totally good; it contains evil, sickness, plague, and death. Nonetheless, the Priestly teaching insists that this world is indeed good and that the so-called evil phenomena of nature are essential for the perpetuation of the

---

[7] See the extensive treatment in Milgrom 1991:704–13, 766–68, 1000–1004.

[8] E.g., Exod 6:12; Jer 17:3; Jonah 2:7 (Eng. 6); Ps 22:30 (Eng. 29); 71:20.

[9] E.g., Isa 26:19; Ps 22:16, 30 (Eng. 15, 29); Job 7:21; 10:9; 17:16; 20:11; Dan 12:2.

cosmos. Because of this assumption, the prophet is able to praise God, who "creates light and creates sickness, makes peace and *creates evil*" (Isa 45:7).

Herein, I submit, lies the main innovation of the Priestly source. All nations believed that the gods exact their retribution on humanity through nature. However, Israel's innovation, as expressed in the Priestly source, went beyond that. It proclaimed that God's will is also revealed through nature. The forces that are beneficial or detrimental to humanity are suspended in a delicate balance. All individuals are capable, with the aid of their rational faculties, to distinguish between the two forces, and thereby to achieve a life that can be adjudged "it was good." In effect, the real contribution of this Priestly theology is that it manifests the beginnings of an ecological doctrine. Thus, whereas every person bears responsibility for differentiating between good and evil, Israel, in addition, is responsible for differentiating between impure and pure. This latter distinction, as well as the former, according to the Priestly source, is implemented in the creation account: all animals are either pure or impure genetically, a quality determined by their origin either from the sea or from the land.

Selected Texts

[11:3] The question arises: Why were not the permitted quadrupeds listed? The answer is that the legist takes the sacrificial quadrupeds for granted, namely, cattle, sheep, and goats. His only concern is to classify the nonsacrificial animals, which, in the main, are wild. This supposition is corroborated by the list of birds (vv. 13-19), which contains only the prohibited species.

[11:4] The camel has a three-chambered stomach, and it chews the cud. The feet have cushionlike soles enveloped in hardened skin. Each foot is cleft into two toes, but it has no hoof.[10]

The impurity mentioned here and for the other enumerated animals (vv. 5-7) applies only to their carcasses (v. 8). "What does Scripture mean by impure? [It means] impure forever."[11] The declaration "it is impure" is found only in cases of impurity that are indefinite and irreversible by humans: for instance, various forms of scale disease (13:11, 15, 31, 44, 46) and moldy fabrics or a fungous house, which, after being declared impure, must be destroyed (13:51, 55; 14:44). Thus certain animals and objects are declared impure irrevocably.

The rock badger has no hoofs but has broad nails. It is not a true ruminant, but only resembles one because in chewing it moves its jaws side to side. Thus the attribution of cud chewing to this animal was made by observing its chewing habits rather

---

[10] The camel of the Bible was probably the single-humped dromedary (see THEME F).

[11] *Sipre Numbers* 126.

than by dissecting it to determine whether it had multiple stomachs, the characteristic anatomical feature of ruminants. Moreover, that this animal is wild, living in craggy regions,[12] indicates that the criteria of chewing the cud and of cloven hoofs came first, and that at a later period the environment was scoured to find the animals that bore one of the two criteria. For the significance of the chronological priority of the criteria, see THEME F.

[11:6] Like the rock badger, the hare is not a true ruminant, but the sideways movement of its jaws gives it the appearance of one. Its habit of regurgitating the food it eats and returning to it later also creates the impression that it is incessantly chewing its food.

[11:7] The pig is the only one of the four named quadrupeds that has cloven hoofs but is not a ruminant. This latter criterion was deliberately formulated in order to exclude the pig. Otherwise, Scripture could have stipulated one criterion—cloven hoofs—and it would have eliminated the other three quadrupeds. It must, therefore, have added cud chewing as a second criterion for the sole purpose of eliminating the pig.

Whenever pigs were used in worship among the Hittites they were offered up to underworld deities. This was also the practice among the Greeks. The pig was considered sacred to certain gods of the underworld, especially Demeter and Dionysus.

The onset of the Iron Age in Canaan is marked by a precipitous drop in pig production. Israel had entered the scene. The stark contrast between the proliferation of the pig at Philistine sites and its near total absence everywhere else in contemporaneous Israelite sites raises the possibility that Israel's aversion to the pig stemmed from two sources that in effect were one: the dietary habits and the cultic practice of the hated Philistines.

In Israel the pig was regarded as repulsive, as is apparent from the following apothegm: "Like a gold ring in the snout of a pig is a beautiful woman bereft of sense" (Prov 11:22). Moreover, the pig was associated with idolatrous worship (Isa 66:3) and with those "who eat pig's flesh, and the šeqeṣ [see v. 11 and THEME H], and the mouse" (Isa 66:17), apparently in a cultic rite. Here too the cult seems to be directed to chthonic deities.

It is clear from the evidence of the ancient Near East that the pig was revered in chthonic cults, which penetrated into Israel as late as the sixth century, arousing the wrath of priests and prophets alike. The latter expressed themselves in denunciatory orations, the former in ritual taboos. By adding the criterion of cud chewing, the priests deliberately excluded the pig from the list of permitted animals, which proves that they were rejecting the pig because it was an abomination both aesthetically and

---

[12] From the Dead Sea to Mount Hermon, Ps 104:18; Prov 30:26.

culturally. The stipulation of the other criterion, cleft hoofs, however, was based on other grounds: to limit the Israelite's access to the main domestic species of the animal kingdom—cattle, sheep, and goats (plus several wild but virtually inaccessible animals, Deut 14:4; for details see THEME F).

[11:8] No sanctions are invoked for eating or touching animal carcasses except if done by priests (Lev 22:8-9). The only penalty—and it is a severe one—is incurred when coming into contact with the sanctuary or its sanctums while in a state of impurity (7:20-21) or if the impurity is not cleansed but allowed to be prolonged (5:2; 17:15-16). The impurity deriving from a carcass may account for the practice of removing one's sandals before entering a sacred precinct (Exod 3:5; Josh 5:15); sandals, being fashioned of animal skins, are *eo ipso* impure, but only in regard to the sacred. This rule is to this day strictly enforced in Islam.

[11:9] Not all marine animals have fins; for example, crustaceans propel themselves by their legs. It is possible that the criteria for fish and, indeed, for all other animal species contained in this chapter are so worded as to emphasize their means of locomotion. Assumed is that those animals are permitted that move in a way that is natural to their environment: land animals walk (on feet, not paws), water animals swim (not crawl), and air animals fly.[13] These criteria effectively reduce edible marine life for the ancient Israelite to a handful of fish (see v. 12).

[11:10] The term *šeqeṣ* ("abomination") connotes something reprehensible and detestable. Yet in this chapter it bears a more precise, technical meaning. It should be noted that *šeqeṣ* is not attributed to all species of forbidden animals. It is reserved for marine animals (v. 10), birds (v. 13), flying insects (v. 23), and reptiles (vv. 41-44), but it is missing in the passages that deal with the quadrupeds (vv. 2-8, 24-28, 39-40) and the eight exceptional vermin (vv. 29-38), where instead the term *ṭame²*, "impure," is employed. There is a legal and ritual distinction between these two terms: *šeqeṣ* refers to animals whose ingestion is forbidden but do not pollute, whereas *ṭame²* refers to animals that, in addition, pollute by contact (see THEME H).

[11:12] Why are the fish unnamed? For my answer, see THEME G.

[11:20] "Winged swarming creatures": in other words, flying insects.

[11:21] Members of the locust-grasshopper family actually have a third pair of long, jointed legs that are attached close to the neck, appear to be above the other legs, and are bent when the insect is in a squat position.[14]

---

[13] Douglas 1966:54-57.
[14] Wessely 1846.

Leviticus 11–16: The Impurity System

[11:22] The reason for exempting the locusts is not clear. It may be related to Israel's pastoral life in its presettlement period, when the community subsided on its herds as well as on the sporadic visits of locusts, just as bedouin do to this day. Indeed, we should remember that one inhabitant of the wilderness, John the Baptist, made "locusts and wild honey" his exclusive fare (Matt 3:4; Mark 1:6) and that Yemenite Jews still eat fried locusts.

[11:24-28] Thus far, only the four named quadrupeds have been declared as *ṭameʾ* (vv. 4-7) and as conveyers of impurity by contact (v. 8). This rule also holds for all quadrupeds that do not possess the requisite criteria, as is made clear by vv. 24-28.

[11:24] That the impure person must undergo bathing is implied not only here but throughout the chapter. Washing is specifically called for in Leviticus 11 only in the case of impure vessels. If washing is required for vessels contaminated by touch, however, all the more so must it be true for persons. Furthermore, one who eats the carcass of a pure animal ostensibly is only "impure until evening" (v. 40), but other texts inform us that he or she also requires bathing (17:15; 22:6). Finally, as all who carry a carcass must launder their clothes (vv. 25, 28, 40b), it is inconceivable that they are not also obliged to undergo bathing (15:5, 6, 7, 8, 10, 11, 13).

[11:25] Because the carcass most likely came into contact with clothes, their bearer must bathe.[15] Or the reason may be the greater intensity of the contact: whereas touching presumes light contact, carrying implies that the pressure of the carcass on the clothes, even indirectly (e.g., when the carcass is wrapped), suffices to transmit the impurity.

[11:32] What accounts for the fact that impure wooden vessels are discarded by the Hittites, purified by the Israelites, and either discarded or purified by the Hindus? The answer may rest on economic grounds. Wooden utensils would rarely be found in the Israelite kitchen. Rather, this concession would have been intended for more costly items, such as the handles of tools and weapons, the beams of roofs and looms, and the like. The same reason that exempted the outside of sealed crockery from being permeable to impurity may have prevailed here as well: to spare the Israelites severe economic loss. Perhaps the same reason obtains among those Indians who permit the reuse of contaminated wooden vessels. Also, one could surmise that the reason that Hittite religion demanded their destruction was that wood in Anatolia was relatively inexpensive. This, however, is but a conjecture and awaits investigation.

---

[15] Ramban.

It is not surprising that metal implements are omitted from this list. Metal articles were not to be found in the ordinary home.[16] Even so, the more likely reason is that, being nonporous, there was no question about whether they could be purified.[17] The enumerated vessels, by contrast, are all organic and their porosity would have made it doubtful whether they could be purified. Metal vessels were, of course, used in the cult and in armaments; hence they are listed among the items requiring purification (6:21; Num 31:22). The question of whether articles of metal (and glass) required purification was the subject of a controversy with the Sadducees.[18]

[11:33] These animals must be small in size because they can fall *into* earthenware vessels. Flat earthenware was apparently rare: "The thin plate such as we use today was a difficult ceramic form to manufacture, and it was little used until New Testament times."[19]

[11:34] Once wetted by any liquid,[20] food becomes susceptible to impurity—even after it has dried.[21] Water embodies an anomalous, indeed, paradoxical status. It is the purifying agent par excellence (v. 32b); yet it is most vulnerable to impurity. The only logical answer seems to be that water used for purification (ablution) does indeed become contaminated by the object it is purifying. Hence it most probably must be drained off without allowing it to come into contact with any person or object.

[11:35-38] The basic principle is that the earth and everything that is embedded in it, such as cisterns (v. 36) and planted seeds (v. 37), are not susceptible to impurity. But objects unattached to the land such as vessels (vv. 32-33), solid food (v. 34a), potable drink (v. 34b), and loose seed (v. 38) are susceptible. The sole exceptions are earthenware ovens or stoves, even if they are embedded in the ground (v. 35b). Strikingly, in various Hindu sects (e.g., Assamese), the soaking of grain also renders it permeable to impurity.[22]

[11:40] Why need "and anyone who eats of its carcass" be mentioned when it is obvious that if a person who touches or carries a carcass is rendered impure (see v. 27), all the more so if one eats of it? Furthermore, as eating was omitted in the case of an impure animal carcass (vv. 24-28), why was the case of the pure animal included here? The answer is obvious: whereas a person would hardly be expected to eat the

---

[16] Finkelstein 1962:1.129.

[17] Wright 1987:11 n. 69.

[18] *t. Ḥag.* 3:35; cf. Finkelstein 1962:1.128–30.

[19] Kelso 1962:3.851a.

[20] *Sipra Shemini* par. 8:1.

[21] *b. Ḥul.* 36a.

[22] Hayley 1980:115.

carcass of an impure quadruped, one might not hesitate to eat the carcass of a pure quadruped on the assumption that it was properly slaughtered. Hence there was a need to specify that the required purification for eating a carcass was equivalent to (but not severer than) that required of one who carried the carcass.

[11:41] The third and final category of "swarmers" (the first being the fish, vv. 9-12, and the second, the flying insects, vv. 20-23) is divided into three categories: the creeping, the four-footed, and the many-footed (v. 42a).

[11:42] A chiastic reprise of v. 41, thus indicating stylistically that vv. 41-42 form an organic unit, the most significant consequence of which is that the following verse (v. 43) heads up a new unit. The purpose of the repetition is not just literary but ideological. It stresses that in contradistinction to the other animal categories (quadrupeds, birds, and fish), which have permissible species, all of the swarming creatures are forbidden as food.

[11:43] Why does the emphasis on the repulsiveness of the land-swarming creatures far exceed that of the previously mentioned creatures? The answer probably lies in the unique nature of the land swarmers.[23] In contradistinction to all the other categories, which can boast of at least several permitted creatures (quadrupeds, v. 3; Deut 14:4; fish, v. 9; birds, Deut 11:11; flying insects, Lev 11:21-22), the land swarmers allow for no exceptions—all are forbidden. Hence they are derisively abhorred. Furthermore, the land swarmers are ubiquitous, especially in the kitchen or wherever food is stored. Yet these reasons still do not explain why all land swarmers were eschewed and none was allowed.

For a possible answer one must resort to the speculative but cogent explanation proffered by Paschen.[24] "Earth" can denote the underworld, the abode of the dead.[25] Even more to the point is that "dust" at times denotes the grave or the underworld.[26] Thus it is the association with the earth, the sphere of death, that led to the exclusion of all land swarmers from Israel's diet. This explanation, admittedly speculative for the present, will take on added force once it is demonstrated that all ritual impurity, embedded and legislated in chapters 11–15, has this as its common denominator: the association with death. Perhaps for this reason, the call to holiness is attached to the blanket prohibition of all land swarmers. The antonym of *ṭameʾ*, "impure," is *qadoš*, "holy." Therefore, if the former stands for the forces of death, the latter symbolizes the forces of life. Israel, then, is commanded here to desist from all land swarmers,

---

[23] Eerdmans 1912:65.

[24] 1970:58.

[25] E.g., Exod 15:12; Jer 17:13; Jonah 2:7 (Eng. 6); Ps 22:30 (Eng. 29); 71:20.

[26] E.g., Isa 26:19; Ps 22:16, 30 (Eng. 15, 29); Job 7:21; 10:9; 17:16; 20:11; Dan 12:2; cf. Ridderbos 1948.

the denizens of the sphere of death, by keeping in mind that its task is to be holy, to seek life, for its God is holy; its God is the source of life.

[11:44] Israel must not contaminate itself by eating land swarmers because holiness, the goal it must seek, cannot coexist with impurity. That Israel is commanded to be holy is the main thrust of chapters 17–27 (H). Israel can become holy by obedience to God's moral and ritual commandments (see THEME D above and chap. 19, THEME A). This objective is adumbrated in earlier sources (Exod 19:6; 22:30 [Eng. 31]) but is assiduously avoided—and by implication, denied—by P, which holds that only the priests (and temporary nazirites) are holy.

The reason that Israel must aspire to holiness is *imitatio Dei*. The call to holiness is attached to the total prohibition of all land swarmers, because the antonym of impure—the status of all land swarmers—is holy. Moreover, Israel is commanded to avoid land swarmers because they are the denizens of the sphere of death, by keeping in mind that its task is to be holy, to seek life, for God is holy and the source of life. This rationale is applied to these diet laws once again (Lev 20:26) and is discussed above in THEME D, and in chap. 19, THEME A.

[11:47] Creation was the product of God making distinctions (Gen 1:4, 6, 7, 14, 18). This divine function is to be continued by Israel: the priests to teach it (Lev 10:10-11) and the people to practice it. The purpose of the discriminations that Israel must impose on the animal world is not explained here. But the rationale is explained unambiguously in 20:24b-26: "You shall distinguish the pure quadruped from the impure, the impure bird from the pure. You shall not defile your throats with a quadruped or a bird or anything else that moves [on] the earth, which I have set apart for you to treat as impure . . . and *I have set you apart from all other peoples to be mine*." The animal world mirrors the human. The separation of animals into pure and impure is both a model and a lesson for Israel to separate itself from the nations. The latter have defiled themselves by their idolatry and immorality. Israel must therefore refrain from partaking of their practices, and thereby become eligible for a life of holiness—the way and nature of its God (THEME D, above) was to limit Israel's access to the animal world.

Childbirth

Chapters 12 and 15 deal with the impurity of genital discharges. Chapter 12 focuses on the impurity of lochial (post-childbirth) blood of the new mother. During the first seven days after the birth of a male child the blood flow is strong, comparable to that of a menstruant (discussed in 15:19-24). On the eighth day the male child is circumcised. Thirty-three days later, presumably after the lochial blood has ceased, the mother brings the prescribed offering to the sanctuary. If the child is female the mother's impurity time is doubled: fourteen days of severe (menstrual) impurity and sixty-six days of lesser (lochial) impurity, after which she brings the required sacrifice. A reduced sacrifice is available for the poor.

Selected Theme

Vaginal Blood

Women who are menstruating are seen as a source of impurity and are forbidden from engaging in sexual intercourse with their husbands. If this smacks of an ancient superstition against menstrual blood, it most likely is, but only in part. In the Bible, the source of the menstruation taboo lies in a deep commitment to life and its perpetuation.

Members of primitive societies have testified to their researchers that menstrual and lochial blood (following childbirth) is dangerous to persons. Written sources give testimony that this view was also held by the ancients, for instance, the Romans and the pre-Islamic Arabs. It is also recorded as a folk belief in the Talmud: "If a menstruant woman passes between two [men], if it is at the beginning of her menses, she will slay one of them, and if it is at the end of her menses, she will cause strife between them."[1] Moreover, menstrual blood was regarded as a powerful charm among the Arabs, and here too we find an echo in rabbinic writings: "If a woman sees a snake . . . she should take some of her hair and fingernails and throw them at it and say, 'I am menstruous.'"[2] Thus it was the worldwide fear of menstrual blood as the

---

[1] *b. Pesaḥ.* 111a.
[2] *b. Šabb.* 110a.

repository of demonic forces that is most likely the cause of the isolation of the menstruant.

Yet Israel's monotheism had exorcised the demons (see chap. 4, THEME A). What dangers, then, continued to lurk in the menstruant's impurity? If there were no demons—if, instead, God was the source of both good and evil—then impurity itself should have been eliminated in the Bible and the menstruant rendered neutral. To be sure, the demons disappeared from the official religion, but the demonic continued in humans. Impurity in Israelite religion was not the purview of the demons; it was a sign of moral failing and physical infirmity in humanity. The former represented Israel's disobedience—their violation of God's prohibitive commandments (chap. 4, THEME A). The latter represented the diminution of life and, if unchecked, destruction and death. Although the loss of vaginal blood and semen is a necessary part of the human cycle, its symbolic value, representing the loss of life, is a process unalterably opposed by Israel's God, the source of its life: "you shall keep my laws and my norms, by the pursuit of which men shall live: I am YHWH" (Lev 18:5).

In the Israelite mind, blood was the chief symbol of life (17:10; Deut 12:23). Its oozing from the body was no longer the work of demons, but it was certainly the sign of death. In particular, the loss of seed in vaginal blood was associated with the loss of life. Bleeding or touching blood was not considered polluting, and people who were wounded and bleeding were not defiled and were not forbidden to come to the sanctuary or partake of the sacrifices. The only bodily emissions that pollute are: (1) menstrual blood and semen—both of which are major pollutants (15:1-13, 19-30); and (2) ejaculation of semen without intercourse, when the man is impure until the evening (15:16). Thus it was that Israel—alone among the peoples—restricted impurity solely to those physical conditions involving the loss of vaginal blood and semen, the forces of life, and to the corpse and to scale disease, which visually manifested the approach of death (see chap. 13, THEME). All other bodily issues and excrescences were not tabooed, despite their impure status among Israel's contemporaries, such as cut hair or nails in Persia and India and the newborn child as well as the mother in Greece and Egypt. Human feces were also not declared impure (despite Deut 23:10-12 [Eng. 9-11]; Ezek 4:12). The elimination of waste has nothing to do with death; on the contrary, it is essential to life. That is why it was decreed from early on that the act of excretion should be accompanied by this blessing: "Blessed is he who has formed a human in his wisdom and created in them many orifices and many cavities. It is fully known before your throne of glory that if one of them should be ruptured or one of them be blocked it would be impossible to survive and stand before you. [Blessed are you] who heals all flesh and performs wondrously."[3]

Thus biblical impurity and holiness are semantic opposites. As the quintessence and source of holiness resides with God, it is imperative for Israel to control the

---

[3] *b. Ber.* 60a.

occurrence of impurity lest it impinge upon the realm of the holy God. The forces pitted against each other in the cosmic struggle are no longer the benevolent and demonic deities who populate the mythologies of Israel's neighbors, but the forces of life and death set loose by people themselves through their obedience or defiance of God's commandments.

Selected Texts

[12:2] That this severe "menstrual" impurity is terminated by immersion is nowhere stated either for the parturient or for the menstruant. But as all statements regarding the duration of impurity automatically imply, if they do not explicitly affirm, that it must terminate by bathing, the mere statement that the period of the parturient's severer impurity lasts seven (or fourteen, v. 5) days assumes that this period ends by bathing. The same holds true for the menstruant (see 15:19). Besides, if a minor impurity such as seminal discharge requires bathing (15:6), all the more so the major genital discharges. By the same token, bathing permits her to have contact with the common, including sexual congress with her husband, though this latter point is disputed by the sectarians, such as the Samaritans, the Falashas (Ethiopian Jews), and the Karaites.

[12:3] This verse, which switches from the mother to the boy, is clearly an editorial parenthesis that interrupts the prescriptive ritual for the mother. It cannot be claimed that the circumcision is a purificatory rite for the boy and thus comparable to the purificatory rites enjoined upon his mother, for there is no equivalent rite for a newly born girl. The purpose of this interpolation is to emphasize the uniqueness of the timing of circumcision, not the rite itself, for the rite of circumcision was practiced ubiquitously by Israel's Semitic neighbors. In Israel alone circumcision was performed in infancy—precisely, on the eighth day. The boy's blood is clean and symbolic of God's covenant (see below), while the mother's blood is contaminating and symbolic of death. Circumcision removes the male from the realm of death by the shedding of his own blood.

The rite of circumcision is attested throughout the world. According to Jer 9:25 [Eng. 26], it was practiced by the Egyptians, Edomites, Ammonites, Moabites, and Arabs as well as by the Israelites. In Egypt, however, it seems—at least in the Hellenistic period—to have been limited to the priests. Everywhere else it is a puberty rite that fits a man for marriage. In Israel alone it is associated with infancy, though originally it may also have been a premarital rite. Such an earlier practice may be reflected in Ishmael's circumcision at the age of thirteen (Gen 17:25). Philology provides even stronger evidence.[4]

---

[4] Snaith 1967:3.

With the transfer of circumcision to infancy, it became a sign of the covenant, an initiation rite into the religious bond between Israel and its God (Gen 17:1-27). That the uncircumcised may not participate in the paschal sacrifice (Exod 12:43-49; Josh 5:2-10) and that, in the oldest narrative stratum, circumcision was required of the non-Israelite bridegroom—if in Dinah's case it was not just a ruse to kill (Gen 34:14-17, 22)—indicate that the covenant idea was associated with circumcision from earliest times.

Israel's ancient custom of taking an oath while holding the circumcised membrum (Gen 24:2-9; 47:29-31) may be related to the Babylonian practice, attested as early as 1700 BCE, of settling matters by means of an oath in the presence of a symbol of the god (e.g., the saw of the sun god, the spear of Ishtar, the mace of Ninurta). As no image of Israel's God was permitted, the circumcision, the sign of the covenant, was employed instead. The circumcised membrum indicates the presence of God as a divine witness who, by implication, will punish the violation of the oath.

[12:4] According to Luke 2:22, Joseph and Mary brought baby Jesus to the temple "when the days of their purification . . . were fulfilled." This was on the thirty-third day after Jesus' circumcision (or forty days after his birth). This is the basis of the Christian feast of Candlemas, celebrated on February 2. The pronoun "their" is clearly a textual error since only Mary required purification. On the other hand, commentator J. A. Fitzmyer suggests that Luke, not being a Palestinian Jewish Christian, was not accurately informed of Lev 12:4.[5]

The parturient's blood discharge (lochia) is mentioned in Leviticus 12 three times (vv. 4, 5, 7), emphasizing its long duration beyond the initial seven/fourteen-day impurity. The first discharge is bright red, then turns brown, and becomes increasingly paler. The total discharge lasts from two to six weeks. Hence the round figure of forty days is quite accurate. Moreover, the bright red of the initial discharge resembles the menstrual flow and is therefore treated as such.

The expression "blood purity," found twice in this chapter (vv. 4a, 5b), is probably a frozen idiom that refers exclusively to the parturient's state following her initial seven- (or fourteen-) day impurity. The use of "purity" here makes sense. It implies that her previous impurity no longer exists, a point that the following verse makes explicit by stating that she remains impure only in regard to sanctums. Thus she now has unrestricted access to the common sphere, including her husband. Indeed, the use of the abstract noun "purity" twice in reference to her blood flow strongly suggests that sexual contact with this blood does not defile.

Comparative material duplicates the disparity in the purificatory periods following the birth of a boy and that of a girl, with the period following a girl's birth

---

[5] Fitzmyer 1981:424.

nearly always being longer. The earlier Hittite civilization (second millennium BCE) also attests a distinction in the purification of the newborn child: three months for a male and four months for a female. Later Hellenistic medicine from Hippocrates (fifth century BCE) to Galen (second century CE) also held that there was a difference: thirty days for a male and forty-two days for a female. Thus the biblical distinction, though with different numbers, is probably based on physiology, that is, early medical science.[6]

[12:5] The term "sacred precinct" is significant here, for in the entire Bible it never stands for the sanctuary or temple building. It refers to all the objects in the sacred area of which the tabernacle is but one. Indeed, the full name for the Second Temple confirms it; it means "the house of the sacred area" (2 Chr 36:17).

[12:6] That these sacrifices are brought after the impurity has totally disappeared is irrefutable proof that their function is not apotropaic or medicinal. In Israel the puerperal period is not feared as governed by the demonic (in polemical opposition to other cultures; see above, THEME). Only ritual impurity adheres, which time and bathing remove (see chap. 15, THEME C). To be sure, no bath whatever is mandated by the text for the parturient; but as already pointed out, the bathing requirement is always omitted for the simple reason that it is taken for granted except in cases in which it is not self-understood (see 11:24). Such will clearly be the case for the menstruant (see 15:19) and a fortiori for the parturient.

[12:7] Now that forty (or eighty) days have elapsed and she has brought her requisite sacrifices to the sanctuary, she is purified completely and is eligible to make contact with sacred objects. Moral impurity, on the one hand, can only be forgiven by God and not by any action of the priest. Hence the verb is in the passive and it means "be forgiven" (see 4:20, 26, 31, 35; 5:10, 13, 16, 18, 26). Physical impurity, on the other hand, is eliminated mechanically by the water and the sacrifice. The process is automatic. Hence the verb for purification is in the active construction and means "is pure." There is no moral consequence, and no judgment of moral or social worth is made here.

---

[6] M. Bar-Ilan, unpublished manuscript.

Scale Disease

Selected Theme
The Symbolism of Scale Disease: Part I

Biblical scale disease is difficult to identify. But one thing is certain: it is ritual, not pathology. To begin with, the scale disease diagnosed here is not leprosy (Hansen's disease). Its positive identification, however, is uncertain. I invited a respected San Francisco Bay Area dermatologist, Marvin Engel, to address my graduate seminar on this subject. After carefully studying the biblical text and its derivative medical literature, he stated his conclusions without any hesitation: the symptoms described in Leviticus 13 do not correspond to any known skin disease. His main difficulty, surprisingly, was not the diagnosis but the treatment. Chronic skin diseases, he claimed, such as psoriasis, favus, and vitiligo, will not disappear or even change appreciably within one or two weeks. Thus, if these are the diseases described in Leviticus 13, the prescribed quarantine period is ineffectual and, indeed, can be misleading. The safest statement that can be made about these diseases is that they share one feature in common: they produce scales. Hence I have rendered the Hebrew term as "scale disease."

The enigma of scale disease cannot be resolved by medical science, but it can, at least, be illumined once the medical approach is abandoned and attention is directed to the text itself. We are dealing with ritual, not medicine. Moreover, the text stresses that it is not the disease per se but its appearance that is the source of impurity. Indeed, it is the focus on appearance that has resulted in condemning clothes infected by mold and houses by fungus, surely not because they are stricken with scale disease but because they bear the appearance of scale disease. The suspicion that we are not dealing with the disease aspect of this phenomenon can be buttressed by yet another consideration. The ancient world was familiar with a wide variety of diseases. In Mesopotamia, for example, a large percentage of its surviving cuneiform tablets deal with the diagnosis and treatment of disease. In Israel these diseases were probably known as well. Yet Scripture concerns itself with just a minute portion.

Furthermore, these skin diseases—if their tentative identification be granted—are mainly not contagious. This medical fact is confirmed by Scripture itself. The Aramean general Naaman, though afflicted with scale disease, was not prevented from leading an army, living with his family, confronting the prophet's servants, and, above all, entering the temple of Rimmon with his king leaning on his arm (2 Kings 5). To be sure, had he been an Israelite he would have been banished like Miriam (Num 12:14-16), the four outcasts (2 Kgs 7:3-10), and Uzziah (2 Kgs 15:5). But this only proves that Israelites bearing scale disease were not banished for hygienic reasons. Indeed, Leviticus confirms the impression that scale disease was not considered a disease: furniture removed from the house before the priest's examination cannot be declared impure (Lev 14:36). The rabbis also presume that scale disease is not a disease, for they declare that its rules are not applicable to non-Jews and their homes in the Holy Land. In short, we are dealing with ritual, not pathology.

Infectious diseases and especially those to which a sexual fault is attached always inspire fears of easy contagion and bizarre fantasies of transmission by non-venereal means in public places. The removal of door knobs and instillation of swinging doors on U.S. Navy ships and the disappearance of the metal drinking cups affixed to public water fountains in the United States in the first decade of the twentieth century were the early consequences of the "discovery of syphilis"—"instantly transmitted infection." The warning to generations of middle-class children always to interpose paper between bare bottom and public toilet seats is another trace of the once rife horror stories about the germs of syphilis being passed to the innocent by the dirty.

AIDS has revived similar phobias and fears of contamination. Some still argue that anyone who is HIV positive (who as yet does not have AIDS) ought to be quarantined. Many still fear being in the presence of someone suffering from a terrible disease; in the case of AIDS or cancer, such fear is irrational.

To be sure, the text specifies that certified carriers of scale disease must rend their clothes, dishevel their hair, veil their mouth, warn persons in their vicinity that they are impure, and isolate themselves outside the camp (13:45-46). All but the last listed, however, are not incorporated into the priestly purification system (chap. 14). Hence they must be folk beliefs and practices, which entered into the text as a concession to the people at large. Even the ostracization of the afflicted outside the camp/city, if the priestly legists had a complete say in this matter, would have been reduced to the level of the *zav* (someone with a chronic genital discharge, chap. 15) and the corpse-contaminated person (Numbers 19), who were not banished but remained at home.

Scale disease is cut from the same cloth as other ritual impurities: carcasses (chap. 11), parturition (chap. 12), and genital discharges (chap. 15). The fact that scale disease (chaps. 13–14) is ensconced within these subjects is in itself sufficient warrant for claiming that ritual impurity is its motivating postulate. The question, then, is not what is scale disease, but what is ritual impurity?

The main clue for understanding the place of scale disease in the impurity system is that it is an aspect of death: its bearer is treated like a corpse. This equation is expressly stated by Aaron in his prayer on behalf of Miriam when she is stricken with scale disease: "Let her not be like a corpse" (Num 12:12). In addition, both scale disease and the corpse contaminate not only by direct contact but, unlike all other impurity bearers, also contaminate by overhang, that is, by being under the same roof. Impurity, in this view, being a gaseous substance, rises upward. But if blocked by a roof it then fills the space below. Furthermore, the purification rites of the corpse-contaminated person and the one afflicted with scale disease are strikingly similar: both require aspersion with animal blood that has made contact with cedar, hyssop, and scarlet thread and has been diluted in fresh water (Lev 14:4-7; Num 19:1-13).

The common denominator of all the skin ailments described in Leviticus 13 is that the body appears to be wasting away. As the continuation of Aaron's prayer expresses it: "Let her not be like a corpse that emerges from its mother's womb with half its flesh eaten away" (Num 12:12). As pointed out by medical authorities, "The most striking external feature of such a stillborn child is the way the superficial layers of the skin peel off."[1] Thus it is the visible "peeling off," the striking characteristic of the scale diseases listed in Leviticus 13—reminders of the disintegration of the corpse and the onset of death—that has led to their impure status and to the banishment of their carriers from the community. Note that the other human sources of impurity—of the parturient (chap. 12), the menstruant, the gonorrhean (chap. 15), and the corpse contaminated (Numbers 19)—are *not visible*. Hence their bearers are not banished but may remain at home. This criterion is also the governing postulate of all the other impurities discussed in chapters 11–15, and its elucidation and confirmation in these impurities as well will serve to support its existence here. In conclusion, the *appearance* of the disease, and not so much the disease itself, is the source of impurity. Bodily impurity stands for the forces of death that are countered and reversed by God's covenantal commandments, the forces of life.

Selected Texts

[13:2-17] Discolorations, scabs, and shiny marks are the main criteria for diagnosing scale disease. If they have turned the hair white and appear deeper than the skin, the priest declares them impure. In the case of white shiny marks, if the scaliness appears only superficial and the hair has not turned white, the patient is quarantined by the examining priest for one week. If the scaliness has not spread, the patient is quarantined for another week. If the affection has faded and not spread, it is considered a scab, and the priest pronounces him pure. In the case of white discolorations, if a patch of raw flesh appears in them that has turned the hair white, it is immediately diagnosed as scale disease. But if white scales have covered the entire body, the person is pronounced pure.

---

[1] Hulse 1975:93.

The text, however, says nothing about how and when this examination takes place. The precise information is provided by the rabbis: "They [the priests] may not inspect skin disease in the early morning or in the evening or within the house or on a cloudy day, for then the dull white would appear bright white; or at midday, for then the bright white would appear dull white. When should they inspect, then? At the third, fourth, fifth, seventh, eighth, or ninth hour. So R. Meir. R. Judah says: At the fourth, fifth, eighth, or ninth hour."

[13:18-28] Scale disease occurring in the site of healed boils and a burn caused by hot coals or ashes, manifesting themselves in white discolorations or reddish-white shiny marks, are to be treated more leniently than the preceding cases. If the hair has not turned white and the lesion appears no deeper than the surrounding skin—the two critical symptoms—the patient is quarantined for one week only, not for two. If after the quarantine the sore has not spread, it is considered a scab resulting from the boil or burn, and the victim is pronounced pure.

[13:29-37] These verses deal with the infections of the scalp and the beard, to wit, the hairy parts of the head. The treatment is the same as for the scale disease described in vv. 2-8, though the priest is told to look out for yellow hair rather than white hair. The yellowing of the hair favors the diagnosis of favus rather than psoriasis.

[13:38-39] A white skin eruption that is faded, not sunken, and does not have white hair is considered pure and requires no quarantine. The question needs to be asked: Why did not the editor first complete his description of impure cases (vv. 42-44) before describing pure cases? Apparently, he ordered his material according to the subject: men and women together first (vv. 38-39), then men alone (vv. 40-44).

[13:40-44] Ordinary baldness, whether it starts from the forehead or the crown, is not impure unless it is marked by reddish-white patches.

[13:45-46] A certified carrier of scale disease must rend his clothes, dishevel his hair, veil his mouth, warn persons in his vicinity that he is impure, and isolate himself outside the camp. These and salient features of his purification are striking reminders of his similitude to the corpse-contaminated person. Both rend their clothes, dishevel their hair (10:6), contaminate by overhang (14:47; Num 19:14), and are sprinkled (Lev 14:7; Num 19:19) with spring water (Lev 14:6; Num 19:17) containing cedar, hyssop, and crimson yarn (Lev 14:6; Num 19:6). However, their differences should not be overlooked: the corpse-contaminated person does not veil his mouth, warn others of his presence, or offer sacrifices for his purification (contrast Lev 14:1-32), but uniquely requires the ashes of a red cow (Num 19:1-12).

[13:45] The practice of certified scale-diseased persons to ward off oncomers by pointing to their impurity is paralleled by this poignant picture of the Jerusalemites after their city was destroyed: "They wandered blindly through the streets, defiled with blood, so that no one was able to touch their garments. 'Away! Unclean!' people shouted at them, 'Away! Away! Touch not!'" (Lam 4:15a). In Lamentations, however, the call has been reversed: instead of the warning being issued by the scale-diseased persons, it originates from passersby—emphasizing the extent to which the Jerusalemites have become repugnant. Later commentators softened the harshness of the ostracism, for example, "He thereby informs others of his sorrow so that they implore mercy on his behalf"; he must call out because being garbed like a mourner others may approach him to offer consolation.

[13:46] That scale disease requires total isolation is not due to its ostensible physical contagion, which must be emphatically denied (see the introduction to this volume), but for the ritual—not medical—reason that its impurity is contagious under the same roof, a postulate not only explicit in the rabbinic system but implicit in the Priestly biblical system (see chap. 15, THEME C). In this regard the scale-diseased person bears the same degree of impurity as the corpse. The question needs to be addressed: Why banish the scale-diseased person if his disease is not contagious? What difference does it make if he is ritually contagious and even contaminates the whole community? The answer rests upon the distinctive virulence of his impurity to contaminate by overhang. If he were to remain in the community, people might be with him under the same roof and be unaware of it and then enter the sanctuary or eat sacred food. It is this fatal contact between the impure and the sacred that had to be avoided at all costs.

[13:47-58] In semitropical climates dampness gives rise to mold or fungus, which affects and destroys fabrics. These infections resemble those on humans and are treated similarly. Two seven-day periods of quarantine are prescribed. If the fungus or mold has not spread after the first seven days, the garment is washed and quarantined for another seven days. If it still has not spread, the affected part is torn out and the fabric may be reused. If, however, the affection has spread or it has failed to fade, the fabric must be burned.

The juxtaposition of the two pericopes on affections of persons and fabrics is most likely due to their strikingly similar symptoms. Both "are abnormal surface conditions that disfigure the outside of the skin or garment. Both cause the surface to flake or peel."[2]

A moldy garment in no way reflects the character of its bearer; otherwise sacrifices or some other rite would have been prescribed for the owners of the garment,

---

[2] Ibid.

so that they could make expiation for their suspected wrong. The nexus between malady and sin has been severed. The malady is diagnosed objectively—scientifically, one might say. The extension of scale disease from persons to garments (and to house, 14:33-53) is artificially drawn, far removed from the original claim that every natural disorder is the result of human willful disobedience.

[13:59] Since the entire topic of scale disease (chaps. 13–14) will conclude with a subscript that enumerates all of its components, including fabrics (14:54-56), why is there a need for this repetitive and, ostensibly, superfluous subscript for fabrics? Several cogent reasons can be offered. (1) It sets off the pericope from chapter 14, which returns to the subject matter of persons. (2) There is no subscript in v. 46, at the end of the discussion of human scale disease, because its purificatory rites continue in chapter 14 whereas this pericope on fabrics is complete unto itself: there is no purificatory rite beyond the burning or washing of the fabric. An additional reason suggests itself: (3) Without this subscript, the impression might be gained that the purificatory rites for humans and houses (chap. 14) also apply to fabrics.

Purification after Scale Disease

Israel's neighbors ascribed illness to a demonic entity that overtook the body. To heal the afflicted person, a healer exorcised the demon, banishing with it the demonic illness. Israel rejected this vision of illness and, with it, the vision of the pagan physician or magician. Healing comes from God alone, either directly (Exod 15:26) or through a surrogate, the prophet (e.g., Moses, Exod 15:25; Elijah, 1 Kgs 17:22; Elisha, 2 Kgs 2:21; Isaiah, 2 Kgs 20:7-8). Disease is not a demonic entity independent of God, nor is ritual an intrinsically effective agency of healing. Both disease and healing, the ailment and what cures it, stem from the one God. The ritual, bereft of its inherent power, is transformed into a symbolic purification; it becomes a religious, and not a therapeutic, act. In a provocative insight about the nature of illness and health, the Leviticus text ascribes them both to the same divine source.

Selected Theme
The Symbolism of Scale Disease: Part II
What is this symbolism, and why does it call for the intervention of the priest? As will be explained in chapter 15, THEME C, the root cause of the priest's intervention in cases of scale disease is the anomalous nature of the impurity. The scale disease, alone among the impurities generated by live persons, contaminates by overhang (the corpse also shares this power), necessitating the banishment of its carrier from the community. The enforcement of the banishment and the comportment of the carrier are matters that are delegated to the priest (13:45-46). Moreover, the bird rite (see v. 4)—though it is extraneous to the Priestly system of impurity and is a residue of a pagan exorcistic rite—is performed under the supervision of the priest (vv. 4-7). Indeed, it is most likely the pagan origins of this rite that motivated Israel's priesthood to take charge of its execution. In large measure, the priests succeeded in excising, and failing that in blunting, the most blatant pagan elements of the rite. The live bird was not offered as a gift to some chthonic deity. In this respect, the transformation of the bird rite into a practice compatible with Israel's monotheism was more successful than the similarly structured scapegoat rite for the purging of the sanctuary,

in which the name of the original divine recipient of the animal, Azazel, was preserved (16:8, 10).

The same transmutation and evisceration are evident in the bird rite for fungous houses (vv. 10-20), but to an even greater degree. The affection itself is not only denied a demonic source, it is drained of any inherent power. At most it communicates a minor impurity to persons and objects, which impurity is eliminated by bathing and sunset on the very day it is contracted. But even more significant is that the impurity does not begin to exist until it is "discovered" by the priest. Of course, the same holds true for the scale-diseased person (13:3, 11, 20, 25, 30), but the legislation on houses takes pains to warn the owner to remove all possessions before the arrival of the priest and thereby save them from possible condemnation (v. 36). In short, we are dealing with an impurity that has been eviscerated of its principal potency.

What then is the meaning of this priestly impurity, and, if there was the danger of confusing it with demonic impurity, why was it retained? A major clue, provided by the text, is that the scale-diseased persons must bring a purification offering, implying that they have polluted the sanctuary. Thus in this case, as in all cases of ritual impurity, we are confronted with the binary opposition between holiness and impurity, which symbolize the forces of life and death, respectively. The bird rite was retained not only for the negative reason that the (mostly, nonmonotheistic) masses insisted on it, but because from the priestly point of view it presented vividly and forcefully the very battle and victory of life over death. All elements employed in the rite were connotative of life: the "live" (wild) birds, the "live" (spring) water, the "life" blood, and the bloodlike ingredients: the red cedar and the crimson yarn. In opposition to this life-affirming ritual stands the scale disease, which itself so clearly illustrates the forces of death.

Thus the entire purification process is nothing but a symbolic ritual, a *rite of passage*, marking the transition from death to life. As the celebrants move from the realm of impurity outside the camp, and are first restored to their community, then to their home, and finally to their sanctuary, they have passed from impurity to holiness, from death to life. In so moving, they are reinstated with their families and are reconciled with their God.

Selected Texts

Three separate purification ceremonies are required: for the first day (vv. 2-8; also invoked for houses, vv. 48-53), for the seventh (v. 9), and for the eighth (vv. 10-32). The first-day ritual is performed by the priest outside the camp (or city) from which the stricken person has been banished. Cedar wood, crimson yarn, and a live bird are dipped into an earthen vessel containing a mixture of spring water and the blood of a slain bird. The cured person (or house) is sprinkled with this mixture seven times, after which the live bird is set free. The healed person is admitted into the camp (or city) after he launders his clothes, shaves all his hair, and bathes, but he is not yet allowed to enter their residence. That is permitted him on the seventh day, after shaving, laundering, and bathing again. On the eighth day he brings to the sanctuary oil, semolina, and sheep for various sacrifices, which are offered up in the following order: reparation, purification, burnt, and cereal offerings. The animals for the burnt and purification offerings may be commuted to birds if the offerer is poor. By contrast, the reparation lamb and the *log* of oil may not be changed, as the blood of the lamb and the oil are needed to daub the person's right earlobe, right thumb, and right big toe.

[14:4] The birds had to be wild, else the ever-present fear would remain that the live bird dispatched to the open country would return to the settlement and bring back the very impurity it was supposed to eliminate. Birds are chosen not because they are favored by chthonic deities or even by celestial deities. They are chosen because they transport the assumed freight of impurity upward and outward, to far-off distances whence the impurity cannot return. That the function of the birds is to carry off the impurity as far as possible is graphically depicted by the two women who "had wings like those of a stork" (Zech 5:9) for the purpose of carrying the tub of wickedness to far-off Babylonia (Zech 5:5-11).

The power of the blood, the symbol of life, was abetted by the addition of two red ingredients, the crimson yarn and the cedar wood, in order to counter and reverse the death process, vividly and visually represented by the deterioration of the body stricken with scale disease. To be sure, in the Israelite system the patient had to be cured before this purificatory rite could be applied. But the rite itself was not created by Israel. Indubitably, it was—as was most of the sacrificial system—a legacy from Israel's pagan past. A similar verdict must be accorded to the use of these same ingredients in the purification of corpse-contaminated persons. Indeed, the fact that the same life-enhancing ingredients are used in purificatory rites for those contaminated by a corpse or by scale disease further supports the theory that the scale-diseased person is regarded as a corpse (chap. 13, Theme) and that impurity, in general, is associated with death (see chap. 15, Theme B).

[14:5] The waters are called "living" because they flow perpetually and do not cease, like the living being whose movements never cease. Spring water was probably an essential element of the original purification rite prior to its incorporation into the Priestly system, and its function in its pagan setting was, together with the other ingredients, to exorcise the disease from the patient. To be sure, things are no longer the same in this Priestly text: the patient is already cured. What, then, is the function of these ingredients here? Although it is subsequently stated that the ritual has purified the patient (v. 7b), it will turn out that this rite is only the first step in the purification process and that nothing of the sort has happened. Nonetheless, the explicit wording of the text is an incontrovertible admission that originally, at one time, purification did indeed occur.

Support for this position can be adduced from the Bible itself. Scale-diseased Naaman is told by Elisha, God's prophet, "Go and bathe seven times in the Jordan, and your flesh shall be restored, and you shall be pure" (2 Kgs 5:10). Now, we should bear in mind that because the Jordan flows, its waters qualify as spring water. Yet the text states unambiguously that these waters will heal Naaman. Thus we see that the folk tradition, ensconced in the book of Kings, is at variance with the official, Priestly tradition, embodied in this Levitical ritual. Nevertheless, each tradition is aware of the other, to judge by the slight concession each accords the other. The folk tradition concerning Naaman's cure repeatedly states that not only will his flesh be healed but that, in addition, he will become "pure" (2 Kgs 5:10, 12, 13, 14).

The Priestly tradition, as we now see, has incorporated an older exorcistic rite, and though it serves no practical function at all—the patient has already been healed and the residual impurity is eliminated by the subsequent baths (see Lev 14:8, 9, 20)—it stands as the indispensable beginning of an eight-day purificatory rite because the people, not the priests, have demanded it. The exorcism for scale disease was allowed to remain at the head of week-long purification rites, but deprived of its originally inherent magical powers. Israelite monotheism, in its Priestly version, had clearly been at work.

The blood of the slain bird absorbs the disease from the patient and transfers it to the water. The live bird reabsorbs the disease when it is dipped into the water and transports it into the open country. Without doubt, in its pagan antecedents, this exorcistic rite was accompanied by incantations, which were subsequently excised by Israel's priesthood (see chap. 16, THEME C, on the original form and function of the scapegoat and its congeners in the ancient Near East). In addition, the rite was thoroughly transformed so that it was no longer a cure for disease but a ritual for purification after the disease was cured. In truth, however, the bird rite plays no role whatsoever in the actual purification of the healed "leper." His purification is effected by immersion into water first following the bird rite (v. 8) and, again, on the seventh day (v. 9). Indeed, that the bird rite turns out to be extraneous to the rest of the Priestly ceremony proves that it has been borrowed from Israel's anterior cultures and it was retained not because Israel's priests wanted it but probably because the people at large demanded it, practiced it, and would not have tolerated its deletion. For them, this rite of exorcism was indispensable.

[14:8] The healed "leper" no longer has to dwell outside the camp. This is the first of three mentions of "he shall be pure" (vv. 8, 9, 20). Each "he shall be pure" indicates that another layer of impurity has been removed. Before this purification, his impurity is that of a corpse. Now, after his first bath, he reenters his community. No one need be concerned about being under the same roof. By the elimination of the initial layer, this first-day purification rite renders the healed scale-diseased person incapable any longer of contaminating persons and vessels by overhang.

[14:9] The second of three occurrences of "he shall be pure" (vv. 8, 9, 20). This declaration of purity again follows a bath (v. 8), proving that the bath always reduces the impurity by one degree. The person need no longer remain outside his tent but can now enter it for he no longer contaminates sanctums by overhang, only by touch (see Figure 5 in chap. 15, THEME C). To eliminate the last vestige of impurity he needs to bring the appropriate sacrifices to the sanctuary on the following day.

[14:10] The biblical day begins at sunrise. This can certainly be verified in P. God made the world only during daylight, allowing nighttime to intervene between one creative day and the next (Genesis 1). Sacrifices may be eaten through the night, but on the following morning—the start of a new day—they must be incinerated. The case in this verse is even more obvious: sacrifices are never offered at night. Technically, nightfall should end all impurities as it does for all minor impurities. It is, then, the need to await daylight before entering the sanctuary that accounts for the additional eighth day.

[14:13] The purpose of the blood rite is both purificatory (note the verb "expiate," v. 20) and apotropaic (8:23). Like the priestly consecration, it is also a rite of passage. The blood on the extremities protects the person as it protects the priestly novitiates during their transition from one status to another: the consecrands from the profane realm to the sacred, the scale-diseased persons from being impure outcasts to full members of their community.

[14:16] The priest faces the adytum and flings the drops of oil on the courtyard floor. The purpose of the rite is to dedicate this oil to God.

[14:18] The forehead is the part of the body that is the focus of oil rituals elsewhere in the ancient Near East. The following is an example from an Egyptian text: "Recitation: 'Oil; oil! You are that which is on the brow of Horus; you are on the brow of Horus.'"[1] Ugarit records the following: "He also took oil in his horn and poured it on the head of the daughter of the King of A[murru]. Whatever si[n she has committed against] me, [you should know that it has been ato]ned."[2] The common denominator of these anointing ceremonials is that they symbolize an elevation in status. The divine statue is consecrated; the divorced queen is restored.

---

[1] Otto, cited by Veenhof 1966:309.
[2] RS 32.124.26–32, cf. Pardee 1979:14–20.

[14:20] Nothing in the text indicates the function of the burnt offering except its expiatory goal. But what does it expiate? It has been suggested that originally the burnt offering was the exclusive expiatory sacrifice, but once the purification and reparation offerings were assigned their specific expiatory functions, the burnt offering retained the remainder of the wrongs requiring expiation (chap. 1, A BRIEF HISTORY). Because the former sacrifices expiated violations of prohibitive commandments (4:2) and known or suspected desecration (5:14-26), the burnt offering retained the power to expiate for neglected performative commandments. The battery of all four expiatory sacrifices—reparation, purification, burnt, and cereal offerings—thereby assures the scale-diseased person that all possible inadvertent misdemeanors have been covered. The wrong is expiated; the disease will not return.

The placement of this final "he shall be pure" is crucial. It occurs at the end of the three rites that mark the stages through which the scale-diseased person passes in his rehabilitation to society and his reconciliation with his God. The initial "he shall be pure" at the end of the first day admits him to the camp (v. 8); the second, to his tent (v. 9); and the third, to his God (v. 20). The first two are preceded by baths that execute the rites of passage. This third "he shall be pure," however, is not preceded by bathing. It signifies the completion of the process: the healed and now purified person is henceforth a full-fledged participant in his community and its worship.

[14:33-53] Bright green or bright red eruptions on the walls of the house warrant a seven-day quarantine. If the infection has not subsided after the period of quarantine, the infected stones are removed and replaced, the interior plaster is removed and recoated, and a second quarantine is imposed. If the infection nonetheless persists, the house is demolished. If instead it is healed, the priest performs a ceremonial that is a duplicate of the first-day rite for the purification of cured scale-diseased persons. Spring water containing the blood of a bird, cedar wood, hyssop, and crimson yarn is sprinkled on the house seven times and a live bird is released into the open country.

Israel's priesthood has eviscerated the magical and demonic from the rites of the fungous house prevalent in the contiguous cultures and, as in the case of the scale-diseased person, has incorporated them into its overarching symbolic system that proclaims the victory of the forces of life over the forces of death (see details in the introduction to this volume).

[14:34-54] The remarkable thing about this pericope is that although God is explicitly included as the author of the injunction, nowhere is it stated or even intimated that the infection comes as a punishment for sin. The owner is enjoined, under the guidance of a priest, to subject his house to an elaborate test to see whether the infection spreads, and, if the examination is positive, to dismantle the house or, if negative, to purify the house. But the owner does nothing to or for himself. He does not bring sacrifices, as does the certified scale-diseased person, a rite that surely would have been prescribed if he were suspected of having sinned. And if he launders and bathes, it will only be for the reason that he, or anyone else, entered the house *after* it was condemned by the priest (vv. 45-46). Thus the disparity between Israel and its neighbors could not be any wider than in this ritual that they observed in common. The Mesopotamians attribute the fungous houses to demons, the Hittites to its occupants, but Israel to neither. YHWH, as the one and only God, must be the source of all that happens in nature. Yet whereas calamitous events are elsewhere in Scripture ascribed to human disobedience of divine law, in this case there is no such attribution. The infection has been diagnosed and treated objectively—in a real sense, scientifically. Human causality has been dismissed.

Although God is clearly the author of the fungi (v. 34), nowhere is it intimated that they are a punishment for sin. The owners must work on the house according to the instructions of the priest, but they never do anything on their own behalf. They do not bring a sacrifice as they would were they themselves inflicted by the disease. Although God punishes sin, this house fungus is not a punishment.

[14:36] There are a number of significant presuppositions ensconced in this verse. (1) Impurity of "scale-diseased" houses, like that of scale-diseased persons, contaminates by overhang, for if even a single stone be certified by the priest as "leprous," then everything within the house is contaminated. (2) The impurity is not retroactive. Only those objects found in the house when the priest condemns it are declared impure, but if these same objects are removed before the priest arrives they are considered pure. (3) Those persons who were in the house before the priest declares the quarantine are also pure, including the investigating priest! Thus there can be no lingering doubt that this impurity is wholly symbolic. To be sure, formal laws and procedures must be followed: the impurity is transmitted by overhang and it must be eliminated by the same bird rite employed for persons. But, in reality, the impurity of the infected stone has not been transmitted to the persons and objects in the house. Transmission occurs only if and when the priest so declares.

[14:40] An "impure place" (also in vv. 41, 45) implies a definite place, known and recognized by everyone, so that it could be avoided, and people would not use its discarded materials for building purposes. This phrase contrasts with "a pure place" (4:12), which was also a definite place. In modern times the former would be known as a dump, the latter as a sacred ash heap.

The implication is that the land itself is neither pure nor impure, neither sacred nor profane. The land is God's land. Sins against God defile the land; obedience to God (i.e., if Israel adheres to the commandments) sanctifies the land.

Thus one can deduce that the land is not inherently holy. That is why in Leviticus—and, indeed in the entire Bible—the land is never called "the holy land." Israel's behavior alone will sanctify the land or defile it.

Genital Discharges

Why are the two chapters that discuss genital discharges separated? If this portion of Leviticus were organized thematically, one would have expected chapter 15 to be joined to the other genital-discharge chapter, chapter 12. However, the sequence of chapters 12–15 seems to have been determined not according to theme but according to the duration and complexity of the purification process, in descending order. The first of this series, chapter 12, deals with the purification of parturients, which takes forty or eighty days. The second, chapters 13–14, deals with the scale-diseased person, who requires eight days, four sacrifices, and anointing for purification. Finally, chapter 15 deals with persons with genital discharges, who, depending on the type of discharge, necessitate eight days and two sacrifices, seven days, or one day for purification.

The laws of sanctum contamination, derived in Theme B, are summarized as follows:

1. The contamination of a sanctum varies directly with the intensity of the impurity source, directly with the holiness intensity of the sanctum and inversely with the distance between them. Also, contamination has a threshold, a fixed value, below which it cannot be activated.

2. The sanctuary is a special case of the general law (1) whereby:

    a. Contamination is a function of the intensity of the impurity source alone, i.e., impurities of a severe amount and from any distance (in the camp) will contaminate the sanctuary.

    b. Contamination takes place at three ascending thresholds: the outer altar, the shrine, or the adytum.

    c. Contamination displaces an equal volume of the sanctuary holiness (the Archimedean principle) until a saturation point is reached.

3. Sanctums are related to common things in regard to their contamination and purification, as follows:

140

a. Sanctums are more vulnerable to contamination by one degree.

b. Each purification stage reduces the communicability of the impurity source to both sanctums and common things by one degree.

Selected Themes

A. The Menstruant

The abhorrence of the menstruant is a cardinal rule among all primitive societies. Across primitive culture, the impurity extends to things she touches, such as eating and cooking utensils, weapons, food, and even footpaths. The effects of her impurity (or neglecting to distance oneself from her impurity) can be deadly: crop failures, disease, military defeat, hunting failures. Because the consequences of even accidental encounters with the menstruant are believed to be so perilous, in most primitive cultures she is isolated to protect the community.

Against the backdrop of Israel's immediate and remote contemporaries and what was probably the dominant practice within Israel itself, the Priestly legislation on the menstruant is all the more remarkable. First and foremost, she is neither banished from the community nor even isolated within her home. The implicit assumption of the pericope on the menstruant is that she lives at home, communicating with her family and performing her daily work. How is this possible, considering the severity of her impurity: even more than having a prolonged discharge, she can contaminate an object she does not even touch if her bed or seat connect with it (v. 23)? The ingenious answer of the legists was to restrict her impurity to that which was underneath her, in effect, whatever might receive a drop of menstrual blood. Of course, she herself was rendered impure and, in turn, could render persons and objects impure. Thus anyone touching her is contaminated (v. 19b). But what if she touches someone? The text is silent. It was not silent on this matter in the case of the *zav*. It stated explicitly that anyone who touches such a person becomes impure but only if one does so with unrinsed hands (v. 11). The conclusion is as inescapable as it is liberating: the menstruant may touch. As long as she is scrupulous about rinsing her hands, she may clean the house, cook and serve the food, and perform any other work. All she needs is a separate bed, a separate chair, and the discretion to stay out of her family's reach. While I do not intend to exonerate the biblical tradition for partaking in the fetishizing of menstruation, one should not pass over Israel's distinction from its contemporaries (and many modern societies) in not isolating its menstruants and in imposing nearly the same impurity rules for male genital discharges (compare vv. 1-17 with vv. 18-30).

B. The Priestly Laws of Sanctum Contamination

The ancients feared impurity because they imputed to it a malignant power of supernatural origin. They conceived of it as demonic, aggressively alive, and contagious not just to touch, but as reaching out through air and solid matter to assail its victims:

Leviticus 11–16: The Impurity System

> The highest wall, the thickest walls
> Like a flood they pass
> From house to house they break through
> No door can shut them out
> No bolt can turn them back
> Through the door like a snake they glide
> Through the hinge like a wind they blow.[1]

That impurity is dangerous from a distance is commonplace in Mesopotamian ritual texts like the one cited above. One is contaminated "if he talked to an accursed man,"[2] or "[Namburbi] for the evil of a dove or strange bird which . . . has hovered [lit. 'stood'] [over a m]an,"[3] or "when a man looketh upon a corpse,"[4] or "The roving Evil Eye hath looked on the neighborhood, and vanished afar, hath looked on the vicinity, and vanished afar, it hath looked on the chamber of the land, and vanished afar, it hath looked on the wanderer, and like wood cut for kindling (?), it hath bent his neck."[5] B. Landsberger could without hesitation speak of the "circumambient danger" of Mesopotamian impurity.[6]

The airborne quality of impurity was amplified many times over in the presence of the sacred: "An impure person has come near the sacrifice";[7] "An impure man or woman must not see (the ritual proceedings)."[8] Moreover, impurity as the embodiment of divine evil was even a threat to the gods themselves, particularly to their sanctuaries. One recalls the images of protector gods, the *šedu* and *lamassu,* set before the entrances of Mesopotamian temples and palaces, and, above all, the elaborate purification rituals for both temples and homes to rid them of demons and prevent their future incursions.[9] Indeed, to say that impurity attacks from a distance is to admit that it is demonically alive.[10]

Turning to Israel, we find that animate impurity has completely disappeared. Its devitalized traces, however, are still detectable in the rules for the scale-diseased person (14:46-47) and the corpse (Num 19:14-16): everything under the same roof is contaminated except the contents of tightly sealed vessels (Num 19:15). Here we can still discern impurity as a gaseous substance, a volatile force, a miasma exuded by the source of impurity. To be sure, this impurity is no longer of pagan dimensions; it has "clipped wings," being airborne only within an enclosure. Above all, it

---

[1] Thompson 1903–14:1.53, V, lines 25-31.
[2] Reiner 1956:137, line 85; cf. 1958:22, III, line 130.
[3] Caplice 1965–71:36.34, lines 1-2.
[4] Thompson 1971:26.
[5] Thompson 1903–14:2.112, lines 6-11; cf. Ebeling 1949:203–6, lines 5-15.
[6] Cited by Ritter 1965:302 n. 13.
[7] *CAD* 4.106.
[8] *CAD* 1/2.8.
[9] Saggs 1962:315–16.
[10] Wright 1987:247–61.

has lost its malignancy; contaminated objects and persons need merely undergo ritual purification.

In the sacred sphere, however, an entirely different situation exists. Upon entering the sacred precincts, the very power that has been stripped from impurity in contact with the common is revealed in all of its primeval force. This fact can be demonstrated by examining the system of scaled sanctum taboos upon which the Priestly legislation is structured. First, however, the nomenclature must be clarified. I begin by noting two sets of opposites: holy and common; pure and impure. Both the common and the holy are presumed pure, unless we have been told that they have become contaminated. The holy is divided into two classes: sacred and most sacred (see 5:15). The latter, found exclusively in the sanctuary, is further subdivided by location, depending on whether the objects of the most sacred are in the outer courtyard, the sanctuary tent, or the innermost shrine.[11]

As the common and the holy are presumed to be pure—their normal and acceptable condition—three of the four categories listed above can interact: the holy (including the sacred and most sacred), the common and the impure. They can interact in five separate pairs: (1) most sacred and common; (2) sacred and common; (3) most sacred and impure; (4) sacred and impure; and (5) common and impure.

Contact 1 (most sacred and common) yields the following correlations. The common object is rendered "holy" on touching all "most sacred" objects—even those in the sanctuary courtyard such as the altar (Exod 29:37) or the sacrifices (Lev 6:11, 20; Ezek 46:20). On the other hand, common people, that is, nonpriests, will pay with their life if they encroach upon the most sacred (Num 1:51; 3:10, 38; 4:19; 17:5, 28; 18:3, 7),[12] even if they do so only by inadvertently gazing upon the sanctums while they are being dismantled (Num 4:20; Neh 6:11). Only the priest may handle the most sacred because he is like them: both having been anointed to sacred status (Exodus 28; Leviticus 8). But even he is barred from the adytum except under severe restrictions (chap. 16).[13]

In the contact between the most sacred and the common, an obvious question presents itself: Why isn't the most sacred contaminated when touched by the common? The sanctums are not being contaminated because the common is an inert category, devoid of active power. Unlike the impure, the common has no power to contaminate. In this relationship, the activity is on the part of the "most sacred," which "sanctifies" common persons (and things) on touch or can kill them on sight if they are inside the shrine. Thus the superholiness with which the most sacred is charged exhibits the same airborne quality as severe impurity.

---

[11] Milgrom 1976a:35–37.

[12] Ibid.

[13] The Levite is like the layman in all respects (Num 18:3) except that, if he is a Kohathite, he carries the most sacred sanctums when the camp is in transit and after they have been covered by priests (Num 4:5-20).

Contact 2 (sacred and common) does not affect either the sacred or the common so long as the common remains uncontaminated. So indeed reads the rule of eating flesh off the well-being offering (7:19b; 10:14). Conversely, the illegitimate contact of the sacred with the common (desecration) is subjected to severe penalties: if inadvertent, a fine of 20 percent and a reparation offering (5:14-16); if deliberate, death at the hands of God (see 5:20-26). Even the legitimate contact of the sacred and the common is subject to the 20 percent penalty (chap. 27).

Contact 4 (sacred and impure) is illuminated in contrast with contact 1 (discussed above). The prescribed penalty is not death by divine agency but excision (*karet*); for example, "the person who, while impure, eats flesh from YHWH's sacrifice of well-being, that person shall be cut off from his kin" (7:20; cf. chaps. 6–7, THEME B).

As for contact 3 (most sacred and impure), our texts are silent, but only because the death penalty is obvious, a deduction a fortiori from the capital punishment prescribed for the contact 1 cases discussed above. We also have the precedent of Nadab and Abihu, whose immediate death was caused by "a strange fire" (10:1), which, whatever its nature, resulted in the contamination of the sanctuary. Perhaps the clash between most sacred and impure results in even greater calamity if we note the frequent reference to the wrath of God punishing not only the offending priest but also his community (e.g., 4:3; 10:6; Num 18:5). Those relationships are also integrated into a dynamic theology that is described and represented diagrammatically in the text on "and between the pure and impure" (Lev 10:10).

Having discussed the penalties for bringing sanctums into contact with the common and the impure, we can now focus exclusively on the contact between sanctums and the impure (3 and 4 above) to study the processes involved, to wit, how a sacred object is contaminated and then purified. Contact 5 (impure and common) need not be discussed here because it has been the subject of all the purity laws in chapters 11–15. It is rarely prohibited (e.g., 11:8) and never penalized, unless the prescribed purification is not observed. When this occurs, even minor impurities become major ones, polluting the sanctuary from afar (5:2-3; THEME B on 5:1-13). But then we are dealing with the contact of the sacred and the impure. The pollution of the sanctuary by airborne impurity has already been discussed in connection with its purification offering (chap. 4, THEME A). It remains to discuss the impact of impurity on Israel's other dominant sanctum, the priest.

It comes as no surprise to find airborne and deadly impurity in texts dealing with the pagan priests of the ancient Near East. The Babylonian *mašmašu* is contaminated if he even glances at dirty water[14] or a person with "unwashed hands."[15] The *šešgallu,* the head priest of Babylon's Esagila, "shall not view the [New Year's]

---

[14] Meier 1937:11, I, lines 105, 107.
[15] Thompson 1903–14:2.139–40.

144

purification of the temple. If he does view (it), he is no (longer) pure."[16] The "loosening" of the impurity from the temple walls and its transfer to the scape-ram has made it doubly dangerous to the holiest of the priests and airborne once again. The human corpse, in particular, can contaminate from afar, but the priest is its special target. Note the alarm sounded in Ur warning of the approach of Dumuzi from the land of the dead:

> O city of Ur! At my loud cry
> lock your house, lock your house! City lock your house!
> O temple of Ur! Lock your house, city lock your house!
> Your *entu* priestess must not go out of her house,
> O Giparu city lock your house![17]

The dead must be kept away from the city and temple, but the chief priestess (*entu*) may not even expose herself to the open air of the street. The susceptibility of the priesthood reaches down to the end of pagan times: the Roman high priest, the Flamen Dialis, sins as did his ancient Babylonian counterpart if he but glances at a corpse.[18] So too in Hellenistic Syria: "Those priests who bore the corpse of a Galloi priest of Syria were not allowed to enter the temple for seven days; if any priest looked at a corpse he was impure for that day and could only enter the temple the following day if he was cleansed."[19]

In these essentials, the priest of Israel is not different from his pagan colleague. His sensitivity to impurity is greater than the layperson's, and the high priest, by virtue of his supreme holiness, is the most vulnerable of all. Accordingly, the ordinary priest is permitted to attend the burial of his immediate blood relatives only (21:1-4); the high priest, not even for his parents (21:11). In Ezekiel's system, the priest is further set apart from the layperson in that his purification from corpse contamination lasts two weeks, climaxed by a purification offering sacrifice (44:26-27), whereas in P the layperson needs only to be sprinkled with purification offering waters on the third and seventh days (Num 19:9). Thus, of the three bearers of corpse contamination—the nazirite, Ezekiel's priest, and the layperson—the two consecrated classes require sacrifices for their purification but the layperson does not. This contrast is dramatically projected by the table in THEME C below (C 4, 5, 7), and it demonstrates the distinction between the contamination of the sacred (contact 2) and the contamination of the common (contact 5). Finally, the prohibition issued to Israel's high priest that "he may not leave the sanctuary" to follow after the bier is strikingly reminiscent of the Babylonian high priestess, who "must not go out of her house" (above). In this instance Babylonian and Israelite law coincide exactly.

---

[16] *ANET*, 33, lines 364-65; see chap. 16, Theme B.
[17] Translation of Jacobsen 1961:208.
[18] Servis, *ad Aeneid* 6.176.
[19] Lucian, *De syria dea* 2.62.

Leviticus 11–16: The Impurity System

The susceptibility of the high priest to airborne impurity persists into rabbinic times: "If any of his [the high priest's] near of kin die he may not follow after the bier, but he may go forth with the bearers as far as the city gate, *if he and they come not within sight of one another*" (my emphasis). So Rabbi Meir. But Rabbi Judah says: "He may not go forth from the Temple, for it is written 'neither shall he go out of the sanctuary' (Lev 21:12)."[20] Rabbi Meir and Rabbi Judah do not differ at all. As the Roman and Babylonian parallels teach us, Rabbi Meir is correctly citing the reason for the biblical prohibition. Moreover, just as the Flamen Dialis was not allowed to spend a single night outside Rome, so Israel's high priest was never allowed to lodge outside the temple.[21]

A residue of the notion of the aerial contaminations of the sanctums in rabbinical times is further evident from the provisions surrounding the Yom Kippur ceremony: One who witnesses the burning of the Yom Kippur purification bull and he-goat (16:27)—laden with the total impurity of the sanctuary and people (on "iniquities" see 16:21)—should not be able to see the high priest while he is officiating;[22] one who defecates or urinates may not face the direction of the sanctuary if it is within sight.[23] Perhaps this is what the Dead Sea sectaries had in mind when they prohibit the slaughter and consumption of a maimed animal at any distance less than thirty *stadia* (four miles) from the temple.[24]

The contamination of Israel's sanctuary, discussed in detail in chapter 4, THEME A, needs only summarizing here: (1) The accidental sins or impurities of the individual contaminate the outer altar, requiring purification blood on its horns (4:22-35); (2) the accidental sins or impurities of the community invade and contaminate the shrine, requiring purification blood on the horns of the inner altar and the veil (4:1-21); and (3) the deliberate sins penetrate the veil into the adytum, requiring purification blood on and before the ark cover (16:14-15). Thus the contamination of the sanctuary varies directly with the intensity of the impurity charge. This law will hold true for all sanctums. The sanctuary, however, is set apart from other sanctums. Instead, as we have already observed, the sanctums are governed by another correlation, that the closer the impurity source to the sanctum and the greater the holiness charge of the sanctum, the more readily contamination takes place. More precisely, the comprehensive law reads, *sanctum contamination varies directly with the charge (holiness) of the sanctuary and the charge of impurity, and inversely with the distance between them.* If we borrow from the vocabulary of electromagnetism (while not equating the phenomena), we could describe the workings of the law as follows:

---

[20] *m. Sanh.* 2:1.
[21] Lieberman 1950:165 n. 12.
[22] *m. Yoma* 7:2.
[23] *t. Meg.* 5:25-26.
[24] 11QT 52:17-19.

opposites attract, and in the Priestly system holiness is opposite in charge to the impure. If either holiness or the impurity source is strong enough or the distance between them small enough, impurity will become airborne, spark the gap, and impinge on the sanctum.

The fixed levels of penetration observed for the contamination of the sanctuary yield a second law: Impurity displaces an equal amount of sanctuary holiness. This correlation is adumbrated, outside P, in the ancient regulation of the holy war camp: "let him not find anything unseemly among you and turn from you" (Deut 23:15b; cf. contact 4). Thus God withdraws from the contaminated camp. In P this general principle becomes mathematical law. Holiness and impurity are finite, quantitative categories; impurity displaces sanctuary holiness in fixed amounts until a saturation point is reached beyond which the sanctuary cannot endure. It might be termed Archimedes' law of holiness displacement. It certifies that holiness can abide with a limited but fixed amount of impurity, and accounts for the repeated admonitions not to pollute the sanctuary (e.g., Lev 12:4; 15:31; 20:1-4; Num 19:13, 20).

In P's own terms this law can be understood as follows: God will tolerate inadvertent wrongs that contaminate the outside altar (Lev 4:22-35) and the shrine (4:1-21), for they can be purged through purification offerings. Conversely, as for the perpetrator of "rebellious acts" (16:16), "who acts defiantly, reviles YHWH" (Num 15:30), personal sacrifice will not avail. The nation as a whole must expiate for him and others like him at the annual purgation rite of the sanctuary (chap. 16), cleansing the contaminated adytum with the purification blood and transferring the released impurities to "the goat for Azazel" (16:10, 20b-22). Even then, only a limited amount of deliberate sin will be tolerated. There is a point of no return. One day, purgation will no longer avail; the impurities, especially the accumulated rebellious acts in the adytum, will rise beyond the set limit; God's endurance of his people's impurities will end; he will forsake his abode to abandon it and his people to destruction (details in chap. 4, THEME A).

In essence, this Priestly theology of sanctuary contamination is structured on the lines of pagan analogues. Indeed, all three laws controlling Israel's system operate with equal validity in the polytheistic world, but with one crucial distinction. The pagans, who gave highest priority to protecting their sanctuary from impurity, believed the latter to be personified demonic forces intent on driving out their patron god from his sanctuary, and they sought magical apotropaic rituals, mediated by the priesthood, to enhance the life force of the deity and shield the sanctuary from invasion. In Israel these universal laws are recast in terms of monotheism: impurity is the outcome not of demonic force but of people's sin. The cause of impurity has radically changed. Humanity has replaced the demon. People have the ultimate power to obey or resist God. If they choose to rebel—to use the Priestly idiom—they will pollute the sanctuary to the point that God will no longer abide in it. But whether the cause is the demon or the person, the net effect is the same: God is evicted from his earthly abode.

Leviticus 11–16: The Impurity System

Only a theological structure such as the one just outlined can explain the thought and imagery of Ezekiel, prophet-priest par excellence. The first section of his book (chaps. 1–11) is a vivid description of Jerusalem's imminent destruction, dramatized by P's conceptual imagery of God's departure from the temple. Equally characteristic of P is Ezekiel's indictment, exclusively stressing the presumptuous, rebellious sin as having contaminated the adytum and forced God's departure (note the similar vocabulary of Ezek 39:24a and Lev 16:16). Six times he explicitly labels the contamination of the temple as the end result of Israel's sin (Ezek 5:11; 8:6; 23:38, 39; 24:21; 44:7), and seven times he prophesies its ultimate purification (11:16; 37:26, 27, 28; 48:8, 10, 21). Indeed, only by recognizing that the Priestly laws of sanctum contamination inform Ezekiel's thought are we able to explain the ideological framework of his book. God's abandonment of his contaminated temple is complemented by an uncontaminable temple, so assured because Israel will never be less than pure. Ezekiel is his own best witness:

> Son of man, do you see what they are doing, the great abominations that the house of Israel are committing here, to drive me from my own sanctuary? (Ezek 8:6)

> They shall not contaminate themselves any more with their idols and their detestable things, or with any of their transgressions . . . but I will purify them . . . and I will set my sanctuary in the midst of them forevermore. (Ezek 37:23a, b, 26b)

Thus the blueprint of the new temple is not a chance appendix to the book; it is a logical, fitting climax to all that has preceded it. First comes the reunification, restoration, and purification of Israel, ending with a promise of a Davidic ruler and a new temple (chaps. 36–37). Then follows the purification of the land after the slaughter of Israel's enemies therein (chaps. 38–39, esp. 39:12-16). With purging of people and land complete, the new temple can be built (chaps. 40–48).

Having described the process and effect of impurity impinging on the sacred and the common, we are now ready to extrapolate a third and final law. So far it has been ascertained that bathing removes impurity to the extent that it can no longer contaminate the common, but it may contaminate the sacred until evening or, in more severe cases of impurity, until sacrificial purification on the following day (see also cols. D-1 and D-2 of the table in THEME C). Prior to the bathing, however, both the common and the sacred are subject to contamination, which can take place from a distance.

Thus the periods before and after bathing offer two new criteria for comparing the realms of the sacred and the common: (1) the sacred is of greater sensitivity than the common to contamination by one degree, and (2) each purification stage reduces contagion to both the sacred and the common by one degree. There are three possibilities for the contamination of an object: from afar, by direct contact, or by overhang. Specifically, a severely impure person contaminates a common object by direct contact and contaminates a sacred object from afar. After bathing, the person is no

148

longer contagious to the common object but can contaminate a sacred object by direct contact (but not from afar). Finally, after the last stage of purification (by that evening or after sacrifices the following day) the person is no longer contagious even to sanctums. If these two correlations are correct, then a reconstruction of the entire system of ritual impurities contained in the Priestly source is now feasible. Despite the large gaps in our biblical data we would need to know only either the number of baths required or the final purification procedure (evening or sacrifices) to deduce the missing stages. This reconstruction is tabulated in columns D-1 and D-2 of the table in THEME C, where the impurities are listed in order of severity (determined by the length and procedure of purification, cols. B and C).

Lacunae are also occasionally filled by the rabbinic evidence, accepted whenever it proves an ancient and uncontested tradition. To our delight it also corroborates our general laws, which nearly always independently predict the same results. For example, early rabbinic sources and Josephus affirm that the scale-diseased person has the impurity status of a corpse and analogously contaminates everything under the same roof.[25] This "overhang" principle creates an extra stage in the contamination scale (see D-1 of the table in THEME C). An additional stage for the scale-diseased person is also predictable, for the person alone among the contaminated requires not one but two baths for purification; and the third law states that each bath reduces contagion by one degree. A third, converging line of evidence stems from the analogy of the "scale-diseased" house, which also contaminates by overhang (14:46-47).

Other correlations with rabbinic tradition will be found in the remarks on the table in THEME C. Differences will also appear. Still, because the biblical assumption of post-bathing sensitivity of sanctums also informs the rabbinic system, the differences are in details rather than in principle. Herein, I maintain, lies the greater harvest of this study. The discovery of the biblical laws of sanctum contamination will lead to the isolation of the rabbinic laws that veer from their biblical predecessors. These can now be studied for the concrete, historical situations that brought about their change.[26]

The laws of sanctum contamination, derived in this THEME, are summarized as follows:

1. The contamination of a sanctum varies directly with the intensity of the impurity source, directly with the holiness intensity of the sanctum, and inversely with the distance between them. Also, contamination has a threshold, a fixed value, below which it cannot be activated.

2. The sanctuary is a special case of the general law (1) whereby

   a. Contamination is a function of the intensity of the impurity source alone,

---

[25] *m. Kelim* 1:4; *m. Neg.* 13:7, 11; Josephus, *Ag. Ap.* 1.31; *Ant.* 3.264.

[26] E.g., Milgrom 1983c.

i.e., impurities of a severe amount and from any distance (in the camp) will contaminate the sanctuary.

b. Contamination takes place at three ascending thresholds: the outer altar, the shrine, or the adytum.

c. Contamination displaces an equal volume of the sanctuary holiness (the Archimedean principle) until a saturation point is reached.

3. Sanctums are related to common things in regard to their contamination and purification, as follows:

a. Sanctums are more vulnerable to contamination by one degree.

b. Each purification stage reduces the communicability of the impurity source to both sanctums and common things by one degree.

The impurity bearers (and their biblical sources) are listed in order of their severity. Severity is determined by the duration and complexity of the purification procedure. Thus the scale-diseased person whose period of impurity is indeterminate and who must undergo a seven-day purificatory rite involving two baths, followed by an eight-day sanctuary rite comprising four sacrifices and two daubings, qualifies for first place in this scheme.

C. The Table of Purification Procedures and Effects

The impurity bearers, twelve in number, fall into two divisions, determined by the way the impurity is terminated. The first six end with sacrifice; the second group of six with evening. Focusing first on the sacrificial group, the most prominent fact to be noted is that each purification rite features primarily the purification offering. The implications of this fact are clear. We are dealing with the phenomenon of the indirect, airborne pollution of the sanctuary. That is, whenever such impurity occurs in the Israelite camp it is powerful enough to convey itself to the sanctuary, and it can be eliminated only by the purgative action of the blood of the purification offering (above, THEME B; chap. 4, THEME A). A corollary implication is that until this sacrifice is offered (and for the lesser impurities, until the prescribed evening), one may not partake of sacred food or enter the sanctuary. Thus the elimination of sanctum pollution must be the final stage in the purification process, a conclusion corroborated by the explicit statement on the parturient who, following the initial period of severe impurity of seven or fourteen days, is now permitted to contact common things but "may not touch any consecrated thing, nor enter the sacred precinct" (Lev 12:4). Additional proof is provided by Ezekiel, who prescribes that a corpse-contaminated priest must first complete his purificatory rites and only then "on the day he reenters the inner court of the sanctuary to minister in the sanctuary, he shall present his purification offering" (Ezek 44:22). On the scale-diseased person see below.

	A. Impurity Bearer	B. Duration	C. Purification Stage (days)	Procedures
MAJOR SACRIFICES	1. Scale-diseased person (Lev 14)	x + 7 (8)	X	
			1st	sp, l, sh, b
			7th	sh, l, b
			8th or [eve]	P.O. ewe/bird + 3 sacrifices + 2 daubings
	2. Parturient (Lev 12) + 33 (66)	7 (14)	7 (14)	
			7th (14th)	[l, b]
			41st (81st) or [eve]	P.O. bird + lamb/bird
	3. zav, person with genital discharges (Lev 15:3-15, 28-30)	x + 7 (8)	x	
			7	
			7th	l, b
			8th or [eve]	P.O. bird + bird
	4. Corpse contaminated priest (Ezek 44:26-27)	7 + 7 (8)	7	[sp on 3rd, 7th]
			7th	[l, b]
			15th or [eve]	P.O. (bird?)
	5. Corpse contaminated nazirite (Num 6:9-12)	7 (8)	7	[sp on 3rd, 7th}
			7th	sh [l, b]
			8th or [eve]	P.O. + bird + bird + lamb
	6. Person whose impurity is accidentally prolonged (Lev 5:1-13)	x + 1	x	
			xth	[b]
				P.O. ewe/bird
			(x + 1)st or [eve]	semolina
MINOR EVENING	7. Corpse contaminated layperson (Num 5:2-4; 19)	7	7	sp on 3rd, 7th
			7th	l, b
			7th	eve
	8. Menstruant (Lev 15:19-24)	7	7	
			7th	[l, b]
			7th	eve
	9. Handler of red cow, scapegoat, or burnt P.O. (Num 19:7-10; Lev 16:27, 28)	1	P-B	
			bath	[l, b]
			eve	eve
	10. Emits semen (Lev 15:16-18)	1	P-B	
			bath	l, b
			eve	eve
	11. Carcass contaminated (Lev 11:24-40; 22:5)		P-B	
			bath	(l), b
			eve	eve
	12. Secondarily contaminated (Lev 15; 22:4b-7; Num 19)	1	P-B	
			bath	(l), b
			eve	eve

FIGURE 6.1 TABLE OF PURIFICATION PROCEDURES AND EFFECTS: PART I

Sigla
[ ] - reconstructed   x - indefinite   zav - one with a prolonged genital discharge
b   - bathing   sh - shaving   eve - evening
sp   - sprinkling   l - laundering   P-B - pre-bath
P.O. - Purification Offering

	D-1 THE EFFECT ON THE COMMON		
	P_1	P_2/H	
MAJOR SACRIFICES	[overhang] Those under same roof may not enter the sanctuary		**1. Scale-diseased person**
	direct, stays outside tent		
	none		
	none		
	direct, at home [wash hands]	[direct] isolated, no leniency	**2. Parturient**
	none, sex permitted	none	
	none	none	
	direct, at home. Wash hands	direct, banished (Num 5)	**3. *zav***
	ditto	ditto	
	none	none	
	none	none	
	direct, at home (Num 19)	direct, banished (Num 5)	**4. Corpse-contaminated priest**
	[none]	[none]	
	none	none	
	direct, at home (Num 19)	direct, banished (Num 5)	**5. Corpse-contaminated nazirite**
	[none]	[none]	
	none	none	
	direct, at home	direct, at home	**6. Prolonged impurity**
	[none]	[none]	
	none	none	
MINOR EVENING	direct, at home (Num 19) but isolated assumed	direct, banished (Num 5)	**7. Corpse-contaminated layperson**
	none	none	
	none	none	
	direct, at home (touch with washed hands)	direct, isolated at home	**8. Menstruant**
	none	none	
	none	none	
	none	[direct] remains outside	**9. handler**
	none	none	
	none	none	
	none	direct	**10. semen**
	none	none	
	none	none	
	none	[direct] for priest?	**11. carcass**
	none	none	
	none	none	
	none	[direct] for priest?	**12. secondary**
	none	none	
	none	none	

FIGURE 6.2 TABLE OF PURIFICATION PROCEDURES AND EFFECTS: PART II

Sigla
[ ]   - reconstructed   x - indefinite   *zav* - one with a prolonged genital discharge
b   - bathing   sh - shaving   eve - evening
sp   - sprinkling   l - laundering

	D-1 THE EFFECT ON THE SACRED		
	P₁	**P₂/H**	
	airborne, must sacrifice		
	[overhang] to sacred food. Hence, outside tent		**1. Scale-diseased**
	[direct] Hence, no sanctum contact		
	none		
	airborne; must sacrifice	airborne; must sacrifice	
	concession: at home	isolate in community (Josephus)	**2. Parturient**
	direct (Lev 12:4)	direct	
	none	none	
	airborne; must sacrifice	airborne; banished (Num 5)	
	concession: at home		**3. zav**
	ditto	ditto	
	[direct] no sancta contact	[direct] no sancta contact	
	none	none	
	airborne; must sacrifice	airborne; must sacrifice	**4. Corpse-**
	at home (Num 19)	banished (Num 5)	**contaminated**
	[direct] no sancta contact	[direct] returns home; no sancta contact	**priest**
	none	none	
	airborne; must sacrifice	airborne; must sacrifice	**5. Corpse-**
	at home (Num 19)	banished (Num 5)	**contaminated**
	[direct] no sancta contact	[direct] returns home; no sancta contact	**nazirite**
	none	none	
	airborne; must sacrifice; at home	airborne; must sacrifice; at home	**6. Prolonged**
	[direct] no sancta contact	[direct] no sancta contact	**impurity**
	none	none	
	direct, at home (Num 19)	airborne; banished (Num 5)	
	isolation assumed		**7. Corpse-**
	none	direct; returns home after l, b	**contaminated**
		(Num 31:24)	**layperson**
	none	none—after eve	
	direct; at home; no sancta		
	touch with washed hands	[airborne] at home; isolated	**8. Menstruant**
	none	[direct] after l, b	
	none	none	
	direct; remains outside	[airborne] remains outside	
	none	[direct] after l, b—returns home	**9. Handler**
	none	none—after eve	
	direct; no sancta	[airborne] at home	
	none	[direct] after l, b	**10. Semen**
	none	none—after eve	
	direct; no sancta	[airborne] for priests?	
	none, even for priests (Lev 22:4-6)	[direct] after l, b	**11. Carcass**
	none	none—after eve	
	direct; no sancta	[airborne] for priests?	
	none	[direct] after l, b	**12. Secondary**
	none	none—after eve (sacrifice for priests?)	

*Left margin labels: **MAJOR SACRIFICES** (items 1–6), **MINOR EVENING** (items 7–12)*

FIGURE 6.3 TABLE OF PURIFICATION PROCEDURES AND EFFECTS: PART III

Sigla   [ ]   - reconstructed   x   - indefinite   *zav* - one with a prolonged genital discharge
        b   - bathing   sh - shaving   eve - evening
        sp   - sprinkling   l   - laundering

153

A further assumption of this table is that the ablution (bathing plus laundering) required in every purification procedure functions to reduce the level of impurity. Thus, since the scale-diseased person must undergo two baths, we must assume that there are four stages in his purification of which the baths constitute the intermediate stages (1C). This, however, creates a problem. Ordinarily, there are only three stages in the reduction of impurity to the sanctuary; it can be polluted by air, by touch, or not at all. Now, however, a fourth stage is required. This new category is supplied by the rabbis, who aver that the scale-diseased person also contaminates by overhang (see above, THEME B). This category can be deduced from the biblical case of the fungous house, which explicitly contaminates by overhang (Lev 14:46-47). Strikingly, the independent testimony of the rabbis about the fourth level in the impurity range of the scale-diseased person jibes perfectly with the four stages of their purification, as required in this table (Fig. 6.1). Also the rabbis' concept of overhang illustrates their awareness that impurity is a gaseous substance that needs to be dissipated in the open air but, if confined in a closed space, will contaminate everything within it. Note their graphic descriptions of impurity's dynamic, airborne power: It "penetrates upward and downward";[27] "its nature is to expand, not to contract."[28]

The ability of the bath to reduce impurity is further supported by the case of the *zav*. His purification, like that of the scale-diseased person, also proceeds in four stages. But unlike the scale-diseased person, he undergoes just one bath (3C). The ostensible discrepancy is resolved once it is noted that the *zav*'s impurity remains the same in both the first and the second stages; during his seven-day purification he continues to contaminate in exactly the same way (see Fig 6.3 – *zav*). Thus only one bath is required, on the seventh day, after which he can no longer contaminate common things.

Perhaps the most significant assumption of the table stems from the last column: each purification stage reduces impurity by one degree, but the sacred is more vulnerable to pollution than the common by one degree. It is the third law of sanctum contamination (THEME B). The case of the scale-diseased person will exemplify this relationship. The scale-diseased person is banished from the camp not because he is contagious, but because he pollutes common things by overhang. Thus he is not allowed to remain in the camp lest he contaminate all persons and objects that are with him under the same roof. The danger becomes lethal if someone unknowingly contaminated by him enters the sanctuary or eats sacred food. The factor of overhang, however, is not present for other impurity bearers, such as the parturient and the *zav*, which accounts for the fact that, though their impurity is severe, they are not banished from the camp. Because they do not contaminate by overhang, they may remain at home. The table also informs us that the scale-diseased person's impurity is more

---

[27] E.g., *m. ʾOhol.* 7:1-2.

[28] E.g., *m. ʾOhol.* 4:1-3.

contagious with respect to the sacred sphere, polluting it from afar (1D-2). Thus no sooner has he been declared impure than his impurity ipso facto pollutes the sanctuary. Consequently, he will have to bring a purification offering to the sanctuary to purge it of the impurity that he has imparted to it.

On the first day of his purification rites, the scale-diseased person enters the camp but may still not enter his tent (Lev 14:8). The reason cannot be that he contaminates the common sphere by direct contact.[29] Note that the *zav* contaminates all that he or she touches (Lev 15:4-12, 25-27), yet is allowed to stay home (3D-1, P_1). The reason for the scale-diseased person's stricter rule is the overhang effect upon the sacred. Sacrificial food may be present in the home, to be polluted as soon as he or she enters. It is this contact between the impure and the sacred that is most dreaded, subjecting the violator to the penalty of *karet* (Lev 7:20) and the nation as a whole to destruction (Lev 15:31; cf. Ezek 9:7). On the seventh day of purification, after the second bath, the scale-diseased person is pure in regard to common objects and persons. Because he no longer contaminates the sacred by overhang, he may enter his tent. Yet, as the sacred is still vulnerable to his touch, he may neither eat sacred food nor enter the sanctuary. This last barrier is lifted the following day, when he purifies the sanctuary of the impurity that he has caused. The rabbis were fully aware of the susceptibility of the scale-diseased person to the sacred as shown by their retelling of his sacrificial rite: "He would bring up his reparation offering and its *log* [of oil] in his hand and set it up by Nicanor's Gate [the entrance to the inner court]. And the priest stands on the inside and the scale-diseased person on the outside . . . for he cannot enter the court until some of the blood of the reparation offering and the purification offering [*sic*] is sprinkled upon him."[30]

What pertains to the scale-diseased person also holds for the other impurity bearers: at every stage of their purification, the sacred is more susceptible to impurity than the common by one degree. The final stage of the purification process always finds the erstwhile impurity bearer pure in regard to the common but still impure in regard to the sacred. If his impurity is major, he has polluted the sanctuary from afar and must purge it with his purification offering. If his impurity is minor, it is incapable if generating airborne pollution to the sanctuary but still defiles by direct contact (e.g., sacred food) until it fades away by evening.

All sources agree, not just the Priestly legislation but also the narratives (e.g., Numbers 12; 2 Kgs 7:3-10), that the scale-diseased person is banished. By contrast, the treatment of other impurity bearers shown in the table is subject to two differing traditions (col. D). The one that unmistakably stems from P is labeled P_1; the other, which also manifests Priestly style and vocabulary, either stems from the school of P

---

[29] Cf. *m. Neg.* 14:2; contra Wright 1987:213.
[30] *t. Neg.* 8:9.

(P_2) or from the Holiness Source (H). Therefore column D is split in two, reflecting the data either stated or inferred from each.

Beginning with the parturient (2D), we note that according to P_1 (chap. 12), she is likened to the menstruant during her initial impurity of seven or fourteen days, which can only mean that, like the menstruant, she may remain at home. This is possible because she most likely only contaminates the objects immediately beneath her but not those she touches with washed hands (see "without having rinsed his hands," v. 11). Again like the menstruant, she is assumed to undergo baths at the end of this first stage, but it is uncertain whether a second bath is required at the end of the next stage (thirty-three or sixty-six days). Numbers 5:2-3 (P_2 or H), however, suggests that there was a coeval tradition concerning the parturient. To be sure, this passage does not mention her, yet the fact that the menstruant is absent implies that the text mandates the banishment of only erratic impurities, not normal ones. Furthermore, that she is required to bring a purification offering implies that the Priestly legislators considered her impurity to be powerful enough to pollute the sanctuary. Theoretically, this should have led to her banishment (like the *zav*, Num 5:2-3). That she was not banished is attributable to the normality of her condition, which would correspondingly evoke less apprehension even from extremists. It is not without significance that the Qumranites also did not banish the parturient and the menstruant from their cities,[31] and Josephus records that only the scale-diseased person and the *zav*—in other words, those with abnormal impurities—were expelled, while others were quarantined.[32] Nevertheless, if the parturient was not banished, she may have been quarantined, if not in her own house then in separate quarters, within her community. The latter expedient was endorsed by many who regarded the parturient (and the menstruant) as a grave source of impurity.[33] That the sacred realm remains vulnerable to her impurity during the intermediate stage is made explicit in 12:4.

The information on the purification of the corpse-contaminated priest (4C) comes from Ezek 44:26-27. That the Priestly writings do not register such a distinction between the priesthood and the laity is not to be explained as a contradiction of sources. Ezekiel may have just chosen to be stricter than his fellow priests. Note that his marriage rules for priests resemble those of the high priest (cf. Ezek 44:22 with Lev 21:14). Thus it may have been as much a matter of predilection as one of tradition. His general outlook was severe, to judge from his book, and he would be expected to eschew lenient observances. In any event, one cannot deny the logic of Ezekiel's ruling: If a layperson of temporary sanctity (the nazirite) is required to bring a purification offering for corpse contamination (Num 6:11), how much more so a priest of lifelong sanctity.

---

[31] 11QT 48:14-17.
[32] *Ant.* 3.261-62.
[33] Josephus, *Ant.* 3.261.

The nazirite who, by definition, is a holy person (Num 6:5, 8) elevates himself into the sacred sphere, the domain of the priest. It is therefore not surprising that the stages of his purification are an exact copy of those of Ezekiel's priest (4D and 5D). Nor should one wonder that the nazirite (after all, a layperson) is required to bring an additional sacrifice for corpse contamination, the reparation offering (Num 6:12a). Precisely because his impurity cancels out his prior naziritic service (Num 6:12b), he is guilty of desecration, the penalty for which is the reparation offering (see Lev 5:14-26 [Eng. 5:14–6:7]). Procedures mandated for the purification of the contaminated nazirite and priest (Ezekiel's) were probably originally followed by all priests. Subsequently P denied them to the priesthood but conceded them to the nazirite, possibly because the laity demanded or, in any event, practiced them. Perhaps, out of fear that sacrificing *because* of the dead could easily become sacrificing *to* the dead, sacrifices were abolished altogether for the laity and priesthood alike. The net result is that, in P, there is no difference between laypersons and priests in regard to purification for corpse contamination.

The last of the major impurity bearers is the one whose minor impurity, incurred by touching a communicable animal or human impurity (5:2-3), has accidentally been prolonged (5:1-13). That such a person is required to offer a purification offering implies that he has polluted the sanctuary, that is, his impurity has become airborne. Also implied is that during this period he has contaminated persons and objects by direct contact (6D-1) and that, even after he bathes, his contagion to sanctums persists until his sacrifice the following day.

So far we have seen that the Priestly laws of impurity are not univocal. Discrepancies and outright contradictions (except for the scale-diseased person) necessitate the supposition of more than one Priestly tradition. When we turn to the minor impurity bearers grouped in the bottom half of the table (7-12), the problem becomes more complex. The corpse-contaminated layperson, to begin with, is an anomaly; he is purified uniquely by being sprinkled with the ashes of a red cow on the third and seventh days (7C). Although these ashes derive from a purification offering (Num 19:9, 17), it has been shown that originally this rite was an exorcism, which was only subsequently adapted to Israel's sacrificial system (chap. 4, THEME B). The law of Num 5:2-3, which links corpse contamination with the major impurities of scale disease and genital discharges, reveals that corpse contamination originally was considered a major impurity. That the banishment of the corpse-contaminated person was actually practiced or that, at least, there was a tradition to this effect, is shown by the campaign against Midian, where the returning soldiers had to remain outside the camp until their purificatory rites were completed (Num 31:24). Moreover, Num 31:24 records another anomaly: the soldiers reenter the camp not in the evening of the seventh day, as would be required by the law of 19:19b, but earlier, after they bathe on that day. This aberration might be dismissed as inconsequential or even erroneous were it not also attested for three other minor impurity bearers: the priest who supervises the incineration of the red cow (19:7, and presumably the one who incinerates it), the one who dispatches the scapegoat (Lev 16:26), and the one who incinerates the animals as burnt offerings (16:28). All three are permitted to return to the camp after their baths even though their impurity lasts until evening (Num 19:7).

Why did P_1 refuse to banish the *zav* and the corpse-contaminated person but allow him or her to stay at home? Why did P_1 not accept the older tradition, which probably required the corpse-contaminated person to sacrifice (as did the corpse-contaminated nazirite and Ezekiel's priest) and, instead, reduce corpse contamination to a minor impurity, requiring solely bathing and sunset but no sacrifice? Finally, why, according to the preceding reconstruction, did P_1 reduce the purification process of minor impurity bearers from three stages to two?

A glance at column D of the table provides the answer: P_1 initiates the long historic process whereby the power of impurity is progressively reduced. From the beginning, Israel eviscerated impurity of its demonic content but allowed traces of its original virulent force in the presence of sanctums. Still, airborne impurity could not remain. It too closely resembled demonic impurity, and the danger persisted that the masses would not be able to distinguish between the two. Slowly, then, almost imperceptibly, airborne impurity was progressively eliminated: all impurity bearers, with the exception of the scale-diseased person, were allowed to remain at home. Impurity to sanctums was restricted to contact, and contact with the common, even in cases of severe impurity, became possible with washed hands. By the time the rabbinic age was reached, airborne impurity had totally disappeared from the scene. And when the temple was destroyed and contamination of the sacred (except for agricultural gifts to the priests) was no longer possible, the very ground for virulent impurity was removed. Except for the menstruant (cf. 18:19; 20:18), it was no longer a sin to remain impure (see chap. 12, THEME). The full development of the historic process in the reduction of impurity is chronicled in 5:1-13.

One presupposition of the table can be called into question: that sacrifices, the final stage for major impurities, are equivalent to evening, the final stage for minor impurities. Implied by this equation is that, for minor impurities, evening combines laundering and bathing to eliminate the last traces of impurity, whereas for major impurity, the evening is never mentioned. Moreover, in the case of the two major impurity bearers, the scale-diseased person and the *zav*, the text explicitly states that the person is purified after laundering and bathing on the day prior to the sacrifice (14:8; 15:13). Thus it demonstrates that the intervening evening does not count in the purificatory process. Furthermore, the text also specifies that the parturient and the scale-diseased person achieve complete purification only after the prescribed sacrificial rites (12:7, 8; 14:20). This can only mean that the last stage for major impurity is indeed the sacrifice; hence it is equivalent to the evening, the last stage for minor impurity.

Corroboration for this thesis is provided by the rabbis' description of the scale-diseased person standing outside the sacrificial court until the purificatory sacrifice is completed[34] and by their categorical statement that the major impurity bearers—specifically the scale-diseased person, parturient, *zav*, and corpse-contaminated nazirite—are forbidden to enter the sacrificial court until their sacrifices are offered.[35]

I have no explanation for the unambiguous and incontrovertible evidence of the text that the sacrifices are brought into the sanctuary court together with their offerers; I have therefore inserted into the final stage (c) of the major impurity bearers the alternative "or [eve]," thereby allowing for the possibility that the evening before the sacrifice, though never mentioned in the text, suffices—just as with minor impurity bearers—to eliminate the last vestige of impurity, which then permits the person to enter the sanctuary with the prescribed sacrifices the following morning. According to this construction, the residual impurity would last only for the few hours between laundering/bathing and evening. The net effect would be total congruence between major and minor impurities: both would cease to pollute the common by the bath and the sacred by the evening.

Selected Texts

[15:2] Being a disease of the private parts, only the person can determine if he or she has a flow. Scientific opinion is nearly unanimous "that the only illness that we know of that can be referred to here is gonorrhea."[36]

[15:4] The use of the imperfect verb, here and throughout this chapter, implies that the bearers of impurity are not banished from the community or even isolated within the community (see THEME A) but remain at home. This fact differentiates the chapter from the rules of the wilderness camp, which expel the *zav*—one with an abnormal genital discharge—(Num 5:2-4) and the rules of the war camp, which even excludes the emitter of semen (Deut 23:10-12). This chapter is primarily concerned with the communicability of impurity, whereas the previous pericope, on scale disease (Leviticus 13–14), says nothing on this matter. This difference can be explained only by the premise that the scale-diseased person is banished from the community and hence has no contact with persons or objects, whereas those experiencing sexual fluxes continue to reside at home.

[15:5] This is the first time we learn about the transmission force of impurity: it can affect persons and objects indirectly, at a second and even third remove (cf. v. 23).

---

[34] *m. Neg.* 14:8-9.
[35] *m. Ker.* 2:1; cf. Maimonides, "Those Lacking Expiation," 1:1.
[36] Preuss 1978:410.

Leviticus 11–16: The Impurity System

This extra-strength impurity is limited to objects directly underneath the *zav* and his congeners: males incurring seminal emissions and females in their menses or discharging abnormally. Their common denominator is that they are discharging from their genitals and hence the objects beneath them are directly contaminated by their genital flow. That is why only the bedding, seat, and saddle are singled out as objects that can be defiled. There is no mention of the table or cup or any other object that is likely to be touched being able to pass on its impurity. To be sure, earthenware and wooden vessels can be contaminated by the *zav* (v. 12), but nothing is said about their ability to contaminate others. Indeed, the only generalization in this pericope is: "Whoever touches anything that was *under him* shall be impure" (v. 10a). The difference, again, is that his discharge is assumed to make direct contact with the objects beneath. The likelihood for this to happen is strong, seeing that underpants were not worn (except by priests while officiating, Exod 28:43), hence there was nothing to stop or impede the flow of genital discharge to the furniture underneath.

[15:11] "Without having rinsed his hands." The implications of this leniency are far-reaching. For if the *zav* takes the precaution of rinsing his hands he can touch persons, vessels, utensils—anything (unless it is underneath him). Thus he can live at home!

[15:13] "Spring water" is found in an artesian well (Gen 26:29) or in running water (Lev 11:36; 14:6). Thus spring water either above the ground or below is what is meant, but stored water or drawn water is excluded.

[15:15] Why birds, the least expensive animal? The reason must surely be economic, not for the sake of the male—gonorrhea being infrequent—but for the sake of the female suffering from an equivalent affliction (v. 2). Because of hormonal imbalances, a woman is more prone to abnormal discharges and hence requires an inexpensive sacrificial procedure.

[15:16] Any discharge of semen, regardless of the circumstances, generates impurity. It must be emphasized, however, that the impurity is solely of a ritual nature: it disqualifies the person from contact with sanctums.

[15:18] Why is the sexual act defiling? One can understand that seminal emissions, being a total loss of life-giving fluid, were regarded as impure. But in conjugal union, the act of procreation? Ramban's reply merits consideration: "The individual does not know if his seed will be wasted, or if a child will result."

[15:24] Her menstrual impurity is transmitted to him. Why is this taboo so severe? All other contacts with the menstruant result only in a one-day impurity, whereas in this case it involves the identical degree of impurity as borne by the menstruant herself: seven days plus contagion to other things and persons upon contact. In his study of the Nuer of Africa, J. W. Burton provides the needed illumination: "The necessity (among the Nuer) of maintaining the distance between bleeding youths (undergoing initiation) and pregnant women, and between bleeding women (menstruants) and potential life (intercourse) is thus a symbolic statement of the necessity for keeping life-creating processes from potentially life-destroying forces."[37] Thus it may be the loss of both life-giving semen and genital blood that evokes the utmost horror of the legislator.

Alternatively, one may argue that if, during normal intercourse, the man transfers his impurity (seminal) to the woman (v. 18), so too in this case, the menstruant transfers her seven-day impurity to her sexual partner.

---

[37] Burton 1974:530

The Day of Purgation
(Yom Kippur)

All year long, Israel's sins have been polluting the sanctuary. True, the pious have been bringing purification offerings, which prove effective because their impurity was caused inadvertently. However, what of the advertent, brazen sinner? Their sins have penetrated into the adytum, the inner sanctum, polluting the very seat of the Godhead, threatening the destruction of the community. Since the brazen sinners are barred from offering sacrifice, how then is the sanctuary purified? The answer is Yom Kippur, the annual Day of Purgation, when the high priest risks his life by entering the adytum—to which entry is forbidden to mortal humans—and purifies the adytum through a smoke screen. The high priest emerges, transfers the removed pollution plus all the sins of the people, which he confesses, onto the head of a live goat, and dispatches the goat to the wilderness. The background of the drama of the sanctuary's purification is found in chapter 4, Theme A.

Selected Themes
A. The Public Fast

The annual Day of Purgation for Israel's sanctuary, the tenth of Tishri, was, at first, entirely dissociated from the notion of public fast. Precisely because it was probably the climax of the New Year Festival, it must have been altogether joyous in nature. The original joyousness of the tenth of Tishri is, to be sure, suppressed in the prescriptions for the day (16:29-34; 23:26-32; Num 29:7-11). Still, the initial intent of the celebration can be adduced from Scripture itself, from the fact that the Jubilee Year was proclaimed on this day (Lev 25:9). The shofar blast proclaimed each fiftieth year as the occasion on which ancestral lands reverted to their owners (25:10-34) and Israelites who, because of indebtedness, were sold into slavery were given their freedom (25:35-59). Surely, the day that heralded this "year of liberty" (Ezek 46:16; Lev 25:10) was a day of unbridled joy and in no way reflected the sober character of the later Day of Purgation. It is, in fact, a later rabbinic source that preserves the best evidence of the original nature of this day: "Rabban Simeon b. Gamliel said: There were no happier days for Israel than the fifteenth of Ab and the Day of Purgation, for on them the daughters of Jerusalem went forth to dance in the vineyards. And what did they say? 'Young man, lift up your eyes and see what you would choose for yourself: Set not your eyes on beauty, but set your eyes on family.'" (The image of maidens dancing in the vineyards recalls when Shilonite maidens dancing in the vineyards on the annual "feast of YHWH" were snatched as brides by the surviving Benjaminites, Judg 21:19-24.)

Thus we can assume that on the tenth of Tishri, the culmination of Israel's ancient New Year Festival (for further details see Lev 23:23-25), the people rejoiced that the new year was successfully launched and that the high priest had emerged safely from his purgations in the innermost shrine. This day, then, was marked by feasting, merriment, and the dancing of maidens in the vineyards, which, no doubt, resulted in many marriages throughout the land—a far cry from the practice of "self-denial" that characterizes this day's successor to the present time. The transformation may have occurred when the emergency contingency for purging the sanctuary was abolished and its somber, mournful aspect was transferred to the "once a year" purgation of the sanctuary on the tenth of Tishri, whose original jubilant character was replaced by fasting and penitence.

B. Temple Purgation in Babylon

It has been averred that rites of penitence marked the New Year Festival in Babylon, hence that there is no basis for presuming that the penitential rites prescribed for the tenth of Tishri emerge at a later date. The text of the Babylonian New Year Festival is unfortunately fragmentary, but it describes the events from the second to the fifth of Nisan in great detail. Because the similarities to Yom Kippur are striking, the pertinent sections, dealing with the rites on the fifth day, are cited herewith in full:

> On the fifth day of the month of Nisannu, four hours of the night (remaining?), the *šešgallu*-priest shall arise and wash . . . he shall put on (*i-de-qu*) a linen robe in front of the god Bel and the goddess Beltiya. . . . When the purification of the temple [of Bel and Beltiya] is completed, he [the *šešgallu*-priest] shall enter the temple Ezida, into the cella of the god Nabu, with censer, torch, and *egubbu*-vessel to purify the temple, and he shall sprinkle water (from) the Tigris and Euphrates cisterns on the sanctuary. He shall smear all the doors of the sanctuary with cedar oil. In the court of the cella, he shall place a silver censer, upon which he shall scatter aromatic ingredients and cypress. He shall call a slaughterer to decapitate a ram, the body of which the *mašmašu*-priest shall use in performing the purgation ritual for the temple. He shall recite the incantation for exorcising the temple. He shall purify the whole cella, including its environs, and shall remove the censer. The *mašmašu*-priest shall lift up the body of the aforementioned ram and proceed to the river. Facing west, he shall throw the body of the ram into the river. He shall (then) go out into the open country. The slaughterer shall do the same with the ram's head. The *mašmašu*-priest and the slaughterer shall go out into the open country. As long as the god Nabu is in Babylon, they shall not enter Babylon, but stay in the open

country from the fifth to the twelfth day (of *Nisannu*). The *šešgallu*-priest of the temple of Ekua shall not view the purification of the temple. If he does view (it), he is no (longer) pure. . . . When he (the king) reaches [the presence of the god Bel], the *šešgallu*-priest shall leave (the sanctuary) and take away the scepter, the circle, and the sword [from the king]. He shall bring them [before the god Bel] and place them [on] a chair. He shall leave (the sanctuary) and strike the king's cheek. . . . He shall accompany him (that is, the king) into the presence of the god Bel . . . he shall drag (him by) the ears and make him bow to the ground. . . . The king shall speak the following (only) once: "I did [not] sin, lord of the countries. I was not neglectful (of the requirements) of your godship. [I did not] destroy Babylon; I did not command its overthrow . . . the temple Esagil, I did not forget its rites. [I did not] rain blows on the cheek of a *kiddinu*. . . . I did not humiliate them. [I watched out] for Babylon; I did not smash its walls.". . . After (the *šešgallu*-priest) says (this), the king shall regain his composure. . . . The scepter, circle, and sword [shall be restored] to the king. He shall strike the king's cheek. If, when [he strikes] the king's cheek, the tears flow, (it means that) the god Bel is friendly; if no tears appear, the god Bel is angry: The enemy will rise up and bring about his downfall.[1]

The similarities between the Babylonian New Year Festival and Israel's Yom Kippur are immediately apparent. On both occasions, (1) the temple is purged by rites that demand that the high priest rise before dawn, bathe and dress in linen, employ a censer, and perform a sprinkling rite on the sanctuary; (2) the impurity is eliminated by means of slaughtered animals; (3) the participants are rendered impure; and (4) the king/high priest submits to a ritual of confession and penitence.

In each of these categories there are also significant differences. (1) Whereas in Babylon the demon-intruder is exorcised, in Israel it is the sin and iniquity generated by humanity that must be expunged. Israel uniquely elevated the people and their behavior to being worthy of divine scrutiny. The fate of the nation rests on the shoulders not of its leadership but of its laity. Moreover, whereas the purgation of the temple is the predominant aim of all of the rituals during the Day of Purgation, the Babylonian purgation rite is relatively minor, preparing one of the many cellas in Marduk's temple, Esagila, for the brief stay of a visiting god, Nabu. (2) In Babylon the detergent itself (the carcass of the ram) is eliminated; in Israel elimination is achieved by dispatching a goat onto which Israel's sins have been loaded. To be sure, Israel's detergent, the carcass of the purification offering, is burned, thereby paralleling the Babylonian elimination procedure (see chap. 4, THEME A). Hence one can infer that the Azazel goat was originally a discrete elimination technique that was artificially attached to the sanctuary purgation in order to focus on Israel's moral failings rather than on the sins and impurities that polluted the sanctuary. (3) In Babylon the impurity of the slaughterer and officiating priest lasts seven days—the remainder of the festival—whereas in Israel the impurity of the dispatcher of the goat and the

---

[1] *ANET* with corrections (orally) by D. P. Wright.

burner of the purification offering carcasses lasts one day. Furthermore, the exact Israelite counterparts, the officiating priest and the slaughterer, are not rendered impure. And in Babylon, because the high priest becomes impure merely by watching the purgation, lower temple officials conduct the ritual. In Israel, by contrast, the entire ritual is conducted by the high priest. (4) In Babylon the king undergoes a ritual of humiliation: the high priest strikes his cheek, drags him by the ears, and makes him bow to the ground; tears indicate the king's penitence and the god's favor. His confession is within a political context; he has been a faithful custodian of the god's temple and city and has not violated the political rights of the *kidinnu* (a protected group). The major difference lies in the self-reflection of the Babylonian king and the fact that he focuses on his own conduct, whereas in Israel the high priest confesses the failings of his people. In other words, in Babylon the viability of the society depends solely on the worthiness of the king; in Israel the national destiny is equated with the moral condition of the people, as articulated through the priest. (5) The Babylonian ceremony lasted eleven or twelve days, whereas the Israelite counterpart was of one day's duration. While this is technically accurate, if the tenth of Tishri is seen not as an isolated day of purgation but as the culmination of a New Year Festival, ten days in duration, then in some senses Yom Kippur is better understood as one day of Israel's ten-day New Year Festival—in particular, the final and climactic one. The first ten days of Tishri are, in Jewish tradition, a penitential period during which people, through their repentance, can alter the divine decree.[2] Its roots could be traced to a putative ten-day New Year Festival ending in the joyous celebration of the sanctuary's purgation on the tenth and last day.

There is no reason to doubt the antiquity of an annual purgation rite for the sanctuary on the tenth and final day of the New Year Festival, which, in accordance with Israel's ancient agricultural calendar, began in the autumn (see Exod 23:16b; 34:22b). Because this day was a national holiday, it was marked by complete cessation from labor. The vestiges of jubilation and merriment that survived even into rabbinic times make it doubtful that the element of "self-denial" is original. Most likely, self-denial played an indispensable role during the emergency situations declared by the high priest when he felt that divine punishment was imminent because the people's sins had polluted the sanctuary. When the high priest's prerogative to declare an emergency "whenever he chooses" (v. 2) was abrogated and the sanctuary's purgation was restricted to an annual observance "once a year" (v. 34) on the tenth of Tishri, then the penitential characteristics of the emergency days were transferred to the annual day, thereby altering its nature from one of unrestrained joy to one of subdued optimism. Yom Kippur, then, reflects the hope that the purgation of the sanctuary, coupled with the people's repentance, as reflected in their acts of self denial, would result in a blessed new year.

---

[2] *b. Roš Haš.* 18a.

C. Azazel and Elimination Rites in the Ancient Near East

The antiquity and ubiquity of the Azazel rite are immediately apparent. Purgation and elimination rites go together in the ancient world. Exorcism of impurity is not enough; its power must be nullified. This was accomplished in one of three ways: curse, destruction, or banishment. The last mentioned was used frequently: evil was banished to its place of origin (e.g., the netherworld, wilderness) or to some place in which its malefic powers could work to the benefit of the sender (e.g., to enemy territory) or in which it could do no harm at all (mountains, wilderness).

The Mesopotamian corpus of ritual texts yields many examples of the elimination of evils by transfer and disposal that relate conceptually to the Azazel rite. In such rites, the demonic illness of the affected patient or building is transferred to another object (a slaughtered animal, bread, dough, figurine, etc.), which is then disposed of in an appropriate place. The example that follows will focus on the conceptual and systemic differences between the Mesopotamian rites and the biblical rites instead of on the purely formal similarities and dissimilarities.

In *Uttuke Limnuti* (lines 115-38), Ea instructs his son, Marduk, on how to purify a patient beset by demons.[3] Among the many rites performed, a *mašḫultuppû*-goat is brought to the patient's body and his head is bound with the animal's headband. The demons are exorcised by incantations: "From the body of the disturbed man, arise . . . whatever evil, [arise, set out] to Ereshkigal's place (i.e., the underworld)."[4] The incantations are followed by the removal of the *mašḫultuppû*'s skin from the patient's body and its disposal in the street, symbolic of the hope that all evil will return to the underworld.

The rite is clearly one of transfer on which the skin serves as the instrument that takes on the evil, thereby cleansing the patient. Becoming thus impure, the skin is discarded. The foregoing example of a Mesopotamian elimination rite parallels the biblical scapegoat rite in that an object that is selected to draw the evil from the affected person is consequently disposed of. The dissimilarities, however, are more significant: (1) In Mesopotamia, the evil removed by such rites is demonic and is considered very real; in the Bible, while the impurity is real, it does not possess the vitality and independence of demonic evil. (2) There are no group transfer rites in Mesopotamia: their rite seeks to remove a demonic impurity that infects an individual. The biblical scapegoat, in contrast, removes the sins of the entire nation. (3) The Mesopotamian rites seek the aid of the deities of the wilderness to accept the evils; in the Bible the entire rite is done under the aegis of its one God. (4) The Bible rejects the idea of substitution, which presupposes demonic attack and the appeasement of threatening demons.

---

[3] Gurney 1935:84–95.
[4] Gurney 1935:84-95

Thus Israel's monotheism and priestly doctrine of collectiveness are the major contributing factors in transforming the elimination rites of the ancient Near East into those of Yom Kippur.

Selected Texts

[16:1] According to this initial verse, chapter 16 follows upon chapter 10 chronologically. Thus chapters 11–15 are an insert specifying the impurities that can pollute the sanctuary (15:31), for which the purgation rite of chapter 16 is mandated. From the point of view of the redaction, the connection of chapter 16 to chapter 10 makes sense. Nadab and Abihu had polluted the sanctuary doubly, in life by their sin and in death by their corpses. Yet chapter 10 has said nothing about the procedure for purging the sanctuary, and in the case of such severe pollution—the sin and subsequent death of Nadab and Abihu occurred in the sacred precincts—the entire sanctuary, including the adytum, would need to be purged. This procedure is detailed in chapter 16. Indeed, that the rite described here could be regarded as an emergency measure originally (vv. 2-3) fits the case of Nadab and Abihu perfectly.

Another reason for regarding the original juxtaposition of chapters 10 and 16 is structural. As was shown in the discussion of the structure of Leviticus (see Introduction, B), chapter 19 is the center of Leviticus. But this leaves the balance lopsided, 18 chapters versus 8 chapters. Removing chapters 11–15 brings chapter 16 closer to the center. Chapters 11–15, then, were a later insertion.

[16:2] It should be noted that nothing is said concerning a fixed time. This fact is observed by the midrash, which makes this striking comment: "He [Aaron] may enter any time he chooses as long as he follows this procedure,"[5] from which Elijah of Vilna concludes that Aaron could enter the adytum whenever he chose, but his successors could do so only on the Day of Purgation. His observation, I believe, is correct, for it points to the possibility that initially the purgation rite for the sanctuary was an emergency measure, a thesis that fits the theory that originally this chapter followed upon the deaths of Nadab and Abihu, and which can be supported on many additional counts.

The term *kapporet* is untranslatable, so far. It refers to the solid gold slab (3.75 feet by 2.25 feet) atop the ark, at the edges of which were two cherubim, of one piece with it and made of hammered gold, kneeling and facing each other with bowed heads and outstretched wings so as to touch in the middle. It can hardly be rendered "mercy seat/throne" or "cover."

Which cloud is meant here, the cloud of incense that the high priest raises in the adytum (v. 13) or the divine fire-cloud that, according to P, descends upon the tabernacle as a sign that Israel is to make camp (Num 9:15-23), and rests upon the ark

---

[5] *Midr. Rab.* 21:7.

whenever God speaks to Moses (Exod 25:22; Num 7:89)? The difference is not inconsequential. The cloud of incense interpretation implies that the high priest may only see the ark if his view is blocked by a screen. The fire-cloud interpretation instead says nothing on this count, but merely states why the high priest may not come at will into the adytum: the divine presence in the form of the fire-cloud rests upon the ark.

The screen interpretation is preferable, for vv. 2-5 are an inventory of the materials the high priest needs to perform his rites, and the screen, this verse tells us, is indispensable. Moreover, there is simply no prohibition against seeing the divine fire-cloud. Every Israelite witnessed its guiding presence through the wilderness (Exod 40:39). Furthermore, all of Israel saw God's *kavod* (fire-cloud) when the tabernacle was first dedicated (Lev 9:23b).

[16:4] How many times did the high priest wash during the day? He bathed his body twice, before and after he officiated in his special linen garments (16:4, 26). He would have washed his hands and feet each time he entered the tent or officiated at the altar (Exod 30:19), that is, the three times he entered the tent to minister in the adytum, and a fourth time when he officiated on the altar. If he also officiated in the morning and evening, he would have washed two more times. Thus, in sum, he would have bathed his body twice and washed his hands and feet six times.

[16:6] The high priest is considered chieftain of the priestly clan; hence all his personal sacrifices are also on behalf of his fellow priests, unless he alone has erred (4:3-12).

[16:8] The purpose of the lots is clearly to leave the selection of the animals to YHWH. Otherwise, if the high priest chose the animals, it would appear that he and the people he represented were offering an animal to Azazel. Thus the text takes pains to state that both animals were placed "before YHWH" (v. 7),[6] that both were designated a purification offering (v. 5), and that the goat of Azazel will be placed alone "before YHWH"(v. 10). Here is clear evidence of the Priestly efforts to alter what was most likely in its original form a pagan rite (see below and THEME C above).

The most plausible explanation is that Azazel is the name of a demon who has been eviscerated of his erstwhile demonic powers by the Priestly legislators. First, the goat sent him is not an offering; it is not treated as a sacrifice, requiring slaughter, blood manipulation, and the like, nor does it have the effect of a sacrifice, namely, propitiation, expiation, and so on. Moreover, an animal laden with impurities would not be acceptable as an offering either to God or a demon (cf. v. 26). Hence the

---

[6] Ramban; *Zohar Aḥare* 63:1.

Israelites could not have been worshiping Azazel. Second, the goat is not the vicarious substitute for Israel, because there is no indication that it was punished (e.g., put to death) or demonically attacked in Israel's place. Instead of being an offering or a substitute, the goat is simply the vehicle to dispatch Israel's impurities and sins to the wilderness/netherworld (v. 21). The banishment of evil to an inaccessible place is a form of elimination amply attested in the ancient Near East (see above, THEME C).

Azazel himself is deprived of any active role: he neither receives the goat nor attacks it. Regardless of his origins—in pre-Israelite practice he was surely a true demon, perhaps a satyr, who ruled in the wilderness—in the Priestly ritual he is no longer a personality but just a name, designating the place to which impurities and sins are banished. As for the survival of the name Azazel, "demons often survive as figures of speech (e.g., 'gremlins') long after they have ceased to be figures of belief. Accordingly, the mention of a demon's name in a scriptural text is no automatic testimony to living belief in him."[7] Azazel suffers the fate of all angels and spirits in Scripture. They can represent the powers of the physical world (Ps 104:4; 148:8), but they are not deified (Deut 4:19; 17:3; Job 5:1) and their worship is prohibited (Exod 20:4-5; 22:19 [Eng. 20]; Deut 5:7-8).

[16:10] In contrast to the bull and other goat, which are about to be slaughtered (vv. 11, 15), the Azazel goat is "stationed alive." An early rabbinic tradition holds that a red ribbon was tied to the horns of the live goat. This practice has confirmed ancient precedents. In Israel the significance of the ribbon was practical: to distinguish the scapegoat from the goat to be slaughtered, for the goats had to be alike in appearance. The use of red ribbons as marks of identification is attested to in the Bible (Gen 38:28; Josh 2:18).

[16:13] The rabbis hold that the cloud "cover[ing] the *kapporet*" was created not by incense but by means of an added ingredient whose sole purpose was to be a "smoke raiser." The "cloud" (v. 2), then, stands for the screen created by the "smoke-raiser" substance, also referred to as "the cloud of incense" (v. 13). According to Albeck,[8] therefore, the Pharisees, in agreement with the Sadducees, maintained that the purpose of the incense was to shield the ark from the view of the high priest. They both agreed that the smoke screen had to be raised outside the adytum and before the entry of the high priest. They differed only concerning the composition of the screen. On the one hand, the Pharisees held that the "cloud" was to be created from the smoke-raising ingredient; but, in keeping with vv. 12-13, the incense should be kindled only when the high priest was inside the adytum. The Sadducees, on the other hand, maintained that the incense plus the smoke raiser should be ignited prior to the high

---

[7] Gaster 1962a:818.
[8] 1952:215n.2

priest's entry. In effect, the Pharisees and the Sadducees were in complete agreement concerning the exegesis of the biblical instructions concerning the "cloud." It stands for the smoke screen that YHWH requires in order to manifest himself to the high priest (v. 2), and it is this same cloud that must cover the ark (v. 13). The cloud, however, must be distinguished from the incense, whose function is not to serve as a screen but to placate God for the high priest's presumption in entering before God's presence.

Thus the rabbis' exegesis of v. 13 must be correct: the ark is covered by "the cloud" and not by "the incense." Moreover, the procedure they prescribe best fits the data. Because YHWH insists that the high priest may enter the adytum only if the ark is shielded by a cloud (v. 2), the high priest produces this cloud by igniting a "smoke-raising" substance just before he enters the adytum; and once inside, in keeping with the sequence of vv. 12-13, he ignites the incense.

It can hardly be overlooked that the Priestly source, as represented in Leviticus 16, is set up in deliberate contrast with the narrative tradition of Mount Sinai. In the latter, Moses alone is permitted to penetrate the divine cloud atop the mountain, but in this chapter, it is the high priest Aaron who is permitted to enter the inner shrine on Yom Kippur. Even then a difference is maintained. Whereas Moses penetrated the divine cloud, Aaron stands in front of the (incense) cloud—a discernible sign that the Priestly source concedes that the prophet (Moses) is superior to the priest (Aaron).

[16:16] Here the "pollution" refers to the ritual impurities described in chapters 11–15 and the moral impurities generated by the violation of prohibitive commandments (see 4:2). The ritual in the sanctuary concerns itself with removing its pollution (also caused by Israel's wrongs; see below); while the rite with the Azazel goat, by contrast, focuses not on pollution, the *effects* of Israel's wrongs, but exclusively on the *wrongs themselves*.

The term rendered "rebellion" or "transgression" originates in the political sphere, where it denotes the rebellion of a vassal against an overlord (e.g., 1 Kgs 12:19; 2 Kgs 1:1; 3:5, 7; 8:20, 22). By extension, it is transferred to the divine realm, where it denotes Israel's rebellion against its God (Isa 1:2; 43:27; Jer 2:8; 33:8). Thus it is the term that characterizes the worst possible sin: open and wanton defiance of YHWH. As intention plays no part in the creation of *physical* impurity, this term must be directed solely to the pollution generated by Israel's *moral* violations. Moreover, as it implies intention to purposely commit the act as well as to flout the law, it is this sin that generates the impurity that not only attacks the sanctuary but penetrates into the adytum and pollutes the *kapporet*, the very seat of the Godhead (see the diagram and discussion, chap. 4, THEME A). One should also note that this term occurs nowhere in P except here, another indication that this text originates in a different provenience and was subsequently adopted and adapted by P. The fact that all of Israel's sins, including the brazen ones, are responsible for the pollution of the

170

sanctuary and are now purged by the blood of the two purification offerings makes it highly probable that *originally* the high priest's confession over the live goat referred only to those purged impurities and that the purpose of the rite was to dispatch these impurities into the wilderness.

The shrine should be purged in the same manner as the adytum. Specifically, one object (the incense altar) is to be purged by direct contact with the purgation blood, and the rest of the shrine is to be purged by a sevenfold sprinkling of the blood on the shrine floor. There is, however, no need to specify how the purgation of the incense altar takes place, for the procedure was already given in 4:6-7, 17-18. The purging of the shrine took place with the blood of the bull and goat separately, just as in the adytum.

One should also note that uniquely in this chapter "the tent of meeting" does not refer to the entire tent of meeting, as everywhere else in P, but only to the outer room, the shrine.

[16:19] The purpose of the dual blood application is neatly caught by the rabbis: "Purify it of the past (impurities) and consecrate it for the future (sacrificial uses)." Of course, it is not consecration but reconsecration that is effected here. The sanctuary and its sanctums were consecrated at the time of their completion and installation (8:10-11).

Only the altar was reconsecrated, to the exclusion of the other sanctums. Manifestly, the altar, the most vulnerable target of the unending impurities generated by Israel (see chap. 4, THEME A), would become so polluted that its very holiness was endangered. Hence a periodic rite of consecration was prescribed.

[16:21] That the text stresses that the hand-leaning rite is executed with both hands is the key to understanding the function of the Azazel goat. It is not a sacrifice, else the hand-leaning would have been performed with one hand (see at 1:4). The two-handed ceremonial instead serves a transference function: to convey, by confession, the sins of Israel onto the head of the goat.

The crucial significance of the confession is accurately pinpointed by this rabbinic comment: "By confessing iniquities and transgressions, they turn them into inadvertences,"[9] thus qualifying them for sacrificial expiation (see at 5:5).

"Iniquities" is the key term in the confession because it is the only category of sin repeated in this ritual's conclusion (v. 22). Thus it parallels and corresponds in importance to "impurities," the term selected in summing up the purpose of the sanctuary purgation (v. 16). Indeed, the only difference between the inventory of wrongs purged by the blood of the bull and the goat (v. 16) and that purged by the scapegoat (v. 21) is that "impurities" is replaced by "iniquities." "Impurities" refers to the effect

---

[9] *Sipra Aḥare* par. 2:6.

of Israel's sins on the sanctuary; "iniquities" refers to the effect of Israel's sins on themselves. Thus it is clear that the blood purges the impurities of the sanctuary and the scapegoat purges the sins of the people. This distinction was perceptively perceived by the rabbis: for *pollution* that befalls the temple and its sanctums through wantonness, atonement was made by the goat whose blood is sprinkled within the adytum and by the Day of Atonement. *For all other wrongs* specified in the Torah, the scapegoat makes atonement.[10]

Purgation and elimination rites go together in the ancient world. Exorcism of impurity is not enough; its power must be eliminated. An attested method is to banish it to its place of origin (the wilderness or the netherworld; see below) or to some place where its malefic powers could work in the interest of the sender (e.g., enemy territory; what the Philistines feared, 1 Sam 5:7). Thus the scapegoat was sent off to the wilderness, which was considered inhabited by the satyr-demon Azazel (see above, THEME C).

[16:24] This is the only time that immersion after sacrifice is mentioned. Its purpose cannot be the removal of the impurity that the high priest purportedly removed from the scapegoat; he is immune to the impurity that he removes. Only one plausible reason remains: to remove the superholiness that he contracted by entering the adytum. This premise would account both for the discarding of his supercharged garments inside the tent and for the need to wash when he resumes his usual operations on the lower level of holiness within the shrine.

[16:28] The one who burns the red cow is also rendered impure (Num 19:8), and one can deduce that the burnt purification offering always contaminates the one who handles it; this, indeed, is the tradition of the rabbis. They also transmit another tradition that neither the scapegoat nor the carcasses of burnt purification offerings transmit impurity while they are still *inside* the sacred precincts. Clearly, this rule guarantees that the high priest and the priestly cadre can handle these sacrifices without fear of contracting impurity.

[16:29] The people are addressed for the first time. Heretofore, they were referred to in the third person. Moreover, they played no part whatsoever in the sanctuary ritual. Even their offerings were not brought by them but by Aaron (see v. 5). Additionally, the entire ritual was addressed to Moses, who, in turn, was to impart it to Aaron but not directly to Israel (vv. 1-2). Thus this switch to second-person, direct address to Israel is the first of several signs that this and the following verse comprise an appendix to the text.

---

[10] *m. Šebu.* 1:6.

More than fasting is required in the process of self-affliction. Daniel "refrained from all choice food, no meat or wine passed my lips and I did not anoint myself." Thus his self-affliction consisted of a partial fast and, in addition, he abstained from anointing his body. The latter deprivation is included among the items enumerated in the rabbinic definition: "Afflict yourselves, from food, drink, and from enjoying bathing, and from anointing, and from sexual intercourse."[11] King David not only fasts but sleeps on the ground, does not change his clothes, and refrains from sex, anointing, and bathing (2 Sam 12:16-20), perhaps serving as a confirmation of the rabbinic definition.

The prohibition directed to the resident alien concerns only his work. He is not required to practice self-denial. This view may be justified on the grounds that the resident alien is bound by the prohibitive commandments and not by the performative ones (see chap. 17, THEME A).

---

[11] *Tg. Ps.-J.;* cf. *m. Yoma* 8:1.

Leviticus 17–27

The Holiness Source (H)

With chapter 17, the verbal and ideological scenery of Leviticus changes. We have entered the domain of H, the holiness chapters. Two critical changes occur: ritual impurity becomes moral impurity; and the domain of the sacred expands, embracing the entire land, not just the sanctuary, and all of Israel, not just the priesthood. The result of these two ideological changes is a decided emphasis on ethical behavior and the granting of civil equality to the resident alien. These changes are marked by a new vocabulary and style; P's terminology is often given a new meaning, as will be shown.

Selected Themes
A. On Being Holy: Part II (continued from chap. 11, Theme D)

These and other characteristics of H were affected, in my opinion, by a new priestly school, H, at the end of the eighth century BCE. This school concerned itself with the people at large. Its goal was revolutionary: the creation of an egalitarian society (see 17:2; chap. 19, THEME A; chap. 20, THEMES B and D). Thus the centerpiece of Leviticus radically alters the presuppositions of all that came before: with H, everyone has access to the holy. The burden now is on the individual to live a life that accords with holiness. It is within everyone's reach.

The common denominator of H's material (chaps. 17–27) is the theme of holiness. Its source and rationale are found in chapter 19. Logically, this chapter should have introduced the holiness material, were it not for the redactor's desire to underscore the chapter's centrality to the entire book of Leviticus by flanking it with two similar collections of sexual prohibitions (chaps. 18 and 20) in chiastic relation. Also, in its present position, as demonstrated in the INTRODUCTION, B, chapter 19 is the center of the book of Leviticus. This is followed by holiness precautions for priests and Israelites (chaps. 21–22), the holiness of time (chap. 23), YHWH's name (chap. 24), land (chap. 25), the covenant (chap. 26), and consecrations (chap. 27). The root *qdš*, "holy," appears in sixteen of the twenty divine speeches. The anomalous chapter 17 was needed by the redactor (H_R) because of its associations with and allusions to P's closing chapter 16 and thus could form a needed bridge between P and H. The theme of holiness thus accounts for the choice of these H chapters.

175

Leviticus 17–27: The Holiness Source (H)

B. YHWH in H: A Survey

In the H chapters, Leviticus 17–27, YHWH is a surprising deity. YHWH does not seem to be a jealous or territorial god: YHWH does not forbid the worship of other gods (with a single, specific exception discussed below). Although not jealous with respect to YHWH's exclusive divinity, the YHWH of H is deeply protective of his terra, the promised land. In H the harm of sin is not only personal but, more importantly, territorial: while sinners may dirty themselves, the great risk of their action is that they will pollute the land and, through the land, the name of YHWH. In line, perhaps, with this primal connection to the land, the YHWH of H prizes fidelity highly and has a tribal sense of justice: it is in the H passages that the measure-for-measure vision for a penal system is laid out. This YHWH has a deep and abiding interest in individual sanctity. Therein lies perhaps the greatest contribution of H's YHWH: ethics achieving sanctity (see also 5:20-26, THEME B).

If the one God, YHWH, forbids the worship of other gods, it is not attested in H except in regard to Molek (20:1-5; see chap. 20, Theme A). Why is Molek worship singled out for unique and virulent condemnation? The reason is that the people practiced Molek worship on the assumption that their behavior was sanctioned (even commanded!) by YHWH, and therefore invoked YHWH's name during the ritual worship. Molek worship was no mere idolatry; instead, it involved the sacrifice (i.e., murder) of children (to earn access to the ancestral spirits)—a further desecration of YHWH's name (18:21). That YHWH is vexed by the illegitimate use of his name is attested by the existence of two categories of blasphemy: whoever curses YHWH (by using a surrogate name, e.g., "God," "the Name," etc.) is punished by YHWH, but if one curses the name "YHWH," the resulting pollution is so powerful that those within earshot must "return" his curse (via hand-leaning; see chap. 1, Theme B), and the community slays him (and his curse) by stoning (24:14-16).

YHWH is a God of fidelity. His signature "I YHWH (have spoken)," except where it reflects his self-presentation (as in 18:2; 19:2), is the equivalent of the prophetic "the declaration of YHWH," indicating that YHWH keeps his word and will punish its violation—again, a sign of his fidelity. His fidelity to his word is so unbreachable that he will keep his covenantal promise to the patriarchs and will restore exiled Israel to God's land, even if it has broken the (Sinaitic) covenant again and again—but only if it shows remorse and repents of its sins (a requirement discussed in more detail below in connection to the pollution of the land). YHWH's reconciliation with Israel is not, as some readers may assume, an act of mercy, but instead bespeaks deep fidelity (26:42-45). Indeed, the words for "mercy" never appear in H (or in P).[1]

H shows no concern at all for the poor other than at harvest time (19:9-10; 23:2), in contrast with D, which shows deep compassion for the poor (Deut 15:7-8),

---

[1] Friedman 1988:238–39.

in the form of interest-free loans (Deut 23:20). Indeed, H denies the poor access to the sabbatical aftergrowth (25:6-7, in contrast with Exod 23:11). However, this may be based on pragmatic grounds: to preserve the meager produce for those under the landowner's exclusive responsibility (family, slaves, and resident workers and aliens).

H's treatment of the poor provides a telling example of the tension between theory and practice. In theory, in the ideal world that H envisions, the landless should be nonexistent because the laws of redemption and jubilee will be in effect. Moreover, in general, the poor will be taken care of by their kin group. However, the reality was much starker. The text testifies that the poor must have existed in large numbers, because of the following conditions: the loss of landed property due to its inability to support growing families; the increased latifundia, which the jubilee laws tried to rectify (chap. 25); and, above all, the massive influx of homeless and land-less refugees as a result of the destruction of the northern kingdom in the eighth century BCE. D had it right: "the poor will not cease from the midst of the land" (Deut 15:11a). Thus the question remains unanswered: Why does H ignore the poor? Rephrasing the question theologically: Why is there no instruction from YHWH—if not a law, at least some concern—for the poor? I have no answer, except for an admonition to all of us not to allow ourselves to be satisfied by laws that should work in theory when their failure is plainly evidenced by the suffering of those who surround us.

YHWH's punishments are mainly exemplified by the principle of measure for measure—the ultimate in precise justice (Lev 26:13-38). He also punishes by vertical retribution, holding the children accountable for their sins and for the sins of their fathers (26:39). This is not unjust. The fathers, presumably, did not atone for their sins. The responsibility, therefore, falls on the children to make amends for the pollu-tion caused by sin that their forebears left behind. In H what matters is that the land is still polluted; if the parent has not remedied the pollution, someone else must take over the responsibility or the land will become polluted and the people and then God will be banished (for details see 18:24-30). Reflected here is an image of disorders in creation that must be rectified. In H's theology, YHWH had created an ordered world. Hence he has prohibited the admixtures of species, even between priests and layper-sons (19:19; 22:10, 12-13). What is true in nature also holds in morality. Sins cause a breach in the world, and they must be expiated, if not by the sinners, then by their children. The required expiation, remorse and confession, is H's contribution to the development of prophetic repentance (see 26:40-41).

H's explicit image for the disruptions caused by sins is the pollution of the land. Here H has expanded the literal pollution caused by homicide (illegally spilled blood) to the surrounding earth (Gen 4:10-12; Num 35:33-34; Deut 31:4) to cover all violations, which metaphorically pollute the entire land (Lev 18:24-30). The land is YHWH's; YHWH has redeemed Israel from Egypt and granted it this land. The peo-ple of Israel are his tenants (25:23-24) and slaves (25:39-43). Hence they must obey

Leviticus 17–27: The Holiness Source (H)

YHWH's laws, specifically, to return the land to its original tenants and release indentured Israelites to their kin groups. The indentured Israelites are not slaves; they receive daily wages as resident hirelings. They are slaves of YHWH, not of anyone else.

The postulate of the land also explains the legal equality of the resident alien and the citizen (24:17-22). Because the resident aliens settled on YHWH's land, they are entitled to the owner's (YHWH's) protection.

YHWH's presence blesses (obedient) Israel by circulating about the land—a literary image that recalls the divine voice circulating in the primordial garden and thereby suggests that paradisiacal conditions can be restored (26:11-12).

Israel in the wilderness is a recalcitrant, rebellious horde (JE). Faithless and feckless, it exasperates its leader Moses. How will Israel become a disciplined people, obedient to YHWH's laws as transmitted to Moses? It is this wilderness dilemma, true also for H in his own time, that may be the basis of H's greatest teaching: the doctrine of holiness (see THEME A above). It serves as a heuristic technique. It is a ladder on which Israel can climb symbolically toward YHWH, the quintessence of holiness (19:2). The totality of commandments needs neither overwhelm nor deter. Step by step, rung by rung, Israel can transform itself spiritually and be ever more deserving of YHWH's blessing.

Nothing better illustrates Israel's immature dependence and dire need for such aid than H's beginning in chapter 17. Israel is incapable of absorbing the divine commandments rationally. Israel has to be told what to do, not why they should do it. Only Moses is provided with rationales (vv. 5-7, 11, 14a). Perhaps it is no accident that the term "holy" appears only two chapters later (19:2). Thereafter, Israel begins to be capable of receiving and internalizing rationales.

Simply put, Israel should strive to attain holiness, and (holy) priests should strive to sustain it (20:8). That is, YHWH awards increased holiness with each ascent of the ladder. Conversely, violation of the divine commandments causes slippage. Thus holiness is a dynamic concept, and priests, no differently from laity, must be on the alert concerning their own spiritual standing. Indeed, their very holiness always stands in jeopardy. Moreover, priests, by virtue of their right to officiate on the altar, are not allowed to make mistakes (10:1-3, P). They are subject to even more severe regulations than the laity (22:1-16).

The essence of divine holiness can be captured in the ethics that Israel is bidden to follow (e.g., 19:11-18). Equally important and even more operative in daily life is negative holiness, namely, the requirement to abstain from violating the divine prohibitions. Here too a divine model is invoked. As YHWH has separated the species (Genesis 1) and separated Israel from the nations, so should Israel separate itself from the contaminating ways of the other nations (Lev 20:24b-26). The more Israel succeeds in abstaining from violating the commandments, the more "I will be sanctified" (22:32), that is, the more YHWH's holiness becomes visible in Israel.

178

In sum, though the text speaks of the YHWH who sanctifies Israel, the reality is that Israel sanctifies itself through YHWH. If it obeys YHWH's commandments, its sanctification is automatic, a built-in result of the commandments. We may recall that the antithesis holy versus impure stands symbolically for life versus death (see above). Thus the self-sanctification produced by observing the commandments is life generating. This is pronounced succinctly and precisely by H: the one who follows YHWH's commandments "shall live by them" (18:5b).

C. Rationales Are Theology

H's rationales (one of its distinctive features), also termed "motive clauses," will be discussed as they sequentially appear in Leviticus.

1. I open this discussion with an out-of-sequence rationale (20:24-25) because it fuses two major theological planks in H's program—separation and holiness—and anchors their foundation in the basic themes of creation and life. Separation (20:24, 25 [bis], 26) is the leitmotif of P's creation story (Gen 1:4, 7, 14, 18). Separation of the elements and species produces order out of chaos[2] and allows for life to multiply and fill the earth (Gen 1:22, 28). Similarly, Israel's dietary code (Leviticus 11), which declares most of the animal kingdom off limits ("abomination" or "impure"), is based on a reverence-for-life principle, an aspect of P's life-versus-death theme that recurs throughout its impurity laws (chaps. 11–15).

The life-death antipodes are the basis of all of the dietary laws. H propels it one giant step forward. It declares "impure" to be the incompatible antithesis of a quality of YHWH expressed by the term "holy," a quality that should be emulated by all of Israel (11:44; 19:2; 20:26). Thus adherence to the dietary laws, namely, eschewing contact with the world of "impure," forms an indispensable step in Israel's ascent on the ladder of holiness (see chap. 19, THEME A).

Israel's separation from the nations is the continuation (and climax) of the cosmic creation process. Just as YHWH has separated the mineral, vegetable, and animal species to create order in the *natural* world, so Israel must separate from the nations to create order in the *human* world. Israel, in its quest for holiness, is simultaneously manifesting the universal or primordial life process. Israel's separation from the nations is the natural culmination of the creation process; it is possible that H carries the belief that the very order of the natural world rests on Israel's ability to maintain its sanctity by separating itself from the nations that surround it.

We should not forget that H was well aware (at least by oral transmission) of the antediluvian legends. The creation of the first human pair ends in failure: the violence of Cain and his descendant Lamech, miscegenation with celestial beings (Gen 6:1-4), and universal "violence" (6:13). The polluted earth requires a cleansing so

---

[2] Cf. Douglas 1966:55–57.

massive that only a flood suffices; God tries again with the righteous survivor Noah, hoping to avert failure by imposing law (9:1-6).[3] This experiment also fails with Noah (9:21) and with his descendants, who defy God by building up instead of spreading out (11:1-9; contra 1:28). Furthermore, H (at least H_R) is fully cognizant of JE's patriarchal narrative. Thus God decides on an individual who willingly "spreads out" (12:1, 4, 5) from his sinful society and builds a model family (18:19). P's Abraham is commanded, "Walk in my ways and be blameless" (17:1). Just as the life of Abraham will be a standard for blessing throughout the nations (12:3), so will be the exemplary life of his progeny (cf. 26:4).

Therefore, if Israel follows YHWH's commandments, it too will evoke admiration and emulation throughout the world (Gen 12:3; 18:18; 22:18; 26:4; 28:14; cf. 48:20; Isa 65:16; Jer 4:2; Ps 72:17). Abraham, Jacob, and their progeny will be a standard for blessing chiefly because they exemplify "justice and righteousness" (Gen 18:18-19; 22:18). Thus when H demands that Israel separate from the nations, it has in mind that Israel's *imitatio Dei* will generate a universal *imitatio Israel*.

While the system above reflects the aspirations of H, the reality does not match up. In the time of H, social injustice and individual criminality are rampant. How can the authors of H reconcile their brilliant and sanctifying world order with a reality that was harsh and unforgiving?

H devises a plan to help Israel build toward and systematically achieve its purpose on earth. To P's life-death principle, which governs its impurity laws, H attaches prescriptions for attaining holiness. The separation from all things "impure" is the first rung on the ladder of holiness; H's rungs are specified in chapter 19 (see below).

When H prescribes separation from Egypt and Canaan (18:3) because of their immoral sexual mores (18:6-23), we should bear in mind that these serve as only an illustration of all the Egyptian and Canaanite practices and laws that Israel should avoid. Instead, H instructs Israel, it should follow the life-giving laws of YHWH (18:5). In truth, nowhere does H state explicitly that the purpose of Israel's separation is to create a model people for nations to emulate. But H did inherit the tradition that the moral behavior of the patriarchs, the model for the descendants, was intended to influence the behavior of their neighbors (Gen 12:3; 22:18; 26:4).

Separation does not mean isolation. Israel is completely integrated into its surroundings commercially and culturally. In H's view, non-Israelites will witness how Israel treats the alien (Lev 24:22; see chap. 17, THEME A) and the poor (19:9-10) and how it abolishes slavery (25:39-43; see chap. 25, THEME B)—for which Israel's God will reward it with prosperity and security (26:3-13). With those examples, H cannot conceive of how the non-Israelites would not be induced to behave similarly (see also Deut 4:8). How far, indeed, is this incipient transnational role from the servant poems of the exilic Isaiah, which predict that Israel will be "a light of the nations" (Isa 42:6-

---

[3] Frymer-Kensky 1977.

7; 49:6; 51:4; cf. 61:1)? After all, the divine promise to the patriarchs (mentioned above) and H's concrete plan of achieving holiness by separation from the ways of others and obeying YHWH's commandments lie before exilic Isaiah. Is he not standing on the shoulders of the patriarchal traditions and H's legislation?

2. Leviticus 17 is short (16 verses), yet rife with rationales—all dealing with the same theme. Since blood is life (v. 14, repeating v. 11a, the aside to Moses) and hence forbidden to be ingested by both the Israelite and the alien (v. 10, repeated in vv. 12, 14, the aside to Moses), then nonsacrificial slaughter is declared a capital crime punishable by YHWH with *karet* (v. 4; see chaps. 6–7, THEME B). Moreover, nonsacrificial slaughter is banned permanently to prevent the worship of chthonic deities (v. 7). The blood of sacrificial animals must be drained on the altar (v. 4a). YHWH has empowered the blood of an animal killed for its flesh to redeem its killer if the blood has been returned to YHWH via the altar (v. 11)—which adds a new dimension to P's function for altar-sacrificial blood: purging the sanctuary of pollution (chaps. 4, 16) and expiating inadvertent wrongdoing (1:4; 5:16, 18, 26).

3. Whereas P speaks of only the pollution of the sanctuary and its sancta, H holds that the entire land of Israel is vulnerable to pollution (18:24b-25). Israel had the right to possess the inhabited land of Canaan because Canaan had polluted the land by its gross sexual misconduct (18:24a, 26-28; 20:22). The resident alien is also subject to this rule because he lives on the land, and violations of prohibitive commands committed by any of the inhabitants pollute the land (18:26).

In essence, H does not differ from P regarding the end result of disobeying YHWH's commandments. P also posits that the pollution of the sanctuary leads to YHWH's abandonment of Israel and its ejection from its land. H does, however, differ in this regard: whereas P presumes Israel's banishment by hostile *human* forces, H presumes a natural ecological cause and effect: Israel pollutes the land; the land becomes infertile; Israel is forced to leave. (H combines the two rationales in the maledictions of chap. 26.)

4. Molek worship is included among the sexual prohibitions (18:21; 20:1-5) because it destroys human seed, thereby aborting procreation and constitutes murder. It also desecrates YHWH's name (18:21b) and pollutes his sanctuary (20:3). The reason for the latter rationale is that YHWH's name is invoked during the worship of Molek on the presumption that YHWH commanded the sacrifice of children to this chthonic god; on the same day, its devotees would ascend from the Valley of Hinnom, where they worshiped Molek, to the Temple Mount to worship YHWH (see Ezek 23:39; and TEXT on 18:21b). Neither H nor its eighth-century prophetic contemporaries condemn any other idolatry, presumably because only Molek worship threatened the true worship of YHWH.

5. Leviticus 19 contains fifty-two laws grouped into fifteen subjects (see the introduction to chap. 19), yet only four laws are given a rationale. The first rational

covers all the others: "You shall be holy, for I YHWH your God am holy" (19:2). YHWH demands obedience to his commandments. Obedience produces godliness, a quality encapsulated by the term "holy" (see chap. 11, Theme D; chap. 19, Theme A; chap. 20, Theme B). Just as the priests, who are innately holy, are qualified to enter into YHWH's presence, so if Israel obeys YHWH's commands (19:37), it will attain holiness (19:2) and qualify for admission into the presence—that is, the providence and protection—of YHWH. H sharply differs from Isaiah on the eligible recipients of holiness. Isaiah holds that only the repentant survivors of YHWH's purge of the wicked will be called holy (Isa 4:3-4; 10:21-22). H rejects this dismal prediction. All of Israel, including its worst sinners, can attain holiness. This optimistic view of the inherent power of the human being to achieve salvation has become a basic plank in Judaism's theology.

6. Two prohibitions are singled out with the rationale that their violators desecrate sanctums: the consumption of sacred food beyond its allowable time (19:7) and the desecration of God's name with a lying oath (19:12). Those who resist harvesting the fruit of a tree during the first three years of its growth and offer YHWH the harvest of the fourth year will be rewarded with an abundant yield in the fifth year (19:23-25). This rational is also practical; it is confirmed by agronomics (see 19:23). H also adapts the rationale for supporting the alien (19:33-34) found in earlier legal tradition—for example, "you should know the feelings of the alien" (Exod 23:9; cf. 22:20 [Eng. 21]). Israel should recall that it was once an alien in Egypt, where it was exploited and persecuted. The concern for the alien is attested in all the pentateuchal codes (Exod 22:20 [Eng. 21]; 23:9; Lev 19:10, 33-34; 24:22; Num 15:14, 15, 29; 35:15; Deut 10:19; 14:21, 29; 16:11, 14; 23:8; 24:19-21). This suffices to indicate the vulnerability of the alien and the necessity for this rationale.

7. The injunctions to the priests (Lev 21:1—22:16) contain four rationales. H uniquely stresses that priests must *sustain* their holiness (21:8, 15, 23), while Israel must *attain* it (19:2; 20:26). Priests, who are holy congenitally, must watchfully avoid impurity because they offer YHWH's food (21:6). Israel, for its part, must show priests respect due to their sacred work (21:8). The high priest may not follow the bier even for his father or mother, because he is anointed with the sacred oil and will "desecrate" himself and the sanctuary (21:12). Priests may eat sacred food after their ablutions from minor impurity (22:7b), as do the Israelites, because this is their major source of food. This is the language of concession: it may indicate that originally priests had to wait until the following morning (see 22:7b). Indeed, purificatory procedures are the same for priests and laypersons (cf. chaps. 11, 14, and 15), though Ezekiel enjoins severer procedures for priests (44:25-27).

8. Since God provided Israel with booths for housing in the wilderness "exile," Israel should recall this event by living in booths (Lev 23:43) in the new exile of Babylonia.

9. Because YHWH owns the land, Israel is his tenant; it may continue to lease the land as long as it fulfills the owner's condition to redeem confiscated land and restore it to its original tenant at the Jubilee (25:24, 38). Thus selling the land is in reality leasing it until the Jubilee, and what is sold is not the land but its usufruct (see 25:24). YHWH is also Israel's owner because he is their redeemer. Hence Israel cannot be owned by any other person or power (25:42, 45), and the enslavement of an Israelite is totally forbidden.

10. In chapter 19 the motive clause "I am YHWH (your God)" appears sixteen times—always where the prohibition can be violated in secret. Violations lead to the disruption of the cosmic balance; because the disruption happens in secret, it goes unremedied. Thus the refrain "I am YHWH (your God)" reminds the infringer that even if by ignorance of intent he is not prosecuted in a human court, he will not escape the attention of the divine judge. This motive clause appears in a similar context in chapter 25 regarding cheating (25:17), taking interest on loans (25:38), and redeeming kin from non-Israelite masters (25:55). In chapter 26 this motive changes complexion: it alludes to the faithfulness of YHWH to fulfill his promises (26:13) and to keep his covenant (26:44-45).[iv] A further rationale appears in explaining Israel's exile: it has loathed YHWH's laws, in particular, by neglecting the septennates (v. 43; cf. vv. 34-35).

---

[4] Cf. Rashi on 26:13; Exod 6:2; and Saadiah on Lev 26:45.

The Prohibitions of Secular Slaughter and Eating Blood

Chapter 17 comprises five laws concerning the prohibition against ingesting blood (see also THEME B). The prohibition itself is confined to the third (middle) law (vv. 10-12). The rest of the chapter, however, either leads up to it (vv. 1-9) or depends on it (vv. 13-16).

The common denominator of all five laws is the ritual procedure in the slaughter and consumption of meat. The first law (vv. 3-7) mandates that permitted domesticated quadrupeds must be sacrificed at a legitimate sanctuary. The quadrupeds permitted for the human table are the very ones permitted for God's table, the altar. The second law (vv. 8-9) prohibits both the Israelite and the resident alien from sacrificing to other gods. The third law (vv. 10-12) lays down the absolute prohibition against ingesting blood, incumbent on Israelite and resident alien alike. The fourth law (vv. 13-14) prescribes that the blood of game killed by the Israelite and resident alien alike must be buried, and the fifth law (vv. 15-16) states that the Israelite or resident alien who eats of an animal that has died must be purified. The first, third, and fourth laws contain rationales (vv. 5-7, 11-12, 14). They take the form of asides to Moses and are not intended to be repeated to Israel.

What is the meaning of this aside to Moses? Surely, it is not H's intention to hide its rationales from Israel; they occur in nearly every law in subsequent H chapters. Note, for example, in this chapter the rationale "he has spilled blood" (v. 4b), and in the next various rationales (18:5, 7b?, 8b, 10b, 12b, 13b, 16b, 21b, 23b, 24-25, 27-29). Here, I submit, the rationales underscore the innovative nature of the law banning nonsacrificial slaughter. H felt that the rationales—chthonic worship (17:5-7), ransoming murderers (v. 11), and the life force is the blood (vv. 11, 14)—were too esoteric and innovative at Israel's initial stage of development.

Verse 11, the center of the larger chiasm (vv. 10-12), has its own chiasm, with v. 11aβ, the ransoming power of the altar (not the blood), as its center. As the rabbis observed, the alien is excluded.[1] This is as it should be. The alien may not worship

---

[1] *Sipra Aḥare* par. 7:5.

other gods (vv. 8-9), but he need not worship Israel's God; neither need he slaughter his animals at the altar, but may slaughter them at home.

Verse 11 is an aside to Moses. Whereas God commands Moses to prohibit the ingestion of blood during the consumption of meat to Israelite and alien alike (v. 10), he confides to Moses the rationale for this prohibition as it concerns his people Israel: the life-blood of an *Israelite's* meat must be offered on the altar to ransom his life. Thus v. 11 complements and completes the law of vv. 3-5. It explains why the Israelite, but not the alien, must first offer up all his meat as a sacrifice (i.e., a well-being offering)—to ransom his life for spilling the life-blood of the animal in order to enjoy its meat.

Selected Themes

A. The Resident Alien

Israel regarded itself as an alien both in its own land (during the time of the forefathers, Gen 15:13; 23:4) and in Egypt (Exod 2:22; Lev 19:34). Moreover, since the land belonged to God, Israel's status on it was theologically and legally that of an alien (Lev 25:23). Aliens had attached themselves to Israel during its flight from Egypt (Exod 12:38, 48; Num 11:4), as did many Canaanites after the conquest (e.g., Josh 9:3-27). Indeed, the Canaanites whom Solomon enslaved for his work projects (1 Kgs 9:20-21) are referred to in the later literature as aliens (2 Chr 2:16).[2] Israel, in H's view, did not own its land but by God's grace was given the land as a permanent lease provided it obeyed God's commandments. Aliens, however, could not own landed property and were largely day laborers and artisans (Deut 24:14-15), or were among the wards of society (Exod 23:12). Indeed, since the Levites—although Israelites—were also landless, they were dependent on the tribes in whose midst they settled, and hence they could be termed "aliens" (e.g., Judg 17:7; 19:1; Deut 18:6). Although some aliens did manage to amass wealth (Lev 25:47), most were poor and were bracketed with the poor as recipients of welfare (cf. Lev 19:10; 23:22; 25:6).[3] These latter verses indicate only too clearly that the alien was landless. Thus the rabbis are at a loss to explain Ezekiel's prophecy (47:22-23) that the alien will inherit the land on a par with the Israelite.[4]

Under biblical decree, the alien enjoyed protection with the Israelite under the law, as it is written: "there shall be one law for you and the resident alien." (Num 15:15; cf. Exod 12:48-49; Lev 24:22; Num 9:14; 15:29-30). However, the admonition of civil equality for the resident alien by no means should be construed as a general statement of parity between Israel and the alien. Whereas civil law held the citizen and the alien to be of equal status (e.g., Lev 24:22; Num 35:15), in the religious

---

[2] Paran 1989:116.

[3] For further details see Seeligmann.

[4] *Sipre* Numbers 78, on Num 10:29.

domain the alien neither enjoyed the same privileges nor was bound by the same obligations. The religious law made distinctions according to the following underlying principle: the alien is bound by the prohibitive commandments but not by the performative ones.[5]

This conclusion can be derived from the following prohibition incumbent on the alien: "Any person, whether citizen or alien, who eats what has died or has been torn by beats shall launder his clothes, bathe in water, and remain impure until the evening; then he shall be pure. But if he does not launder (his clothes) and bathe his body, he shall bear his punishment" (Lev 17:15-16). Thus the alien and the Israelite are not forbidden to eat carrion, but are required to clean themselves of the impurity. Aliens living on the land must keep themselves free from impurity for the same reason that Israelites must: failure to eliminate impurity threatens God's land and sanctuary. The welfare of all of Israel residing in God's land and under the protection of God's sanctuary is jeopardized by the prolongation of impurity. This principle is underscored by the requirement to bring a communal purification offering to atone for the individual wrongs not only of the Israelites but of the aliens as well (Num 15:26).

No wonder, then, that the alien and the Israelite are equally obligated to refrain from violations that produce impurity. Moreover, the requirement of a purification offering is imposed for the inadvertent violation of any prohibitive commandment (Lev 4:2, 13, 22, 27), whether the polluter is Israelite or non-Israelite. Anyone in residence on YHWH's land is capable of polluting it or the sanctuary. Since a later view is that the entire planet is YHWH's (Ps 24:1), the priestly theology would imply that physical (e.g., ecological) or moral (e.g., genocidal) crimes anywhere on earth pollute it (ultimately causing YHWH to abandon it) and render it uninhabitable (see chap. 4, THEME A).

Performative commandments, however, are violated by refraining or neglecting to do them. These violations are sins not of commission but of omission. Because these are acts of omission, of nonobservance, they generate no pollution either to the land or to the sanctuary. Thus, while their nonobservance can lead to dire consequences, these consequences are reserved for the Israelites who are obligated by their covenant to observe them. The alien, however, is not so obligated, because the alien, the resident non-Israelite, does not jeopardize the welfare of the Israelite neighbor by not complying with the performative commandments. As a result, for example, the alien need not observe the paschal sacrifice. But if he wishes to observe it, he must be circumcised (Exod 12:48) and, presumably, must be in a state of ritual purity (Num

---

[5] For example, the alien is under no requirement to observe the festivals. The paschal sacrifice is explicitly declared a voluntary observance for the alien (Exod 12:48; Num 9:14). Whereas an Israelite abstains on pain of *karet*, the alien may participate in the voluntary sacrificial cult if he or she follows its prescriptions (Num 15:14-16; Lev 22:17-25). Details in Milgrom 1982.

9:6-7, 13-14). However, under no circumstances may the alien violate the prohibition to possess leaven during the festival (Exod 12:19; 13:7).

The alien never lost the connotation of "resident alien" in the Older Testament.[6] The first glimmer of a new status for the alien is found in the words of Second Isaiah at the end of the sixth century BCE. In the Babylonian exile, non-Jews had been attracted by the Jewish way of life, particularly by the Sabbath. Isaiah calls on these would-be proselytes to "make ʿaliyah" with the Israelites. Although he cannot promise them that they will be part of the peoplehood of Israel—conversion as such was unknown—he assures them that the temple service will be open to them because "My house will be called a house of prayer for all peoples" (Isa 56:7).[7]

One postexilic passage, however, states unequivocally that the alien will become part of the Israelite people: "and the resident aliens shall join them and attach themselves to the house of Jacob" (Isa 14:1).

The assimilation of the alien may also be intimated in Ezek 47:22-23: "You shall allot it [the land] as an inheritance for yourselves and the aliens who reside among you, who have begotten children among you. You shall treat them as Israelite citizens; they shall receive allotments along with you among the tribes of Israel. You shall give the alien an allotment within the tribe where he resides—declares YHWH your God." With this last barrier between the social status of the Israelite and the alien removed, total assimilation is apparently envisioned.

The way is now open to the next stage of religious conversion, a stage discernible by the year 200 BCE. At that time, Antiochus III issued a decree fining any foreigner who entered the Israelite court of the temple (equivalent to "the entrance to the tent of meeting") the sum of 3,000 silver drachmas, payable to the priests[8]—a far cry from the biblical alien, who could enter the tabernacle court to offer sacrifices. Clearly, the Jews of the third century BCE were not in violation of the Torah, for by then they had reinterpreted the Torah's "alien" to denote the convert. That the institution of religious conversion was heretofore unknown not just in Israel but also in its contemporary world is indicated by the need of the Septuagint translators to invent a new word, "proselyte."[9]

B. Blood Is Life: Part II (continued from chap. 11, Theme B)

The fundamental question is this: Why does the Priestly account concede meat to Noah rather than to Adam, who instead is explicitly ordained as a vegetarian (Gen 1:29)? Was there an earlier tradition that carnivorous humans represent a later stage

---

[6] M. Smith 1971:178–79.

[7] See also Ezra 6:21; Neh 10:29-30 (Eng. 28-29); 2 Chr 30:25; and a discussion in Japhet 1977:286–99.

[8] Josephus, *Ant.* 12.145-46.

[9] Tov 1982:793.

in the history of the human race? There is a Mesopotamian text likely known to the Israelites that strikes pervasive roots into much of the Bible's antediluvian epic: the Epic of Gilgamesh.

The key to this channel of influence is that after the flood the animals will be in "the fear and dread of you" (Gen 9:2a*a*), implying that heretofore humans were not just vegetarian but friends of the animals. However, with the concession of meat, humans became hunters. Note the relevant passage from *Gilgamesh:*

> "On seeing him, Enkidu, the gazelles ran off. The wild beasts of the steppe drew away from his body. . . . But now he had [wi]sdom, [br]oader understanding. . . . [The harlot] says to him, to Enkidu: 'Thou art [wi]se, Enkidu, art become like a god! Why with the wild creatures dost thou roam over the steppe? . . . Food (meat) they placed before him. He gagged . . . nothing does Enkidu know of eating food."[10]

Biblical Adam was modeled on Mesopotamian Enkidu. Before each of them experienced sex, they were vegetarians (Gen 1:29; *Gilgamesh* I, iv, 2-4), naked (Gen 2:25; *Gilgamesh* II, ii, 27-28), and friends and protectors of the beasts (Gen 2:20; 3:1-41; *Gilgamesh* I, iii, 9-12). After sex, they eat meat (conceded to Noah, Gen 9:3, but presumably illegally eaten by Adam and his progeny [see below]; *Gilgamesh* II, ii, 3-7), wear clothes (Gen 2:24; 3:21; *Gilgamesh* II, ii, 27-29, iii, 26-27), and have become enemies of the beasts (Gen 3:15; 9:2; *Gilgamesh* I, iv, 24-25; II, iii, 28-32).

However, the most significant parallel between the protagonists of the two epics is that sex makes them wise and thereby enables them to become civilized. "Thou art wise Enkidu, art become like a god" (*Gilgamesh* I, iv, 34) is matched by Adam and Eve's eating the forbidden fruit that was "desirable for wisdom" (Gen 3:6), for it empowered them to "know good and evil" (Gen 2:7, 17; 3:4, 21). That the latter expression is a euphemism for sex is proved by Deut 1:39, especially 2 Sam 19:36,[11] and by the more obvious euphemism that they were naked (see Lev 18:6) before they ate the fruit and immediately afterward realized their nakedness (Gen 2:25; 3:7). Also the woman had her name changed to Eve, "the mother of all living," only after she ate of the fruit (Gen 3:19), implying that previously she had been a "helpmate (helpmeet)" (Gen 2:20), but not a sexual partner.

This insight enables us to penetrate the metaphoric imagery of the garden of Eden story. The serpent revealed to Eve that eating the fruit would endow her with creative power—a divine characteristic (Gen 3:5, 22). And if Eve, and subsequently Adam, yielded to this temptation, it is precisely because they wanted that power. Life in the garden was paradisal bliss, but it was limited, repetitive, and boring. Adam and Eve already had immortality, presumably by having eaten of the tree of life, which was not forbidden to them. Only the tree of knowledge of good and evil was forbid-

---

[10] I, ii, 24-34; II, iii, 3-7 (*ANET,* 75, 77).

[11] Milgom 1994.

den (2:16-17). Having eaten of the latter tree, if they continue eating from the tree of life, they will possess both immortality and creativity. In short, they will be gods! Their banishment from Eden thus became inevitable: "Now that the man has become like one of us . . . the Lord God banished him from the garden" (3:22-23).

The creative impulse can be either constructive or destructive. This then is the meaning of the biblical idiom "knowledge of good and evil": the creative impulse as manifested in sex (knowledge) can either build a world (good) or destroy it (evil).

To be sure, the line of Cain also knows both good and evil—Cain himself is "a builder of a city" (Gen 4:17), and his progeny create the first arts and sciences of civilization (4:20-22). But Cain also commits the first murder, and his descendant Lamech more brazenly follows suit (4:23-24). Thus the sapiential empowerment from "eating the fruit" certainly leads to good and/or evil consequences.

It is probable that with their eviction from paradise, man and woman illicitly begin to eat meat.[12] With Noah, the carnivorous appetite of the human being is legitimized (Gen 9:1-4). This concession forms part of the first law code (9:1-6). Humans will kill to have meat. Therefore let them do so only if they drain the animal's lifeblood and return it to its divine Creator.

Selected Texts

[17:2] As a signature of H, this salutation is theologically significant. P carefully distinguishes between Moses' statements to priests and to laity. Even where priests and laity share a concern, either one party or the other is addressed (Num 2:2; 5:6, 12; 6:2). Indeed, on two such occasions, Moses directs the priests to speak to the Israelites (Lev 11:1-2; 15:1-2). H, however, breaks down this distinction. On issues of common concern, priests and laity are addressed simultaneously; for example, see the headings to sacrificial slaughter (17:1-7) and sacrificial defects (22:17-25).

H's egalitarian thrust is clear: All Israelites, not just priests, are enjoined to follow a distinctive regimen of holiness (19:2). No matter that concerns the sanctuary and its personnel is out of their purview. Indeed, the sociopolitical implications are even more fundamental: the laity is divinely ordained to *supervise the priests* while they carry out their functions (see 21:24).

[17:3] The requirement to offer the blood of the sacrificial animals on the altar falls solely on the Israelites. This forms another bond between the first and third law of the chapter. The resident aliens are bound by the Noachian law to drain the blood (Gen 9:4), but since they are not required to worship Israel's God, they do not need to bring the blood to an altar (see above, THEME A).

This law prohibits to Israel all common, nonsacrificial slaughter and, instead, demands that the meat for the table initiate as a sacrifice.

---

[12] Brichto 1976.

This triad—ox, sheep, or goat—comprises all the sacrificial quadrupeds.
The phrase "outside the camp" always implies the vicinity of the camp.

[17:4] The expression "the entrance to the tent of meeting" and its synonym "before the tent of meeting" are used solely for the slaughter of well-being offerings (3:2, 8, 13), whereas the slaughter of other sacrifices take place "before YHWH" (1:5, 11; 4:15), another indication that the subject of this law—as, indeed, of the entire chapter—is procuring meat for the household, the chief function of the well-being offering.

The accusation "bloodguilt" is of murder, "equivalent to the one who by spilling blood of a human being forfeits his life."[13]

Verses 5-7. Nonsacrificial Slaughter Banned:
An Additional Rationale

This is the first aside to Moses (also vv. 11-12, 14). The initial rationale "he has shed blood" (v. 4) is now supplemented by a second one. As this pericope explicitly states further on (v. 7), the blood of the slaughtered animal is suspect of being offered to chthonic deities. The word for sacrifice, *zebah*, denotes a well-being offering, the meat of which is eaten by the offerer—another indication that the subject of this law is the proper procedure for providing meat.

[17:7] The plain meaning of this text is that the ban on nonsacrificial slaughter is to be permanent. It is the pragmatic consequences of H's assumption that there always will be multiple sanctuaries, one in easy access of every Israelite.

Verses 8-9. The Second Law:
No Sacrifices to Other (Infernal) Gods

[17:8] Schwartz suggests that vv. 5-7, H's rationale for the ban on nonsacrificial slaughter, is an aside to Moses and is not intended to be delivered to Israel.[14] That is, Israel is informed of the law (vv. 3-4), but only Moses is told its rationale (vv. 5-7). Thus "say to them further" indicates a change in the recipient of the message, from Moses (vv. 5-7) to Israel (vv. 8-9). The same literary phenomenon surfaces twice more in a subsequent law of this chapter: Moses alone is privy to the rationales (vv. 11-12, 14a).

Verses 10-12. The Third Law:
The Blood Prohibition and Its Rationale
Regarding Sacrificial Animals

[17:11] Both animals and people have a *nefeš*, "soul." *Nefeš* refers to the life essence of both human and beast as distinct from the body. It is the part of the person or ani-

---

[13] Rashi.
[14] Schwartz 1991:45–46.

mal that does not disintegrate into dust, but departs the body (see "as her *nefeš* departed," Gen 35:18). It is presumed that the *nefeš* is contained in the blood.

As observed by the rabbis,[15] the alien is excluded in this law. This is as it should be. The aliens may not worship other gods (vv. 8-9), but need not worship Israel's God; neither need they slaughter their animals at the altar, but may slaughter them at home (see v. 3). This is an aside to Moses. Whereas God commands Moses to prohibit the ingestion of blood during the consumption of meat to the Israelite and alien alike (v. 10), God confides to Moses the rationale for this prohibition as it concerns God's people Israel: the life-blood of an *Israelite's* meat must be offered on the altar to ransom the Israelite's life. Thus v. 11 complements and completes the law of vv. 3-5. It explains why the Israelite, but not the alien, must first offer up all his meat as sacrifice (i.e., a well-being offering)—to ransom the Israelite's life for spilling the life-blood of the animal in order to enjoy its meat.

Anthropological evidence reveals that the fear of killing an animal harks back to a very early period in the history of humanity. Indeed, an early Sumerian myth relates that a ritual and sacred meal are devised by the gods in order to sanction the killing of an animal.[16] However, *Israel is the only people* that codifies this sensitivity to animal life, *converting this ethic into law*. Life is inviolable. Hence all people must eschew the blood, the symbol of life (Gen 9:4). Israel is enjoined to obey an additional safeguard: the blood must be returned to God on the altar.

Verses 13-14. The Fourth Law: No Ingestion of Blood; Game

Hunting is attributed in the Bible to pre-Israelite personalities—Nimrod (Gen 10:9) and Esau (Gen 25:27)—an indication that it played an important role in early times. After the settlement in Canaan and certainly by the monarchic period, hunting became an insignificant factor in the national economy. To be sure, the royal menu featured specimens of game: deer, gazelles, and roebuck (1 Kgs 5:3). These three animals are supplemented by four others whose identification is uncertain in the list of wild animals, and are permitted in the Israelite cuisine (Deut 14:4-5). Once Israel's pastoral economy shifted almost exclusively to agriculture, hunting also changed from a necessity to a sport, one that could be indulged in only by a leisure class, namely, the royal aristocracy. Nevertheless, this law and the one specifying the permitted game, mentioned above, demonstrate that since hunting continued to be practiced—even by relatively few—it had to be controlled by legislation.

[17:13] The fact that the phrase "that may be eaten" is used indicates that the subject here and throughout the chapter is meat for the table. Indeed, the absence of any

---

[15] *Sipra Aḥare* par. 7:5.
[16] Hallo 1987; elaborated in 1996:217–20.

reference to predatory (hence, forbidden) animals shows that the notion of hunting as sport is not even envisaged—a far cry from the practices of Israel's neighbors.

[**17:14**] All blood must be drained, but only blood on the altar is endowed with the power to expiate or ransom. Moreover, certain bloodless offerings also expiate (5:13). This can only mean that *it is the altar, not the blood, that expiates*. For this reason, the alien, who does not have to resort to the altar (vv. 3-4), requires no ransom for slaughtering a sacrificial animal. This is his divinely endowed right (Gen 9:3); he drains the blood and need not bury it. Only the Israelites risk their life in taking the life of an animal: a higher order of morality is incumbent on Israel.

Once the sanctuary is centralized (in Jerusalem) as mandated by Deuteronomy 12, this law changes radically. Erstwhile sacrificial animals may now be slaughtered profanely. In effect, the Israelite adopts the previous position of the resident alien. As long as the Israelite abstains from ingesting the blood, the flesh of permitted animals need not be sacrificed but may be slaughtered and eaten at home. This is the position in Judaism to this day.

Verses 15-16. The Fifth Law: Eating of a Carcass Requires Purification

Since the Israelite is not forbidden to touch a human corpse (only a priest is prohibited, 21:1-4), touching an animal carcass is, a fortiori, also not forbidden. Of course, he *should* not touch a carcass or eat of it. If he does, he is impure and must undergo laundering and washing (11:40; 17:15). It is only if he contacts a sanctum or prolongs his impurity that sanctions are imposed (7:20; 11:16).

[**17:15**] For an explanation of the method of purification "launder his clothes, bathe in water," see 11:25. Bathing the whole body is required.

[**17:16**] "He shall bear his punishment" is a nonexpiable, irremediable divine sentence. In all cases where punishment is not stated, it is forthcoming—irrevocably. In theological terms, one might say that the punishment expiates the sin.[17]

---

[17] Explicitly, *m. Yoma* 8:8, but the punishment itself is unavoidable.

Illicit Sexual Practices

Chapter 18 touches on some of the most intimate and complicated social issues of its time, as well as our own. Its verses discuss family relationships, sex, homosexuality, and worship practices. Given the way the Bible is mentioned in conjunction with these issues in modern discourse, it would be natural to think that the Bible enjoins all homosexuality, imposes sexual prohibitions arbitrarily, and prohibits intermarriage between Jew and non-Jew. However, a close reading of this chapter reveals that none of these presuppositions holds true. Instead, what we find is the redactors of H trying to protect the Israelites, especially women, against what they perceived as the great vices of the era. From their struggle and their method, we can take instruction even as we question their ultimate decisions.

Chapter 18 comprises three parts: (1) exhortation (vv. 2b-5); (2) prohibitions (vv. 6-23); and (3) exhortation (vv. 24-30). That only one prohibition in part 2 is called an abomination (v. 22), whereas all of them are labeled as such in part 3 (vv. 26, 27, 29), indicates editorial activity: an older list has been incorporated by the H redactor into his exhortations. I have chosen to delve deeply into four questions posed by chapter 18: What is the Levitical view of intermarriage, of the need for sexual prohibitions, of homosexuality, and of Molek worship?

Selected Themes
A. Did H Permit Intermarriage?
The absence of a ban against intermarriage among the sexual prohibitions of Leviticus 18 and 20 demands explanation. Given the vehemence of later admonitions against intermarriage in Deuteronomy (7:3-4) and Deuteronomistic (Josh 23:12; 1 Kgs 11:1-2) and proto-Deuteronomistic sources (Exod 34:11-17),[1] and the prevalence of sexual impropriety among the other nations living in and around Canaan (Lev 18:3, 24, 27-28), we would expect to find H restricting marriage to non-Israelites as part of the sexual credo. After all, if the Canaanites were violating the

---

[1] Langlamet 1969; cf. Caloz 1968; Reichart 1972.

sexual prohibitions, thus causing impurity—both to the land and to those who reside on it (vv. 24-30)—wouldn't it be natural to protect Israel from this impurity by prohibiting the Israelites from marrying into those communities in which such impurity was commonplace?

The glaring omission of intermarriage in H (and in P as well; see below) is especially striking to a social anthropologist: "What is unusual in the biblical laws of purity is they do not set members of the congregation apart from one another. The laws specify prohibited degrees of closeness, but not intermarriage with outsiders or lower classes."[2] Indeed, the need for *Jubilees* (30:10), the rabbis,[3] and other Second Temple sources[4] to concoct a forced interpretation of Molek worship (Lev 18:21) as a ban against intermarriage can be attributed to their embarrassment at not finding intermarriage among the prohibited sexual liaisons (see 18:21).[5] How can we account for its absence?

The answer, I submit, can be found by facing the fact that there is no absolute ban against intermarriage in preexilic times, and an absolute ban against intermarriage did not emerge until postexilic times. Even Deuteronomy limits the prohibition against intermarriage to Canaanites (Deut 7:3-4), Moabites, and Ammonites (23:4-7), but not to others, expressly exempting Egyptians and Edomites (23:8-9). The priestly sources (H and P), on the contrary, express neither opposition to nor prohibition of intermarriage. Endogamy is not a prerequisite for holiness, and, as noted by Kugel, contact with other nations—presumably including intermarriage—is not proscribed.[6] God has separated Israel from the nations solely to protect Israel from following their ways (Lev 20:23, 24b); intermarriage is not a concern. Of course, evidence of aversion to exogamous marriage on ethnic grounds exists (e.g., Gen 27:46—28:2; Judg 14:3), but it does not achieve legal codification until the postexilic age.

H's only concern, as demonstrated throughout its legislation, is to maintain the purity of the land. As a consequence, even the resident alien who observes all the prohibitive commandments is permitted to remain on the land and is accorded complete civic equality with the Israelite (with the exception of land inheritance; see chap. 17, THEME A). During the period of the monarchy, with full political control in the hands of the Israelites and the Canaanites reduced to a small subservient minority (particularly in Judah, the probable provenance of H), intermarriages—the relatively few that would occur—would have been unidirectional: the resident alien would have become a worshiper of YHWH, and a (possibly zealous) follower of his laws (e.g., Uriah, 2 Sam 11:11). This type of intermarriage posed no threat to the Israelites of the biblical redactors.

---

[2] Douglas, forthcoming.

[3] *b. Meg.* 25a; *Tg. Ps.-J.* on 18:21.

[4] E.g., Philo, *Spec. Laws* 3.29.

[5] Cf. Vermes 1981; S. J. D. Cohen 1983.

[6] Kugel 1996:23. Note that Num 33:50-55 (probably) exhorts Israel to expel the Canaanites (cf. Exod 23:27-33) but is conspicuously silent on intermarriage (contrast Exod 34:11-17; Deut 7:3-4).

This state of affairs changed radically in the postexilic era. The relatively few returning exiles found the land occupied by many of the neighboring peoples. Their socioeconomic and political situation would be best described by the Deuteronomic curse: "The alien in your midst shall rise above you higher and higher, while you sink lower and lower; he shall be your creditor, but you shall not be his; he shall be the head and you, the tail" (Deut 28:43).

Under these circumstances, intermarriage was also likely unidirectional, only this time the arrow pointed the other way. The new alien—politically independent, socially secure, economically better off—had become a desirable spouse. Israel, though in its own land, was now threatened with assimilation. Thus among Ezra's first tasks was to stem this assimilationist tide. Without the benefit of an explicit legal precedent, he had to create a halakic midrash (Ezra 9:2, 12), combining D's declaration that the people of Israel are holy and P's dictum that the desecration of a sanctum merits divine punishment, to outlaw marriage to the non-Israelites living on the land. But in the case of inadvertence—Israel being innocent of Ezra's "law" and intermarrying—the sin is expiable by the dissolution of the illicit marriages, followed by a reparation offering (Lev 4:14-16; cf. Jer 2:3; Mal 2:11).[7]

B. The Hidden Purpose of the Sexual Prohibitions

The key that opens up the question of the hidden purpose of the sexual prohibitions is found in the idiom "uncover nakedness," which occurs in all the prohibited copulations with women (vv. 6-19). Ziskind offers an attractive rationale for the use of this idiom:

> [Its author] intended these prohibitions to be absolute, to transcend the laws of rape, seduction or adultery and to be lifelong, i.e., from the time that the relationship was established by either birth or marriage, and not to end with death or divorce. . . . Accordingly, a man would now be forbidden to have sex with his stepmother not only in his father's lifetime, but after his father died. He was barred from sex with his daughter-in-law and sister-in-law on the death of his son or brother (hence no levirate). . . . Women could no longer be handed around to other men in the family as wives and concubines. A widow could now marry anyone she wished outside the family or could be free not to remarry at all. . . . The rules forbidding a man to marry a woman and then to marry or make a concubine of her mother, daughter or sister prevented the unseemliness of a man moving from one member of a woman's family to another, and thus ended an abuse in the practice of polygamy (Lev 18:17-18). P [rather, H] did not wish any dilution of affection to take place among sisters or between mother and daughter by reason of a circumstance in which these women were forced to compete for the attention of the same man.[8]

---

[7] For the details of this exegetical tour de force, probably the first inner biblical midrash, see the discussion in Milgrom 1976a:70–74; 1991:359–61.

[8] 1996:128–29.

Maimonides seems to have alluded to the same rationale:

All illicit unions with females have one thing in common: Namely, that in the majority of cases these females are constantly in the company of the male in his house and that they are easy of access for him and can easily be controlled by him—there being no difficulty in making them come to his presence; and no judge could blame the male for their being with him. Consequently if the status of the woman with whom union is illicit were that of any *unmarried woman,* I mean to say that if it were possible and that the prohibition with regard to them were only due to their *not being the man's wives,* most people would have constantly succumbed and fornicated with them.[9]

I submit that Zuskind and Maimonides are correct, and I can bring support from the text itself. It should be noted that "uncover nakedness" occurs in every heterosexual prohibition but one—the last, adultery (18:20). There is only one possible reason: Since adultery means cohabiting with a married woman, "uncover nakedness" does not apply. Therefore, since the previous cases contain this expression, they are dealing with a woman who is no longer or has never been married. This conclusion is also deducible on purely logical grounds. The fact that the legist found it necessary to include a prohibition of adultery implies that all other prohibitions deal with cases where the woman is unmarried. Indeed, the expression "uncover nakedness" is apparently an organizing factor in this list, which explains why adultery, being without it, is found at the bottom of the list (v. 20).

Ziskind's and Maimonides' view is further supported by the sequence of incest prohibitions in chapter 20, where adultery precedes all others, implying that the following prohibitions focus on cases where the woman is again unmarried, namely, if she is divorced or widowed but still living in the family compound.

In essence, the purpose of this list is to protect the defenseless single woman from the male members of the resident males of her clan, especially the clan head, the paterfamilias.

C. Does the Bible Prohibit Homosexuality?

Of course it does (18:22; 20:13), but the prohibition is severely limited. First, it is addressed only to Israel, not to other nations. Second, compliance with this law is a condition for residing in the Holy Land, but is irrelevant outside it (see the closing exhortation, 18:24-30). Third, it is limited to men; lesbianism is not prohibited. Thus it is incorrect to apply this prohibition on a universal scale.

Moreover, as pointed out by my erstwhile student, Dr. David Stewart, both occurrences of the prohibition (18:22; 20:13) contain the phrase "as one lies with a woman" (lit. "lyings a woman"), an idiom used for only illicit heterosexual unions. Thus one could argue that carnal relations are forbidden only if their correlated

---

[9] *Guide* 3.49 (my italics).

heterosexual unions would be in these lists. For example, the Bible lists the following prohibited relations: nephew-aunt, grandfather-granddaughter, and stepmother-stepson. Thus, according to this theory, nephew-uncle, grandfather-grandson, and stepfather-stepson are also forbidden. This implies that the homosexual prohibition does not cover all male-male liaisons, but only those within the limited circle of family. However, homosexual relations with unrelated males are neither prohibited nor penalized. Admittedly, more than two occurrences of the phrase "as one lies with a woman" (Gen 49:4; Lev 20:13) are needed before accepting this argument as definitive.

As I mentioned above, in the entire list of forbidden sexual unions, there is no prohibition against lesbianism. Can it be that lesbianism did not exist in ancient times or that Scripture was unaware of its existence? Lesbianism existed and flourished, as attested in an old (pre-Israelite) Babylonian omen text[10] and in the work of the lesbian poet Sappho (born c. 612 BCE, during the time of the First Temple), who came from the island of Lesbos (hence "lesbian"). But, in the eyes of the Bible, there is a fundamental difference between the homosexual acts of men and women: in lesbianism there is no spilling of seed. Thus life is not symbolically lost, and it is for that reason, in my opinion, that lesbianism is not prohibited in the Bible.

Thus, from the Bible, we can infer the following: the female half of the world's homosexual population, lesbians, are not mentioned. Over ninety-nine percent of the remaining gays, namely non-Jews, are not addressed. This leaves the small number of Jewish gay men subject to this prohibition. To those who argue that the Bible enjoins homosexuality, a careful reading of the source text offers a fundamentally different view. While the Bible never applauds homosexuality, neither does it prohibit most people from engaging in it.

D. Molek Worship

Idolatrous worship is not enjoined in Leviticus, but Molek worship is, and with staccato emphasis. As will now be shown, Molek worship was egregiously sinful for multiple reasons. "Molek worship may be associated with ancestral worship, making it more understandable why these laws against Molek have been placed with other laws regarding intimate family matters."[11] As I will show (see chap. 20, THEME A), the assumption that Molek was an underworld deity associated with the worship of the dead can be validated. I will also show that ancestor worship was rife in ancient Israel (chap. 20, THEME C), particularly during the eighth century, the time of the composition of most of H, and that, plausibly, Molek was a vaunted instrument by which the departed ancestors could be consulted (hence the juxtaposition of necromancy with Molek, 20:1-6). What singles out Molek from all other necromantic mediums is his

---

[10] TCS 4, 194:XXIV 33'; Bottéro and Petschow 1975.
[11] Hartley 1992:336–37.

identification with YHWH, the God of Israel, as intimated by the motive clause attached to the Molek prohibition (v. 21b).

Finally, what makes Molek worship such an egregious crime is that it was practiced in God's land by the Canaanites, causing pollution and the expulsion of its inhabitants,[12] a fate that awaits Israel if it does the same (Lev 18:24-30).

In sum, H found it necessary to incorporate Molek into this chapter because it held that the violation of two prohibitions incumbent on and practiced by the Canaanites—Molek worship and illicit sexual unions—would also condemn Israel to destruction and exile.

Another question is: Why is Molek worship called a desecration of God's name, while the other prohibitions in chapter 18 (and in chap. 20; see v. 3) are not? To put the question differently: What is it about Molek worship that warranted this designation? The instance of the false oath (19:12) is illuminating. It involves using the name of God in a false oath—that is, making YHWH an accomplice in a crime—most likely, in offering false testimony in court. The tentative conclusion derived from the analogy is clear: the sin of Molek worship is egregious because the name of YHWH is associated with it.

Can this conclusion be substantiated? Three passages from Jeremiah can be marshaled for support:

> And they built the shrine [singular with LXX and Tg.] of Topheth, which is in the valley of Ben-hinnom, to burn their sons and daughters in the fire—which I did not command, and which did not come into my mind. (Jer 7:31)
>
> And they built the shrines of Baal to burn their sons in fire as burnt offerings to Baal—which I did not command, and did not decree, and which did not come into my mind. (Jer 19:5)
>
> They built the shrines of Baal that are in the valley of Ben-hinnom to offer up their sons and their daughters to Molek—which I did not command, and which did not come into my mind (that they should) do this abomination. (Jer 32:35a)

The explicit mention of Topheth, Hinnom, and Molek in Jer 7:31 and 32:35 ensures the identification of these two verses with the Molek cult. The occurrence of the phrase "which I did not command, and which did not come into my mind" in all three passages realizes the possibility that Jer 19:5 is also a reference to Molek worship. This possibility turns to probability in view of the following verse: "Assuredly a time is coming—declares YHWH—when *this place* shall no longer be called Topheth or valley of Ben-hinnom, but valley of Slaughter" (19:6; cf. 7:32). The reason that in the future Topheth will be called "valley of Slaughter" is explicated further on in the chapter: God will place Jerusalem under siege when "I will cause them to eat the flesh of their sons and the flesh of their daughters" (19:9). God punishes by the prin-

---

[12] A view also held by D; cf. Deut 18:9-12.

ciple of measure for measure. They who cause Molek to eat the flesh of their sons and daughters will now be compelled to do the same.

Thus there can be no doubt that the phrase "which I did not command, and which did not come into mind" can only mean that the Molek devotees harbored the belief that YHWH had acquiesced to, and even commanded, this worship, which Jeremiah vigorously and repeatedly repudiates.

The thesis must therefore be seriously considered that many Israelites saw no incongruity in worshiping YHWH and Molek simultaneously. This practice is clearly what Ezekiel had in mind when he condemns those who "on the very day that they slaughtered their children to their fetishes, they entered my sanctuary to desecrate it. That is what they did in my house" (Ezek 23:39). This interpretation is buttressed by another Ezekielian statement: "And you shall not desecrate my holy name with your gifts and your fetishes" (Ezek 20:39b). In this verse, the prophet declares explicitly that the syncretic practice of serving YHWH with gifts and at the same time worshiping idols constitutes a desecration of God's name! By the same token, then, the labeling of the Molek worship in Lev 18:21 as a desecration of God's name is due to the notion current in the popular mind that the worship of Molek is not incompatible with the worship of YHWH. In the popular mind, YHWH and Molek were distinct deities, governing distinct spheres—the world and the underworld, respectively (cf. Ps 6:6 [Eng. 5]; 88:11-13 [Eng. 10-12])—each making demands (human sacrifice for Molek), offering rewards (consultation with departed ancestors through Molek), and being worshiped at discrete sites (the Topheth in the valley of Ben-hinnom for Molek). Moreover, if the distinction between the worship of celestial and that of chthonic deities (on an altar versus in a trench) that prevailed in the Greek world also held in Israel, then even in official religious circles YHWH was a celestial deity (Gen 11:5, 7; Exod 19:11, 18, 20; 20:22; etc.), whose control did not extend into the underworld.[13] This incipient dualism is forcefully repudiated by H (and other monotheistic circles), which labels it a desecration of God's name.

The two postulated reactions to Molek worship are polaric and either compatible or incompatible with the worship of YHWH. Can this antimony be resolved? The answer I would suggest is that each view reflects a different circle of eighth- and seventh-century Judah. Those adhering to pure monotheism held that Molek and YHWH are incompatible (see above), but the people at large apparently believed that the two are bridgeable. Their position is not represented in Scripture, but it is ensconced in the popular pronunciation of Molek, which they pronounced with different vowels, as *melek*, "king." Whereas in priestly and prophetic circles Molek and YHWH were discrete deities, in the popular mind Molek was "the king" *appointed* by YHWH to rule the underworld. Molek held a status equivalent to that of other negative, malevolent

---

[13] Cf. Zevit 1996:57.

forces in the divine pantheon, such as "the Destroyer,"[14] the executioner of YHWH's death sentence, and "the Adversary,"[15] YHWH's prosecutor and persecutor of humanity. It should not be overlooked that these divine agents possessed some autonomy so that YHWH, in effect, had to defend Israel against the Destroyer's wanton force (Exod 12:23; see "a paschal offering," Lev 23:5) and to check the Adversary's desire and power to harm the human race (Zech 3:1-2; 1 Chr 21:1). It is this autonomy that Molek possesses *in his realm*. It is he whom his devotees beseech by child sacrifice, a crime compounded by being performed in YHWH's name, and which brings down the wrath of Israel's priests and prophets. Herein may lie the difference between Molek and the other malevolent forces. The latter are not worshiped; their demonic intent cannot be blunted by sacrifice. But Molek controls access to the ancestral spirits, and to attain his intervention, sacrifice—child sacrifice—is essential.

Thus both factors combine to create the enormity of the sin of Molek worship: ascribing to Molek the attributes of a deity who can demand child sacrifice, and, at the same time, averring that Molek is an agent of YHWH who carries out his will.

Selected Texts

Verses 2b-5. The Opening Exhortation

[18:2] The formula of God's self-identification is usually rendered as either "I am YHWH your God" or "I YHWH am your God." Both renderings presume that this formula is equivalent to God's self-declaration at the beginning of the Sinaitic covenant (Exod 20:2; Deut 5:6). Its import would therefore be that which was aptly expressed by the rabbis: "I am the one who said (at Sinai) 'I am YHWH your God' and you accepted my hegemony; henceforth, then accept my decrees."[16] The inclusion vv. 2a, 4b, 5b gives literary expression to the divine source of the laws. It states the reason why Israel must follow the specified commandments. In that sense, it is equivalent to the prophetic expression "the declaration of YHWH." Therefore, when two formulas are found at the end of a law pericope, they should be regarded as ellipses for "I YHWH your God (have spoken)" (v. 4b) and "I YHWH (have spoken)" (v. 5b).

[18:3] Egypt was reputed for its licentiousness (Ezek 16:26; 23:3, 20-21; see also Potiphar's wife [Gen 39:7-12], and Sarah in Pharaoh's harem [Gen 12:14-15]). That brother-sister marriage prevailed among Egyptian royalty was well known. It was even practiced by the patriarch Abraham.[17] Moreover, consanguineous marriages (father-daughter, brother-sister, aunt-nephew, uncle-niece, and others) prevailed in Egypt in every period, in nonroyal as well as royal cases.[18]

---

[14] Exod 12:23.

[15] Job 2:1.

[16] *Mek. Baḥodeš* par. 6; *Sipra*, addition.

[17] Gen 20:12; cf. Lev 18:9.

[18] As shown by Monkhouse 1989. See also, e.g., Breasted 1906:386–88, 390–91; Murray 1927:45–46; Černy 1954.

The sexual immorality of the Egyptians and the Canaanites is attributed to their ancestors Ham (Gen 9:22; the father of Egypt, 10:6) and his son Canaan (9:25). Indeed, since only the Canaanites are responsible for polluting the land and being expelled from it (Lev 18:24-25, 27) the purported sexual debauchery of the Egyptians has no function in chapter 18 except to allude to Ham's sin with Noah (but see below).

That Canaan was cursed (Gen 9:25) instead of his father Ham, the real perpetrator of the sexual crime against Noah (Gen 9:22), has been a conundrum that has vexed the ages. Now, however, a likely explanation is at hand. According to the pesher on Genesis published in 1992, 4Q252, col. 2,[19] Canaan was cursed instead of his father Ham (Gen 9:20-22), because the sons of Noah were blessed by God (Gen 9:1); thus Ham's curse was passed down to his son Canaan.[20]

It could therefore well be that the editor of the exhortatory envelope (Lev 18:1-5, 24-30) had the Noachian episode in mind. Canaan and Egypt (Ham's sons, Gen 10:6) lost their rights to the land of Canaan because their sexual immorality polluted the land, and the land vomited them out (Lev 18:25). Israel is therefore warned that it faces the same fate if it behaves similarly.

In addition, the priestly memory that the land of Canaan was once an Egyptian province (the borders of the promised land, Num 34:1-5 [P], correspond to those under New Kingdom Egypt)[21] may be responsible for the inclusion of Egypt in our verse.

Canaan was identified with homosexuality (Gen 9:20-26; 19:5-8) and bestiality.[22] But there is no extrabiblical evidence that the Canaanites were steeped in sexual immorality.[23] Where, then, did H get that idea?[24] Sexual depravity was a means of both stigmatizing an ancient enemy, the Canaanites, and sending a dire warning to Israel that it will suffer the same fate, expulsion from the land, if it follows the same practices. Alternatively, H may have exaggerated the sexual sins of the Egyptians and the Canaanites so that Israel would cut off all ties with them.[25]

[18:5] The fulfillment of these laws gives life. In other words, life is built into these laws. Not God but the laws give life to those who fulfill them. Thus disobeying these laws by engaging in foreign incest practices shortens or deprives life.[26]

---

[19] Wacholder and Abegg 1992:2.212–15; Eisenman and Wise 1992:86–89, as analyzed by Fröhlich 1994.

[20] Confirming R. Judah, *Gen. Rab.* 36:7.

[21] See B. Mazar 1954; de Vaux 1968.

[22] Van Selms 1954:81–82.

[23] Nussbaum 1974:34–89.

[24] See Nussbaum 1974:90–115.

[25] Schwartz 1999:225.

[26] R. Simeon, *m. Mak.* 3:15.

Leviticus 17–27: The Holiness Source (H)

Verses 6-23. Forbidden Sexual Relations

Carmichael observes that the incest rules of the Bible, and Leviticus 18 and 20 in particular, have left a greater impact on Western law than any comparable body of biblical rules.[27] For example, the Table of Levitical Decrees set out by the Church of England held sway until 1907.

The basic sociological unit in Israel was the "father's house." It included three to five generations consisting of fifty to a hundred people living in close proximity. Although the average Israelite house could accommodate four persons (father, mother, two children), the kin-related group, numbering about twenty persons, lived in close quarters, around a common courtyard.[28]

The prohibitions are listed in the following order:

1. Verses 6-11: your closest blood relations: mother (7), stepmother (8), the addressee's: half sister (9), granddaughter (10), stepsister (= sister, 11).

2. Verses 12-14: your parent's closest blood relations and affines: father's sister (12), mother's sister (13), father's brother's wife (14).

3. Verses 15-16: your relatives by marriage: daughter-in-law (15), brother's wife (16).

4. Verses 17-18: your wife's closest relatives: wife's daughter (17a), wife's granddaughter (17b), wife's sister (18).

5. Verses 19-23: unrelated: copulation with a menstruant (19), someone's wife (20), a male (22), an animal (23). Molek worship is placed among these copulation prohibitions (21).

The main distinction between these laws is that nos. 1-3 (vv. 6-16) concern relations between the addressee and a forbidden woman, whereas nos. 4 and 5 (vv. 17-23) focus not on the relations but on the act.[29]

H presumes that its shame rationales will fall on disciplined ears, a situation that can prevail only when the extended family is a cohesive, communal unit, an intimation that this list may stem from early or even premonarchic times. The power of a shame culture to control societal behavior is witnessed in modern Japan, where individual honesty and a low crime rate prevail. The series of shame rationales is a further indication that incest was prevalent and that the text had to appeal repeatedly to Israel's shame culture in order to win obedience.

The prohibitions can be divided into two groups: vv. 6-16 and 18-23; v. 17 is a transitional verse. The order in the first list is logical: mother, stepmother, sister, granddaughter, aunt (both), step-aunt (father's), daughter-in-law, sister-in-law.

---

[27] Carmichael 1997:1–3.
[28] Milgrom 1978; 1990:335–36; van der Toorn 1996b:204.
[29] Schwartz 1999:132; Hartley 1992.

[18:6] This verse serves as a heading for the list of the forbidden unions with kinswomen. It automatically implies, as Lev 21:2 specifies, that all close blood relatives absent from the list are also included.

"Approach" is a euphemism for sex. Here it means "encroach sexually." "Uncover nakedness" is another euphemism for "copulate."

It may seem puzzling that five of the listed prohibitions were blatantly violated in the narratives about Israel's founding fathers. Abraham's marriage to his half sister, Sarah (Gen 20:12), is forbidden in Lev 18:11 and punished by *karet* in 20:17. That such unions were the accepted practice is directly proved by Tamar's statement to her half brother, Amnon, that their father, King David, would not object to their marrying (2 Sam 13:13). Jacob's marriage to Rachel in the lifetime of her older sister, Leah (Genesis 29), is prohibited by Lev 18:18. Moses, Aaron, and Miriam were the offspring of a union between an aunt and her nephew (Exod 6:20) forbidden in Lev 18:12 and punishable in 20:19. Tamar is vindicated for having seduced her father-in-law, Judah (Gen 38:26), a liaison condemned in Lev 18:15 and punishable with death in 20:12. Judah admits his wrong in withholding his last surviving son from performing his levirate duty with Tamar (Gen 38:26), a union prohibited by Lev 18:16 and punished with *karet* in 20:21.

The answer to these incontrovertible contradictions rests with Ziskind, who concludes that H's laws of forbidden sexual unions constitute nothing less than a reform: "The priestly writer was not only compiling the rules relating to the purity of family life but was reforming them with the objective of improving the status of women within the framework of ancient Israel's patriarchal family structure."[30]

Since the blood relatives in this list (vv. 6-16) live in the family compound, they are under the authority and complete control of the addressee, the paterfamilias. The forbidden liaisons may be consensual, and, even if discovered, there will be no one to bring the paterfamilias to justice, except YHWH; and he will punish.

[18:7] "The nakedness of your father" is an interpolation by the H redactor[31] who thereby connected the exhortatory prelude (vv. 1-5), alluding to the homosexual crime of Ham (Egypt) and Canaan (Gen 9:22) regarding their father Noah, with the palpably older list of sexual prohibitions. This structural link, however, was not the redactor's only objective. This verse and equivalent statements in vv. 8, 12 (cf. vv. 10, 16) may also imply that a liaison with one's mother is tantamount to having sex with one's father—a taboo so deeply embedded in the Israelite (and universal) psyche that it requires no legislation.

[18:8] It is clear from the law codes that the violation of copulating with the stepmother was a major concern. It is punishable by death (20:11) and national

---

[30] 1988:104.
[31] Cf. Elliger 1966.

destruction (Deut 27:20; Ezek 22:10) and it is the only incest law mentioned in the prohibitions of Deuteronomy 23 (v. 1, a clear sign of its prevalence).[32] The matter is unclear whether the addressee's mother is alive. Clearly, there is no ban on polygamy (it may even be assumed in Lev 18:9, 11). That is, she need not be his stepmother, whom his father marries after his uterine mother dies. Indeed, it is a polygamous marriage that evokes a grown son's interest in a stepmother, for no blood relationship would be violated. This prohibition, then, would follow from the experience that such unions lead to disaster, as attested by the cases of Reuben (Gen 35:22; 49:4) and Adonijah (1 Kgs 2:13-25). Furthermore, this prohibition may also include concubines[33] in order to prevent a son from usurping his father's position (2 Sam 16:21-22; 1 Kgs 2:22; cf. 1 Sam 20:30; 2 Sam 12:8). "All these references indicate that such relations were a real possibility. This is probably due to the young age at which girls were married, which often resulted in a situation where a later wife of a man would be about the same age as his son by an earlier wife, if not younger."[34]

[18:9] The emphasis of this prohibition is on "outside clan": Even though your half sister belongs to another clan, she is your mother's daughter and therefore forbidden.

[18:11] Once she enters the father's family—even though her own father is of a different clan than your father, no matter how distant—she is your sister and prohibited to you. However, if she is of a different clan—there being no common blood—the implication is clear: she may marry you.[35]

[18:12] Normally, aunts would not reside with the family, which indicates that these incest laws applied to blood relations regardless of where they lived. Another factor may be the high status held by a paternal uncle (v. 14), which also extended to a paternal or maternal aunt (v. 13). It is perhaps no accident that although Saul was sent by his father to look for lost donkeys, he reported back to his uncle (1 Sam 10:14-16).

How did Moses feel when he learned through this law that he was a bastard? His mother Jochebed was his father Amram's aunt (Exod 6:20). For that matter, some of the patriarchs were also guilty of illicit unions: Abram married his half sister (Gen 20:12; cf. Lev 18:9), Jacob married two sisters (Genesis 29; cf. Lev 18:18), and Judah had sex with his daughter-in-law (Genesis 38; cf. Lev 18:15)—thereby bastardizing all their progeny, the people of Israel! Comparing the books of Exodus and Numbers helps resolve this paradox. Israel's murmuring against God before receiving the law at Sinai goes unpunished; after Sinai the same offenses are severely punished (com-

---

[32] See Driver 1895:259.

[33] Keil and Delitzsch 1956:2.414.

[34] Tigay 1996:209.

[35] Ehrlich 1908–14:2.82.

pare Exod 15:24-25 with Num 21:4-6; Exod 16:1-12 with Num 11:1-5, 31-34; Exod 16:22-27 with Num 15:32-36; Exod 17:1-7 with Num 20:1-13). Sinai is the watershed for Israel; its laws do not apply ex post facto.

[18:13] However, unions between uncles and nieces were permitted after Sinai—for example, Othniel and Achsah, daughter of Caleb, brother of Kenaz (Josh 15:17; Judg 1:13). Indeed, such marriages were considered meritorious by the rabbis,[36] perhaps because the affection a man has for his sister will be extended to her daughter.[37] Marriages between uncles and nieces were repeatedly and emphatically forbidden at Qumran[38] and by early Christians (Matt 14:4; Mark 6:18).

[18:18] This prohibition bans marriage to a sister-in-law during the lifetime of the wife.[39] This, the plain meaning of the words, is reinforced by the context: the women are related to each other (as in v. 17) and the prohibition is not permanent but time-conditioned (as in v. 19). Sororate marriage (after death) is known among the Assyrians and Hittites,[40] but forbidden during the wife's lifetime.[41] The rabbis regard such a union as meritorious: no other woman would show the same affection to the orphaned child of a deceased sister.[42] In other cultures as well, it is considered a preferred marriage.[43]

[18:20] This wording might imply that sexual relations with a widow or divorcee are forbidden.[44] Thus this prohibition must be time-conditioned: it is operative only as long as she is his wife. One should keep in mind that adultery does not apply to the extramarital relations of a married man with an unmarried woman. Since it was essential to be certain of the paternity of heirs, only the extramarital affairs of the wife concern the legislator.[45]

[18:21] The prohibition against offering child sacrifices to Molek adds a new rationale for eschewing Canaanite practices. The Canaanites were expelled from the land for polluting it not only by their sexual aberrations, but also by their Molek worship. A lopsided imbalance, however, is thereby created: one idolatrous practice over

---

[36] *b. Yeb.* 62b.
[37] Rashi.
[38] CD 5:8; 11QT 66:16-17; 4Q274, fr. 7:2-3, 4-5.
[39] Philo, *Spec. Laws* 3.27; *m. Qid.* 2:7.
[40] MAL A §31; HL §192.
[41] Inferred from HL §194.
[42] Hertz 1941:1.180.
[43] Murdock 1949:13, cited by Rattray 1987:539.
[44] Ehrlich 1899–1900 (H): 1.280.
[45] Cf. Abarbanel on Deut 24:1; Coulanges 1956:97.

against seventeen itemized sexual violations, which the redactor tried to rectify in chapter 20 by placing Molek prohibition first and expanding it over five verses.

Concerning the nature of Molek worship, its place among forbidden sexual practices, and its banning as a desecration of YHWH's name, see THEME D above.

There is no doubt that child sacrifice was practiced in the ancient world[46] (see chap. 20, THEME C). Especially impressive are the archaeological excavations in Phoenician colonies, particularly Carthage, that have unearthed special precincts in cemeteries containing hundreds of urns, dating as early as the eighth century BCE, that contain bones of children and animals (but no adults), many of which are buried beneath steles inscribed with dedications to gods.[47] Reliefs from about 500 BCE found at Pozo Moro, Spain, a site bearing Phoenician influence, show an open-mouthed, two-headed monster receiving offerings of children in bowls.[48]

Neither can there be any question that the practice of "burning babies" in pagan worship is attested in the Bible.[49] Particularly strong is the evidence of 2 Kgs 23:10: "He also defiled Topheth, which is in the valley of Ben-hinnom, so that no one might consign his son or daughter to the fire of Molek." All the identifying words are here: Topheth (cauldron, see below), Ben-hinnom (the site of the cult), "consign to fire" (burning), and Molek (the god). This cited verse, 2 Kgs 23:10, is embedded in a chapter that contains bona fide historical information. Moreover, the fact that the cultic practice described in this verse is attributed to Josiah's immediate predecessors, who did, indeed, sacrifice their children (2 Kgs 16:3; 21:6), lends weight to the identification of the other instances of sacrificing children with Molek worship (Deut 12:31; 18:10 [a legal passage!]).

Thus the evidence tilts toward the view that Lev 18:21 is expressly prohibiting the practice of sacrificing children to Molek.

[18:22] Sodomy is attested in all periods (e.g., Gen 19:5; Judg 19:22; Rom 1:27; 1 Cor 6:9; Gal 5:19; 1 Tim 1:10) and is most often reviled, if not proscribed. The sodomy or rape (Gen 19:5) of the Sodomites (hence its name) is a cause for their destruction.[50] The homosexual drive of the men of Gibeah,[51] protected by their tribe, Benjamin, leads to the tribe's proscription. (It can hardly be accidental that Gibeah is the city and the capital of King Saul. Whether historical or fictional, this story is an attempt to taint the Benjaminites, Saul's tribe, with a repulsive crime.)

---

[46] Ackerman 1992:117–26.

[47] Stager and Wolff 1984.

[48] Almagro-Gorbea 1980; Kennedy 1981.

[49] Deut 12:31bβ; 18:10; 2 Kgs 16:3b (= 2 Chr 28:3); 17:17a, 31; 21:6; 23:10; Isa 30:33; Jer 7:31; 19:5; Ezek 16:21; 20:31; 23:37; Ps 106:37-39.

[50] Milgrom 2000:1788–89.

[51] Judg 19:22.

Egyptian mythology relates that the god Seth had carnal relations with his younger brother Horus.[52] The Book of the Dead (§125) includes the confession: "I have not copulated with a boy"; however, an adult consenting man is omitted. The Hittites declare sodomy with one's son—but not with any other male—a capital crime.[53] Thus sodomy (like heterosexuality) is subject to regulation, but not to interdiction.

Therefore the difference between the biblical legislation and other Near Eastern laws must not be overlooked. The Bible allows for no exceptions: all acts of sodomy are prohibited, whether performed by rich or poor, higher or lower status, citizen or alien.

The common denominator of all the prohibitions, I submit, is that they involve the emission of semen for the purpose of copulation, resulting in either incest and illicit progeny or, as in this case, lack of progeny (or its destruction in the case of Molek worship, v. 21). In a word, the theme (with Ramban) is procreation. This rationale fully complements (and presupposes) P's laws of 15:15-18. Semen emission per se is not forbidden; it just defiles, but purificatory rites must follow. In certain cases of sexual congress, however, it is strictly forbidden, and severe consequences must follow.

Indeed, the assumption that H is fully cognizant of P throws light on the question: Why is masturbation—the willful spilling of seed—not proscribed? First, we must recognize that the ancients did not condemn masturbation. What Hippocrates considered harmful is not masturbation, but excessive expenditure of semen.[54] In Israel, moreover, the spilling of seed, by itself, is not the issue. As illustrated by the story of Onan, sin occurs if seed is deliberately spilled during coitus (Gen 38:9-10). Indeed, all the cases cited in our chapter refer to illicit intercourse. But the ejaculation of semen results in only a one-day impurity that requires laundering and bathing (Lev 15:16-18), regardless of whether the act takes place during legitimate intercourse, or by the self, deliberately (masturbation) or accidentally (nocturnal emission).

An ancillary question concerns birth control. May a married couple practice coitus interruptus? The example of Onan (Gen 38:8-10) is irrelevant. His act is condemned because he refused to act as the levir and thus denied an heir to his deceased brother. Analogous to the case of masturbation, the silence of our text would permit the inference that birth control was not prohibited as long as the couple had reproduced. This, indeed, is the opinion of the tannaitic rabbis: two males according to R. Shammai (on the basis of Moses' two sons, 1 Chr 23:15), and one male and one female according to R. Hillel (Gen 1:27b-28a).[55]

---

[52] Westerndorf 1972:2.1272–73.

[53] HL §189.

[54] Marcus and Francis 1975:384.

[55] *m. Yeb.* 6:6; *t. Yeb.* 8:4.

If the rationale of procreation proves correct, I would have to presume that Israel's priests might have frowned on sexual congress during the certified pregnancy, but they would not have forbidden it; their prohibitions focused on illicit intercourse. They would, however, have had only a positive attitude concerning sexual relations after the onset of menopause. They would have held up the example of Abraham and Sarah, as passed down by tradition, who by the grace of God were blessed with a child despite their advanced age (Gen 18:9-13). Similarly, as I have argued (see 12:4), with the rabbis (versus the sectarians), the priests would have permitted the parturient to reengage sexual union with her husband, despite her lochial, after the initial seven or fourteen days of severe impurity had passed.

Female sexual relations are nowhere prohibited in Scripture, nor anywhere else (to my knowledge) in the ancient Near East. Surely, lesbianism was known. Hebrew Scriptures ignored it (contrast Rom 1:26) because in the act no genital fluids are lost.[56]

Verses 24-30. Closing Exhortation

The violation of prohibitions listed in chapter 18 leads to banishment from the land (see also 20:22-23). The rationale is that the land becomes polluted and vomits out its inhabitants. This ecological theology is not the innovation of H. It is already adumbrated in the punishment for the first human sin: "Cursed be the ground because of you" (Gen 3:17). As pointedly observed by R. Meir, "Three entered to be judged at the beginning of creation and four emerged condemned. Adam, Eve, and the serpent entered to be judged and the earth was cursed because of them."[57] Not by accident, I submit, is sex the first couple's sin: they engaged in it, defying God's prohibition. This is the probable meaning of the "good and evil" (see chap. 17, THEME B). Neither, I submit, is it accidental that the flood is triggered by an egregious sexual crime (Gen 6:1-4). To be sure, the earth is polluted (Gen 6:11, 13), probably by an accumulation of violent crimes committed by the offspring of divine and human beings, a boundary-crossing cohabitation that pinpoints this act as the immediate cause of the flood. But I must reserve this subject for separate treatment. In any event, that sexual violations can pollute the land is found in Deuteronomy (24:1-4) and the prophets (Jer 3:1-10). But only here, in H, are they itemized, categorized, and penalized (cf. Lev 20:10-21).

That human sin pollutes the land is an axiom that pervades all of Scripture.[58] But nowhere is it so clearly stated as here that exile is the automatic, built-in punishment for land pollution.

---

[56] Cf. Pope 1976:417.

[57] *Abot R. Nat.* B, chap. 42, p. 116.

[58] E.g., Gen 4:12; 8:21; Lev 26:34-35, 43 (presumed); Num 35:33-34; Deut 2:23; 24:4; Isa 24:5-6; Jer 3:2; Ezek 36:17; Ezra 9:11; cf. Frymer-Kensky 1979:223.

The verb "defile" therefore must be understood in a real but noncultic sense.[59] Supporting this view is the fact that H never calls the land "holy." As a priestly source, which held that the contact between "holy" and "impure" is dangerous and at times fatal (see 22:3), H had no choice but to avoid any reference to the land as holy. Indeed, the concept of "holy land" is totally absent from the Hebrew Bible (even though it is implied; see on 25:23) and does not surface until the Apocrypha (2 Macc 1:7) and Philo (*Spec. Laws* 4.215).[60] Indeed, as a matter of principle, H rejects the notion of innate holiness in nature. This perhaps also explains why H never designates God's land as holy (for other reasons see below on Lev 25:23).

Ritual impurity always allows for purification and atonement. But the sexual abominations of Leviticus 18 (and 20) are not expiable through ritual. There is but one solution; the land must disgorge its inhabitants: "Land was rendered unfit for habitation *by them*, not permanently polluted (land waste) but polluted remediably in that it was cleansed of them."[61] The violation of the Sabbaths (both weekly and septennial) also lead to exile, but in this case a healing period is specified: the time the land was worked on the Sabbath is prescribed for its rest (26:34-35).[62] No period, however, is set for the pollution limits of the land. God alone keeps the reckoning: "And they shall return in the fourth generation, for the iniquity of the Amorites is not yet complete" (Gen 15:16).

Murder also allows for atonement—the death of the murderer(s) (Num 35:33). Otherwise, destruction and exile are once again the consequence (see Ezek 24:6-14). The punishment decreed upon Cain, wandering, and his ultimate settlement in the land of the "wanderer" (Gen 4:16), is, in reality, not exceptional. His homicide is declared involuntary, for he knew not the consequence of his act,[63] and his punishment is codified in the prescribed exile to the asylum city for the involuntary homicide (Num 35:22-28).

In sum, ritual purity (P) is always subject to ritual purification, but no ritual remedy exists for moral impurity (H). Indeed, the sinner cannot expunge moral impurity. It is a capital crime. If committed by the individual, it is punished by God with *karet* (e.g., sexual offenses, Lev 18:29) whenever humans overlook or neglect it (e.g., Molek worship, 20:1-5). If, however, the entire community is guilty of moral impurity, the irrevocable result is the pollution of the land (18:25; Num 34:3-34) and the exile of its inhabitants (Lev 18:28; 26:14-38). These radically differing concepts of "impurity" are one of the terminological hallmarks that distinguish H from P.

---

[59] Cf. Wright 1991:162–63; see "defiled themselves," v. 24.

[60] As Weinfeld 1993:203 pointed out, the term *ʾadmat haqqodeš* (Zech 2:15) refers to the land around the temple.

[61] Goodman 1986:26.

[62] Cf. *Abot R. Nat.* A, chap. 38, p. 115.

[63] *Gen. Rab.* 22:26.

Leviticus 17–27: The Holiness Source (H)

Concerning the expulsion of the Canaanites, H expresses itself once again in Num 33:50-56. As pointed out by Schwartz,[64] this passage agrees with the earlier epic tradition (JE) that the Canaanite cultic objects must be destroyed and the Canaanites themselves must be forcibly expelled by Israel and/or by God (cf. Exod 23:24-33; 34:11-13). Our pericope, however, presents a different view: Just as the Canaanites were not ejected by the Israelites, but beforehand by the action of the land, so Israel will not be ejected by some outside invading force, but by the automatic regurgitation by the land of the pollution inflicted on it by sinful Israel. This implies that Israel would be forced to leave because the consequent sterility of the land would no longer yield any produce. This notion, adumbrated in the first homicide (Gen 4:11-12) and developed by the Holiness tradents for all subsequent homicides (Num 35:33-34), is fully exposited in H's blessings and curses (Lev 26:3-5, 10, 19-20). Here, however, the pollution of the land is not caused by homicide (Numbers 35) or by Israel's neglect to drive out the Canaanites (Numbers 33) or by the adoption of Canaanite cultic practices (Exodus 21, 34) but by its sexual aberrations (and Molek worship).

Leviticus 26 modifies H's metaphysical hypostatization of the land as the agent of Israel's expulsion (chaps. 18 and 20) by adopting a position closer to Numbers 33. The process is initially begun by natural causes blighting the land's fertility (Lev 26:16-22), leaving the coup de grace to the human enemy (vv. 25-32). Even at this point, Israel's woes are not at an end. YHWH is portrayed graphically as pursuing Israel in exile, breaking its ethnic cohesion by scattering the people (v. 33a) and its psychological stability by destroying their morale (vv. 36-37) until they rot (v. 39).

In effect, Leviticus 18 (20) adheres to P's conceptual explanation of Israel's expulsion by its image of impurity "forcing" YHWH to abandon the sanctuary, but it transfers the barometer of Israel's moral and spiritual status from the sanctuary to the land. But in contrast to P's imagery, which pictures the sanctuary as evicting its resident, YHWH, Leviticus 18 images the land as evicting its resident, Israel (and previously the Canaanites). Both Leviticus 26 and Numbers 33, however, realistically attribute the expulsion to human agency. Numbers 33 is closer to the older narratives in that it too lays down one condition for Israel's residence in the land—the expulsion of the Canaanites. Leviticus 26 is rooted more in actual historical experience—the destruction and exile of north Israel. But the entire scenario, as in Numbers 33 (see v. 56) is directed by YHWH.

[18:24] The use of the term "impurity" in H constitutes a radical departure from its usage in P. No ritual, be it bathing or sacrifice (P's purification technique), can expunge the pollution of the land (v. 25). The violator is punished with *karet* (v. 29), and the community with exile (v. 28). H, however, is not negating P. Each source

---

[64] Schwartz 1999:232.

speaks of a different kind of impurity: in P it is concrete, cultic—ritual impurity; in H it is abstract, inexpungible—moral impurity.

One should not, hence, conclude that H's impurity is only metaphoric. It is just as real and potent as P's impurity. It is engendered by wide-ranging violations that, in effect, are congruent with all the divine prohibitions. This is also true for P. Its effect, however, is more devastating. It leads not only to the pollution of the temple (20:3) but explicitly, as emphasized in this pericope, to exile from the land. Moreover, H's impurity is nonexpiable. Perhaps it is analogous to the final stage in the pollution of the sanctuary, according to P. Once the impurity has accumulated to a sufficient degree, the consequence is inevitable and irreversible. God abandons his sanctuary (in H's theology, God's land is his sanctuary; see 25:23) and his people, unprotected and vulnerable, are subject to invasion and exile.

There is no doubt that according to Leviticus 18 and 20, Israel will not wage a war of conquest. Both the metaphors of the land spewing out its inhabitants and, explicitly in the verse, that YHWH himself will drive out the Canaanites "from before you" imply that Israel will meet no resistance upon entering the land.

[18:25] It can hardly go unnoticed that H's doctrine of land corresponds with P's doctrine of the sanctuary. Both function as the *Picture of Dorian Gray:* as Israel's evil, ostensibly unpunished, continues to mar that face of God's sanctuary, so does the (sexual) evil of the inhabitants of God's land mar the face of the land.[65] In either case, purgation must take place by either ritual (P) or exile (H).

[18:28] Note that H consistently refrains from calling the land holy. The reason, I submit, is that H is a priestly document. If the land were a sanctum (*qodeš*, "holy") then ritual impurity—menstruation, for example—would automatically defile the land, mandating Israel's expulsion.

[18:29] How much pollution can the land tolerate before it vomits out its residents? How many violations are required before they cause the exile of the nation? The text is silent. Perhaps H is following P's model of the pollution of the sanctuary. Just as one can presume that YHWH tolerates a low level of pollution in the sanctuary as long as it is purged by the purification offerings of the inadvertent wrongdoers (Leviticus 4) and advertent miscreants (by the high priest, Leviticus 16), but will abandon the sanctuary (and the nation) if the pollution level of the sanctuary reaches a point of no return, so the progressive pollution of the land ultimately leads to its regurgitation of the pollution together with its inhabitants. H, then, has merely borrowed P's theology of the sanctuary and applied it to the land.

---

[65] See Milgrom 1991:258–61.

Ritual and Moral Holiness;
Ethics

"You shall be holy, for I, YHWH your God, am holy." Thus opens chapter 19, direct-
ing the people of Israel to model themselves after their God and to aspire to holiness.
But what does it mean to imitate a deity in holiness? The rest of the chapter sets the
people of Israel on the road to holiness. Unlike all the other priestly pericopes (in
both P and H), which expound a unified theme, this chapter comprises a miscellany
of laws (ritual and ethical, apodictic, and casuistic, directed to the individual and to
the collective).[1] Its guidelines, ranging from the mundane to the profound, the
obscure to the prosaic, spoke powerfully to the ancient Israelite, enabling the common citizen to achieve the holiness that had hitherto been limited to the priests. Similarly, the directives speak powerfully to us as we wonder how to make our own lives
unique and meaningful.

"Respect your mother and father. Make one day every week separate from the
others and sanctify it with your rest. When you reap your harvest, always leave a seg-
ment for the poor and the lonely. Deal honestly with all those you encounter. Pay people their wages before they go home at night, so they should not want for money or
food. Judge others fairly and love your neighbor as yourself. Remember that you
were a stranger in the land of Egypt and treat the stranger as a citizen."

I follow Schwartz, who divides the chapter into eighteen units flanked by a
heading and a closing;[2] each one, I shall demonstrate (see THEME A), is subsumed
under the inscription "You shall be holy" (v. 2aβ, b):

1. The heading (v. 2aβ, b)

2. Unit 1 (v. 3)	6. Unit 5 (vv. 11-12)
3. Unit 2 (v. 4)	7. Unit 6 (vv. 13-14)
4. Unit 3 (vv. 5-8)	8. Unit 7 (vv. 15-16)
5. Unit 4 (vv. 9-10)	9. Unit 8 (vv. 17-18)

---

[1] See Schwartz 1999.
[2] 1999:241–49.

10. Unit 9 (v. 19)	15. Unit 14 (v. 30)
11. Unit 10 (vv. 20-22)	16. Unit 15 (v. 31)
12. Unit 11 (vv. 23-25)	17. Unit 16 (vv. 32)
13. Unit 12 (vv. 26-28)	18. Unit 17 (vv. 33-34)
14. Unit 13 (v. 29)	19. Unit 18 (vv. 35-36)

20. The closing (v. 37)

Each of these eighteen units can be regarded as Israel's directives for achieving holiness. Since, as I will show, these units comprise ethical as well as ritual commandments—indeed, more of the former (units 1*, 4-8, 13, 16-18) than of the latter (units 1*-3, 9-12, 14-15)—we are given a glimpse of the revolutionary step taken by H: H proclaims that holiness, hitherto limited by P to the sacred sphere (the sanctuary) and its officiants (the priests), is now within the reach of every Israelite provided that he or she heeds cultic prohibitions and fulfills the ethical requirements specified in this chapter (see THEME A).

Selected Themes

A. On Being Holy: Part III (continued from chaps. 17–27, Theme A)

The call to holiness is found only in chapters 19–22 (19:2; 20:7, 8, 21; 21:16, 23; 22:16, 32) and in two other H passages (11:44-45; Num 15:40) at the beginning or the end of units. The peroration "I YHWH" is found eighteen times in this chapter and is sprinkled liberally throughout chapters 18–26. The laws incorporated into chapter 19 were chosen for their aptness to be subsumed under the rubric of holiness or its negation, impurity and desecration.

Leviticus 19 provides the prescription to effect a transformation to holiness. Under the call to holiness (v. 2), chapter 19 enumerates sixteen units (with two amendments) containing commandments by which holiness can be achieved.

The first two units echo the Decalogue. The Sabbath (v. 3b) must be sanctified (Exod 20:8-11; Deut 5:12-15), and parents must be honored and revered (v. 3a; Exod 20:12; Deut 5:16). The worship of other gods or of images of Israel's God (v. 4) is strictly forbidden (Exod 20:3-6; Deut 5:7-10). Obedience to the covenantal Decalogue renders Israel "a holy nation" (Exod 19:6).

Unit 3, the well-being offering (vv. 5-8), expressly mentions the terms "sacred" and its violation "desecrate" (v. 8). Unit 4, horticultural holiness (vv. 9-10), lacks these terms, but its inclusion under the call to holiness is significant. The emulation of God's holiness, *imitatio Dei,* must include practicing God's concern for the indigent. Also setting aside part of the harvest might be equivalent to firstfruits and tithes; thereby, symbolically, YHWH has assigned some of his due to the poor.

Unit 5, ethical deeds (vv. 11-13), includes oath desecration (v.12), implying the concomitant diminution in holiness. The remainder of this ethical series (vv. 14-18) includes unit 6, exploitation of the helpless (v. 14); unit 7, injustice and indifference (vv. 15-16); and unit 8, reproof and love (vv. 17-18), all of which emphasize the divine attribute of compassion, essential to God's holy nature. The rabbis neatly encapsulated it: "As he [YHWH] is gracious and compassionate (cf. Exod 34:6), so you should be gracious and compassionate."[3] "As he clothes the naked (Gen 3:21), you should clothe the naked; as he nurses the sick (Gen 18:1), you should nurse the sick; as he comforts the mourners (Gen 25:11), you should comfort the mourners; as he buries the dead (Deut 34:5), so you should bury the dead."[4]

Unit 9, mixtures (v. 19), proscribes the breeding of different animals, sowing mixed seed, and weaving fabrics made from mixed seed because these mixtures are reserved for the sacred sphere, the sanctuary and the priests. Unit 10, the betrothed slave woman (vv. 20-22), involves a reparation offering prescribed in cases of desecration (5:14-16). Unit 11, horticultural holiness (vv. 23-25), focuses on the fruit of the fourth year, which is declared "sacred" and belongs to YHWH (v. 24). Unit 12, eschewing the chief form of impurity, death and the dead (vv. 26-28), is essential in emulating the God of holiness, because holiness is inextricably linked to our pursuit of life. Unit 13, prostitution (v. 29), is a form of desecration (cf. 22:7, 9). Units 14-16, Sabbath and sanctuary (also 26:2), consulting the dead (also 20:1-17), and respecting elders (vv. 30-32), parallel the opening verses (vv. 3-4) and hence reecho the Decalogue, the basic prescription for holiness. Units 17-18, the resident alien and business ethics (vv. 33-37), are appendices.

To recapitulate, in Leviticus 19 H in effect writes a new "Decalogue." YHWH's self-declaration becomes a call to holiness, followed by a series of commandments (addressing the most pressing problems in H's time; see below) by which holiness may be achieved.

The basic text of Leviticus 19 (vv. 1-32) and, indeed, the bulk of H reflect the priestly response to the indictment by the prophets of the eighth century BCE (especially by Isaiah of Jerusalem) of Israel's cultic and socioeconomic sins. Isaiah's revelation of the thrice-repeated declaration of YHWH's holy nature (Isa 6:3), to judge by the prophet's reaction (v. 5), indicates to him that the divine imperative for Israel is to be ethical: "YHWH of hosts shall be exalted by his judgment and the holy God shall be shown holy by his righteousness" (5:16), a statement that is both a prediction of doom upon unrighteous Israel (vv. 24-30)[5] and an indictment of the moral failings of Israel's corrupt judicial leaders, who blur the distinction between right and wrong (v. 20) and pervert justice for the sake of bribes (v. 23). Isaiah's indictment of the leadership includes the prophet *and the priest* (28:7), but it is especially directed against the civil leaders (3:14) and the rich (5:8), who rob the poor and seize their land. That is, for Isaiah the Trisagion implies that YHWH, who governs his world by justice, expects Israel to do the same in its domain. In Isaiah's gloomy forecast, only

---

[3] *Mek. Šira* par. 3; *b. Šabb.* 133b.

[4] *b. Soṭ.* 14a.

[5] See Milgrom 1964:167–72.

those who do not participate in these social evils will survive the forthcoming purge, and these few—provided they truly repent—will be called "holy" and will be admitted into the new Zion (4:3).[6]

The text of H testifies that its priestly authors have been stung by their fellow Jerusalemites' rebuke. Their response is twofold. First, they adopt Isaiah's revelation that YHWH's holiness implies that Israel must be ethical. Then they go beyond Isaiah by prescribing specific commandments (Leviticus 19) by which holiness can be attained and by prescribing a revolutionary program that will reverse the extant socioeconomic wrongs (Leviticus 25). Finally, H takes issue with Isaiah's pessimism concerning Israel's inability to repent. (Note that after pronouncing Israel's irrevocable doom in chap. 6, Isaiah never again calls on his people to repent.)[7] In Leviticus 19 H brims with hope that all Israel will heed the divine call to holiness. Hence there is no reason to anticipate a purge of the nation.

B. H and Ethics

The bonding of ethics and ritual is not unique to Israel. It abounds in Mesopotamia—for example, Šurpu tablet II;[8] the Bilingual Hymn to Nanurta, II.3-7;[9] the Nanshe Hymn, 136-71[10]—and is exemplified in Egypt's sacral sphere by an inscription on a door of the temple of Edfu.[11] Unique to Israel, rather to H, though, is the subsumption of rituals *and ethics* under the rubric of holiness. All the pentateuchal codes raise the issue of holiness. Here H takes a giant step forward. Other codes restrict holiness to ritual commandments (abstention from Sabbath labor: Exod 20:8-11 [JE]; Deut 5:12-15 [D]; eating carcasses, Exod 22:30 [JE]; Deut 14:21 [D]; idolatry and mourning rites, Deut 7:5-6 and 14:1-2 [D]), whereas H lists ethical prescriptions alongside rituals as determinants of holiness. H also differs from the prophets, but in the other direction. The prophets rank ethics as supreme. YHWH's holiness is characterized mainly by ethics: "YHWH of hosts is exalted by justice and the holy God is shown holy by his righteousness" (Isa 5:16). Indeed, for some of the prophets, Israel's national destiny is determined exclusively by its ethical behavior.[12] H, however, insists on the equal and inseparable role of ritual in the prescription for the holy life. Possibly, the fourth and fifth commandments of the Decalogue (Sabbath and parents) were chosen to head the list of prescriptions of holiness (Lev 19:3), even ahead of the first and second commandments (19:4), in order to illustrate from the start that ethics (respect for parents) and ritual (Sabbath observance) are of equal importance.

---

[6] See ibid.
[7] See ibid.
[8] Reiner 1958.
[9] Lambert 1960:119.
[10] Heimpel 1981:90–93.
[11] Weinfeld 1982:233–35.
[12] Kaufmann 1937–56:3.76–79; 1960:365–67.

Leviticus 17–27: The Holiness Source (H)

H's concern for the underprivileged and helpless is illustrated not only by its numerous citations of them, but also by its formulaic and lexical expressions. A number of examples should suffice. The closure of nearly every prescription in chapter 19 is "I YHWH your God (have spoken)." This formula is explicitly defined at the opening of the chapter by the declaration "I YHWH your God am holy" (v. 2). Hence anyone who disobeys YHWH's injunctions concerning the care of the underprivileged and the alien is desecrating YHWH's holiness. Similarly, chapter 25 resorts to this formula to close its major units (vv. 17, 38, 55) and uses exhortative admonitions as an inclusion: "do not cheat/oppress" (vv. 14, 17); "do not rule over him with harshness" (vv. 43a, 46bß). Both chapters also utilize the closing formula "you shall fear your God" (19:14, 32; 25:17, 36, 43). It is no accident that this formula is attached to those prescriptions involving the handicapped and the most vulnerable (the deaf and blind, elders, indentured servants). Their case cannot be adjudicated in a human court, but YHWH has witnessed the exploitation *and will prosecute.*

H also has a penchant for generalizations (in contrast to P). Thus the injunction "do not curse a deaf person, and before a blind person do not place a stumbling block" (v. 14) cannot be taken literally; rather, "deaf" and "blind" are metonyms for all the helpless, and "curse" and "stumbling block" stand for abuse and harm, respectively. The full importance of this injunction is that, though the deaf do not know who insulted them, or the blind who hurt them, God knows and he will punish accordingly. In contrast to the codes of the ancient Near East, in which only verifiable injury or loss is adjudicable, Israel's law has moved beyond them to ethical laws under the surveillance of a caring God.[13]

To be sure, concern for the underprivileged—the poor, the widow, the orphan, and the alien—is consistently reiterated throughout Scripture (Exod 22:20-23 [Eng. 21-24]; Lev 19:9-10, 13, 33-34; Deut 15:18-19; 24:14, 17; 27:15; Jer 7:6; 22:3; Zech 7:10). The prophets repeatedly rail against their neglect and exploitation (Isa 1:17, 23; 3:14-15; 10:2; Jer 5:8; Ezek 16:49; 18:17; 22:7, 29; Amos 8:4; Mal 3:5; cf. Ps 82:3; 94:6). H differs from them in going beyond outcries and implorations. It legislates concrete measures in order to prevent their impoverishment (see the Jubilee laws, chap. 25).

Ostensibly, H has no concern for the needy persons listed above, since they are not mentioned in H, except for a single law affirming the indigent's rights to the "leftovers" of the harvest (19:9-10; repeated in 23:22). But one must bear in mind that H discards empty implorations and focuses on concrete efficacious measures. Moreover, H is mainly the product of the eighth century BCE, when family ties were strong and the patriarchal structure was still in place. The widow and the orphan would be the charge of the nearest relative of the deceased (see Ruth 3:13; 4:4). The alien would be the responsibility of the owner of the land on which he resided (Lev 25:6),

---

[13] D. Steward (orally).

and the Levites would be mostly employed in the flourishing regional sanctuaries throughout the land.

The eighth century BCE was characterized by national prosperity, which brought in its wake urbanization, latifundia (the rich swallowing up the land of the poor), and other social injustices decried by the prophets (cited above) and solved (in theory) by the priestly H (see the Jubilee laws, chap. 25). In the main, however, every poor Judahite belonged to some household, or, if that was wanting, to a kin group. The situation changed rapidly for the worse when Judah was inundated by hordes of landless, destitute northern refugees (following the fall of northern Israel), among whom the widow, orphan, alien, and Levite abounded.

The paucity of references to the poor in H (a single verse and its copy, 19:10; 23:22) should not be misjudged. On the one hand despite D's plethora of references to gifts from the produce for the orphan and the widow, namely, of tithes (Deut 14:29; 26:12, 13), of the harvest (24:19-21), and of the Festivals of Weeks and Booths (16:11, 14), the poor are excluded from these gifts. Instead, Israel is exhorted to grant the poor interest-free loans (15:7-11; 23:20-21; 24:10-13; cf. Exod 22:24-26 [JE]), the assumption being that the poor can work off their debts but the orphan and widow cannot. H, on the other hand, does not discriminate between these groups. As long as they are poor, they are entitled to glean from the crops; they need not depend on the unpredictable beneficence of the rich.[14]

The refinement and sensitivity of H's concerns toward the helpless can be illustrated by the following examples:

1. "You shall not stand aloof by the blood of your fellow" (Lev 19:16b). If this rendering is correct, then one is not permitted to remain on the sidelines of one's endangered fellow. The rabbis correctly infer: "If one sees someone drowning, mauled by beasts, or attacked by robbers, one is obligated to save him, but not at the risk of one's life."[15] In H's court, the "silent majority" would be guilty (see also chap. 4, THEME A).

Not surprisingly—though I was surprised when I realized it—a similar ethical law derives from P's concept of sin: the *inadvertent* sinner also pollutes the sanctuary and must "repair" the damage by an appropriate purification offering.[16] Nonetheless, it should be clear that H has raised the culpability to unparalleled heights. It includes not only unintentionality but also passivity, a nonexistent legal category, as far as I can tell, in world jurisprudence, both late and modern.

2. The structured sequence in Lev 19:17-18 clearly addresses the needs of the helpless. It is spelled out in the text and repeated here for convenience:

---

[14] But see my reservations, Milgrom 2000:1437.

[15] *b. Sanh.* 73a.

[16] Milgrom 1991:254–61.

19:17

Prohibition:	You shall not hate your kinsperson in your heart;
Remedy:	reprove your fellow openly,
Rationale:	so that you will not bear punishment because of him.

19:18

Prohibition:	You shall not take revenge or nurse a grudge against members of your people.
Remedy:	(Rather) you shall love your fellow as yourself.
Rationale:	I YHWH (have spoken).

These two verses form parallel panels[17] that may aid in discerning the intent of the author. For example, the remedy for taking revenge and nursing a grudge is extending love (for the meaning of love, see below). The ethical emphasis here is on thought, the perils of which were sensitively apprehended by the rabbis who declared that "causeless hatred" was responsible for the destruction of the Second Temple.[18]

3. The verb "love" (19:18) signifies not only an emotion or attitude, but also deeds. Such is its meaning in suzerainty treaties (i.e., the pact between a suzerain and his or her subject state)[19] and elsewhere. The medieval exegetes come to the same conclusion by noting that the Hebrew word for "love" takes the preposition *le*, which they render as "for," that is, "do good as you would do for yourself." Indeed, all four attestations of "love" with the preposition *le* (19:18, 34; 1 Kgs 5:15; 2 Chr 19:2) imply doing, not feeling.[20] This, arguably, is the ethical summit not only in this chapter but in all of Scripture.[21]

4. The theological innovation of H's law of redemption is that YHWH is the ultimate redeemer (25:24). If indebtedness causes the sale of any of YHWH's land, the nearest kinsperson is obligated to redeem it and return it to the owner. He may retain it only to cover his costs, but by the unilateral decree of the divine owner, he must return it to the human owner at the Jubilee. Though the redeemer is a member of the same clan, he cannot retain it. Here H has broken with the hoary institution of clan ownership of property (cf. Jeremiah 32). Henceforth, the concern of the law is to guarantee property rights for the individual.

5. "Do not charge the Israelite debtor interest as if he were a resident alien" (Lev 25:35). This constitutes a reversal of antichresis (confiscating usufruct in lieu of

---

[17] Schwartz 1999:317–21.
[18] *b. Yoma* 9b.
[19] Moran 1962.
[20] Malamat 1990.
[21] Cf. Milgrom 2000:1656.

interest) prevalent elsewhere. In this way, whatever the debtor earns amortizes the principal in addition to supporting his family. If his destitution forces him to become an indentured servant, his status is that of a hireling, not that of a slave. He may not be treated "harshly" (25:43, 46b). Implied is that if he finds the creditor's conditions too severe or the wages too low, he can seek another employer. Again, his work amortizes the principal, pays off the loan, and retrieves his land so he can make a fresh start. If he does not succeed on his own, the safety net of the Jubilee awaits him (or his heirs). The institution of slavery is totally abolished for the Israelite. This constitutes a practical advantage over the slave laws of Exodus 21 (JE) and Deuteronomy 12 (D). The latter legislation does not provide him with resources, there is no indication that his land is returned to him, and the probability is strong that it will not be long before he is indentured once again.

Selected Texts
Verses 1-2. Opening: Call to Holiness

[19:2] This unique heading in Leviticus provides one of the reasons why its author(s) wished to communicate the notion that this chapter is central to the entire book. The rabbis stress this fact: "Holiness (chap. 19) was not only given to priests but to priests, Levites, and Israelites";[22] this chapter was recited to the entire Israelite community "because most of the commandments are derivable from it,"[23] because the Decalogue is contained in it.[24]

The rabbis interpret Lev 19:2[25] by stating that "Israel's behavior is different from that of other nations"[26] and by connecting this verse with the preceding chapter 18, namely, "from illicit sexual unions."[27] When we scan the contents of this chapter, although most of the commandments are negative (about thirty), many are positive (about fourteen). Thus holiness implies not only separation from but separation to, and since YHWH is the standard by which all holiness is measured, the doctrine of *imitatio Dei* takes on wider dimensions: "It is comparable to the court of a king. What is the court's duty? To imitate the king!"[28] "As YHWH is gracious and compassionate (Exod 34:6), so you should be gracious and compassionate."[29] The observance of the commandments will lead Israel, negatively, to be set apart from the nations (Lev 20:26), as God is set apart from his creatures and, positively, to acquire those ethical qualities, such as those indicated in the divine attributes enumerated to Moses (Exod

---

[22] *Seder Elijah Rab.* 145.
[23] *Sipra Qedošim* par. 1:1.
[24] *Lev. Rab.* 24:5; see above.
[25] *Sipra Qedošim* par. 1:1.
[26] *Num. Rab.* 10:1.
[27] *Lev. Rab.* 24:6; cf. *y. Yeb.* 2:4.
[28] *Sipra Qedošim* par. 1:1.
[29] *Mek. Šira* par. 3; *b. Šabb.* 133b.

34:6), cited by the rabbis, above. This dual obligation of both withdrawal and partic-
ipation inherent in the nature of the Deity was fully captured by Buber: "God is the
absolute authority over the world because he is separated from it and transcends it but
He is not withdrawn from it. Israel, in imitating God by being a holy nation, similarly
must not withdraw from the world of the nations but rather radiate a positive influence on them through every aspect of Jewish living."[30]

The positive aspect of *imitatio Dei* is spelled out in Deut 10:18-19: YHWH
"executes justice for the fatherless and the widow, and *loves the alien*, giving him
food and clothing. *Love the alien*, therefore, for you were *aliens* in the land of Egypt."
Note that the term "alien" occurs three times. Since YHWH related to you with love
when you were aliens in Egypt, you should relate to aliens in your midst with love.
Since the alien is not an Israelite, he should not be treated with hostility or with indifference, but with love. The rationale is *imitatio Dei*. Love, meaning compassionate
deeds, is specified as the basic essentials for life: food and clothing.[31]

In Lev 19:33-34 *imitatio Dei* is stated, rather implied, prohibitively: Since
YHWH redeemed you from oppression when you were aliens in the land of Egypt, so
you should not oppress him but "redeem" him by granting him equivalent civil rights.
Thus both aspects of *imitatio Dei*, performative and prohibitive, are specified in the
two cited passages through the medium of YHWH's love of the alien.

Israel should strive to imitate God, but, on the other hand, it should be fully
aware of the unbridgeable gap between them: "(One may think that) one can be
(holy) like me? Therefore, it is written 'for I am holy.'"[32] This chapter, therefore,
stands in sharp contrast to the previous chapter, which is headed by YHWH's self-
declaration, as found in the Decalogue (18:2b). The importance of this change cannot
be overestimated: for H, the God of the covenant is demanding more than obedience
to his commandments (v. 37). He is also stating the rationale or, rather, the goal, the
end product, of the commandments. Obedience produces godliness, a quality encapsulated in the word "holy." Just as the priests, who are innately holy, are qualified to
enter into God's presence ("those near to me," 10:3), so Israel, in following all
YHWH's commandments (19:37), will attain holiness (v. 2), thereby also qualifying
for perpetual admission into the presence—that is, the providence and protection—of
the holy God (see further 20:7).

Verse 3. Unit 1: Revere Parents and
Keep the Sabbath (Ethics and Cult)

Elsewhere, the mother precedes the father only in 21:2. What could be its rationale
here? The rabbis posit the following reason: "A man honors his mother more than his

---

[30] 1964:96.
[31] See on 19:18.
[32] *Lev. Rab.* 24:9.

father because she sways him with persuasive words. Therefore in the commandment to honor (Exod 20:22) he [God] mentions the father before the mother. . . . A man is more afraid of his father than his mother because he teaches him the Torah. Therefore in the commandment (Lev 19:3), he mentions the mother before the father. . . . Scripture thus declares that both are equal, the one as important as the other."[33]

However, the most plausible answer is a structural one: The Decalogue is inverted here both in the order of father and mother and in the order of the Sabbath and parents commandments to indicate that the author has the Decalogue in mind.[34] Indeed, there can be no doubt that H was aware of the Decalogue and alluded to it in vv. 2-4 (and in the inclusio in vv. 30-32). Note the following:

1. The only other time that "I YHWH your God" (v. 2) occurs at the head of a group of laws is in the Decalogue (Exod 20:2; Deut 5:6). Whereas in the Decalogue YHWH identifies himself as the God of the exodus, here he is identified as God the Holy.

2. The fact that commandments 1, 2, 4, and 5 are reversed in vv. 2-4 alludes to Seidel's law, namely, that the author of Leviticus 19 is referring to an earlier list of these commandments, the Decalogue.

3. The puzzle concerning the omission of commandment 3 can now be solved. The legist only wanted to focus on an aspect of commandment 3, the false oath. He therefore brought it down to its proper context, v. 12.

Thus the first five commandments are accounted for. It therefore stands to reason that the author of Leviticus 19 knew the Decalogue and made use of it.

Respect for parents and other family authorities was a sine qua non in the ancient world. Note this sensitive statement in the Sumerian hymn concerning those unacceptable to the goddess Nanshe: "a mother who shouts at her child, a child who talks obstinately to his mother, a younger brother who talks arrogantly to his elder brother, talks back to his father."[35] For biblical examples, see Gen 45:11; Ruth 4:14-15 (cf. Tob 4:3; 14:13; Sir 3:1-16). One should not overlook, though, a different perspective concerning filial duties to the father recorded in the Ugaritic Epic of Aqhat:

Who erects the stela of his god-of-the-father, in the sanctuary the symbol of his ancestor; who on earth makes his smoke emerge, on the dust tends his place; who crushes the jaws of those who revile him, and drives away those who act against him; who takes him by the hand in his drunkenness and supports him when he is sated with wine; who eats his emmer in the temple of Baal [and] his part in the temple of El; who plasters his roof in the [fou]l season, and washes his garments when they are dirty.[36]

[33] *Mek. Baḥodeš* 8.
[34] Paton 1897:53; Seidel 1978:2; Weiss 1984:96; Paran 1989:10.
[35] Nanshe Hymn, II, 168-71 (Heimpel 1981:93).
[36] *CTA* 17 I:26-33.

Leviticus 17–27: The Holiness Source (H)

This text presupposes a time when the father will no longer be able to care for himself. He is concerned that his son will keep up the ancestral cult (see 2 Sam 18:18; Absalom, having no son, erects the stela himself) at the sanctuary and at the family hearth; will defend his honor; will hold him up whenever drunk (cf. Gen 9:21-27); will celebrate festive meals at the sanctuary (cf. 1 Sam 1:4-5); and will perform mundane but essential tasks, such as doing roof repairs and laundering the father's clothes.[37]

Why were the fourth and fifth (Sabbath and parents) commandments of the Decalogue chosen to head the list? As indicated above, the inversion (the first and second commandments follow in the next verse) implies consciousness of the Decalogue. An ancillary purpose may have been to illustrate from the start that ethics (respect for parents) and ritual (observance of the Sabbath) are of equal importance.

All the laws in chapter 19 are unenforceable in human courts; hence the emphatic: "I YHWH (your God will enforce them)." Note that this formula is absent in vv. 5-8 because in the law the divine punishment *karet* is specified.

Verse 4. Unit 2: Worship of Other Gods and Images of Israel's God

As will be discussed in units 12 and 15 (vv. 26-28, 31), certain forms of idolatry, such as Molek and ancestor worship, negate the holiness of YHWH, the God of life. This unit is clearly a reworking of the first and second commandments.

A "molten god" was made by pouring molten metal either into a cast or over a wooden frame. The latter apparently describes the metal-plated idols mentioned in Scripture (Deut 7:25; Isa 30:22; 40:19-20; 44:9-20; Jer 10:3-4). Indeed, the golden calf was, in most likelihood, fashioned the same way because it could be burned (Exod 32:20).

Verses 5-8. Unit 3: The Well-Being Offering

The glaring contrast between the preceding paraphrases of the Decalogue (vv. 2-4) and the ostensibly picayune sacrificial detail discussed in this unit has led most commentators to suggest that these verses are a secondary interpolation by a later redactor.[38] Thus the question of what this unit is doing here must be addressed. Even the commentators who regard this unit as an intrusion have to face this question.

The answer, I submit, lies in the nature of the sacrificial procedure detailed in this unit. It speaks of the well-being offering and the need of the offerer to beware *lest he desecrate it*. It must be kept in mind that the meat of the well-being offering is the

---

[37] Translation and discussion in van der Toorn 1996b:154–65.

[38] E.g., Dillmann and Ryssel 1987; Wellhausen 1963:155; Baentsch 1903; Elliger 1966; Cholewiński 1976. Eerdmans 1912 alone defends its integrity.

only sacred food that the layperson is allowed to eat. And he is most likely to be tempted to desecrate it when, after the two-day limit for its consumption has expired, a portion of it remains. (After all, how much of a whole animal can a family consume in two days?) Moreover, he is allowed to bring the sacred meat home and eat it with his family as long as they are all in a pure state (7:19b). In a sense, the sacred meat has transmitted the holiness of the sanctuary into the home. Thus the family must treat every act of eating a meat meal as a sacred rite. In my opinion, it foreshadows and supplies the precedent for the rabbinic doctrine (but not innovation!) that the home has replaced the nonexistent temple.[39]

In any case, it is holiness that is uppermost in the legist's mind, holiness that is commanded to the entire people of Israel. For this reason, the author/redactor inserts this unit close to the overarching command "You shall be holy" (v. 2a). And his logic is unassailable. After laying out his paraphrase of the most important (for him) part of the Decalogue (commandments 5, 4, 1, 2), he then proceeds to caution his people: you cannot begin to climb the ladder of holiness until you take precautions that the one sanctum you have a right to possess is never desecrated.

Supporting my view is the fact that although this unit is a near verbatim repetition of 7:16-18, the major difference between the two is that this unit also adds a rationale: "Because he has desecrated what is sacred to YHWH" (v. 8aβ). Thus it is the fear of cultic desecration, which totally and irrevocably cancels the degree of holiness reached by the Israelite, regardless of how many of the ensuing commandments he has faithfully observed, that is responsible for the insertion of this unit near the head of the list.

At what point does the well-being offering become sacred? Ibn Ezra's answer, once the suet is offered up, is not correct. Rather, it is when the priest, together with the offerer, performs the elevation rite with the sanctified pieces. How long does its sanctity last? According to this verse, it lasts as long as it exists. Thus it must be either eaten or eliminated (by burning); otherwise, even in a putrefied state, it is technically still "holy"! The result of allowing the meat to remain beyond its legal time is that the entire sacrifice is invalidated. No wonder, then, that H places its emphasis on the offerer, for it lies within his responsibility that he and all those whom he has invited to partake of the sacrifice must eliminate their sacrificial portion by ingestion or fire before the third day. It is thus hardly imaginable that the offerer parcels out the sacrificial meat and lets the participants go their merry way. Rather, a feast at or near the sanctuary is presumed, lasting one or two days while the meat remains under the supervision of the offerer (and perhaps the priest).

---

[39] *m. Ber.* chaps. 6–7; *b. Ḥul.* 105a.

Verses 9-10. Unit 4: Horticultural Holiness and Required Gifts to the Poor and Alien

Attempts have been made to find the logical connection between this unit and the preceding ones:

1. As you give God the suet of your well-being offering, give to the needy—at God's behest—of your produce (Ibn Ezra).

2. In contrast to the well-being offering, which is completely eliminated (by the ingestion of fire), the field and the vineyard should not be stripped, but some produce should be left for the needy (Hoffmann).

3. Since the offerer of the sacrifice cannot possibly consume the entire animal in two days, but must invite others to his feast, so a portion of the field's produce should be left for the needy (Shadal).

Perhaps the placement of this unit here may have more to do with the following verses than the preceding ones. Verses 11-18 are characterized by their purely ethical nature. The preceding verses (2-8) deal with religious duties. This unit belongs to both categories: not to harvest the entire crop is a religious duty; leaving the remainder for the poor is an ethical duty. Thus vv. 9-10 form a bridge between the two categories.

The roots "holy" and "desecrate" do not appear in this unit. Their very absence is significant: an indispensable step toward the achievement of holiness is concern for the indigent. Stated differently: as was demonstrated in THEME A, "I YHWH your God," with which this unit ends (v.12bβ), as do most of the others (vv. 9-10, 13-14, 15-16, 17-18, 32, 33-34, 35-36), is synonymous with otherness or holiness, as explicitly defined in the generalizing principle "I, YHWH your God, am holy" (v. 2). YHWH has symbolically taken the poor and alien into his domain. Hence anyone who disobeys commandments concerning their care is desecrating, as it were, his holiness. This theme runs through all the ethical commandments (vv. 11-18). The implication is clear: YHWH is the protector of the defenseless, and only those who follow his lead can achieve holiness.

[19:9] Only one side of the field is intended,[40] probably at the far end.[41] The rabbis find practical reasons for this specification:

> R. Simeon said: There are four reasons why the Torah said that *pe'a* should be at the end of the field: so that he will not rob the poor, keep the poor waiting, give the wrong impression, cause deception. How (can he) rob the poor? By waiting till no one is around and then telling his relative, "Come and take this *pe'a*." Cause the poor to wait?

---

[40] *Tg. Ps.-J. 'umana ḥada'*, "one furrow."

[41] *Tg. Yer. 'oman 'oḥaray*, "last furrow."

The poor might sit and keep watch on his field all day, thinking, "Now he will set aside *pe²a*, now he will set aside *pe²a*": however, if he sets aside the end of his field, the poor man does his work all days and at its end (comes) and takes it. Give the wrong impression? People may pass by his field and say, "See, this person has harvested his field and has left no edge for the poor despite the Torah's injunction 'Do not destroy the edge of your field.'" Cause deception? So that they [the field owners] should not say "we have already given" or they will not leave the (part whose crop is) good but only the bad.[42]

The gleanings are "that which falls (from the reaper) during the harvest."[43] Inevitably, stalks will be dropped during the harvesting. Deut 24:19 forbids the owner to return to the field in order to retrieve them. They belong to the poor.

Concern for the poor, the widow, and the orphan is widespread throughout ancient Near Eastern codes and edicts. Israel, however, is unique in its solicitude for the alien. It is of interest to note the impact of this law on the contemporary American scene. Under the headline "Needy Americans Gleaning Unwanted Agricultural Harvest," an article in the *Los Angeles Times* (Aug. 31, 1983) reports that "active gleaning programs have now taken hold in 11 states . . . that take its guidance from Leviticus 19:9-10 . . . in response to what the General Accounting Office calls an 'unmet need' for food among Americans who do not qualify for government food systems."

[19:10] In the priestly texts, this is the only place (and in its copy, 23:22) where the poor are mentioned. H does not mention the widow and the orphan because during its time (mainly, the latter half of the eighth century), the kin group[44] and the household were tightly controlled (see 18:6-23). The widow and orphan automatically would have been taken care of by the nearest relative(s) of the deceased. The cracks in the patriarchal control barely visible in the eighth century (Isa 1:17, 23; 10:2) become a searing fissure a century later, when increasing latifundia and urbanization led to the dissolution of family and clan structure, leaving the widow and orphan open prey to exploitation (Jer 7:6; 15:8; 22:3, 16; Ezek 22:7, 25).

Why is the Levite conspicuously missing from H's humanitarian concerns? The dating of H mainly in the eighth century provides the answer. The Levites are gainfully employed in Judah's regional sanctuaries, residing in their own compound in the Levitical cities (Lev 25:32-34; Num 35:1-8). The influx of Levites among the northern refugees had hardly begun, and it is a century before (Josiah's) centralization throws Judah's Levites among the ranks of the unemployed.

Note that the alien is considered among the poor, a sign that he is landless and has no independent source of income.

---

[42] *t. Pe²ah* 1:6; cf. *Sipra Qedošim* 1:10; *b. Šabb.* 23a, b (bar.).

[43] *m. Pe²ah* 4:10. The act of harvesting explains its occurrence: the reaper grabs a bundle of sheaves with one hand and swings his scythe with the other.

[44] See Milgrom 1978:79-81.

Verses 11-18. Ethical Duties: Introduction

This is an organic section concerning deeds (vv. 11-13), speech (vv. 14-16), and thought (vv. 17-18).[45] The unit on deeds can be subdivided into furtive deeds (vv. 11-12) and nonfurtive deeds (v. 13). The chances are that H has not innovated these ethical prescriptions but has selected them from another (perhaps oral) source in order to group them under the rubric of holiness. Just as H has not invented the procedure with the well-being offering (vv. 5-8), but has borrowed it from P (7:16-18) to subsume it under the rubric of holiness, so H may have borrowed and expanded all the commandments in this chapter (from P?) for this purpose.

These ethical commandments had a profound effect on the rabbis who expounded and expanded them. They had no less an impact on early Christianity, as exemplified in the Epistle of James. "James made conscious and sustained use" of vv. 12-18: If one loves one's fellow as oneself (Jas 2:8), one avoids treating people with partiality (2:1, 9), defrauding others or holding back a hireling's wages (5:4), uttering oaths and dissembling (5:12), slandering others (5:9), and speaking evil of them (4:11).[46]

Verses 11-13. Unit 5: Deeds

Many of the categories in vv. 11-13 are found in 5:20-26 (P), and there can be little doubt that the latter passage was clearly in the mind of the writer (H) of the former.[47] However, whereas 5:20-26 deal with one theme, the illegal expropriation of property, I will show that vv. 12-13 break out of the constricting mold of the punishment for specific acts of expropriation by converting them into basic ethical prohibitions.

[19:11] The category of theft is missing in 5:20-26, where instead we find "robbery." The reason is that vv. 11-12 deal with furtive acts, whereas 5:20-26 deal with undisguised, open use of force. The category of robbery is listed among the nonfurtive acts of v. 13.[48] These violations may elude human jurisdiction. But God will assuredly punish, as implied by the "I YHWH" ending of each section (vv. 3, 4, 10, 12, 14, 16, 18, 25, 28, 30, 31, 32, 34, 36).

That the persons intended by these ethical demands are not limited to Israel is mandated by vv. 33-34, which apply them to the resident alien. What, however, of "the foreigner"? Are we to infer that the Israelite is free to lay aside any of the ethical rules in dealing with him? Here is where abstract logical reasoning leads astray. The forgotten factor is that the H school probably had no contact with foreigners.

---

[45] Cf. Ibn Ezra on Exod 20:2.

[46] L. T. Johnson 1982:399. But as Hartley 1992:325 has cautioned, James's ethical pronouncements are actually "filtered through the teachings of Jesus."

[47] Details in Milgrom 1976a:84–101.

[48] Milgrom 1976a:89–93.

Sequestered in the Jerusalem temple or, at best, having on occasion visited regional sanctuaries and the surrounding countryside, the only persons *of concern* would have been Israelites (and the resident alien). It was Israel's spiritual status, which priestly teaching tried to elevate, that ultimately determined whether YHWH would remain in his sanctuary, in his land, and among his people. It is hardly accidental that the only mention of the foreigner is as the sender, not the presenter of sacrifices (22:25). Contrast Isaiah of Jerusalem, a contemporary, in my opinion, and his wide-ranging knowledge of the surrounding nations and of the empires beyond. But then there is a quintessential distinction between the priest and the prophet, whose commission is, in Jeremiah's words, "I have appointed you a prophet to the nations" (Jer 1:5).

[19:12] The false oath. The rabbis see in vv. 11-12 a series of connected events: "If you have stolen, you are likely to deny, then to lie, and end by taking a false oath."[49]

The importance of H's innovation cannot be overestimated. By unhitching the false oath from the crimes of misappropriation (Lev 5:20-26 [P]), H declares that the latter in themselves are sinful, not just against persons and hence adjudicable in the courts, but against YHWH by preventing his holy presence from residing among Israel.

Just as commentators have found the prohibition against theft (v. 11a) to echo the eighth commandment of the Decalogue, and the prohibition against lying (v. 11b) to paraphrase the Decalogue's ninth commandment (false witness), so they find the false oath in this verse to be imitative of the Decalogue's third commandment (Exod 20:7). The third commandment has been rendered variously as: "You shall not make wrongful use of the name of the Lord, your God, in vain" (NEB, NRSV); "You shall not take the name of the Lord, your God, in vain" (KJV, NAB). NJPS, however, renders: "You shall not swear falsely by the name of the Lord your God," thereby equating "lie" (*šeqer*) here with "in vain, falsely" (*šawʾ*) in the third commandment. But are they equivalent?

In general, the rabbis define *šawʾ* as an aspect of falsehood:

1. It differs from an accepted truth (e.g., the stone pillar is made of gold).

2. It projects an impossibility (e.g., seeing a flying camel).

3. It annuls a commandment (e.g., not to build a booth; cf. 23:42).

4. It involves swearing contradictory oaths, inevitably having to violate one of them.[50]

The accepted meaning of *šawʾ* (whose etymology is unknown) is "useless, worthless." Mowinckel proposed that *šawʾ* also means "magic, evil" (e.g., Hos 10:4;

---

[49] *Sipra Qedošim* par. 2:5; cf. Philo, *Spec. Laws* 4.40.
[50] *m. Šebu.* 3:8-9.

Job 7:3), and in that sense it refers in the Decalogue to the illicit use of God's name.[51]

In any event, it is clear that in the Decalogue, the use of God's name is forbidden over a wide area, including oaths, prayers, curses, and blessings, if its purpose is worthless, false, magical—in a word, if its use is inimical to the revealed will of God. Here, however, the prohibition deals with lying oaths. I would agree that its range is not limited to property, as in 5:20-26. It constitutes a generalization. Lying oaths are forbidden in any situation: on the witness stand for any crime or in private exchange with one's fellow. Thus we must conclude that our verse and the third commandment are not equivalent.[52]

Herein may lie the reason why H had to omit the third commandment from his reprise of the first half of the Decalogue at the head of this chapter. He wanted to focus on only lies, an aspect of the third commandment, and perforce had to place it here, where he needed it in connection with his supplementation (vv. 11-12) to 5:20-26.

"Lest you desecrate the name of your God." This is the rationale for the prohibition against taking a false oath. Notice how different it is from the rationale for the illicit use of God's name in the third commandment of the Decalogue. There it is a threat of punishment that acts as a deterrent. Here the result, desecration, is the deterrent. God's name is the only sanctum other than the meat of the well-being offering (discussed in vv. 5-8) that the laity can utilize. Its desecration nullifies whatever holiness has been achieved through the observance of the other injunctions in this chapter. For this reason, the well-being offering was given such play in this chapter. Now once more the Israelite is warned that his attempt to climb the ladder of holiness is futile if he commits an act of desecration for which there is neither remedy nor expiation (contrast 5:20-26).

A bothersome question is the occurrence of the clause "I YHWH (have spoken)" here rather than at the end of v. 13, which terminates the unit. The likely answer is that v. 13 deals with nonfurtive crimes, which, because they are known, fall under the responsibility of the court. Verses 11-12, however, deal with furtive crimes, and although they escape the notice of the authorities, they are known to God, who will exact retribution from the offender.[53] If this interpretation is correct, it serves as strong evidence that the main function of this phrase is to warn Israel that no violation of God's commandments will go unpunished.

[19:13] The general connotation of the verb ʿašaq is "oppress, extort."[54] H adopts this connotation. P, as is its wont, has a more specific meaning in mind: withholding pay-

---

[51] Mowinckel 1921:50–57. But see Childs 1974:11.

[52] Cf. Schwartz 1999:306–10.

[53] Wessely 1846.

[54] E.g., Jer 21:12; 22:3; cf. Deut 28:29, 33; 1 Sam 12:4; Hos 4:2; Amos 4:1; see Milgrom 1976a:101 n. 376.

ment or property that has come into one's possession legally (5:21, 23). In this case, there is no need for the miscreant to take an oath (contrast 5:22, 24), since he freely admits possessing the other's property or money.[55]

For a discussion of the socioeconomic status of the hireling, see 25:40. There, however, the "slave" is on a long-term hire until the Jubilee or until he repays his loan. Here the subject is the day laborer, who is one of the poorest members of society. He works only intermittently and consequently is in the greatest need of his daily wage for the support of his family.[56]

Verse 14. Unit 6: Exploitation of the Helpless

The literal meaning of the text is a prohibition against playing cruel practical jokes, saying mean things in front of the deaf, or tripping the blind. Thus the appended "but you shall fear your God" takes on an enhanced meaning: although the deaf does not know he was insulted nor the blind who hurt him, God does know and will punish accordingly.[57] H's penchant for generalizations favors a broad definition, "insult, abuse, ridicule." Indeed, as I argue below, it is hardly conceivable that H literally meant that one is forbidden only to place a stumbling block before the blind. That the verse ends with the admonition "but you shall fear your God" implies that the weak and helpless, namely, the deaf and the blind, are under divine protection. This warning is given again in similar circumstances: the elderly (v. 32), cheating in land transactions (25:17), interest on loans (25:36), and exploiting the indentured Israelite (25:35-36).[58]

Since the deaf cannot hear a curse, they cannot ward it off by a blessing (Judg 17:2; Ps 109:28). The likelihood, however, is that the term "deaf" stands for all the helpless.[59]

"One who is blind about anything. . . . Do not give him advice that is not suitable for him";[60] the rabbis generalize this to include all forms of temptation.

"But you shall fear your God" reappears in v. 32 and in 25:17, 36, 43, but nowhere else. They all deal with the exploitation of the helpless: the elderly as well as indebted Israelites forced to sell the land and from whom usury and enslavement are exacted. The rabbis also apply this to those whose "deafness" and "blindness"— that is, weakness—are exploited.[61] Those who are exploited cannot defend themselves, but God will come to their aid;[62] he will hear them when they cry out (Deut

---

[55] Bekhor Shor.
[56] Telushkin 1997:459.
[57] Ibid.
[58] Schwartz 1999:310–13.
[59] *b. ʿAbod. Zar.* 6a, b; Maimonides, *Book of Commandments,* §317; Ramban.
[60] *Sipra Qedošim* par. 2:14; cf. Rom 14:13.
[61] *Sipra Qedošim* par. 2:14.
[62] Ramban, Bekhor Shor.

24:15)—be they Israelite or resident aliens (Exod 22:20-22 [Eng. 21-23]). The defense of the poor is an aspect of the divine holiness that Israel must emulate to attain its holiness (see further Lev 25:36).

Verses 15-16. Unit 7: Injustice and Indifference

The God of justice will not tolerate injustice. This is another aspect of YHWH's attribute of holiness.

[19:15] The NJPS confines this prohibition to judicial procedure, rendering "You shall not render an unfair decision," following the rabbis, who exemplify: "so that one (litigant) will be sitting and the other standing; one (allowed to) speak all he wants, the other who is told (by the judge): 'make it short.'"[63] This crime "leads to five things. It pollutes the land, desecrates the Sabbath, removes the divine presence, defeats Israel by the sword, and exiles it from the land."[64] For the rabbis, this is the cause célèbre for the curses of Lev 26:14-38.

"You shall not be partial to the poor," literally "lift the face," is apt for one whose face has "fallen," namely, the weaker party (cf. Gen. 19:21; 32:21; 1 Sam 25:35), but this idiom is also used for the stronger, respected party (Job 32:21; 34:19; Lam 4:16). Deuteronomy uses the neutral expression "recognize the face" (Deut 1:17), which applies to all parties, rich and poor alike.[65]

[19:16] The noun "slanderer" literally means "merchant, peddler" (Ezek 27:15; Song 3:6),[66] perhaps a variant of "slander, calumniate" (Ps 15:3; Sir 4:28; 5:4). Like a peddler, a slandermonger transfers gossip from one to another (Rashi). The rabbis interpret this verse similarly: "This is peddling slander [lit. 'the evil tongue']."[67] Of him who slanders, the Holy One, blessed be He, says: He and I cannot live together in the world. . . . Whoever speaks slander increases his sins even up to (the degree of) the three (cardinal) sins: idolatry, incest (including adultery), and the shedding of blood. . . . Slander about third (persons) kills three persons; him who tells (the slander), him who accepts it, and him about whom it is told."[68]

Do not "stand idle" when your fellow is in danger. Thus "if you are in a position to offer testimony on someone's behalf you are not permitted to remain silent."[69] "If one sees someone drowning, mauled by beasts, or attacked by robbers one is

---

[63] b. Šebu. 30a.

[64] Sipra Qedošim 4:1.

[65] Gruber 1983b.

[66] Saadiah, Radak, Ramban, Abravanel.

[67] y. Peʾah 1:1; cf. Sipra Qedošim 4:5; b. Ket. 46a.

[68] b. ʿArak. 15b; cf. Tg. Ps.-J.

[69] Sipra Qedošim 4:8; Tg. Ps-J.; see Lev 5:1.

obligated to save him, but not at the risk of one's life."[70] In contrast, "contemporary American law is rights-, rather than obligation-, oriented. For example, if you could easily save a child who is drowning, but instead stand by and watch it drown, you have violated no American law. Under biblical law, however, you have committed a serious crime."[71]

Verses 17-18. Unit 8: Reproof and Love

[**19:17**] The section on ethical duties reaches its climax with this final unit. A more precise analysis finds that the two verses of the unit form parallel panels.[72]

	17	18
Prohibition	You shall not hate your kinsperson in your heart	You shall not take revenge or bear a grudge against members of your people
Remedy	(Rather) reprove your fellow openly	(Rather) you shall love your fellow as yourself
Rationale	so that you will not bear punishment because of him	I YHWH (have spoken)

This unit focuses on one's thought, the perils of which were sensitively apprehended by the rabbis, who declare that "causeless hatred" was responsible for the destruction of the Second Temple.[73]

Wisdom tradition interprets "hate . . . in your heart" to mean that the outlawed hatred "in the heart" is covered under a veil of lying hypocrisy (Prov 10:18; 26:24-25).[74]

It is doubtful if the term "kin" is limited to members of one's kin group or clan.[75] Its probable intent is to include all Israelites, particularly those belonging to other clans. If it were limited to "your kin" this would imply that Israelites from other clans would be the responsibility of *their* kin. Thus v. 17 would also imply that one is free to hate any Israelite who is not one's own kin. This is certainly not the intention.

"Reprove your fellow openly" is the answer to the prohibition against harboring hatred. One detects in this phrase a natural resistance or reluctance to bring one's grievances out in the open, especially to the offending party directly. To overcome

---

[70] *b. Sanh.* 73a.

[71] Telushkin 1997:461.

[72] Schwartz 1999:317; cf. Saadiah, Bekhor Shor.

[73] *b. Yoma* 9b.

[74] Kugel 1997:351–52.

[75] As argued by Cross 1998:4.

this psychological barrier, the offended party must be urged.[76] Note also that open reproof not only dispels hate but engenders love (Prov 9:8). Thus it throws light on the meaning of "love your fellow" (Lev 19:18). The latter injunction is neither wishful nor impractical. One of the ways to love your fellow, according to this unit (vv. 17-18), is to reprove him openly for his mistakes. Conversely, the only admissible rebuke is that which is evoked by love, not by animosity, jealousy, or lust for power.[77]

The sectaries of Qumran make reproof a cardinal requirement for its members, "to reprove each man his brother according to the commandment [i.e., Lev 19:17], and not to bear a grudge [v. 18a] from one day to the next." However, the one giving reproof (for a capital offense) must also report it to the overseer, who dutifully records it.[78] Need it be said that this was hardly the intention of the priestly legist, who contemplated that the reprover would share his complaint with no one else.

"So that you will not bear punishment because of him." If you do not reprove him, you will bear his punishment. Alternatively, the rationale is that you yourself are likely to take action against him, which may prove sinful.[79] Two more literal readings of this clause have also been proposed: "And do not carry (his) sin against him,"[80] that is, do not carry a grudge against him (cf. v. 18a); and "you should not put upon him (his sin)"; that is, do not embarrass him in public.[81]

Another rendering is implied by Sir 19:17a: "Reproach a friend before getting angry." That is, by not reproaching your friend, your anger may lead you to harm him and because of it incur sin.

At Qumran, a reproof was not only a moral duty, but a prerequisite for all offenses:

> Any man from among those who have entered the covenant who shall bring a charge against his fellow that is not without reproof before witnesses . . . if he kept silent about him from day to day, and accused him of a capital offense (only) when he was angry with him, his [the accused's] punishment is upon him [the accuser], since he did not fulfill the commandment of God who said to him: "Reprove your fellow openly so that you will not bear punishment because of him (Lev 19:17)."[82]

The manner of the reproof is also specified by Qumran: "To reprove each his fellow in truth, humility, and lovingkindness to a man: Let him not speak to him in anger or complaint or stub[bornly or in passion] (caused) by an evil disposition. Let

---

[76] S. Greenberg (orally).
[77] M. Aron, personal communication.
[78] CD 9:17-19; cf. 9:2-8, discussed below.
[79] Schwartz 1999:317.
[80] *Keter Torah*; Mendelssohn 1846.
[81] *Sipra Qedošim* 4:8; *Tg. Ps.-J.; b. ʿArak.* 16b.
[82] CD 9:2-8.

him not hate him intrac[tab]ly, for on that very day shall he reprove him so that he will not bear punishment because of him."[83]

Judicial procedure at Qumran required that charges could not be brought before the court, which constituted the full assembly of the sect, unless witnesses (other than those who saw the offense) would testify that they had reproved the offender for a similar offense. In many ways, Qumran's reproof resembles and anticipates the rabbinic "warning," which provided that no one might be convicted of an offense without first having been warned. A major difference between the two is that for the sect reproof followed a first offense, whereas for the rabbis reproof was essential for even a first offense.[84]

[19:18] Verses 17-18 form a unit. Both vengeance and nursing a grudge are products of hate, the former in deed and the latter in thought,[85] connecting with v. 17a. Neither vengeance nor bearing a grudge is permitted even if the reproof proves ineffectual, and the harm done has not been effaced, connecting with v. 17b. The rabbis distinguish between the two concepts:

> You shall not take vengeance. "What is the extent of vengeance? One says to another: Lend me your sickle, and the other refuses. On the morrow, the latter says: Lend me your axe; and the former replies, I shall not lend (it) to you since you did not lend me your sickle. Hence it is written "You shall not take vengeance."
>
> You shall not nurse a grudge. "What is the extent of nursing a grudge? One says to the other: Lend me your sickle; and the former replies, Here, take it, I am not like you who didn't lend me your axe. Such behavior is condemned by "You shall not bear a grudge."[86]

The word "revenge" implies extralegal retribution, which, although forbidden to humans, may be exacted by God. Indeed, "the sign of a saintly, noble person [is] that he commits his revenge to God (David, 1 Sam 24:12; Jeremiah, Jer 15:15; etc.). For YHWH is properly God of *nqm* [revenge] (Nah 1:2; Ps 94:1); to him belongs the ultimate redressing of all wrongs, and by whatever means he wills,"[87] unless he explicitly assigns the task to humans (Num 31:2, 3; Josh 10:13; 1 Sam 14:24; 18:25).

"(Rather) you shall love." The juxtaposition of the two halves of this verse prompts R. Hillel to declare, "That which is hateful to you, do not do to your fellow,"[88] as the central tenet of the Bible (and Judaism). Bekhor Shor asks, however: How does God expect one who has been wronged to the point of wanting to take

---

[83] 1QS 5:25—6:1.
[84] Schiffman 1983:97.
[85] Cf. Rashi, Rashbam, Hazzequni.
[86] *Sipra Qedošim* 4:10-11; cf. *b. Yoma* 23a.
[87] Greenberg 1983:13.
[88] *b. Šabb.* 31a.

revenge to love one's fellow? Bekhor Shor finds the answer in the final, overlooked clause of this verse: "'I YHWH.' Let your love for me overcome your hatred for him . . . and keep you from taking revenge, and as a result peace will come between you."

How can love be commanded? The answer is simply that the verb "love" signifies not only an emotion or attitude but also deeds. This is especially true in Deuteronomy, which speaks of covenantal love. The alien is "loved" by providing him with food and shelter (Deut 10:18-19). God is "loved" by observing his commandments (11:1; cf. 5:10; 7:5-6, 9), and God, in turn, "loves" Israel by subduing its enemies (7:8).[89] "Covenantal love," as Moran has demonstrated, is found and perhaps originates in suzerainty treaties.[90] To select one example out of many, the closest to Lev 19:18b is: "You will love Ashurbanipal . . . as yourselves."[91]

That "love" implies deeds was taught by both Hillel and Jesus: Hillel, negatively, "What is hateful to you do *not do* to others,"[92] and Jesus, positively, "*Do* unto others as you *would do* unto yourselves."[93] Qumran, as well, insists that love must be translated into deeds: "To love each his brother as himself by supporting the poor, the destitute, and the convert."[94]

A number of renderings of "as yourself" have been proposed, each of which changes the meaning of the injunction:

1. Muraoka suggests that it is adjectival, modifying the noun, and is equivalent to "who is a person like you" (Deut 5:14; 18:15). He was anticipated by Wessely, who adds "who is like you," since he too was created by God.[95] Ehrlich nuances it differently: "who is the like of you"—that is, an Israelite, in contrast to the alien (v. 34).[96]

2. Most commentators (including myself) understand "as yourself" adverbially, modifying the verb: "Love (the good) *for* your fellow as you (love the good for) yourself," shortened to "Love your fellow as yourself." This interpretation is earliest attested in *Jub.* 30:24: "And among yourselves, my sons, be loving of your brothers as a man loves himself, with each man seeking for his brother what is good for him, and acting together on the earth, and loving each other as themselves."

3. Kugel[97] cites two examples illustrating that a reflexive sense is intended:

---

[89] Cf. Weinfeld 1972:8–13.

[90] 1963.

[91] *VTE,* iv, 266-68 (Wiseman 1958:49–50).

[92] *b. Šabb.* 31a; *y. Ned.* 9; cf. Sir 28:4.

[93] Matt 7:2; Luke 6:13; Rom 13:8-10.

[94] CD 6:20-21.

[95] 1846:144.

[96] Ehrlich 1908–14:vol.2:65. See also Derrett 1971.

[97] 1997:456.

The way of life is this: First, you should love the Lord your maker, and secondly, your neighbor as yourself. And whatever you do not want to be done to you, you should not do to anyone else.[98]

And love your neighbor; for what is hateful to you yourself, do not do to him, I am the Lord.[99]

Both interpretations are based on older versions; the most celebrated is R. Hillel's reply to the challenge of a potential convert to teach him the entire Torah while standing on one foot: "What is hateful to you do not do to your fellow."[100] Note that this version is cited as early as Tob 4:15: "What you yourself hate, do not do to anyone."

A most illuminating exposition of this injunction is recorded in the names of R. Akiba and Ben Azzai: "R. Akiba says: This is (the most) basic . . . law in the Torah. Ben Azzai says: (Rather) 'When God created Adam, he made him in the likeness of God' (Gen 5:1), so that you should not say: 'Since I despise myself, let my fellow be despised with me; since I am cursed, let my fellow be cursed with me.' This is a more basic law."[101] Ben Azzai, in my opinion, decisively tops R. Akiba.[102] If you do not love yourself, asks Ben Azzai, how can you love someone else? Having penetrated beyond the outer rational capabilities of the human being to his possibly disturbed psychic condition, he proposes his therapy: First, make such a (and every) person aware that he is of ultimate worth because he bears the likeness of God, that regardless of his condition he has the divinely endowed potential to achieve joy and fulfillment in life, and only then, after having learned to love himself, will he be capable of loving others.

Israel Baal Shem Tov, the eighteenth-century founder of Hasidism, would have taken issue with Ben Azzai. His sanguine view of human nature led him to rephrase the golden rule as follows: "Just as we love ourselves despite the faults we know we have, so we should love our fellows despite the faults we see in them."[103]

This injunction (v. 18b) falls in the middle of chapter 19, which contains thirty-seven verses. It is "the culminating point" of H as well as the apex of Leviticus, the central book of the Torah.[104] Within its own pericope (vv. 11-17), it serves as the climax in the series of ethical sins: deceit in business (vv. 11-12), oppression of the weak (vv. 13-14), evil judgment, and hatred leading to planning and executing

---

[98] *Didache* 31:1-2.

[99] *Tg.-Ps. J.* on Lev 19:18.

[100] *b. Šabb.* 31a.

[101] *Sipra Qedošim* 4:12; cf. *y. Ned.* 9:4; *Gen. Rab.* 24:7.

[102] See also *Jub.* 20:2; 36:34; Philo, *Spec. Laws* 2.63; Matt 22:37-40; Mark 12:20-31; Luke 20:27-28.

[103] Cited in Telushkin 1997:466.

[104] Radday 1981:89.

revenge. The remedy: doing good (love). The result: a giant step toward achieving holiness.

Verses 19-29. Miscellaneous Duties

These verses deal with the person's relationship with possessions: animals, crops, clothing (v. 19), slaves (vv. 20-22), land (vv. 23-25), body (vv. 26-28), and daughter (v. 29).

Verse 19. Unit 9: Mixtures

[19:19] It is of utmost significance that the cherubim flanking the ark were mixtures (Ezek 1:5-11), as were the divine guardians in Mesopotamia.[105] This is the initial indication, which will be corroborated in the two following prohibitions, that mixtures belong to the divine realm, on which the human being (except for divinely consecrated persons, the priests) may not encroach.

The most favored explanation for the prohibition against mixtures is that it is a violation of the order God brought into the world by separating the species (Genesis 1) and hence a symbol of disorder, the reversal of creation.[106] This theory could explain the mating prohibition, but as pointed out by Boleh,[107] it has no relevance for the two following prohibitions because mixed seeds in the ground are not "mated" (i.e., grafted) but are kept apart.

Another popular explanation is that mixtures in nature are symbolic of mixtures of human beings, thus a prohibition against intermarriage and assimilation.[108] It is hard to believe, however, that a prohibition against intermarriage would be expressed metaphorically. To the contrary, the question should be reversed: Why is there no explicit prohibition against intermarriage in H, particularly in chapters 18 and 20 dealing with illicit sexual unions, where such a prohibition could be expected? (See chap. 18, THEME A.)

As intimated above, the most plausible explanation, in my estimation, is that mixtures belong to the sacred sphere, namely, the sanctuary, as do its officiants, the priests.[109] Thus the lower cover of the tabernacle and the curtain closing off the adytum are a mixture of linen and wool (Exod 26:1, 31). The high priest's ephod, breastplate, and belt contain the same mixture (28:6, 15; 39:29); for the ordinary priest, this mixture is limited to his belt (39:29); and the Israelite is conceded this mixture by the insertion of a single blue thread of wool in his linen tassels (Num 15:39), as recog-

---

[105] Cf. Freedman and O'Connor 1982:330–34.

[106] b. Qid. 39a; b. Sanh. 60a; Ibn Ezra, Ramban, Bekhor Shor; Kalisch 1867–72:2:419; Dillmann and Ryssel 1897; Douglas 1966:53; Magonet 1983; Houtman 1984; Schwartz 1999:324–28.

[107] 1991–92:2:69–70.

[108] Ehrlich 1899–1900 (H):1.232; cf. Num. Rab. 10:3; Wenham 1979; Carmichael 1982; Eilberg-Schwartz 1990:123; cf. also Carmichael 1995; 1997:87–104; Milgrom 1996.

[109] Cf. Josephus, Ant. 4.208.

nized by the rabbis: "since linen is flax, blue must be wool,"[110] and as astutely perceived by Bekhor Shor: "It is as if it [the tassel] served him [the layman] as a royal scepter."

Whenever the Israelite sees the blue thread in any of his tassels (Num 15:37-41 [H]), he is reminded of the blue cord banding the plate that bears the inscriptions "holy to YHWH" (Exod 28:36-37 [P]), and thus he is constantly called to seek holiness by fulfilling the divine commandments.[111] Once again, H has overruled P: Holiness is not the exclusive property of the priesthood; it is attainable by all of Israel. The blue cord is not even mentioned among the high priest's garments in Lev 8:9, indicating its auxiliary nature. The pericope Num 15:37-41, indisputably attributable to the hand of H, echoes H's primary goal to set Israel on the path of holiness (v. 40b). Thus departing from P's consistently rigid separation between the priesthood (whose garments symbolize the right to enter the sacred sphere) and the laity (barred from entering the sacred sphere, i.e., the inner sanctuary), H prescribes that all (lay) Israelites insert a woolen thread into the linen tassels of their outer garments as a perpetual, visible sign that they must strive for a life of holiness.[112]

Of the three colors in the tabernacle curtains and priestly clothing, the blue is always listed first, thereby signifying its greater importance (cf. Exod 25:4; 26:1, 31, 36; 27:16; 28:5, 6, 15, 33, etc.; note, however, that its primacy breaks down in 2 Chr 2:6, 13). Furthermore, the high priest's robe and the uppermost ark cover are composed of "pure blue" (Exod 28:31; 39:22; Num 4:6), indicating the high priest's unique responsibility to officiate at the inner sanctum and, on Yom Kippur, to enter the holy of holies. Even more telling evidence of the higher status of blue over other colors is that a blue cloth covers all the inner sanctums during the wilderness journeys. But only the ark is covered with a blue cloth (as a symbol of the divine presence, it is crucial that it always be visible), whereas the inner sanctums (the table, incense altar, and candelabrum) are bedecked with fewer cloths, the uppermost being of leather.[113] Thus the priestly (H) command to add a blue thread to the fringes that must be worn by all Israelites indicates H's avid desire to inspire all Israelites to aspire to a life of holiness—the theme of this chapter.

Above all, this explanation clarifies the insertion of this prohibition in this chapter. Israel is commanded to be holy, but is warned that it is not allowed the privilege of breeding different animals, sowing mixed seed, or wearing fabrics of mixed seeds—for these are reserved for the sacred sphere, and, in the case of clothing, for the priests. The mythology of the ancients was rife with mixtures: hybrid animals (cherubim) guarding temple entrances and flanking royal thrones; gods mating with

---

[110] *b. Yeb.* 4b.

[111] S. Tupper, personal communication.

[112] Cf. Milgrom 1983a:61–65; 1990:410–14.

[113] Details in Milgrom 1990:25–28 on Num 4:5-14.

humans and animals or changing into human form. There are biblical allusions to this background, as in the myth of celestial beings mating with earth women (Gen 6:1-4). Cherubim exist in Israel's cult—more precisely, inside the sanctuary, in woven form, on the inner curtains and veil of the tabernacle; carved on the inner walls and doors of the Solomonic temple; and, in sculpted form, inside the adytum of both sanctuaries. Being ensconced inside the sanctuary, all these cherubim were visible only to priests (the cherubim inside the adytum to no one), who were admitted to their presence because they too, wearing garments of mixed seed, symbolically became cherubim (see below), qualified to attend to the service of YHWH. The cherubim themselves, however, were not visible to the laity; they could not become objects of worship.

Mixtures, then, characterize the holiness of the sacred sphere and those authorized to enter or serve in it. The laity, however, dare not cross its boundary. No differently from the cherub guarding the entrance to the sacred garden, armed Levites guard the entrance into the sacred enclosure, "and the unauthorized encroacher will be put to death" (Num 1:51; 3:10, 38; 18:7).[114]

Thus there is no need to explain this prohibition as a metaphor for disorder or intermarriage. It is but a warning to the Israelite that one's holiness is not achieved by penetrating into the sacred realm, but by practicing the proper ritual and ethical behavior as specified in this chapter.

Verses 20-22. Unit 10: The Betrothed Slave Woman

[19:21] The reparation/offering brought by the paramour or seducer of a slave woman rests on the assumption that in Israel adultery was considered a violation of the Sinaitic covenant. In the ancient Near East, although adultery was considered a sin against the gods, it had no juridical impact, whereas in Israel its inclusion in the covenant guaranteed legal consequences. The death penalty for clear-cut adultery could never be commuted. However, in the case of Lev 19:20-22, where investigation shows that the betrothed slave woman had not been emancipated, her paramour or seducer could not be punished. He is not an adulterer because she is not a legal person. Nevertheless, he has offended God by desecrating the Sinaitic oath and must bring his sacrificial expiation.[115]

Verses 23-25. Unit 11: Horticultural Holiness (continued)

As concern for the poor during harvest time (vv. 9-10) is an essential characteristic of a holy people, so is the dedication of the first yield of the fruit trees to the sanctuary. Other firstfruits (the grain, must, oil, and firstlings) are not mentioned because it is presumed that the people are aware of them and, in the main, observing

---

[114] Cf. Milgrom 1970:1–22.
[115] For further details see Milgrom 1977; 2000:1665–77.

them. But waiting for an additional, fourth, year to enjoy the fruit of one's trees may have found few adherents. Hence its mention here and its promise of a reward. R. Akiba neatly captured the issue "The Torah addressed (man's) temptation so that he should not say: For four years I sorrow over it in vain."[116]

The foreskin is the fruit while it is enclosed in its bud, and *Keter Torah* has it right when it interprets this cognate accusative construction as: "Don't let the fruit ripen (open) but pluck it while it is closed." The closed bud, then, is the foreskin that should be plucked before the fruit (i.e., the penis) emerges. I checked with the Berkeley Horticultural Nursery, and this is precisely what is done. The juvenile tree is not pruned—the branches are not thinned or trimmed—but its buds are removed (alternatively, the buds are allowed to flower, and only those that are pollinated and bearing fruit are removed).[117]

[19:24] The firstfruits of produce belong to God (Num 18:12-13), as do the tithe, according to H (Lev 27:30), and the firstlings (27:26; Exod 13:2, 12; Num 18:17). However, the fruit of trees during their first three years is unworthy as an offering to God,[118] and like the impure firstling, according to the epic tradition (Exod 13:13), it must be destroyed.[119]

Horticultural facts also correspond with the biblical injunction regarding the taboo concerning the fruit of the juvenile tree. In the land of Israel, fruit trees reach maturity only after several years: an average of five years for date palms, five to seven years for figs and pomegranates, three to six years for grapes, and four to five years for almonds.[120] Ancient sources confirm this practice. In Babylonia a date orchard ripens in five years,[121] and a rabbinic source testifies that grapevines ripen in five years, figs in six, and olives in seven.[122]

The import of this unit was neatly captured by Philo.[123] His exposition of the text is in italics (although his claim that the young trees need to be pruned[124] is in error):

> Thus many farmers during the spring season watch the young trees to *squeeze off at once any fruit they bear* before they *advance in quality and size,* for fear of weakening the parent plants. For, if these precautions are not taken, the result is that when they

---

[116] *Sipra Qedošim* par. 3:9.

[117] Rattray (orally).

[118] Cf. Ibn Ezra, Bekhor Shor, esp. Ramban.

[119] Cf. Driver and White 1898:90; but the priestly tradition allows impure firstlings to be redeemed, Lev 27:27; Num 18:15.

[120] Bibliography in Eilberg-Schwartz 1990:150–52.

[121] CH §60.

[122] *t. Šebi.* 1:3.

[123] *Virt.* 157-59.

[124] *Virt.* 156.

should bear fully ripened fruit they bring forth either nothing at all or abortions nipped in the bud, exhausted as they are by the laborer of prematurely bearing crops which lay such a weight upon the branches that at last they wear out the trunk and roots as well. But after three years when the roots have sunk deep in and are made firmly attached to the soil, and the trunk supported as it were on immovable foundations has grown and acquired vigor, *it will be able to bear fully in the fourth year. . . . But in this fourth year,* he commands them not to pick this fruit for their own enjoyment but to *dedicate the whole of it as a first fruit to God,* partly as a thank offering for the past, partly *in hope of fertility to come and the acquisition of wealth to which this will lead.*

Verses 26-28. Unit 12: Eschewing Death and the Dead

Neither the word nor the subject of holiness is mentioned in this unit. There is no need. The God of holiness/life negates all forms of impurity/death, of which the corpse is the chief repository.[125] Abstaining from rites in which the dead are consulted or worshiped is therefore indispensable to achieving holiness.

[19:26] The expression "you shall not eat over the blood" may signify a form of divination, namely chthonic worship involving the consultation of ancestral spirits, as developed, with ancient Near Eastern parallels, especially from the Grecian sphere, by Grintz.[126]

Divination, of which augury (the reading of omens) is a branch, must be scrupulously distinguished from sorcery; the latter attempts to alter the future; the former, to predict it.[127] The magician who claims to curse or bless is a sorcerer, whereas the one who foretells events but cannot affect them is a diviner. In Israel sorcery is not only banned (Deut 18:10), but punished with death (Exod 22:17 [Eng. 18]). In biblical religion sorcery in any form was, by definition, deemed ineffectual since all events were under the control of the one God. It was also deemed heretical because any attempt to alter the future purported to flout and overrule the will of God. A sorcerer's techniques (still not fully understood) are both condemned and ridiculed by Ezekiel: "Woe to those who sew cushions on the joints of every arm, and make rags for the head of every stature to entrap persons . . . sentencing to death persons who should not die, and to life persons who should not live, as you lie to my people who listen to lies!" (Ezek 13:18-19). Yet despite the official ban on sorcery (rather, because such legislation was necessary), we infer that it was widely practiced (see 2 Kgs 9:22; Jer 27:9; Mic 5:11; Mal 3:5; 2 Chr 33:6).

Divination is predicated on the assumption that the course of events is predictable: Its advance notices are imprinted in natural phenomena or discernible in

---

[125] See Milgrom 1991:270–78, 986–1000.

[126] 1966:1–17.

[127] Cf. Kaufmann 1937–56:1.350 n. 1, 458 n. 1.

humanmade devices. Divination could be tolerated in Israel[128] since, theoretically, it was not incompatible with monotheism—the diviner could always claim that he was only trying to disclose the immutable will of God. Divination was practiced and permitted not only in Egypt (Joseph, Gen 44:5) and Aram (Laban, Gen 30:27) but also in Israel (Jonathan, 1 Sam 14:9-10; Eliezer, Gen 24:14). As acknowledged by Rashi, "An omen that is not according to the form pronounced by Eliezer, Abraham's servant, or by Jonathan son of Saul is not a (permitted) divination."[129] That is, to interpret an event as an omen of good or evil is not prohibited. Indeed, according to one source, the prophet was originally called a diviner (1 Sam 9:9). Thus the diviner, in contrast to the sorcerer, was never subject to sanctions, either judicially or divinely. The exception was the necromancer, who was executed judicially (Lev 20:27) because he laid claim to the sorcerer's power to raise up the dead even against their will (1 Sam 28:15); his clients, however, were punished by *karet* (Lev 20:6). Molek worship was singled out as a greater capital crime (20:1-5) because it constituted both murder and desecration of YHWH's name (see on 18:21). However, other diviners summed up by the terms "augurer" and "diviner" (19:26) were prohibited but not sanctioned, hence tacitly accepted by H.

Certain religious circles condemned divination as an abominable heresy (Deut 18:10-12; 1 Samuel 15–23)—not that they doubted its efficiency. Rather, God had granted Israel a special boon: He communicated with them directly, through prophets or dreams (Num 12:6; Deut 12:6-8; 13:2-6). The case of Balaam is illustrative of the pentateuchal nonpriestly sources. Although a pagan, Balaam was a worshiper of YHWH (Num 22:13, 18-19; 23:12, 26), and YHWH responded positively to him (22:20) and negatively, when he attempted to play the sorcerer by "compelling" YHWH to curse Israel against his will—something that Balaam knew full well was bound to fail. Balaam reaches the full stature of an Israelite prophet when he abandons his divinatory techniques and seeks a direct revelation (24:1; cf. 23:23).[130] The official cult did sanction one divinatory medium, the Urim and Thummim carried on the (high) priest's ephod (Exod 28:30-35; 1 Sam 2:28; 14:3; 23:6, 9; 28:6; 30:7).

[19:27] The hair symbolized the life force of the individual, and locks of hair were laid in tombs or funeral pyres in pre-Islamic Arabia[131] and ancient Syria[132] as well as brought to the sanctuary as dedicatory offerings (details in 21:5). In other words, these prohibitions ban idolatrous rites. However, they are so entrenched in Israelite life (Ezek 7:18; Mic 1:16) that H and D are forced to limit baldness to part of the head, leaving total proscription of baldness (of any degree) to the priests (Lev 21:5;

---

[128] Contra Kaufmann 1960:87–92.
[129] *b. Ḥul.* 95b.
[130] Details in Milgrom 1990:471–74.
[131] W. Robertson Smith 1927:324 n. 1.
[132] Lucian, *De dea syria* 60.

Ezek 44:20). In any event, it should be clear that the ban on cutting hair at the corners and gashing oneself for the dead originate with the priesthood (Lev 21:5), to judge by its rationale (21:6). That H and D follow suit (though in less extreme form) is due to their extension of (priestly) holiness to all Israel.

In some ancient societies, including Israel, the beard was the prized symbol of manhood, and its mutilation was considered the greater disgrace and punishment (2 Sam 10:4-5; Isa 7:20). Among the Greeks, an old Spartan law forbids the *aphori*, from the moment of their taking office, to clip their beards; and those who fled before the enemy in battle were forced to appear in public with half-shorn beards.[133]

[19:28] That laceration and tonsure (v. 27) were common mourning rites in Israel is attested by Jer 16:6: "Great and small alike shall die in this land. They shall not be buried; and no one shall lament them, nor lacerate and tonsure themselves for them." Schmidt suggests a plausible rationale for laceration rites during mourning: "self-mutilation might be more appropriately viewed as an attempt to assuage the envy which the dead possesses for the living by inflicting suffering on oneself or as a desperate attempt to disguise oneself from ghosts on the haunt by making oneself unrecognizable. . . . Thus, self-mutilation as mourning so blurred the worlds of life and death in the tightly constricted and distinct worlds mapped out in the priestly and deuteronomic legislations that they were singled out for censorship."[134] The binary opposition of life-death is congruent with the thrust of the entire chapter, whose central theme is the opposition of holiness/life to impurity/death.

The prohibition of tattoos bans the legally accepted practice of marking a perpetual Israelite slave (Exod 21:6; Deut 15:17 [J]). This fact alone should indicate that H abolishes the statute of perpetual slavery entirely. Since H maintains perpetual slavery for a resident alien or foreigner (Lev 25:44-46), we can presume that it also permitted such slaves to be tattooed. This practice is confirmed by the rabbis: "[The owner] who marks his slave so that he does not run away is *exempt* [from the prohibition on Lev 19:28]."[135] Thus instead of searching (in vain) for a mourning rite to explain the juxtaposition of tattooing to laceration, tattooing should be regarded as an independent prohibition aimed, perhaps among other objectives, at the abolition of slavery in Israel.

Verse 29. Unit 13: Prostitution, Cultic or Secular?

Cultic prostitution, meaning intercourse with strangers as a sacred rite to increase fertility, is nonexistent in the ancient Near East. This is the conclusion arrived at by the most recent investigators of the subject.[136]

---

[133] Cited by Kalisch 1867–72:2.429.

[134] Schmidt 1996:287, 290. See also Feldman 1977:79–108; for other explanations see Tigay 1996:136.

[135] *t. Mak.* 4:15, a reference I owe to Greengus (orally).

[136] Hooks 1985; Gruber 1983a, 1986; Goodfriend 1992; van der Toorn 1989, 1992.

Verse 30. Unit 14: Sabbath and Sanctuary

The Sabbath took on heightened importance for the prophets of the seventh century who declared that its observance was essential as an antidote to the rampant assimilation under King Manasseh (Zephaniah 1) and hence a determinant of Israel's national destiny (Jer 17:19-27).[137] It became indispensable to Israel's survival during the Babylonian exile when all the festivals were suspended because of the loss of the temple (see Lev 23:3). This may be the reason why this verse is repeated verbatim in 26:2, which serves the purpose (with 26:1) of summoning up the essence of the Decalogue and of adding the weekly Sabbath to the yearly Sabbath as factors in Israel's national survival.

The Sabbath is indispensable to achieving holiness, for by observing it Israel sanctifies it, as expressly commanded in the Decalogue (Exod 20:8; Deut 5:12), and by violating it, Israel desecrates it (Ezek 20:16, 21, 24; 22:8). Reverence for the sanctuary adds a new aspect to holiness in this chapter, indicating that holiness has both a spatial and a temporal dimension.

"Sanctuary" here refers to the *temenos*, the sacred precincts, as it does in 12:4; 20:3; 21:12.[138] At the end of the First Temple period, the people frequented the temple on the Sabbath (Ezek 46:3). The priority of the Sabbath over the sanctuary in this verse is the basis for the rabbinic rule that the Sabbath may not be violated, even for the building of the sanctuary.[139] Indeed, the placement of the Sabbath commandment (Exod 35:1-3 [H]) at the head of the instructions to erect the tabernacle, and before its construction (Exod 31:12-17 [H]), also serves the same purpose.

Verse 31. Unit 15: Consulting the Dead

Necromancy was as pervasive in Israel as in the ancient Near East. Because it was associated with ancestor worship, it was condemned in H. The necromancers had the ability to raise the dead against their will (1 Sam 28:15).

Another motivation may underlie the official opposition to consulting ghosts and wizard spirits: it was presumed that they could read into the future. Thus their activity was a form of divination. As I argued, divination as opposed to sorcery was a legitimate practice, since it did not attempt to change the divine decisions (sorcery), but only to read them in advance of their announcement—in other words, to predict the future. Thus these magicians were in competition with the prophets, who claimed the role of authorized conveyors of YHWH's will, and with the priests, who in their turn restricted divination to the operation of the Urim and Thummim. Thus there may have also been an economic factor that accounts for the repeated official opposition to these competitive diviners (19:31; 20:6, 27; Deut 18:10-12).[140]

---

[137] Greenberg 1971.

[138] Cf. Milgrom 1970:23 n. 78.

[139] *Sipra Qedošim* 7:7.

[140] Cf. Olyan 1997:85.

H's "impurity" is metaphoric: no purificatory rites are prescribed. Neither can the penalty be erased: for polluting the land, expulsion is mandated for the people (18:25) and *karet* for the individual (18:29). The same penalty of *karet* holds for individuals turning to mediums (20:6). Note, however, that although punishment by God is certain, there is no punishment by humans.

Verse 32. Unit 16: Respect for Elders

The same warning "you shall fear your God" is found in v. 14. Both the blind and deaf (v. 14) and the aged (v. 32) cannot enforce the dignity they merit, but God will punish those who deny it.[141] "What if one shuts his eyes and makes believe he didn't see him (the elderly)? Therefore it is written: 'you shall fear your God.'"[142]

Verses 33-34. Unit 17: The Resident Alien

In a paper presented in Jerusalem, Dandamaev described the legal status of aliens in sixth-century Mesopotamia.[143] They were deprived of civil rights: they could not be members of the *puḫru* (city assembly), own property, or have access to the Babylonian temples. Indeed, the temples were not interested in proselytes with whom they would have to share privileges; there was no proselytism. Instead, the aliens made up their own assemblies.[144] Thus not only in Israel but elsewhere in the ancient Near East, aliens were kept ethnically apart and only subsequently absorbed through intermarriage.

[19:33] "In your land." But not in the diaspora, where Israel has no authority. In fact, Israel's status in exile is that of a resident alien, the same status it had in Egypt (v. 34a?), the patriarchs had in Canaan (Gen 15:13; 23:4), and Moses had in Midian (Exod 2:22; 18:3).

"You shall love him as yourself" is the counterpart to v. 18, the same command regarding Israelites. Here, however, the command is practical, not platonic:[145] it specifies cheating him in business dealings (vv. 35-36). This verse also confirms the practical implications of "love"—it must be expressed in one's behavior (see v. 18).

Schwartz points out that there is a reciprocal relation between the alien and the Israelite: It is incumbent on the Israelite to love him (Deut 10:19), not to oppress him (Exod 22:20 [Eng. 21]; 23:9), support him (Lev 19:10 = 23:22; Deut 14:28-29; 24:19), include him in festival celebrations (Deut 16:11; 26:11), allow him to rest on

---

[141] Dillmann and Ryssel 1897.
[142] Rashi.
[143] Dandamaev 1993.
[144] E.g., the Egyptians under Cambyses; Ezekiel and the elders, Ezek 8:1.
[145] Wellhausen 1963:155; Elliger 1966.

the Sabbath (Exod 20:10; 23:12), and provide him safety (Num 35:15).[146] It is incumbent on the alien to follow the same sacrificial procedures as the Israelite (Exod 12:48-49; Lev 17:8, 12, 13; Num 9:14; 15:14, 29), observe the same prohibitions (Lev 16:29; 18:26), and receive the same punishments (20:2; 24:6, 22).

Verses 35-36a. Unit 18: Business Ethics

The opportunity (and hence the temptation) to cheat in commercial transactions was greatest with the measuring instruments used by the seller. Thus the focus of this unit is on honest scales, weights, and other measuring instruments. The declarative statement here for honest measures is repeated in Deut 25:13-16, beginning with a prefatory warning against dishonest measures and, in typical Deuteronomic fashion, ending with a promise of rewards for observing this commandment and condemnation for its violation.

Dishonest measures are vigorously condemned both in prophecy (Hos 12:8; Amos 8:5; Mic 6:10-11) and in wisdom (Deut 25:13-16; Prov 11:1; 16:11; 20:10, 23). A pointed indictment by Amos (8:4-5) is directed against those who hypocritically observe the Sabbath while using false weights and measures.

As aptly noted by Knohl, chapter 19 constitutes the priestly (H) answer to Amos, emphasizing the importance of keeping the Sabbath (vv. 3b, 30a?) and employing honest business practices.[147]

Verses 36b-37. Closing Exhortation

[**19:37**] "You shall heed all my statutes and all my rules, and you shall do them." This statement should be compared with: "My rules alone you shall observe and my statutes shall you heed . . . you shall heed my statutes and my rules . . . if one does them . . ." (18:4-5). These words of v. 37 speak eloquently of this verse's conscious imitation of all cited words of 18:4-5. What is new is the twice-repeated particle "all." Thus the close of the inclusion is, in effect, saying: not only should the prohibitions of chapter 18 be observed, but all the injunctions of chapter 19.[148]

---

[146] 1999:358–61.
[147] 1991:33.
[148] Hoffmann 1953:2.48.

Penalties for Molek Worship, Necromancy, and Sexual Violations

Selected Themes
A. Molek Worship and Ancestor Worship

This chapter describes some of the worst violations of biblical law. Heading the list is Molek worship. Molek worshipers commit two capital crimes in their single act of devotion: idolatry and murder. Molek worship constitutes murder, since the sacrificed child is burned to death, as is explicitly stated in Ps 106:38: "They *shed* innocent *blood*, the *blood* of their sons and daughters, whom they sacrificed to the idols of Canaan so that *the land was polluted* with bloodguilt." The murder must be punished by a human court (Num 35:31-33).

Moreover, the crimes of Molek worship and necromancy are not listed according to their previous order (Lev 18:21 and 19:31, respectively), but are placed at the head of chapter 20 (vv. 1-6), because the entire chapter is ordered according to the severity of the incurred penalties.[1] For the Molek worshiper, the death penalty is prescribed as in the cases that follow (vv. 9-16). In the instance of Molek, however, God supplements death by *karet,* the termination of the line (v. 3a). Indeed, failing immediate action by the judicial authorities, God will personally intervene (vv. 5a, 6b) by imposing *karet* on the violator's family and followers (v. 5).

The rationale is specified: the worshiper's crime against God is that he polluted YHWH's sanctuary and desecrated his name (v. 3b). The issue is that the Molek worshiper invokes YHWH's name, under the erroneous impression that YHWH sanctions (or even commands) Molek worship (see 18:21). The sanctuary (clearly the Jerusalem temple) has been defiled, possibly because the worshiper would likely ascend from the valley of Hinnom to worship YHWH in the temple—both on the same day (Ezek 23:38-39). The necromancy prohibition (v. 6) is coupled with Molek (vv. 1-5), even though its *karet* punishment technically belongs with the other *karet* penalties (vv. 17-18), because Molek and necromancy share the same motivation—ancestor worship.

---

[1] Hoffmann 1953:2.48-49.

A clear example of ancestor worship is Isa 8:19-20a, which also associates ancestor worship with necromancy: "When they say to you: Consult ghosts and wizard-spirits who chirp and mutter; shall not a people consult its ancestral spirits on behalf of the living, (consult) the dead for an oracle and a message?"

Ancestor worship was considered compatible with the worship of YHWH. There is sufficient biblical evidence to support the thesis that in preexilic times, according to popular belief, the dead existed outside YHWH's realm (Isa 38:18-19; Ps 6:6 [Eng. 5]; 88:11-13 [Eng. 10-12]; 115:17).[2] However, voices arose in the eighth century BCE, stemming from prophets (Isa 8:19-20) and priests (e.g., Lev 19:31; 20:6), that, in opposition to this dualism, extended YHWH's domain into the underworld and condemned Molek worship as a "desecration of the name of God" (see 18:21b). However, monotheism is theoretically consistent with ancestor worship, since the departed spirits, even if semidivine and capricious, are subject to YHWH's overall control. Moreover, if van der Toorn is proved correct—and I believe he is—that theophoric names embody family gods, (e.g., the names Abinadab and Ahinadab are equivalent to Jonadub and refer to deified ancestors), then the continued attestation of these names in the biblical onomasticon implies that the cult of the ancestors endured throughout preexilic (and, even later) times, even into the rabbinic period.[3] Caution is recommended, however, because a name can persist long after its original meaning has been forgotten (Anat, a Canaanite goddess, in modern Israel; Beulah, "impregnated," among African Americans). In any event, as Isa 57:9 testifies, the worship of the underworld god Molek persisted into postexilic times. In other words, the battle against necromancy formed a distinct phase in the monotheistic revolution, a battle—to judge by the biblical record—that was never won.

B. On Being Holy: Part IV (continued from chap. 19, Theme A)

Only H could have written: "You shall sanctify yourselves and be holy" (v. 7; also 11:44): Israel can achieve holiness only by its own efforts. YHWH has given it the means: the commandments. All other occurrences of "sanctify oneself" are nonpriestly, and the meaning is different, namely, "purify oneself." The one exception is Ezekiel, who was heavily influenced by H. Ezekiel, however, has God speak in the first person, literally, "I will make myself great and make myself holy and (thus) become known" (Ezek 38:23). Whereas Israel makes itself holy obeying YHWH's commandments, YHWH makes himself holy by his might—in this instance, by his devastation of Gog. That is, the nations will now acknowledge his greatness and holiness (cf. Ezek 36:23-30, 36). In Ezekiel, holiness means YHWH's dissimilarity, and total otherness, the realization of which inspires wonder and awe.

---

[2] Cf. van der Toorn 1991b.
[3] Van der Toorn 1996. Cf. *b. Sanh.* 65.

Leviticus 17–27: The Holiness Source (H)

All four pentateuchal codes differ on the concept of holiness. P limits holiness to consecrated objects and persons, namely, sanctums and priests. For the priests, consecrated once by Moses (Leviticus 8), their holiness is permanent and is automatically bequeathed to their male descendants.[4] D declares that all Israel is inherently holy (Deut 7:6; 14:2; 26:19). While bestowing holiness on a wider group of people, D shares with P a conviction that holiness is static. In contrast, H's concept of holiness is dynamic. Laypersons can attain it, and priests must sustain it, for holiness is diminished or enhanced by violating or obeying, respectively, the divine commandments. In my view, the dynamism of holiness is not entirely the innovation of H. It is adumbrated in JE, where holiness is achievable by observing the Decalogue and the firstfruits and firstborn offerings (Exod 22:28-30 [Eng. 29-31]). H expands these requirements to all of God's commandments.

In H holiness is no longer a priestly prerogative. It is available to and attainable by everyone. What could have motivated H to legislate such a far-reaching doctrine? Here I can only surmise. H is mainly the product of the end of the eighth century BCE. Holiness may be another plank in H's overall program to rectify the socioeconomic injustice prevailing among the people. The growing number of small farmers who lost their inherited land to rapacious creditors (25:25-43) must have produced widespread destitution and despair. In practical terms, H proposed a land reform, the laws of the Jubilee, as laid out in chapter 25. However, it would take effect only in fifty years. What of the immediate need to raise morale and hope? H's answer: the wide accessibility of holiness.

For H holiness was not like its predecessor P's holiness. It was not enough to be descended from the priestly line. It was insufficient only to serve YHWH inside his earthly sanctuary. Instead, in H's view, holiness was a spiritual, metaphysical thing. By following the commandments one could enter the presence of the one who proclaimed, "I am holy." It made one equal to "the holy ones" (Ps 89:6, 8 [Eng. 5, 7]) who serve YHWH in his divine realm. Furthermore, neither financial success nor social prestige nor priestly pedigree was a prerequisite for its attainment. Only adherence to the divine commandments was required. By observing them, an Israelite would become holy.

We should not forget that there was an ethnic exclusivity to the divine gift of holiness. Only a member of the covenantal community could qualify. This contrasts with H's position on the alien. Simply speaking, H accorded the alien the full civil rights and religious privileges enjoyed by native Israelites (see chap. 17, THEME A), but it denied him holiness. Strive as he may to worship YHWH with zeal and to observe all his commandments, the alien still could not become holy.

It should not go unnoticed that the participial expression "YHWH the sanctifier" represents the first of seven such occurrences in H (20:8; 21:8, 15, 23; 22:9, 16,

---

[4] Each high priest, however, must undergo consecration; see Milgrom 1991:555.

23). It is also noteworthy that the outer two are directed to all of Israel, including the priests; the second, third, fifth, and sixth occurrences refer to the priesthood;[5] and the fourth, the middle occurrence, probably refers to the sanctums. It is also no accident that the two outer passages are extensive, giving initially the method by which God sanctifies all of Israel, namely, by their following his commandments (20:7 8), and closing with the rationale for YHWH's indisputable right to impose his holiness demands on Israel, namely, by freeing them from Egyptian bondage and thereby acquiring his lordship over Israel (22:32-33).

H's achievements (or at least H's demands) cannot be fully appreciated unless one realizes that H, in effect, has democratized Israel. The priests, to be sure, reign supreme in the cult: the sanctuary is their exclusive province; the altar is their monopoly. However, to retain their privileges, the accident of birth is necessary, but insufficient. As much of Israel is enjoined to attain holiness, the priests are required to sustain it.

C. Ancestor Worship in the Biblical World

Both archaeology and written records supply unambiguous evidence of the prevalence of ancestor worship in the ancient Near East. Excavations at Ebla have revealed a Middle Bronze sanctuary and an adjoining graveyard devoted to the deceased ancestors (on which see below). Their worship included the consumption of ritual foods, rites in which the names of the dead were recited, offerings of animal and vegetables sacrifices, and the worship of small cultic images of royal ancestors.[6]

Regarding possible archaeological remains of ancestor worship among the Canaanites, it has been argued that the schematic statues found alongside the stelae in Hazor are ancestor idols. According to this theory, their function is equal to that of the stelae, thus strengthening the arguments in favor of the interpretation of the Stelae Temple at Hazor as related to the cult of the dead.[7]

There are widespread literary references to libation pipes to the dead: "On this day stand before Šamaš and Gilgamesh [gods of the underworld] . . . I will pour cool water down your water pipes; cure me that I may sing your praises";[8] "May Šamaš never let the pipe for him receive cool water down below in the netherworld";[9] "May Šamaš uproot him from the land of the living and leave his ghost to thirst for water in the world below."[10] In Sumerian temple hymns, Enegi is described as the "big pipe of Ereškigal's underworld"—an allusion to the clay tube into which liquids for the dead were poured.[11]

---

[5] Reading 21:8 with the LXX; see Milgrom 2000:1809.
[6] Matthiae 1979.
[7] Beck 1990:94.
[8] KAR 227 iii 14-15, 24-25, cited in Bayliss 1973:118.
[9] *CAD* 1/2.324b s.v. *arūtu*.
[10] *CAD* 4.399a s.v. *etemmu* = CH, Epilogue 34-40.
[11] Lambert 1980.

Leviticus 17–27: The Holiness Source (H)

The obvious purpose of the ancestor cult was to secure favors from the deceased for the present life: "Come (O dead ancestors), eat this, drink this, (and) bless Ammisaduqa the son of Ammiditana, the king of Babylon."[12] A second, equally important purpose was to invoke the name of the dead to keep alive their memory: "The invocation in the funerary cult was the only means available to most people to perpetuate their names after their death."[13] Panammu entreats his sons "to invoke the name of Panammu as well as (the god) Hadad."[14]

The chances are that the biblical writers, though fully aware of the popular food offerings to the dead, put a different face on it by referring to them as acts of veneration. What choice had they, considering that any attempt to ban them would have been totally ignored by the populace? The hitherto uninterrupted, long tradition in the ancient Near East, that worshiping the dead would guarantee their guardianship of and benefactions to their living descendants, continued unabated. The pure YHWHists, represented by H and D, could do no more than mask this practice with an interpretation compatible with their theology, similar to the one expressed by Kaufmann: "Burying the deceased in a family grave, giving him food, raising a monument for him, and the like, are deeds of devotion toward the dead through which the living maintained a connection with them."[15] An equivalent example of ritual masking is Maimonides' treatment of incantations:

> Whoever is bitten by a scorpion or a snake is permitted to recite a charm over the bite, even on the Sabbath, in order to calm his spirit and bolster his courage, even though it is of no help whatever. Since it is life threatening, it was permitted him[16] so that his mind does not become deranged. [However, those who] recite a charm over the injury and [add] a verse from the Torah . . . they are among the deniers of Torah (heretics), for they turn the words of Torah, which are only cures for the spirit, into cures for the body. . . . But the healthy person who reads (Torah) verses and Psalms so that he will be protected by the merit of his reading them and be saved from woes and injuries—it is permitted (him).[17]

Although reciting a spell is forbidden (Deut 18:11),[18] Maimonides had to concede to the widespread use of such charms, which he interpreted not as cures but as psychological supports; if a Torah verse was co-opted it could only serve as an apotropaic, a verbal amulet. Thus, no differently from Maimonides, the biblical authors had to improvise an acceptable rationale that could mask the real reasons why the people at large utilized them.

---

[12] Cf. Finklestein 1966.

[13] Bayliss 1973:117.

[14] *KAI* 214.16, 21.

[15] 1960:314.

[16] Cf. *b. Sanh.* 101a.

[17] *Mishneh Torah,* Idolatry 11:11-12. I owe this reference to Moshe Greenberg.

[18] Maimonides, *Mishneh Torah,* Idolatry 11:10.

The necromancer, however, infringed on the sole sovereignty of YHWH. He usurped YHWH's exclusive authority to direct Israel's destiny via the appointed agents, the prophets, and it is no accident that the wholesale ban against all mantic practitioners (Deut 18:10-14) is followed by a designation of the prophet as the only legitimate carrier of YHWH's message (18:15-22; cf. 13:2-6 [Eng. 1-5]).

Therefore, there exists a world of difference between the guardian-dead, the ancestor spirit, and the diviner of the dead, the necromancer. The former was a family benefactor who would focus his blessing on his living descendants. The latter, however, might misread God's intention and mislead an entire nation. For example, the king might consult a necromancer (1 Samuel 28) rather than a true prophet or the official oracle, the Urim and Thummim (Deut 33:8; 1 Sam 14:41 LXX) and, as a result, die in battle with his army (1 Kgs 22:10-23) or cause the destruction of the state and the exile of its inhabitants (Jer 28:1-11). The necromancers, like false prophets, thus had to be extirpated (Lev 20:27; Deut 13:2-6 [Eng. 1-5]; 18–20), if for no other reason than that Israel might be preserved.

However, a deeper, politically motivated cause may lie beneath the ban on necromancy. The cult of the dead was a potential and potent threat against the political establishment, the state, which had endorsed the worship of YHWH as the sole legitimate cult in Israel: "The ancestors might inspire resistance to the leadership of the national administration, or even foment revolution. The suppression of necromancy was not an act of demonstrated piety on the part of Saul, but instead an attempt to secure the state monopoly on divination."[19] Ancestor worship was the bastion of family religion, and it would have been a prime objective of the monarchy from its inception with Saul to ban necromancy (1 Sam 28:9) and contain ancestor worship so that the worship of YHWH could become the national religion of Israel.

Were these instructions effective? Not at all. Ancestor worship continued to flourish, and the prohibitions against necromancy proved a dead letter.

D. Sex and Food

The dynamic quality of H's holiness is evident in its concept of space and also comprises the same tripartite divisions: humanity, Israel and priests. Both points are demonstrated schematically in Figure 7 on the following page.

H harbors an old tradition that the entire camp of Israel in the wilderness cannot tolerate severe impurity (Num 5:1-4; cf. 31:19). This tradition is echoed in D, which states explicitly that the camp must remain holy (Deut 23:10-15 [Eng. 9-14]). It is H, however, that extends this view logically and consistently to the future residence of Israel—the promised land. Hence impurities produced by Israel by violating the Lord's prohibitions—both moral and ritual—pollute not only the sanctuary but

---

[19] Van der Toorn 1996b:318–19.

EARTH (Humanity)

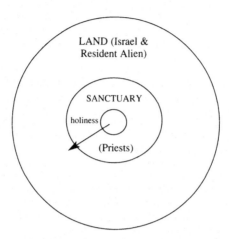

Figure 7. Organization of Space in H

the entire land. Because God dwells in the land as well as in the sanctuary (e.g., Lev 25:23; 26:11; cf. Josh 22:19; Hos 9:3-4), the land cannot abide pollution (e.g., Lev 18:25-30; cf. Num 35:33-34). It is therefore no accident that H enjoins upon both the Israelite and the resident alien, that is, all those who live on the land, to keep the land holy by guarding against impurity and following the prescribed purificatory procedures (e.g., Num 15:27-29; 19:10b-13). Without the commitment of every individual to eschew impurity and purify if necessary, YHWH would be driven from the land and would not bless the land and its inhabitants with fertility and security (Lev 26:3-11).

The bond between Israel and the dietary restrictions is intimated in the Deuteronomic code, as it heads the list of prohibited animals with a notice concerning Israel's election as a holy people: "For you are a holy people to the Lord; the Lord your God chose you from among all the peoples on earth to be his treasured people" (Deut 14:2). Furthermore, Israel's designation as "a holy people" concludes the Deuteronomic diet list, thereby framing it as an inclusion (14:21). What is merely implicit in D, however, is forcefully explicit in Leviticus 20 (H): "I am the Lord your God who set you apart from other peoples. So you shall set apart the pure quadrupeds from the impure, the pure birds from the impure . . . which I have set apart for you to treat as impure. You shall be holy to me, for I the Lord am holy and I have set you apart from other peoples to be mine" (20:24b-26). What could be clearer! Israel's attainment of holiness depends on setting itself apart from the nations and the prohibited animal foods. The dietary system thus both reflects and reinforces Israel's election.

This motif of separation in Leviticus 20 (it occurs four times in two and a half verses, 24b-26) is further extended and underscored by the context. Leviticus 20 is the peroration to the pericope on forbidden sexual unions (20:7-21), which are attributed to the Canaanites, Israel's predecessors in the land, and to their neighbor, Egypt (18:3; 20:23). The implied nexus between sex and food, on the one hand, and apostasy, on the other, is expressly stated elsewhere in Scripture, for example: "You must not make a covenant with the inhabitants of the land, for they will lust after their gods and sacrifice to their gods and invite you, and you will eat of their sacrifices. And when you take wives from among their daughters for your sons, their daughters will lust after their gods and will cause your sons to lust after their gods" (Exod 34:15-16; cf. *Let. Aris.* 151-52; *Jub.* 22:16).

Thus sex and food, bed and board, are intimately related. In *Marjorie Morningstar,* the Jewish heroine finally succumbs to her seducer when she tastes pork for the first time.[20] It is no accident that the author is a learned and observant Jew who understands that a breach in the dietary system may endanger one's entire religious structure.

It is also no accident that one of the early acts of Christianity was to abolish the dietary laws (but not the blood prohibition [cf. Acts 15:20]—significantly because it is incumbent on humanity). Historians have claimed that the purpose was to ease the process of converting the gentiles. This is, at best, a partial truth. Abolishing the dietary laws, Scripture informs us, also abolished the distinction between gentile and Jew. And that is exactly what the founders of Christianity intended to accomplish, to end once and for all the notion that God had covenanted himself with a certain people that would keep itself apart from all of the other nations. It is these distinguishing criteria, the dietary laws (and circumcision), that were done away with. Christianity's intuition was correct: Israel's restrictive diet is a daily reminder to be apart from the nations (cf. Acts 10:9-16, 27-28; 11:4-12).

Selected Texts

[20:2] "The people of the land" means the adult male populace at large. It refers to any unofficial, unauthorized body of Israelites, in contrast to the ʿedah, "council,"[21] which is authorized and official, probably a representative body of all the tribal and clan chieftains. In reality, we are dealing—to use a derogatory term—with a lynch mob.

The sin of the Molek worshiper is exceptionally grievous because of its severe consequence: pollution of the sanctuary and desecration of the name YHWH. The sinner must be killed immediately; any delay jeopardizes the welfare of the entire nation. Hence the prolonged judicial process necessary for the summoning of the

---

[20] Wouk 1955.
[21] In its restricted meaning; Milgrom 1990:335–36.

ᶜ*edah* may, in this singular incident, be bypassed. After all, witnesses are not required. If he is not caught in flagrante delicto, the erection of the Topheth and, above all, the charred remains of his child are evidence enough.

[20:3] The punishment of excision falls into the measure-for-measure category: If the Molek worshiper thought that by sacrificing one of his children he would be granted more,[22] God will see to it that death will terminate his line (*karet*). Also, he hoped that the progeny Molek would grant him would guarantee earthly immortality. Instead, he will be denied access to his deceased ancestors. That is, he will be "cut off" from the past as well as the future. It is an *additional* punishment: he will suffer both execution and excision.[23] However, if the people fail to stone him, then his family and all those who protected him will also suffer *karet* (vv. 4-5).

Here is the first (and in the Torah, the only) explicit statement that idolatry pollutes the sanctuary (see Jer 7:30; 32:34; Ezek 5:11; 23:38). The importance of this verse should not be overlooked. It is the first time that any non-YHWHistic worship is impure. I would suggest that it constitutes a precedent for the seventh-century prophets to extend H's limited usage of "impure" to idolatry in all its forms and consequences, namely, that idolatry henceforth will become a factor in Israel's destiny.

"Desecrating my holy name" indicates that holiness is the quintessential nature of YHWH, which distinguishes him from all other beings. It is ironic yet characteristic of H that it, rather than P, adopts a "name" theology and the use of "desecrate" instead of "pollute," proving that H is just as opposed to anthropomorphism as P, if not more so.

[20:4] If the family engages in a cover-up,[24] it is guilty even if it ignored the crime and did nothing (see 1 Sam 12:3; Isa 1:15; Prov 28:27). Although collective punishment is a basic doctrine in the priestly texts,[25] it probably does not apply here, since by their silence the family members acquiesced in his crime and hence were guilty on their own accord.

Verses 7-8. Sanctification and Opening Exhortation

[20:7] This verse can best be seen as the opening exhortation regarding the illicit sexual practices that follow (vv. 9-21), corresponding to the opening exhortation of 18:1-5, which explicitly admonishes the Israelites not to follow the (sexual) mores of their Egyptian and Canaanite neighbors. These same peoples are also rife with necromancy

---

[22] Ramban, Abravenel.
[23] Shadal; cf. Milgrom 1991:460.
[24] Cf. *Sipra Qedošim* par. 10:13; *Tg. Ps.-J.*
[25] Cf. Milgrom 1990:444–48; and 24:14.

and ancestor worship (see above, THEME A). Perhaps, then, vv. 7-8 should also be regarded as a bridge, connecting the two seductive practices that perpetually threaten to assimilate Israel with its neighbors: idolatry and sexual license.

Verses 9-21. Penalties for Sexual Violations

The order of these prohibitions clearly differs from that in chapter 18 because its organizing principle is also different. Chapter 18 is ordered by family relationships: the closest (vv. 7-11), parents (vv. 12-14), their wives (vv. 15-16), wife (vv. 17-18); and by nonrelatives: menstruant (v. 19), married woman (v. 20), Molek worship (v. 21), sodomy (v. 22), bestiality (v. 23). Chapter 20, though, is ordered according to punishments, based on the severity of the crime: death (three kinds of adultery, vv. 10-12; sodomy, v. 13; mother-daughter, v. 14; bestiality, vv. 15-16); excision (half sister, v. 17; menstruant, v. 18; aunt, v. 19?); childlessness.

[20:9] The fact that a law regarding dishonoring parents heads a list of prohibited sexual unions is hardly an accident, but, on the contrary, is crucial in understanding the provenance of the entire list. It reflects a patriarchal society that relates all familial relationships, by the twin principles of consanguinity and affinity, back to one's father and mother. It adverts to the unstated premise that dishonoring parents—that is, the breakdown of obligations to one's father or mother—is able to lead to the breakdown of relationships with the other members of the familial chain, including the sexual taboos.

"He must be put to death" not at the whim of the parents, but by the decision of the authorized court. That a father *theoretically* had the authority to put a son to death even for noncapital offenses, see Exod 21:15; Deut 21:18-21 (cf. Gen 38:24). Indeed, the very absence here of any statement regarding the executioner can lead to the assumption that the sentence rested exclusively with the family patriarch, who had absolute control over all those who lived together as a "father's house," under his authority. However, the prohibition against copulating with one's daughter-in-law (v. 12; 18:15) is clearly directed to the father himself. Thus there is no alternative but to presume that the elders of the kin group or, in a later period, of the city (Deut 21:19) would constitute the judiciary.

The idiom "his bloodguilt is upon him" assures the court-appointed executioner that he will not be held responsible for slaying the convicted person—his blood(guilt) remains with him. This idiom also implies that the death penalty will befall the miscreant whether or not the elders put him to death. The death sentences prescribed in vv. 9-16 are therefore parallel to that explicitly stated for Molek worship (vv. 4-5): unless the authorities execute the convicted party, God will.

The wording of this law makes clear that the plaintiff is not the husband, who might be willing to accept compensation (Prov 6:32-35), but the community, which

255

must carry out the death sentence.[26] McKeating raises the possibility that the formulation of this law guarantees that the wife can be put to death only if the same end is meted out to her paramour.[27]

[20:11] "The man who lies with his father's wife": *Tg. Ps.-J.* assumes that it is his own mother; hence this verse is parallel to 18:7, 8.[28] The implication of the missing "who is his own mother" needs to be underscored. It means that incest with one's mother is such an egregious crime that the death penalty is taken for granted. This supposition can also explain the absence of the daughter and full sister from this list—and also from chapter 18. Sex with mother, daughter, or sister was abhorred in the ancient Near East, the rare exception in Egypt notwithstanding (see 18:3).

[20:13] Those opposed to homosexual rights, in general, and to professing gays and lesbians in the military, in particular, have resorted to the biblical interdiction of their practice on pain of death. In an op-ed piece, James Michener provides this rebuttal:

> Two other verses from the same chapter of Leviticus bring into question the relevance of these edicts today. Verse 9 warns: "For every one that curseth his father or his mother shall be surely put to death" [KJV]. Would we be willing to require the death sentence for boys who in a fit of rage oppose their parents? How many of us would have been guilty of that act at some point in our upbringing?
>
> Just as perplexing is verse 10: "And the man that committeth adultery with another man's wife . . . the adulterer and the adulteress shall surely be put to death." Can you imagine the holocaust that would ensue if that law were enforced today? . . . We do not kill young people who oppose their parents or execute adulterers. (*New York Times,* March 30, 1993)

As Michener notes, the biblical ban on homosexual acts must be considered in the context of all the other forbidden behaviors of Leviticus 18 and 20. Furthermore, it must be kept in mind that these regulations were binding only in Israel (and its resident aliens, 18:26), not in other countries. Thus prima facie it is illegitimate to apply these prohibitions on a universal scale. Note that lesbianism, though prevalent and known, was not banned (contrast Rom 1:26).

Israel's territory was pocketed by numerous Canaanite enclaves, not to speak of more populous nations on its borders. It was therefore understandable that Israel was obsessed with increasing its birth rate without endangering harmonious relations within the extended family, especially among those who lived in the same household.

---

[26] Loewenstamm 1968:631–32.

[27] 1979:58–59.

[28] Dillmann and Ryssel 1897; Elliger 1966.

[20:14] Daube has argued that the bestiality cases that follow (vv. 15-16) must be an appendix, since the punishment by fire in this verse ostensibly has brought to an end the prior "must be put to death" series.[29] However, bestiality is an old taboo, attested at length not only in the Hittite laws but also in the oldest biblical legislation.[30] It therefore is not a priestly innovation.

Execution by burning is attested in early narratives (Gen 38:24; Judg 14:15; 15:6). The severity of the punishment, death by fire, predicates that the two women conspired with the man. Perhaps it was reckoned as a form of harlotry, which may have put this case into the same category as the priest's daughter who committed harlotry (Lev 21:9).

[20:15] According to the rabbis, the death of the beast serves as a moral lesson to humankind. More likely, however, the animal dies because it has sinned, as does the goring ox (Exod 21:28-32).

[20:17] Presumably, the addressee thought that marriage with a half sister was not a violation. Indeed, if she is a stepsister—that is, both her biological parents are of a different clan—marriage with her is permitted.

Sexual congress with a full daughter or sister is missing from the list, just as in chapter 18. However, this chapter lists penalties. Surely, incest with a full sister (same father and mother) or daughter (issue of his loins) should incur the death penalty. The only solution that occurs to me is that these two unions were not subject to human sanctions. A full sister and an unmarried daughter are under the complete control of the addressee. These unions would be conducted secretively. Even if they became known, who would or could prosecute him? Although the perpetrator cannot be penalized by a human court, he is subject to *karet* in the divine court.

This double euphemism "seeing nakedness" is employed to indicate that the marriage was desired and consummated by both parties.[31] This sentence is exceptional because "he sees her nakedness" does not mean he has jurisdiction of her sexual organs (as in 18:10, 14, 16). Instead, it indicates an equality between man and woman. Both are equally guilty in their sexual behavior.

[20:20] How do the punishments "childless" and "excised" differ from each other? The difference, I would suggest, is slight but crucial. The one who is excised not only suffers the termination of his lineage, but is "excised" from joining his ancestors (rather than being "gathered to his fathers"). The one who is "childless" joins his

---

[29] 1947:79.

[30] HL §§187-200; Exod 22:18 (Eng. 19).

[31] *Sipra Qedošim* 11:11.

ancestors. But what good does it do him? He can only echo Absalom's lament: "I have no son 'to keep my name in remembrance'" (2 Sam 18:18; cf. Isa 56:4-5)—that is, to perform the ancestral rites.

[20:21] Does this verse reject the levirate institution? Elliger answers in the negative on the presumption that this law speaks of a case where the woman already had a child and is ineligible for marriage with a levir (Deut 25:5).[32] However, the lack of such specification would argue the reverse: Leviticus's opposition to the levirate, support for which is the penalty that they will be childless. A better answer is that this is a classic case of measure for measure. They thought that the levirate marriage would produce a child. Instead their marriage will be childless.

Verses 22-26. Closing Exhortation

Here the dimension of holiness is extended to the entire dietary system. Thus H supplements chapter 19. It declares that eschewing impure flesh is indispensable to attaining holiness. A most logical assumption: impure is the antonym and mortal enemy of holy. Moreover, the separation of Israel from the nations accomplished by Israel's separation from much of the animal world consumed by the nations helps complete the divine process of creation.

The connection between separation and creation is demonstrated by the frequent use in the creation story of the verb "separate" (Gen 1:4, 7, 14, 18). Separation creates order, and the distinctions between the elements must be maintained lest the world collapse into chaos and confusion. What holds for nature also holds for humanity. The separation of Israel from the nations is a sine qua non for the maintenance of order within the human world.

Furthermore, the diet laws associate separation with holiness. The doctrine of holiness is extended from the concept *of imitatio Dei* to the concept of separation. Just as God's holiness is a model and mandate for Israel, so is God's act of separation—first, in the creation of the world, and subsequently in the creation of Israel. In the latter case, however, the injunction is stronger. Whereas holiness is God's nature and is apprehensible solely from his self-revelation, separation is the result of his act, visible in the creation of the world (nature) and in the creation of Israel (history). Thus both positive holiness (*imitatio Dei*) and negative holiness (separation) must be reckoned as cardinal planks in H's theology; they are the divine imperatives for Israel. Israel is enjoined to live a life of imitation and separation, the former by fulfilling God's commandments, and the latter by separating from impure food as a reminder to separate from the destructive folkways of other peoples. Indeed, separation is inherent in holiness. Israel's attainment of holiness depends as much on Israel's resis-

---

[32] 1966:276.

tance to the moral impurity of others (symbolized by abstention from impure foods) as on its adherence to the attributes of God's being (concretized in his command-ments).

[20:25] The juxtaposition of the dietary prohibition and the holiness and separation requirements (v. 26) does not categorically mean that Israelites may not dine at the same table with others,[33] but that they must be wary of the meat being served. A deeper implication, however, can be drawn from the association of both the holiness and dietary demands with the moral life, one well understood in Hellenistic times: "An additional signification [of the diet laws] is that we are set apart from all men. For most of the rest of mankind defile themselves by their promiscuous unions, work-ing great unrighteousness, and whole countries and cities pride themselves on these vices. . . . But we have kept apart from these things."[34]

The sociocultural implications of separation through ritual have been fully drawn by Turner,[35] who postulated that many rituals arise to prevent the breakdown of the social order. As encapsulated by Moore and Myerhoff, "every ceremony is par excellence a dramatic statement against indeterminacy in some field of human affairs. Through order, formality, and repetition it seeks to state that the cosmic and social world, or some particular small part of them are orderly and explicable and for the moment fixed."[36]

The significance of this reading is not trivial: It continues H's theological pos-tulate that it is Israel's responsibility to realize on earth the divine attributes of holi-ness and separation. God has by fiat created pure and impure animals. It is now for Israel to live a holy life by distinguishing every day at mealtime between impure and pure animals and thereby remind itself to make distinctions between practices that enhance holiness and those that desecrate it.

---

[33] Gerstenberger 1996:291.
[34] *Let. Aris.* 151-52; see also *Jub.* 22:16.
[35] 1979:75-85.
[36] 1977:17, cited in Gorman 1990:26–27.

Instructions for the Priests

In the priestly tradition, the priesthood is hereditary, limited to the descendants of Aaron. In this respect, Israel differs radically from its neighbors. In Egypt, for example, the priesthood had a lay character. Priests were in office for a limited time, perhaps three months a year; thereafter, they returned to their normal occupations.[1] In Mesopotamia the priestly officials were appointed by the king. In Israel too this was a royal prerogative (2 Sam 8:18; 20:26; 1 Kgs 12:31). Why, then, was Israel's main, ongoing priesthood limited to one family (or tribe)?

A practical reason surfaces at once. If a priest was court appointed, then his office could be bought, as occurred with annoying frequency in Egypt,[2] precisely as occurred during Israel's second commonwealth, when the high priest was chosen by the (foreign) ruler—for a price. However, there is a more positive reason: the unique function of Israel's priest. First, he was bound by many prohibitions, as detailed in chapters 21–22. Above all, he had to know the laws of impurity (e.g., the laws of scale disease, chaps. 13–14)—*and live by them* lest their violation pollute the sanctuary. Moreover, the priest had to be a master of Torah, the entire compendium of Israel's law, so that he could teach it to his fellow Israelites (10:10-11; cf. Deut 33:10; Jer 18:18; Ezek 7:26; Mal 2:6-9; 2 Chr 17:8-9).

Selected Theme

Blemished Priests: A Comparative Survey

One should not be surprised to find that the ancients took pains to compose detailed lists of the blemishes that disqualified their priests and all others (e.g., Mesopotamian diviner) who claimed to have access to the gods. After all, they also required physical perfection for royal attendants (Dan 1:4) and leaders (e.g., Absalom, 2 Sam 14:25). Is modern society much different? Recall how President Franklin Roosevelt's paralyzed legs were carefully (and successfully) hidden from the American public during his long political career.

---

[1] Sauneron 1960:15.
[2] Ibid.

The sectaries of Qumran modeled their list on Leviticus 21. But they were also punctilious about spelling out some of the latter's obvious lacunae. For example:

> And no man smitten with human impurity shall enter the assembly of these (men), no man smitten with any of them shall be confirmed in his office in the midst of the congregation. No man smitten in his flesh, or paralyzed in his feet or hands, or lame, or blind, or deaf, or dumb, or smitten in his flesh with a visible blemish; no old and tottery man unable to control himself in the midst of the congregation; none of these shall come to hold office among the congregation of the men of renown, for the Angels of Holiness are [with] their [congregation].[3]

The Mesopotamian documents are rich with bodily disqualifications, particularly as they pertain to the diviner. They are summarized by van der Toorn,[4] with my amendments, as "who is not of pure descent,[5] or is not perfect as to his appearance and his limbs,[6] who is cross-eyed,[7] has chipped teeth,[8] a mutilated finger, who suffers from any disease of the testes(?) or of the skin." Another Mesopotamian text specifies that only if the diviner "is without blemish in body and limb may he approach the presence of Šamaš and Adad where live inspection and oracle (take place)."[9]

The candidate for the priesthood in the temple of the Babylonian god Enlil has to be inspected "from the edge of his head to the tips of his toes" and must not have a face disfigured by mutilated eyes, irregular features, or brands.[10] What is of special significance in this text is its concern for proof that he has no police record, but not for personal morality, namely, that he is not "a bloodstained person, who has been apprehended in theft or robbery, a condemned person who has been thrashed or lashed."[11]

While I have not found an equivalent list for the Hittite world, other evidence makes clear that one must have existed. The Hittite laws declare unambiguously that bestiality with a horse or mule is permitted, but that such a person may not approach the king, *nor may he ever become a priest.*[12] Moreover, an unfavorable omen is on one occasion attributed to "two mutilated men (who) came into the temple."[13]

To judge from Egyptian papyri of the Roman period, which undoubtedly preserve ancient practice, there were priestly specialists in the temples whose function was to inspect sacrifices. They were called "seal bearers" because they would stamp

---

[3] 1QS[a] 2:4-9 (cf. Vermes 1987:102).
[4] 1985:29.
[5] Preferable to "descendant of a free [*ellu*] man," *CAD* 2.123a.
[6] *BBR* 24:30; *CAD* 4.106a.
[7] *zaqtu;* see *CAD* 21.64a.
[8] *BBR* 24:31.
[9] Lambert 1967:132, II.22-29.
[10] Borger 1973:164, I, 11-12; 165, I, 33, 41-42.
[11] Ibid. 165, I, 29-32.
[12] HL §200A; cf. Hoffner 1973:85 n. 2; Moyer 1969:61.
[13] *ANET,* 497, corrected by R. Stefanini.

the animal without blemishes.[14] The Greeks also required physical perfection in both animals and priests.[15]

The absence of any moral requirements in amply attested Mesopotamian texts is striking, particularly since one text, cited above, requires only that the aspirant for the priesthood not be a criminal. Still, in view of the same silence in Leviticus 21, we should not be too hasty in concluding that moral qualities were not required of Babylonian priests. Indeed, the clue may be hidden in the fact that both lists, Mesopotamian and biblical, were written by priests who may have taken moral requirements for granted. After all, prophets, who were outside observers and critical ones at that, could lambaste priests for their moral dereliction (e.g., Hos 4:6-8) and heap paeans of praise for their moral perfection (Mal 2:4-7). Still, one cannot but harbor the suspicion that because the biblical priesthood was hereditary, in the Israelite tradition, too—no differently from its Mesopotamian counterpart—the priest would be disqualified on moral grounds only if apprehended and convicted of some egregious criminal act.

Selected Texts
Verses 1β-11

A polemic may underlie these verses against the Egyptian cult, which was obsessed with death and the afterlife and which contained in every temple a cadre of special priests involved in funerary rites.[16] Also, underlying these verses is the lethal contact between holiness and impurity, which, if not expunged quickly (lest it fester) and effectively (by the ordained purificatory rites), can lead, in the priestly view, to the destruction of Israel.[17] The priests are innately holy—an axiom that H, a priestly document, accepts. Therefore, theoretically, they should not come into contact with or even be under the same roof as a corpse. This prohibition applied to everyone, all the more so, therefore, to priests.

This law effectively ruled out any funerary role for the priesthood.[18] However, a concession—and that is all it is, a concession—is granted to the ordinary priest but not to the high priest (v. 11), that he may defile himself with his closest kin. It is assumed that the priestly mourner undergoes the required seven-day purificatory rite (Num 19:14, 16).[19]

---

[14] Cf. Licht and Leibowitz 1962.

[15] Plato, *Laws* 6.759-60.

[16] Bergman et al. 1995:63.

[17] Milgrom 1991:254–61, 307–18, 766–67, 953–1004.

[18] Levine 1992:316.

[19] Ezekiel requires an additional week, terminating with a purification offering (Ezek 44:26-27), before he may resume his priestly functions.

[21:1] The contrast between Mesopotamia and Israel is striking: "The Mesopotamian texts hardly refer to the defilement incurred by contact with a human corpse. The ideal of a swift and proper burial of the dead is apparently owing more to a concern for the welfare of the ghosts of the deceased than to a fear of contamination."[20] Conversely, Israel was obsessed with fear of contamination of the dead for precisely the opposite reason: to wean Israel from the worship of the dead.

[21:5] The purpose of the cut hair for the dead is most likely the same as that of the well-attested donation of hair to the sanctuary. Since hair continues to grow throughout life (and appears to do so for a time after death), the ancients considered it to be the seat of a person's vitality and life force, and in ritual it often served as the substitute for a person. A bowl dating from the ninth century BCE found in a Cypriot temple contains an inscription on its outside surface indicating that it contained the hair of the donor. It was placed there, if the reconstructed text is correct, as a "memorial" to Astarte, as a permanent reminder to the goddess of the donor's devotion.

What I am suggesting is that shaving the head or cutting the beard for mourning the dead is simply an aspect of the cult of the dead. Let us keep in mind that these rites are not the impulsive, anguished acts of grief (contrast Ezra 9:3). Shaving and polling hair is performed carefully, deliberately. And, I submit, there is good chance that this hair—the symbol and essence of life—was offered as a sacrifice to the god(s) of the dead.[21] Israel's priests and, in particular, H, intent on eradicating the pervasive and tenacious cult of the dead, would have spared no effort to inculcate that these mourning rites were forbidden by YHWH.

Indirect supporting evidence may be derived from the fact that the ordinary priest is not forbidden to dishevel his hair and rend his clothes, as is the high priest (v. 10b). The ordinary priest is therefore permitted to indulge in all other rites of mourning that do not involve cutting his hair (or his flesh; see below). Thus there has to be a specific reason why the removal of hair is proscribed. I submit that lurking in the background is the cult of the dead, a possibility that, I believe, is enhanced by the prohibition to gash the flesh (see below).

The prohibition "shave off the edge of their beards" is functionally equivalent to that imposed on the laity: "You shall not destroy the side growth of your beard" (19:27b). Cutting or shaving the edge of the beard was practiced in mourning (Jer 41:5) and was a regular practice among some of Israel's neighbors (Jer 9:25 [Eng. 26]; 25:23).

The prohibition, "make gashes in their flesh," also holds for the laity (Lev 19:28). It is repeated here because it disqualifies the priest,[22] or because pagan priests

---

[20] Van der Toorn 1985:37.

[21] On the sacrifice of hair, see Milgrom 1990:356–57.

[22] Ibn Ezra.

engaged in such a practice in the cult (1 Kgs 18:28).[23] As pointed out in Lev 19:28, however, this practice was commonly followed by worshipers at the altar as a means of offering up their life, symbolized by the blood, to their god(s). In this respect, it was functionally equivalent to pulling or shaving the hair and, as part of the funeral rites, may have served as an integral element in the cult of the dead.

The prohibition against tattooing (19:28aβ) is lacking here. Rather than suggesting that it was not considered a mourning rite,[24] it might have been encompassed by the prohibition against gashing the flesh, since it too involved blood-letting incisions.[25]

[21:6] Note the similar injunction to the laity: "You shall be holy to me" (20:26). Thus both have to aspire to holiness: the priests to retain it, the laity to attain it.

[21:7] In Second Temple times, the lineage of a woman marrying a priest was carefully investigated.[26] The precedent, however, had already been set at the beginning of this period when the exiles returned from Babylon (Ezra 2:61-63).

In the ancient Near East, rape was considered a stigma. In the laws of Ur-Nammu and Sumer, deflowering is described in the context of rape.[27] In Israel, however, there is no stigma attached to a raped (or seduced) single girl (Deut 22:28-29) —if she is the daughter of a layman. But a stigma may very well exist if she is the daughter of a priest. (She may even be suspect of complicity.) Consider the case of a husband who finds that his bride is not a virgin; for her deception, she is put to death. However, a priest's daughter who is neither married nor betrothed, but just promiscuous, is burned by fire (v. 9). Finally, in view of the high degree of purity demanded of a priest's bride in Second Temple times (see below), it is altogether plausible that in the biblical period rape disqualified a woman from marrying a priest.

[21:9] I must reckon with the possibility that by "harlotry," premarital sex is intended. It has been shown that although some societies may be permissive in sexual matters in regard to commoners, they are restrictive in regard to royalty. For example, the Samoans prescribe the death penalty to royal girls who engage in premarital sex.[28] Thus, as far as H is concerned, JE and D's laxity (Exod 22:15-16 [Eng. 16-17]; Deut 22:28-29) does not apply to daughters of Israel's royalty, the priests.

---

[23] Hoffmann 1953:2.65.

[24] Elliger 1966.

[25] W. Robertson Smith 1927:334.

[26] Philo, *Spec. Laws* 1.101 (who insists on a virgin, the high priest's requirement of Lev 21:13); Josephus, *Ag. Ap.* 1.31-36; *m. Qid.* 4:4; *t. Qid.* 5:4; but see Lieberman 1967:295.

[27] *ANET,* 524, 526.

[28] Cohen 1969:673.

Her action casts a stigma on her father. In all likelihood, he has no desire to be seen in the company of his fellow priests; it is as though he were disqualified.

"She shall be burned by fire." The unfaithful *married* or *betrothed* daughter of a layman (Lev 20:10; Deut 22:23-24) was put to death by stoning, whereas even a promiscuous single daughter of a layman was probably stigmatized socially but was unpunished by the court. However, the older practice for punishing adultery was death by fire (Gen 38:24; Judg 15:6). The Samson incident (Judges 15) shows that the instigator of the adultery, in this case the father, is also burned. Note that in contrast to the lay bride, who is stoned at her father's house (Deut 22:21), indicating his culpability in fomenting the deceit that she was a virgin, the burning of the priest's daughter does not take place at the father's home; he is not held responsible for her harlotry.

[21:10] The purpose of mentioning the specific rite "on whose head the anointing oil has been poured" is to distinguish the high priest, who exclusively is anointed on the head, from ordinary priests, who are anointed only on their clothing (8:30).

The high priest donned ordinary clothes when he left the sanctuary.[29] Thus, when Mark 14:63 declares that the high priest rent his clothes because of Jesus' blasphemy, these were not his sacred vestments, since the blasphemy was uttered in the high priest's home (v. 53). Gerstenberger expresses surprise that Ezra, a priest, rent his clothes (Ezra 9:3, 5).[30] However, he was not in mourning but in dismay, and, above all, these were his ordinary clothes, not priestly vestments.

[21:11] The principle of areal impurity or, to be more exact, overhang, is operative here. The severe impurity of the corpse fills the house in which it lies.[31] The same prohibition is enjoined upon the nazirite (Num 6:6b). It is not a coincidence. In his or her taboos, the nazirite approximates the greater sanctity of the high priest.

Verses 16-23

The requirements that priests bear no physical blemish is not limited to Israel, but is attested universally. Examples from Israel's neighbors discussed in the THEME above include moral requirements. I cite one to underscore the paradox. According to Plato, a prospective priest "must be screened to see to it that he is sound of body and of legitimate birth, reared in a family whose moral standards could hardly be higher."[32] Why is the biblical list of priestly blemishes restricted to the physical body, whereas blemishes of character and piety are omitted? A possible answer is that moral and

---

[29] Maimonides, *Temple Service*, Temple Vessels, 1:5, 7; cf. *m. Hor.* 3:5 and *b. Hor.* 12b.
[30] 1996:312.
[31] Milgrom 1991:986–1000.
[32] *Laws* 6.759.

spiritual requirements are subsumed in the word "holy": Since Israel is required to be a moral and devout people in order to attain holiness (detailed in chap. 19), ipso facto, the same holds true for Israel's priests. The lacuna, however, is so gaping that to assume it is taken for granted will not do.

The list of blemishes for priests (21:17-23) was compiled to match that for sacrificial animals (22:22-24). Since animals have only physical imperfections, but no moral ones, the compiler of the priestly defects was constrained to limit himself to physical imperfections.

[21:17] The base meaning of "blemish" is physical deformity (cf. Deut 17:1; 2 Sam 14:25; Song 4:7; Dan 1:4). It is also attested for moral deficiencies (Prov 9:7; Job 11:15), but these two citations stem from wisdom literature, where the term acquires an extended meaning. Thus the limitation of "blemish," by definition, to physical defects signifies that moral defects, which may also have disqualified a priest, were not the concern of this list.

[21:18] The deaf and dumb, among others, are missing because this list is arbitrary to match the twelve animal defects with equivalent ones for the priests. Besides, the list consists of *visible* deficiencies. Obviously, one cannot discern deafness and dumbness by the priest's appearance.

[21:20] The defect "a crushed testicle" proves that the common denominator of the list is not an aesthetic or a visual criterion.[33] However, this ostensibly exceptional defect was arbitrarily chosen to match its equivalent defect in the animal list (22:24).

[21:23] This prohibition of entering before the veil applies only to the blemished high priest[34]—that is, to his ritual acts inside the shrine: daily at the menorah and incense altar (Exod 30:7-8), weekly at the table (Lev 24:5-9), and, in cases of impurity generated by him or the people, at the incense altar and before the veil (Lev 4:3-21). The prohibition, however, would cover all the other rites of the high priest inside the shrine, because all the inner sanctums stand close to the veil: the incense altar (Exod 30:6), the menorah (Exod 27:21; Lev 24:3), and the table (Exod 26:35).

The reference to the altar must be directed to the high priest and is a continuation of his prohibitions: If he is blemished, he may officiate neither inside the shrine nor at the altar.

[21:24] This is a statement by the H redactor that priestly disqualifications—in all other cultures the private responsibility of their priestly elites—are the concern of all

---

[33] Ellliger 1966.
[34] Ibn Ezra, Abravanel; see Milgrom 1970:40 n. 154.

Israel. That this represents the quintessential viewpoint of H is strikingly demonstrated by H's appendix to chapter 16, vv. 29-34a.[35]

The body of chapter 16 (vv. 1-28 [P]) is addressed to the high priest, Aaron, via Moses (v. 2). But in the appendix (vv. 29-34a [H]), the address shifts to the plural, to Israel—without any introduction or proleptic preparation.[36] In this appendix, Israel is given collateral commandments (self-denial and cessation from labor, vv. 29, 31). In addition, a seemingly irrelevant summary of the high priest's rites is cited (vv. 32-33), followed by a notice that his performance is a binding statute for Israel (v. 34a). This can only mean that the high priest's precise performance in purging the sanctuary and transferring its impurities as well as Israel's sins to the scapegoat is ultimately the responsibility of the entire community. Thus the impeccable appearance and behavior of the ordinary priest, as detailed in chapter 21, is a fortiori Israel's responsibility. The two pericopes are related: all priests, including the high priest, are answerable to the people.

Moreover, as Gerstenberger pointed out, the behavior of priests was not a matter of indifference to the public.[37] Reprehensible priestly deeds, such as those exhibited by Eli's sons, involving illicit ritual procedures and sexual practices (1 Sam 2:12-17, 22 LXX), became the subject of gossip. The prophets frequently berated the priests on similar grounds (Hos 4:4-11; Mal 1:6-13).

---

[35] Milgrom 1991:1054–59.
[36] Gorman 1990:66; Milgrom 1991:1054–55.
[37] 1996:307–8.

Instructions for the Priests
and Laypersons

Chapter 22 clearly is a continuation of chapter 21, which ends with priestly blemishes and continues here with priestly impurity. The previous chapter closes with a concession to blemished priests that they may partake of sacred food (21:22), but in this chapter that privilege is denied to impure priests.[1]

Selected Texts
Verses 2-3. Introduction
[22:2] "sacred donations (that the Israelites)." This term is all inclusive, denoting both the sacred and the most sacred offerings (as in 21:22).[2] This conclusion will be made even more evident by the expression "he may not eat of the sacred donations" (v. 4), which surely refers to *all* sacred food.[3]

[22:3] "Say (further) to them." The previous verse constitutes the general notion of scrupulousness regarding the sacred donations falling under the control of the priests. Moses and Aaron are free to word this generalization as they please. But beginning with this verse, the ipsissima verba of YHWH's commands (i.e., his laws) must be recited. The switch to second person is another indication that the following verses constitute a direct address to the priests.

The term "encroaches" implies the illegitimate use of a sacred object.[4] The priest is differentiated from the layperson in regard to encroachment on the sancta. The latter is put to death[5] whereas the priest suffers *karet*, implying the end of his

---

[1] Bekhor Shor.
[2] With *Sipra Emor* par. 4:5; *Keter Torah;* Wellhausen 1963; Elliger 1966; Porter 1976.
[3] *Seper Hamibḥar*; cf. Exod 28:38 (twice); Num 5:9, 10; 18:8.
[4] Milgrom 1991:351–56.
[5] *yumat, Hiphil*; e.g., Num 18:7.

line[6] (see 20:3), and death by divine agency.[7] This punishment of *karet* falls on all the violations enumerated in vv. 4–8. However, the layperson is subject to the same *karet* penalty as the impure priest for contacting the sacred (7:20). The difference between them lies only in regard to eating from a carcass or torn beast: the layperson undergoes baths (17:15); the priest is subject to death (22:8–9).

Verses 4-9. Priests Eating Sacred Food

[22:4] Saadiah correctly notes that the impurities in vv. 4–5 are listed in descending order of severity. It has been shown that ancient Israel and its Near Eastern contemporaries were aware of many diseases and had diagnosed them,[8] which gives further support to the theory that Israel's impurity laws, in general, and the skin diseases, in particular, are part of a symbolic system.[9]

"may not eat of the sacred donations." The contaminated priest obviously has to subsist on nonsacral food during the period of his impurity. He need not, however, be faced with hunger or starvation.[10] If necessary, he has access to the sanctuary's store of monetary fines (v. 16; 27:13, 27, 31) with which to purchase his basic dietary needs. We must keep in mind that none of the "severe" impurities are long lasting.[11]

"until he is pure." No time limit is cited, as in the case of the one-day impurities (v. 6), since the duration of the impurity is indeterminate. The purificatory period, however, is the same: seven days.

[22:5] "touches any swarming thing by which he is made impure." The qualification "by which he is made impure" is a clear indication that the reference is to the eight enumerated swarming animals of 11:29–31. Only these eight swarmers defile by touching them (11:31). All other swarmers fall under the category of *šeqeṣ*: They are forbidden as food, but they do not defile.[12] This is another example of H presupposing P. Contact with "swarming things" is nigh unavoidable, since the priest may encounter them in the sanctuary itself.[13] Hence the priests are instructed on the required purificatory procedures for touching a dead swarming thing. By the same token, sanctuary animals—which by definition are pure—might have died in the sanctuary. Why, then, is there no prohibition against touching the carcasses of pure animals? One must conclude that although the priest is forbidden to eat of such a carcass, he is permitted to touch it. This must be the case, since the sacrificial animal

---

[6] Milgrom 1991:457–61.

[7] *yamut, Qal;* 22:9; Num 18:3.

[8] Zias 1991.

[9] Milgrom 1991:766–68, 1000–1004.

[10] Gerstenberger 1996:324.

[11] Contra Gestenberger 1996; see discussion above on chaps. 13–15.

[12] For greater detail and analysis see Milgrom 1992a, 1992b.

[13] Cf. *m. ʿErub.* 10:15.

becomes a carcass the moment it is slaughtered. Yet there is no indication that touching it renders the priest impure. Otherwise, he would not be able to continue officiating! The problem of a priest handling a sacrificial carcass may be resolved only by presuming that the holiness of the animal or of the priest himself overrides and cancels the impurity of the carcass.

[**22:7**] "and the sun has set." The verse adds the quintessential information that evening alone does not suffice for purification, but it must be preceded by bathing (v. 6b). However, bathing by itself also does not suffice; the bather must wait until sunset before partaking of any sacred food.

"for they are his food." Rabbinic logic would dictate that all sacred food (produce and meat alike) should have to wait for morning, the end of the calendar day, but since a priest may be totally dependent on sacred food for his sustenance, he is allowed to eat some of it after sunset the previous evening.

One also can argue that originally the purificatory process of the priest was severer than that of a layperson: instead of having to wait until the sunset of the day of his bath, he would have to wait until the following morning.

[**22:8**] H's impurity rules for the priesthood are equivalent to those for the laity regarding contact with sacred donations in a state of impurity (v. 3), regarding purificatory procedures for major (v. 4a) and minor impurities (vv. 4b-7), and regarding contact with carcasses of (pure) animals (v. 8, by implication). In regard to the eating of the latter, however, there is a major difference: laypeople need only purify themselves (17:15-16), but priests are subject to death by divine agency (vv. 8-9).

[**22:9**] This hortatory verse is appended to the laws of vv. 4-8 as a warning to the priests that because of their status any impurity prohibition they violate is deserving of capital punishment at the hands of God. The wording of this verse parallels that of v. 16, thereby indicating that both verses end their respective pericopes.

"and die." It should not go unnoticed that the penalty for the priest is much severer than that for a layperson for a similar violation. Indeed, the layperson who eats carrion is impure for a day (11:39-40), and if he fails to purify himself, he is subject to a purification offering (5:2; 17:16). In reality he suffers no penalty at all; his sin is remediable. But the priest's sin is inexpiable: he will suffer death.

The magnified risk of priests who work inside the sacred sphere is best illustrated by the tragedy of Nadab and Abihu (10:1-3). Gerstenberger supplies an apt modern parallel: "The x-ray physician is far more at risk than is the patient. Thus those who work directly at the hearth of danger must implement heightened precautions."[14]

---

[14] 1996:306.

"I am YHWH who sanctifies them." Who or what is the antecedent of "them"? The change of object from singular to plural indicates, on purely grammatical grounds, that the referent is the plural subject of all the verbs in this verse, namely, the priests. Logic also dictates that the priests are the antecedent: since the priests are holy, their contact with impurity can be fatal. Once again, the consistent use of the participle "sanctifies" indicates H's basic theology: though priests are innately holy, they can enhance or diminish (and even suspend) their holiness by keeping or violating YHWH's prohibitions.

Verses 10-16. Nonpriests Eating Sacred Food

[22:11] "purchases a person with money." Does the slave have to be circumcised, as in the law of the paschal sacrifice (Exod 12:44)? One would certainly think so, since the slave is permitted to eat sacred food, including the sacrificial meat of the well-being offering and the firstling. Of course, H may be assuming that God's command to Abraham to circumcise his slaves (Gen 17:13, 23, 27) should be taken for granted. But its inclusion in the law of the paschal sacrifice and its exclusion in this law regarding the priest's sacred food are most puzzling.

In any event, this phrase proves that the institution of slavery was fully accepted by H in regard to non-Israelites (25:45-46), whereas it was totally prohibited in regard to Israelites (see 25:39-43).

Verses 17-25. Blemished Sacrificial Animals

After forbidding blemished priests to officiate at sacrifices (21:16-23) and impure priests (and nonpriests) to eat sacred food (22:1-16), the text turns to the topic of blemished animals. The list of animal blemishes (vv. 22-24) matches the list of priestly blemishes (21:18-20).

[22:18] There are three recipients of Moses' speech: Aaron, his sons, and the new component—Israel. The significance is clear: both the priesthood and the laity are held responsible for detecting sacrificial blemishes by the offerer, when the animal is chosen, and by the priest, when the animal enters the sanctuary grounds. This three-fold address is also found in 17:2-3, which stresses that both lay offerers and priestly officiants are responsible for carrying out H's fundamental tenet: all meat for the table must initially be sacrificed on a legitimate altar so that its blood will ransom the offerer's life from the charge of murder (17:11).

[22:19] "without blemish." Why does H and not P name the blemishes? P surely had criteria (even if they were not the same), since the qualification "unblemished" is attached to each of the sacrificial quadrupeds (1:3, 10; 3:1, 6; 4:3, 23, 28, 32; 5:15, 18, 25). The probable answer is that P takes them for granted, and it finds no need to list them because the examination of the animal is done by the sanctuary priest. H, however, will have nothing to do with priestly exclusivity. It regards the inspection of the animal to be the shared responsibility of the lay offerer and the officiating priest.

[22:22-24] In addition to physical defects, there was universal concern that the sacrificial animal had not been stolen. In the instructions for the priestly staff at the temple of Philae, Egypt, "watchmen and hour-priests . . . must inspect everything [i.e., the sacrifices] that are brought in for impurity and for stolen property."[15] And in Israel, a prophet fulminates against those who bring to the temple blemished or stolen animals (Mal 1:13-14a).

As noted in chapter 21, the common denominator among the twelve blemishes listed here is that they are noticeable to the observer. This also holds true for the twelve priestly blemishes (21:18-20), with the exception of "a crushed testicle," which indicates that the list of animal blemishes (22:23-25) is original and the priestly blemishes were chosen subsequently to match the animal blemishes in number and kind.

This conclusion compels me to rethink 11:5-6; I had previously implied that the priestly legists erred in labeling the camel, rock badger, and hare as ruminants.[16] It is entirely possible that they knew the truth, but it sufficed that these three creatures gave the appearance of ruminants by the sideward movement of their jaws. In other words, appearance was as much a criterion for the prohibited edible animals as for the prohibited sacrificeable animals.

[22:23] "sacrifice as a freewill offering . . . but it will not be accepted as a votive offering." The reason for this distinction is not self-evident. Abravanel, I submit, offers the most plausible reason: the freewill offering, being the result of a spontaneous declaration, falls on the animal at hand, whether of good or poor quality (but not if it is defective). Under these conditions, a concession is allowed for an extended or a shortened limb, the least of the blemishes. (After all, this limb is not inherently defective, but only so in comparison with others.) But the fulfillment of a vow is set in the future, and the offerer has ample time to find an animal of the finest quality for a votive offering. Hence the votive offering is subject to more rigorous standards than the freewill offering.

[22:24] "You shall not do (this) in your land." I propose, with due reserve, that "in your land" means *at any other sanctuary* in your land. I have argued that H is written from the point of view of an important—probably Jerusalem, the most important—*regional* sanctuary. If I am correct, a rigorous logic is preserved in H: gelded animals

---

[15] Lines 8-10 (Junker 1959).
[16] Milgrom 1991:648–49.

and castrated priests are barred from the altar, but not from the land. Moreover, a sanctuary could own gelded beasts of burden, castrated priests could benefit from the sacrifices (20:22), and castrated Israelites could offer their sacrifices.

[22:25] "any of these." This verse answers the question: What if the animal with defective genitals comes not from the land of Israel, but from foreigners outside the land?[17] Thus vv. 24-25 comprise a single taboo of increasing range: sanctified animals (v. 24a), all the animals in the land (v. 24b), imported animals (v. 25).

"and from the hand of a foreigner." May a foreigner offer sacrifices at the sanctuary? It should be recalled that the alien may offer (17:8-9; Num 15:14) and, for the violation of prohibitive commandments, *has* to sacrifice (Num 15:30-31). The resident alien, however, has a different religious status than the foreigner. Precisely because the alien is obligated to observe the prohibitive commandments, he can be trusted as much as the Israelite to enter the sacred compound in a pure state with an unblemished sacrifice. Not so the foreigner. He therefore can only *send* his sacrifices (which would be carefully inspected), as implied by this verse.

Verses 26-30. Additional Criteria for Sacrificial Animals

[22:27] "seven days." Humanitarianism is the most frequently proposed rationale, beginning with Philo[18] and echoed by Clement of Alexandria, Ibn Ezra, Rashbam, and the moderns. The theory is that the newborn should be allowed to suckle for seven days, to spend one Sabbath with its mother (Zohar), or to teach Israelites not to be cruel to one another.[19] But on the eighth day, it may be brought to the altar, even though it is still suckling! Similar flaws attend the other laws explained by a humanitarian reason.[20] A completely satisfying rationale has yet to be supplied.

[22:28] Here too the humanitarian rationale fails: one may not slaughter the dam and its young on the same day, but it is surely permitted on successive days. Similarly, the analogous prohibition against taking the mother bird and her fledglings or eggs together (Deut 22:6) permits them to be taken separately. Moreover, the tannaitic rabbis sharply rebuke anyone offering a humanitarian rationale in his prayers: "If a man says [i.e., prays] 'To a bird's nest do your mercies extend,' they [the congregation] silence him."[21]

Maimonides echoes the rabbinic view in his law compendium and gives an additional reason: "If [the rationale] were mercy, he [God] should not have permitted

---

[17] Ehrlich 1899–1900 (H):1.236.
[18] *Virt.* 143.
[19] Bekhor Shor.
[20] Milgrom 1991:738–39; see v. 28.
[21] *m. Ber.* 5:3; cf. *b. Meg.* 25a.

animal slaughter at all!"[22] In his *Guide to the Perplexed*, however, he writes: "animals feel very great pain, there being no difference regarding this pain between man and other animals. For the love and tenderness of a mother for her child is not consequent upon reason, but upon the activity of the imaginative faculty, which is found in most animals just as it is found in man."[23]

Verses 31-33. Exhortation

[22:32] "You shall not desecrate." Abranavel claims that this injunction is addressed to the priests. This can hardly be the case, since God's redemptive act in the exodus (v. 33) embraced all Israel. Are all of YHWH's commandments within the purview of the injunction, as proposed by Hoffmann?[24] Again, the answer is negative: the other eighteen occurrences in H of "desecrate the name of YHWH" always refer to a specific context.[25] Here too the immediate context is intended, namely, regarding the Israelite's indispensable responsibility in the sacrificial service: regarding an unblemished animal (vv. 17-25), its minimal age (v. 27), its slaughter (v. 28), and its consumption (vv. 29-30), and the priests' indispensable responsibility to supervise all these acts.

"that I may be sanctified in the midst of the Israelites." YHWH is sanctified when Israel performs his commandments (v. 31), not that he thereby increases his own sanctity.[26] Rather, Israel is more scrupulous in preventing the desecration of his name (21:8a). The result is that the appearance is given that YHWH's sanctity is increased.

Let it suffice here to understand the ideological thrust of this verse: If all Israel refrains from desecrating God's name by faulty sacrificial procedures, it will hasten its progress toward the divine goal, the attainment of holiness (19:2). The only other instance in H that speaks of God's grace in bestowing sanctity on Israel is in connection with its observance of the Sabbath (Exod 31:13).

---

[22] *Prayer* 9:7.

[23] 3.48.

[24] 1953:2.84.

[25] Milgrom 1976a:86 n. 302.

[26] Knohl's (1995:183) daring suggestion; see also Kugler 1997:16.

The Festival Calendar

Each festival begins with an introduction: Sabbath (vv. 1-3), Paschal Offering and Unleavened Bread (vv. 4-8), Firstfruits of Grain (vv. 9-22), Alarm Blasts (vv. 23-25), Day of Purgation (vv. 26-32), and Booths (vv. 33-43). These introductions betray the viewpoint of their author that Paschal Offering and Unleavened Bread, on the one hand, and Barley and Wheat, on the other hand, had each become fused into a single festival.

This chapter is addressed to the Israelites. The priests are not included, even though they are indispensably and inextricably involved in the cultic offerings (v. 11). Nonetheless, the priests' role is deliberately muffled. Center stage is occupied by the people. Israel is responsible for maintaining the *public* cult. To be sure, H, no differently from P, presumes that sacrificial service is conducted exclusively by priests. However, maintenance of the public cult and, presumably, supervision over the priestly order are ultimately the people's responsibility.

Selected Texts

Verse 3. The Sabbath

The Sabbath is the only holiday commanded in the Decalogue (Exod 20:8-11) and the only command grounded in creation (v. 11). It is mentioned by all sources and genres: prophecy (Isa 56:2-6; Jer 17:21-27), history (2 Kgs 11:5-9), poetry (Ps 92:1 [Eng. superscription]; Lam 2:6), narrative (2 Kgs 4:23; Neh 13:15-22), and law (Exod 23:12; Neh 10:32-34 [Eng. 31-33]). The Sabbath stands out from all other holidays by its egalitarian character. All laborers, regardless of status, even animals, rest on this day. It occasions no surprise to learn that in the Babylonian exile it was the Sabbath that attracted non-Israelites to cast their lot with the returning exiles (Isa 56:2-6) and that by the end of the Second Temple period many Hellenistic communities had adopted the Sabbath as a day of rest. As claimed by Josephus: "there is not one city, Greek or barbarian, nor a single nation to which our custom of abstaining from work on the seventh day has not spread."[1]

---

[1] *Ag. Ap.* 2.282.

275

Verses 5-8. The Paschal Offering and the Unleavened Bread

[23:5] "a paschal offering." The common but erroneous rendering "Passover" was first introduced by the LXX. The rabbis, however, comment on Exod 12:13 and 23: "The word means nothing but protection, as it is said 'Like the birds that fly, even so YHWH of hosts shields Jerusalem,' 'shielding and saving, *protecting* and rescuing' (Isa 31:5)."[2] To be sure, in Exod 12:13, 23, it makes no sense that YHWH skipped over Israel's homes, thereby leaving them vulnerable to the Destroyer. Rather, YHWH protects them against "the Destroyer."

The Paschal Offering and Unleavened Bread festivals are discrete in all the early sources (Exod 12:1-13, 14-20, 21-28, 40-51; 13:3-10; Lev 23:5, 6-8; Num 28:16, 17-23). They are fused together first in Deuteronomy (Deut 16:1-7) and in the postexilic sources (Ezek 45:21; Ezra 6:20-22; 2 Chr 30:2, 5, 13, 15; 35:17). The evidence for the discreteness of the two festivals is indisputable. The eating of unleavened bread, according to the priestly texts, is not bound up with sacrifice and therefore does not mandate the state of purity required for visits to the sanctuary. The Israelite and resident alien (Exod 12:48; Num 9:14) need but cleanse their homes of all leaven and eat unleavened bread instead of bread during the seven-day period (e.g., Exod 12:15-20). Even impure persons, such as the corpse contaminated (Num 9:6), could observe this practice in their homes. But they could not make the pilgrimage to the sanctuary in order to sacrifice the paschal offering. Those whose impurity had invalidated them from sacrificing the paschal offering are still enjoined to remove the leaven from their homes and eat unleavened bread for seven days at the same time as their fellow Israelites, whereas their paschal offering is postponed for one month (Num 9:10-11).

The consensus holds that both the Paschal Offering and the Unleavened Bread originated as firstfruit festivals, the former observed by shepherds and the latter by farmers to ensure the fertility of their respective flocks and crops. Thus the Israelite transhumant pastoralists combined their observance of the Paschal Offering (cf. Exod 5:1; 10:9) and the Unleavened Bread festivals after they had abandoned their wilderness wandering and had settled permanently in Canaan. Indeed, the fact that the two festivals were originally separate enabled the rabbis to enjoin the celebration of the seven-day Unleavened Bread Festival (subsequently and erroneously termed Passover), even after the cessation of the sacrifices with the destruction of the temple.

[23:6] "the Pilgrimage Festival of Unleavened Bread to YHWH." On what day(s) was the pilgrimage? The biblical sources provide three different answers. (1) the first day (Exod 12:14, 17 [H?]; Lev 23:6 [H]; Num 28:17 [P]; Deut 16:16 [D; by inference from vv. 2, 7-8]); (2) the seventh day (Exod 13:6 [JE]); and (3) all seven days (Ezek 45:21; Ezra 6:22; 2 Chr 8:12-13; 30:13, 21; 35:17).

---

[2] *Mek. Boʾ* par. 7.

Clearly, Exod 13:6, the epic source (JE), is the oldest. There can be only one reason why the pilgrimage takes place on the seventh day: the Paschal Offering is observed at home, in keeping with the regulations of Exod 12:1-13, 22-27a, 28—which reflect the evidence of local altars and sanctuaries. The Paschal Offering would be offered at a local altar, or, more likely, at an improvised one, in any case near enough to bring the paschal blood back home to smear it on the entrance. The centralization of worship made a pilgrimage to the temple for the Paschal Offering mandatory and necessitated the shift of the pilgrimage to the first day.

Finally, it is hardly a coincidence that the extension of the one-day pilgrimage to embrace all seven days is documented in late biblical sources beginning with Ezekiel. For it is in the Babylonian exile, when the pilgrimage (to a destroyed temple) could no longer be practiced, that the term changes its meaning, from "pilgrimage festival" to "festival." Henceforth, it refers to all seven days during which the eating of leaven is proscribed.

[23:8] "The seventh day is a sacred occasion." Why? This is not true for the other seven-day holiday, the Festival of Booths (the eighth day, which is a sacred occasion, is a different festival; see vv. 34b, 36b). I submit that the sacredness of the seventh day is a remembrance and commemoration of an earlier period when the pilgrimage required during the Festival of Unleavened Bread (Exod 23:15; Deut 16:16), took place on the seventh day (Exod 13:6).

The fifty-day period following the Passover is fraught with peril to the ripening grain lest it be devastated by the dreaded sirocco (*hamsin* = *hamiššim,* "fifty") winds (see v.15, below). Equally significant, this period marks the onset of the dry season. The condensation of the dew each night is generally adequate to bring the crops to fruition. However, any dimunition will also abort the ripening. Thus an "assembly" (D's term) on the seventh day would be convened in each city and town to supplicate God for a "safe passage" on behalf of the crops.

Verses 10aβ-14. The First Barley Offering

[23:10] The first grain is barley, as proved by the comment on the plague of hail: "Now the flax and barley were ruined, for *barley was in the ear* and the flax was in bud; but the *wheat* and the emmer were not hurt, for they *ripen late*" (Exod 9:31-32 [my emphasis]). Also note that Ruth (and Naomi) "arrived in Bethlehem at the beginning of the barley harvest" (Ruth 1:22b), and "she gleaned until the barley harvest and the wheat harvest were finished" (Ruth 2:23aβ).

"the first sheaf of your harvest." The first of the ripened and processed fruits belong to the Deity (Exod 22:28 [Eng. 29]; 23:19a; 34:26a; Deut 26:1-11) so that "a blessing may rest on your home" (Ezek 44:30; cf. Lev 19:24-25). Note also the pragmatic advice of the wisdom: "Honor YHWH with your substance and with the first-fruits of all your produce; then your barns will be filled with plenty, and your vats will be bursting with wine" (Prov 3:9-10).

277

[23:11] "For acceptance on your behalf." Thus the cereal offering of the barley (and of the wheat) not only functions as a sign of thanks for the new crop, but also expresses the hope that God, in turn, will bless the new crop (Ezek 44:30; Prov 3:9-10). The rabbis were unambiguously frank concerning this purpose: "The Holy One Blessed Be He has said: Bring before me a sheaf on the Festival of Protection so that you will be blessed with grain in the fields."[3]

Verses 15-22. The First Wheat Offering (Pentecost or Weeks)

The name Festival of Weeks first appears in the Deuteronomic sources (Deut 16:10, 16; Exod 34:22; cf. Jer 5:24). In the earliest calendar it is called "The Pilgrimage Festival of the Harvest" (Exod 23:16). In P it is referred to as "The Day of the Firstfruits" and "your (Festival of) Weeks" (Num 28:26). H alludes to both of P's names by a seven-week counting and expressly by the word "firstfruits" (vv. 17, 20). The word "Pentecost" from the Greek *pentekoste,* "fifty," first appears in Tob 2:1 and 2 Macc 12:31-32 (books for which we do not have the original Hebrew).

[23:15] "you shall count for yourselves." I admit that I cannot fathom the purpose of the fifty day counting, and the literature I have consulted is of no help. But I suspect that, originally, there was some incantation recited each day to ward off the demons of the weather; with the triumph of Israelite monotheism, however, the magical incantations were excised and all that survived was the counting. But what could be the cause of the fear that would grip the farmer during these days? It is no accident that the sirocco, the hot dry Egyptian east wind, is called in Arabic and Hebrew "fifty." The fifty-day period when the sirocco blows occurs between April and June, when these winds suddenly cause the temperature to rise and the humidity to plummet overnight, resulting in the withering and killing of plants (Gen 41:6, 23; Isa 27:8; Ezek 17:10; 19:12; Hos 13:15; Jonah 4:8), and weakness, heat stroke, and death to humans (2 Kgs 4:18-20, during the grain harvest!).[4]

Thus one cannot be but struck by the stark differences in the Deuteronomic calendar (Deut 16:1-17) between the Pilgrimage Festival of Unleavened Bread and the Pilgrimage Festivals of Weeks and Booths. In the latter, the legist takes pains to emphasize that everyone in the household, including the slaves, and even the underprivileged in the community—Levite, orphan, and widow—should accompany the head of the household in a pilgrimage to the central sanctuary (vv. 11, 14). But in the prescription for the Pilgrimage Festival of Unleavened Bread, this stipulation is conspicuous by its absence. The only possible explanation is that the householder is eager to return to his fields. The text therefore states: "in the morning you may start

---

[3] *t. Suk.* 3:18.
[4] Cf. Dalman 1928:1/2.318–29, 460–61; Keel 1972.

back on your journey home" (v. 7b). At first blush, a totally superfluous statement! It reveals, however, the legist's assurance that the Paschal Offering sacrifice and the Unleavened Bread pilgrimage can be fulfilled by a one-night and one-person stand. The householder's family and retainers can stay home. He need but offer the sacrifice, eat of it, and see the light of day at the sanctuary, thereby fulfilling the ancient commandment to observe the Festival of Unleavened Bread beginning that morning (v. 16a; cf. Exod 23:17; 34:23)—and then hasten home.[5]

To be sure, during Second Temple times, particularly at the end of this period, large-scale family pilgrimages to the temple took place for the Paschal Offering.[6] By then, however, political and economic circumstances had changed. The economy of the large diaspora and of much of the land was no longer agricultural but mercantile. Celebrating the seven-day Unleavened Bread Festival, paralleling the required seven-day Booths Festival, in Jerusalem was now possible.

[23:22] This verse should be compared with its prototype, 19:9-10, from which it is clearly copied. The most obvious change is the omission of 19:10a, since it includes the grape harvest, an event that does not occur until midsummer; hence its omission is logical.[7] The direction of the borrowing is also indicated by the same switch in numbers from the first plural clause to the singular, which dominated thereafter.[8] As demonstrated by Knohl, the addition of a verse ending "I am YHWH your God" (v. 22) following a passage ending with "an eternal law throughout your generations" (v. 21) is indicative of H's legal style.[9] What purpose did H have in mind in repeating an injunction that it already ordained? Greenberg argues cogently that this verse was deliberately appended to the pericope on the firstfruits of the grain (vv. 9-21) in order to underline God's sovereignty over the land: Israel may farm God's land (25:23) only if it brings its firstfruits to YHWH and provides the specified gifts to the poor.[10] H may also have had a larger purpose in mind. In order to induce the landowner to observe the sabbatical prescriptions, H alters the old (reigning?) law of Exod 23:10-11 (JE), which assigns the entire produce of the sabbatical to the poor (and the beasts), so that the sole beneficiaries are the landowner and all those under his control. The poor, however, are thereby excluded. Hence H repeats the injunction to help the poor (19:9-10) in the festival calendar as a reminder to the landowner that sharing the grain harvest with the poor and the alien is not just an ethical desideratum but a specific, time-bound, yearly obligation, even on the sabbatical.

---

[5] See also Bekhor Shor on Deut 17:11, 16.

[6] Cf. 2 Chronicles 30; Josephus, *Ant.* 17.214.

[7] Wenham 1979:305.

[8] Noth 1977.

[9] 1995:52–53. E.g., in Num 10:1-10 (H), see vv. 1-8, 9-10; and in Lev 23:39-43, see vv. 39-41, 42-43.

[10] 1985:115.

Verses 23-25. The Festival of Alarm Blasts

That the number seven bears special, and, perhaps, sacred significance in the calendar (and in progeny) has long been recognized.[11] The seventh month is set apart just as the seventh day, the seventh year, and the Jubilee (the end of the seventh week of years). Moreover, note that the offerings listed for the first day of the seventh month almost duplicate the offerings of a normal new moon (cf. Num 28:11-15; 29:1-6). Thus the seventh new moon is to the ordinary new moon as the seventh day is to the ordinary day (Num 28:3-10), thereby preserving the sabbatical cycle in the lunar calendar. However, this can be accredited as only an ancillary factor. More central is the reality that it is inextricably associated with the other festivals of the seventh month— the Day of Purgation and the Festival of Booths (see below). That this month is replete with festivals (ten days, fully one-third of the month) should not surprise. It is the only month that follows the harvests and precedes the rains. Still, the common denominator that binds these festivals into a single unit is something else, as will be explained below.

In first-millennium Uruk, two New Year festivals were celebrated, one in Nisan (the first month) and the other in Tashritu (the seventh month), and both months qualified as "the beginning of the year." In addition, third- to second-millennium Ur also held two New Years annually that can only be explained as the beginning of the agricultural year (the seventh month) and the beginning of the civil year (the first month).[12] Also, chronological considerations can lead to the conclusion that the royal year in Judah began in the spring, whereas the royal year in north Israel began in the autumn.[13] Nor should it be forgotten that rather recently, in our time, multiple New Years (civil, legal, and fiscal) were normative in the Western world. Finally, I must frankly state that there exists not a single hint in all of Scripture that the first day of Tishri, the seventh month, was New Year's Day. In sum, the text must be taken as it is: it prescribes the rites for the first day of the seventh month, which falls at the end of the harvests (the old agricultural year) and before the onset of the rainy season (the beginning of the new agricultural year).

The purpose of the alarm blasts is to arouse the Deity's attention. But what are Israel's pressing needs that surface on the first day of the seventh month? The Mishna *Ta'anit,* in my opinion, strikes the mark.[14] It deals with the sounding of the shofar at the assembly of a community engaged in a fast to implore God for rain.[15] All three festivals of the seventh month—the alarm call on the first day, the fast day on the tenth, the circumambulation of the altar with waving fronds and other vegetation for seven days, from the fifteenth through the twenty-second, as well as the tradition of a

---

[11] For the earliest source see *Lev. Rab.* 29:11.

[12] Klein 1992; M. Cohen 1993:300–306. Cf. van der Toorn 1991a:331.

[13] Tadmor 1962:267.

[14] *m. Ta'an.* 1:1—3:3.

[15] This will be discussed in detail at v. 40 on "you shall rejoice before YHWH your God."

water libation offered during these days—combine into a single-minded goal: to beseech God for adequate and timely rain in the forthcoming agricultural year.

The "alarm blasts" for rain do not imply a somber celebration. For example, the Feast of Booths is the most joyous festival of all despite its central focus on rituals for rain. Thus Ezra and Nehemiah urge the people: "Go, eat choice foods and drink sweet drinks and send portions to whoever has nothing prepared, for the (New Year) day is holy to YHWH. Do not be sad, for your rejoicing in YHWH is the source of your strength" (Neh 8:10). These instructions echo those issued for New Year celebration among the Hittites,[16] an indication that the joyous nature of the New Year was nigh universal. It was uniquely in Israel, however, that the anticipatory note for the forthcoming rains was added. The alarm blasts, then, served to warn the people that in the midst of their rejoicing over the conclusion of the agricultural season just passed they should not forget that in the days ahead they should implore God's mercy for adequate rain for the new season.

Verses 26-32. The Day of Purgation

[23:26] "you shall afflict yourselves." See the discussion of 16:29.

[23:29] "will be cut off from his kin." The presumed parity between the severity of the Sabbath and that of the Day of Purgation breaks down at this juncture. It is true that both are called days of "complete rest," when absolutely no work is permitted (cf. v. 3 with vv. 31-32), and, ostensibly, the Day of Purgation has a slight edge on the degree of severity because of its requirement to practice self-denial. It turns out, however, that the Sabbath is severer because of the differentiation in penalties. Although both days invoke the *karet* for their violation, the Sabbath violator also incurs the death penalty carried out by the court (Exod 31:14-15; Num 15:32-36), which means that he is immediately put to death as well as being punished with the excision of his line ("and cut him off," 20:3). Thus since the severity of a law is determined by the penalty for its violation, the Sabbath must be adjudged severer than the Day of Purgation. Indeed, originally the Day of Purgation was a day of rejoicing and dancing at the sanctuary (see chap. 16, THEME A).

[23:32] "from evening to evening." As discussed in v. 5,[17] the biblical day began at dawn. Thus the Day of Purgation, like the Festival of Unleavened Bread, is a pointed exception—one that is not difficult to fathom. Its purpose is to limit the fast to twenty-four hours. Otherwise, the Israelite would begin to fast on the ninth day at bedtime and not break his or her fast until the morning of the eleventh—a period of thirty-six hours.

---

[16] Otten 1956.
[17] Also recognized by Rashbam on this verse.

"your Sabbath." But not the Lord's Sabbath.[18] This distinction explains why the Day of Purgation can be shifted to begin the previous evening: it is not YHWH's Sabbath (v. 3), which begins at daybreak. This distinction provides another reason why the Sabbath day is superior to the Day of Purgation: it inheres in creation (Gen 2:1-3) because it became sanctified as YHWH's day of rest (Exod 20:11), whereas the "complete rest" of the Day of Purgation was ordained subsequently, for Israel's benefit, to purge the people and its sanctuary from their sins so that YHWH might continue to abide in their midst.

Verses 33-36a. The Festival of Booths

[23:34] "the Pilgrimage Festival of Booths." The only other pentateuchal code that calls this festival by this name is Deuteronomy (16:13, 16; 31:10). Afterward, this name occurs only in postexilic sources (Zech 14:16, 18, 19; Ezra 2:4; 2 Chr 8:13). The significance of this distribution cannot be overestimated. It indicates that the name became preferable at the Jerusalem temple (H) and subsequently became mandatory there (D). It is missing in the precentralization calendars of Exodus (E) and Numbers (P)—another piece of evidence that P does not presuppose a single sanctuary. The importance of this fact in understanding the origin and meaning of the festival's name is discussed at v. 42.

[23:36] "a solemn assembly." The assembly that marked the end of the Festival of Booths would have been celebrated at the temple, and on the day that the pilgrims were free to return to their homes (cf. Deut 16:8; 1 Kgs 8:66). But would it be far afield to suggest that those who did remain also gathered for prayer—but this time exclusively for rain? On the last day before the Israelite landowner returns home (or while he is doing so), his thoughts and concerns would be focused on the prospects of his forthcoming plowing and sowing being blessed with an adequate supply of rain. Prayer would have been in his heart and verbalized communally at the assembly.

The sharp contrast in the number of sacrificed bulls, seventy during the seven days and only one on the eighth day, should suffice to indicate that the temple early on recognized this sacrificial distinction. That the total number of bulls amounts to seventy, not by mandating ten bulls for each of the seven days but by an arithmetically reduced progression (n-1) beginning at the arbitrary number thirteen, can only mean that the total of seventy was aimed for at the outset. It can also be no accident that the number seventy corresponds—in biblical times—to the assumed number of nations in the world.[19] After all, the Festival of Booths, focusing on a person's needs and desire to give thanks to God for the year's harvest, is of universal appeal. It is small wonder that Zechariah prophesies that this festival would become observed uni-

---

[18] Ibn Ezra.
[19] Genesis 10; Deut 32:8-9 LXX, Sam.; 4QDeut 32; Dan 10:13, 20; cf. Fensham 1977.

versally (Zech 14:16). The eighth day, by contrast, prescribes only one bull—for Israel. Israel, in its rain-dependent land—contrast Egypt—has a need for a separate dialogue with God.

Verses 39-43. Addendum on the Festival of Booths

[23:39] "when you have ingathered the yield of the land." The purpose of the ingathering is for storage, as the Deuteronomic prescription mandates: "when you gather in from your threshing floor and your vat" (Deut 16:13). The grain kernels and the grapes and olives pressed into wine and oil, respectively (Jer 40:10, 12), including, presumably, the summer fruit, are brought into storage.

[23:40] "the boughs of majestic trees." This rendering resolves the age-old crux of Neh 8:15: "Go out to the mountains and bring leafy branches of olive trees, pine trees, myrtles, palms, and [other] leafy trees to make booths as it is written." The fundamental question is: Is there any relationship between the lists in Leviticus 23 and Nehemiah 8? Ostensibly, the differences are irreconcilable:

1. In Nehemiah, there are five species; in Leviticus, four.

2. Olive branches and pine branches (lit. "leafy branches of an oil tree") are not in Leviticus.

3. Conversely, the fruit of the majestic tree and the willows of the brook are not in Nehemiah.

These discrepancies lead most scholars to conclude that the two lists are independent; that is, Ezra's Torah was not equivalent to the MT, hence the canonization of the latter was a subsequent development.

These seemingly irreconcilable differences, I submit, are surmountable, once we reckon with the rendering of the first four species as "the boughs of majestic trees." With one stroke, we eliminate the incongruity of constructing booths with fruits and, at the same time, allow for this term to be a generalization, which can include more than the three enumerated plants. (Indeed, "the branches of a leafy tree" is also a nonspecific category, and is therefore not limited to one species.)

"and willows of the brook." They must have been tall, even longer than palm fronds, for according to the rabbis: "There was a place below Jerusalem called Motza. They [the gatherers] went down thither and collected thence young willow-branches, and they came and set them upright along the sides of the altar with their tops bent down over the top of the altar."[20] The purpose of taking this species of vegetation will be discussed below.

---

[20] *m. Suk.* 4:5.

"and you shall rejoice before YHWH your God seven days." The theme of rejoicing predominates in D's description of visits to the temple during the pilgrimage Festival of Weeks (Deut 16:11) and, especially, Booths (16:14, 15). The theme of rejoicing is totally absent from D's description of the Festival of Unleavened Bread (16:1-8). The midrash casts light on this distinction: "The expression of rejoicing occurs three times in connection with the Festival of Booths, 'You shall rejoice in your festival' (Deut 16:14); 'You shall only rejoice' (Deut 16:15); 'And you shall rejoice before the Lord your God seven days' (Lev 23:40). But no such expression occurs once regarding the seven-day Unleavened Bread Festival. This is because the fate of man's crops is still in the balance then—and he does not know whether there will be a yield."[21]

To "rejoice before YHWH" always means in the sanctuary. But how should one rejoice? It is too late for bringing firstfruits (as in the case of the earlier grain harvests, the omer of barley and the two loaves of wheat). Of course, feasting is always implied (cf. Deut 14:26). But the command to rejoice follows and must result from the command to take the enumerated plants.

That the circumambulation of the altar with these plants was an ancient rite is attested by *Jubilees*, which attributes it to Abraham: "And Abraham took branches of palm trees and fruit of good trees and each of the days [of the Festival of Booths] he used to go around the altar with the branches."[22]

The rabbis were fully cognizant that the theme that unites all these rituals is a supplication for rain. The waving of the branches in all directions is a summons to the four winds to bring rain or "to hinder the bad winds and the bad dews."[23] The blowing of the shofar is mandated for the production of rain: "A city upon which no rain has fallen . . . blows [the shofar] and fasts."[24] The water libation unique to this festival speaks for itself: Water brought from the Pool of Shiloah through the Water Gate "for the libation on the Festival of Booths"[25] could be only for one purpose: "so that the rain would be blessed on its account";[26] "Why did the Torah enjoin us to pour out water on the Booths Festival? The Holy One, Blessed Be He, said: Pour out water before me on the Booths festival, so that your rains this year may be blessed";[27] "By these four species which grow near water, therefore they serve as pleaders for water."[28] And the Mishna states categorically: "in the days of the Festival [Booths], the sentence on the waters will be passed."[29]

---

[21] *Yal.* 654.
[22] *Jub.* 16:31; cf. 2 Macc 10:7; Josephus, *Ant.* 3.245.
[23] *b. Suk.* 37b-38a.
[24] *m. Taʿan.* 3:3; cf. *t. Taʿan.*2:8.
[25] *t. Suk.* 3:3.
[26] *t. Suk.* 3:18.
[27] *b. Roš Haš.* 16a; cf. *t. Roš Haš.* 1:12-13.
[28] *y. Taʿan.* 1:1.
[29] *m. Roš Haš.* 1:2. For further sources, rabbinic and modern, see Milgrom 1983b:170 n. 38.

The rabbis acknowledged that the water libation rite had been performed from the earliest times: "The laws . . . of the willow branch and the water libation were given to Moses at Mount Sinai."[30] They, of course, had Samuel's emergency water libation before them (1 Sam 7:6). They also had the more explicit eschatological statement of the prophet: "All who survive of all those nations that come up against Jerusalem shall make a pilgrimage year by year to bow low to the King Lord of Hosts and to *observe the Festival of Booths.* Any of the earth's communities that does not make the pilgrimage to Jerusalem to bow low to the King Lord of Hosts *shall receive no rain*" (Zech 14:16-17 [my emphasis]).

The streams of "living waters" (Zech 14:8) that will flow out of Jerusalem during this eschatological Festival of Booths is reinterpreted by Jesus in his sermon in the temple during the festival: "On the last day of the festival [the seventh], the great day [when the altar was circumambulated seven times], while Jesus was standing there, he cried out, 'Let anyone who is thirsty come to me, and let the one who believes in me drink. As the scripture has said, "Out of his belly shall flow rivers of living water"'" (John 7:37-38; see 19:34).

There is little doubt that these rites have a magical origin: setting up the branches on the altar (Ps 118:27), beating them at the altar, circumambulating of the altar, pouring the water libation on the altar, all accompanied by shofar blowing, can each be traced to equivalent rites of sympathetic magic. However, the magical origin had been expunged in biblical times,[31] all the more so in the rabbinic period. Let us take the instance of the circumambulation of the altar each day and seven times on the seventh day. The parallel of the story of the conquest of Jericho immediately comes to mind. That, too, involved a daily circumambulation, seven times on the seventh day (Josh 6:3-4, 14-18), accompanied by blasts on the shofar (vv. 8-9, 16, 20). However, the magical circle augmented seven times on the seventh day notwithstanding, the rite was executed at the command of YHWH (vv. 2-5). Similarly, we can assume that all the nonbiblical rites of the Festival of Booths, though undoubtedly originating in popular worship and rooted in magical practices, were ultimately assimilated into Israel's official monotheism so that the rabbis could say with confidence that they were revealed to Moses at Sinai.

Perhaps the most instructive passage of all is: "Blow a horn in Zion, solemnize a fast, proclaim an assembly" (Joel 2:15; cf. 1:14). The purpose of these three actions is to supplicate God for rain: "O children of Zion, be glad, rejoice in YHWH your God. For he has given you the early rain of kindness, now he makes the rain—the early rain and the late—fall as formerly" (2:23). As astutely noted by Knohl,[32] all three actions—horn blowing, fasting, and assembling—characterize, respectively, the

---

[30] *b. Suk.* 44a; *t. Suk.* 3:2.
[31] Milgrom 1990:353, 438–56.
[32] 1987:95; 1995:37.

three festivals of the seventh month: the first day, "commemorated with short blasts" (Lev 23:24); the tenth day, "you shall practice self-denial" (vv. 27, 32); and the twenty-second day, the "solemn assembly" (v. 36), following the seven-day Festival of Booths.

To convey some impression of the unprescribed, nonsacrificial festivities indulged in by the laity and clergy alike during the water-libation rites, I conclude with this probable eyewitness description:

> Anyone who had not witnessed the rejoicing at the Libation Water-Well had never seen rejoicing in his life.
>
> At the close of the first holy day of the Festival of Booths they went down to the Court of the Women where they had made an important rearrangement. And golden candlesticks were there with four golden bowls at their tops and four ladders to each one, and four youths from the young priests with pitchers of oil, holding a hundred and twenty logs, in their hands, which they used to pour into every bowl. From the worn-out drawers and girdles of the priests they made wicks and with them they set alight; and there was no courtyard in Jerusalem that was not lit up with the light of the Libation Water-Well ceremony.
>
> Pious men and men of good deeds used to dance before them with burning torches in their hands and sang before them songs and praises. And the Levites on harps, and on lyres, and on cymbals, and with trumpets and with other instruments of music without number upon the fifteen steps leading down from the court of the Israelites to the Women's Court, corresponding to the Fifteen Songs of Ascent in the Psalms; upon them the Levites used to stand with musical instruments and sing hymns. And two priests stood at the Upper Gate that led down from the Israelites' Court to the Court of the Women with two trumpets in their hands. At cockcrow they sounded a prolonged blast, a quavering note, and a prolonged blast. When they reached the Forecourt they blew a prolonged blast, a quavering note, and a prolonged blast. They kept up prolonged blasts and proceeded until they reached the gate that led out to the east; when they arrived at the gate that led forth to the east they turned their faces to the west and said, "Our ancestors when they were in this place turned 'with their backs unto the temple and their faces toward the east and they prostrated themselves eastwards toward the sun' [Ezek 8:16], but as for us our eyes are turned to the Eternal."[33]

[23:42] "In booths shall you live seven days." The booth refers to the shelter built by pilgrims to the Jerusalem temple for the one festival during which there were too many of them to be accommodated in the city.[34] To be sure, after centralization, the imperative to offer the paschal sacrifice would have brought large numbers to Jerusalem, but this occasion was limited to a one-night observance by the farmer without his family. If booths were erected, they would have been dismantled by the

---

[33] *m. Suk.* 5:1-4.
[34] Ehrlich 1908–14:2.85–86; Licht 1968:1042; Ginsberg 1982:60.

morning. The booths of the autumn festival, however, had to last for seven (and probably eight) days. Strewn on the hillsides that surrounded Jerusalem, they would have been the distinctive visual characteristic of the festival. Jerusalem was not unique in this regard. In ancient Greece, at the Carnea festival, the Spartans "dwelt in tentlike bowers after the fashion of a military camp."[35] It is therefore of ultimate significance that the name "the Festival of Booths" occurs solely in Lev 23:36 and Deut 16:13, 16, the only legal corpora in the Pentateuch that presume regional preference over national centralization. But when the festivals became national celebrations at the capital, the booths erected by pilgrims probably would match and outnumber the residences in the city.

---

[35] Kedar-Kopfstein and Botterweck 1980:205.

Tabernacle Oil and Bread;
Blasphemy; Talion Laws

Selected Texts
Verses 1-9. Introduction

Israel's responsibility for observing the festival calendar and its required sacrifices and offerings (chap. 23) continues here in vv. 1-9 with Israel's responsibility to supply the daily oil for the tabernacle lamps and the weekly bread for the tabernacle table—both located in the shrine. Since this pericope prescribes the people's obligation in maintaining the sacrificial rites in the shrine, why are they not also obligated to supply the needs for the remaining sanctum in the shrine, the daily incense offered on the inner, gold altar (as implied by Exod 35:8)? If the answer is ventured that the incense was provided by the chieftains and not by the entire people (Exod 35:27-28), these verses prescribe—ostensibly, in contradiction to our pericope—that the chieftains also supplied the lighting oil! The resolution of this apparent contradiction is that the chieftains contributed the initial supply, but thereafter the responsibility falls on the entire nation, and this permanent arrangement is reflected in Lev 24:1-9. This being so, the question still remains: Why is the incense omitted from Israel's obligations in this pericope?

I can only conjecture an answer. Perhaps this pericope reflects reality. Olive oil, even the best quality, was relatively cheap; the land of Canaan abounded in olive groves (Deut 6:11; 8:8; 28:40; Josh 24:13; 2 Kgs 18:32). Excavations at Tel Miqne-Ekron, nearby Timnah, and other locations reveal that in the seventh century BCE, this region was the center of a vast olive-oil industry. At Ekron, for example, over one hundred oil presses were discovered in surface surveys. At all these sites, the oil presses were "inside ordinary houses, indicating that the manufacture of live olive oil was a cottage industry practiced by families at their homes."[1] Not so with spices, which were imported and therefore costly. It is no wonder, then, that the list of gifts

---

[1] Mazar 1990:490; cf. Eitam and Shomroni 1987.

of the tribal chieftains to the tabernacle expressly (and consistently) singles out spices (Num 7:14).

Support for this conjecture may lie in the fact that the anointment oil, initially brought by the chieftains (Exod 35:27-28), is also missing from this inventory. Here too the answer may be that the anointment oil contained spices (Exod 30:22-25), thus effectively putting it out of people's reach.[2]

The presence of the menorah, the incense altar, and the Bread of the Presence inside the sanctuary originally may have represented, respectively, the light, aroma, and food offered to the resident Deity. A deeper symbolism, however, may have been understood. One such possibility for the menorah is suggested by Gerstenberger: "God forfeits none of his power, even if the sun itself 'goes down.' The lamp before the holy of holies extends this daylight symbolically through the darkness, signalling thus God's unbroken life: in this sense it is an 'eternal light.'"[3]

Verses 5-9. Bread for the Tabernacle Table

The table on which the bread was always present—even when the table was transported (Num 4:7b)—was, perhaps for that reason, the most important sanctum except for the ark. It follows the ark in all accounts (prescription, Exod 25:29-30; construction, Exod 37:10-16; installation, Exod 40:4, 22; and transport, Num 4:7-8). Its relative importance is further underscored by its being covered during transport. It joins the ark in meriting three coverings, whereas the other sanctums—the menorah and the two altars—rate only two coverings (cf. Num 4:5-8 with vv. 9-14).

There can be no doubt that the display of bread before a deity is an ancient practice. In Egypt the offerings are placed on the outer altar, but only the fresh bread and cakes are brought into the sanctuary and laid on mats (together with incense) before the god's table,[4] where they are burned and sprinkled with wine, as surety for the eternal duration of the sacrificial worship.[5]

Hittite religion also evidences the centrality of a bread offering laid out on a table before the deity.[6] The Hittite king Murshili II attests that "the offerers of sacrificial loaves and the offerers of libations were giving bread and making libations to the gods, my lords."[7] Ritual bread laying was an early custom in Mesopotamia, appearing in a Sumerian inscription of Urukagina of Lagash (c. 2340 BCE).[8] Babylonians

---

[2] If this surmise has merit, then the incense for the temple would have fallen into the same category as the wood for the altar, which Scripture relates was supplied by a few families at fixed times during the year (Neh 10:35 [Eng. 34]; 13:31; *m. Ta'an.* 4:5).

[3] 1996:356.

[4] Sauneron 1960:84.

[5] cf. Dommershausen and Fabry 1995; Blackman 1918–19; Erman 1907:44.

[6] Hoffner 1974:216.

[7] Ibid.

[8] Cooper 1983:60.

laid sweet unleavened bread before various deities, in twelves or multiples of twelve.[9] A table for the bread is also attested in the Greek temple at Delphi that, according to Josephus, was precisely of the same dimensions as that prescribed for the tabernacle.[10]

Thus there can be no doubt that the bread display was integral to Israelite worship from earliest times. It is first attested for the Nob sanctuary, where the bread was given to David and his soldiers (nonpriests!), apparently as an emergency measure to prevent starvation (1 Sam 21:7).[11]

It is important, however, to recognize the wide gulf that separates the bread rite prescribed for the tabernacle from its counterparts in the neighboring cultures. Whereas the latter baked bread for the god's table daily, Israel prepared it once weekly—clearly a token offering whose purpose was exposure, not food.[12] Indeed, even the term, literally "bread of the face" or "personal bread"[13]—a gross anthropomorphism—is missing in this pericope, probably deliberately.[14] The classic polemic against the pagan notion that the sacrifices and food offerings actually fed the deity was penned by the psalmist: "If I were hungry I would not tell you, for mine are the world and its fullness. Do I eat the flesh of strong bulls, or is the blood of goats my drink?" (Ps 50:12-13).

Nonetheless, vestiges—though only fossils—of such earlier beliefs in ancient Israel are evident from the cultic apparatus of the table, which included libation bowls (Num 4:7). Since they were made of gold (Exod 25:29; 37:16), they were not originally intended for the wine libations on the outer altar (Num 15:5, 7, 10), for its vessels were exclusively bronze (Exod 27:3; 28:3). Being of gold, they could be used only inside the shrine. Only there—and nowhere else—was gold used on the cult objects (candelabrum table, incense altar) and structure (inner curtains, planks, pillars, bars, hooks, and rings). Where this libation was offered is not clear. The obvious place, the inner altar—to correspond with the libation on the outer altar—is strictly forbidden by Exod 30:9 (which perhaps betrays that it originally was done there).

Another verse, however, furnishes stronger evidence that a libation on the inner altar originally did take place: "in the sanctuary the pouring of a libation of beer to YHWH" (Num 28:7b). Although the beer and ale industry is attested from early on in the predominantly grain-growing countries of Egypt and Mesopotamia (whereas Canaan was celebrated for its wine as among its chief exports in every age), archaeology reveals that beer was undoubtedly also manufactured in Canaan. Typical of Philistine pottery is a jug "usually provided with a strainer spout . . . in order to strain

---

[9] Zimmern and Wincklen 1905:600; cf. Blome 1934:247–50.
[10] *Ant.* 3.139.
[11] Cf. *b. Menaḥ.* 95b-96a.
[12] Barr 1963.
[13] A. Johnson 1947; de Vaux 1964:39 n. 35.
[14] Kalisch 1867–72:2.522.

out the beer without swallowing barley husks. It is not difficult to infer from the ubiquity of these . . . beer jugs that the Philistines were mighty carousers. In this respect again, archaeology is in full agreement with biblical tradition, as we see from the story of Samson, where drinking bouts are mentioned several times in connexion with the Philistines [Judg 14:10, 12, 17], though it is said emphatically of Samson that he drank neither wine nor beer [Judg 13:14]."[15]

The beer libation must have taken place inside the shrine on the inner altar. However, after it was forbidden as a gross anthropomorphism, lest one think that YHWH—in his private chambers—actually imbibed the brew, the libation was set on the table together with its loaves of bread, and neither was offered on the altar. And just as the bread was assigned to the priests, one may assume that, originally, the beer also became a priestly prebend. Perhaps at some subsequent juncture the beer was altogether eliminated, since it did not fit with the priestly sacrificial system: the bread, being a cereal offering, could be assigned to the priests, but the beer, being forbidden to the priest while officiating, was eliminated. The golden cups on the table remained, but were empty.

It can be no accident that in contrast to all other bread offerings, at least part of which is consumed on the altar (2:2, 9, 16; 6:8), only the frankincense placed alongside (but not on) the table is burned on the altar, but none of the bread. In sum, the bread and the beer are displayed to the Deity and not "consumed" by the Deity. The bread (and, originally, the beer) is given to the priests in its entirety, but only after being displayed before YHWH for an entire week. Being unleavened, the bread would not go stale.

The twelve loaves displayed on the table in the inner shrine probably had the same function as the two onyx stones attached to the two shoulder pieces of the high priest's ephod and, most likely, as the twelve stones mounted in his breastpiece of decision as a "remembrance of the Israelites . . . before YHWH" (Exod 28:12; cf. v. 21). This interpretation is reinforced by the association of the loaves with the covenant (Lev 24:8b). They are a constant reminder to YHWH of his "eternal covenant" with his people. Finally, the two pericopes on the oil and bread (vv. 1-9) emphasize Israel's everlasting obligation to supply the requisite oil (v. 2) and bread (v. 8b) for the inner sanctums.

Verses 10-16, 23. The Case of Blasphemy

Law is inextricably bound to narrative—that is, the set of circumstances that engender it. Thus, as I will demonstrate, all seven laws that emanate from this single case of blasphemy (vv. 15-22), even though they are general in form, can never be dissociated from the narrative framework in which they are embedded (vv. 10-14, 23).

---

[15] Albright 1949:115.

Leviticus 17–27: The Holiness Source (H)

Even the generalization "You shall have one law for the alien and citizen alike" (v. 22a), which is frequently repeated in the H corpus,[16] always applies to the case under discussion.

[24:11] Why was cursing God such a heinous offense? I believe D. N. Freedman is on the right track: "How is it possible, first of all, to bless God when he himself is the source of blessing? . . . Perhaps it is a hangover from primitive views that indeed human beings could confer blessing on God, just as he could confer them on human beings. [It betokens] a certain reciprocity, corresponding to the sacrificial system, which somewhere in its roots had the idea of providing the God with nourishment."[17] Conversely, a curse was believed to be so powerful that is was conceived to be efficacious against a deity. How does one curse God? Presumably, the name of God would be used, and one would say something like "may God be damned."

[24:15] "(curses) his God." This is a euphemism, so that YHWH would not become the object of "curse." Alternatively, the H legist restated the older prohibition, "You shall not curse God" (Exod 22:27 [Eng. 28]), in order to add the element missing in Exodus—the punishment.[18]

"shall bear his punishment." It is assumed that the blasphemer cursed God in secret; hence God alone can punish him.[19] Thus this verse does not repeat the case cited in v. 11, which presumes that the pronunciation (and cursing) of God's name was done in public. There is one severe objection, however, to this interpretation: it requires eisegesis. In v. 15b the curse was uttered privately; in v. 16a, publicly. Nothing in the text warrants such a distinction. Thus an alternative solution must be sought. Perhaps both cases presuppose public acts. That is, even if one curses God without pronouncing his name (v. 15b), he is not subject to the jurisdiction of the court. He is liable for punishment, but only at the hands of God. The implication of this interpretation is that the powers of the court are not unlimited. Witnesses would have to step forward and testify that they have heard God's name pronounced as he was being cursed. If, however, the witnesses admitted that the curse omitted God's name, their testimony would be rejected. The court would reply that it had no authority to encroach on God's domain. It was for God to punish the miscreant who cursed him.

The demarcation between the two jurisdictions depends on whether the sin is committed against God or against a human,[20] and in the latter case, whether the

---

[16] See 19:34; 24:22; Exod 12:49; Num 15:15-16; cf. Exod 12:19, 48; Lev 16:29; 17:15; 18:26; Num 9:14; 15:29-30; cf. also Josh 8:33; Ezek 47:22.

[17] Personal communication.

[18] M. Segal 1964:1.93.

[19] Ibn Ezra (first comment); Wessely 1846.

[20] Milgrom 1970:6–7.

alleged sinner was apprehended. A parade example is the suspected adulteress of Num 5:11-31. An irate husband suspects that his wife has been unfaithful. Having no proof, his only recourse is to bring her to the sanctuary, where she undergoes an ordeal. The priest makes her drink a potion of sacred water to which the dust from the sanctuary floor and a parchment containing a curse have been added. The curse spells out the consequences: if she is guilty; her genital area will distend and she will no longer be able to conceive; if, however, the water has no effect on her, she is declared innocent and she will be blessed with seed.

The key to unlocking this trial by ordeal is the fact that her alleged adultery was unapprehended. Had there been witnesses, there would be no need to cite this case: she would summarily have been put to death. Instead, her case is transferred to divine jurisdiction. But why this unique (in biblical jurisprudence) ordeal? And why consult God at all? Since he will decide the case, let him decide her judgment; and, if she is guilty, let her be put to death.

To pose these questions is to answer them. Since the purported adulteress has not been apprehended—as the text repeats with staccato emphasis (Num 5:13)—then the community and, especially, the overwrought husband may not give way to their passions and lynch her. Indeed, even if she is proved guilty by the ordeal, they may not put her to death. Unapprehended adultery remains punishable only by God, and there is no need or warrant for human mediation.[21] Thus a cardinal principle of biblical jurisprudence is that the unapprehended criminal is not subject to the jurisdiction of the human court.

In the long run, however, it makes little difference in our case whether the curse was uttered in public or private. There are no witnesses who can testify that the curse was hurled against God while pronouncing his name. Whether one curses God in private, even if he pronounces the divine name, or in public, but without pronouncing the name, he is punishable—but only by God. Nevertheless, the second alternative is preferable, because, as indicated above, it does not require the assumption of a switch from a private to a public setting in vv. 15b–16a.

Verses 17-22. The Talion Laws

The import of the uniform application of talion to injuries is eloquently expressed by Hartley: "This principle does not imply that punishment was carried out by inflicting bodily injury in kind, but that punishment for harm to a person is to be commensurate with the harm done, not greater as revenge dictates, nor less as indulgence desires. This principle was a great advance in law codes, for it raised personal injury from a civil tort to criminal law, increasing the social worth of a citizen."[22]

---

[21] For a detailed analysis of this extraordinary trial, see Milgrom 1990:346–54.
[22] 1992:LXII.

The point was raised by my student R. Pinchover that talion in the story of the blasphemer is inexact; the punishment, stoning, does not correspond to the crime, cursing! Moreover, God, the object of the curse, but not the community, should have cursed the blasphemer. Finally, talion, the law applied to the blasphemer, does not even allude to his crime. As a reply to all these points, Pinchover has brought to my attention a fascinating page from the Vassal Treaties of Esarhaddon: "Just as one cuts off the hands and feet and blinds the eyes of those who blaspheme against the god or the lord, so may they bring about your end."[23] Thus the talion law, which begins "Fracture for fracture, eye for eye" (v. 20), where "fracture" replaces "hand" and "foot," actually corresponds to the punishment meted out by the god to a blasphemer.

Nonetheless, these points remain unanswered. The blasphemer does not have his limbs broken or his eyes blinded. He is stoned to death: "life for life" is, indeed, applied to him.

The question we must address can be summed up as follows: What is it about cursing God that corresponds to and warrants death, and why is the talion law employed to specify the penalty? The answer is: If the community had not put the blasphemer to death, the inexpiable impurity generated by the curse would have caused the destruction of the community.[24] Thus one might even say that the community had to kill the blasphemer in self-defense. Another approach is taken by Douglas, who opts for true talion: "the blasphemer has hurled insults at the name of God, let him die by stones hurled at him."[25] The advantage of both suggestions is that they explain the insertion of the talion laws into the narrative. Nonetheless, the more likely answer is that YHWH's talion need not always be precise. He punishes collectively (note Moses' complaint, Num 16:22), and his punishment, unless it is graded as a series of warnings (Lev 26:14-38; cf. Isa 9:7 [Eng. 8]—10:4; Amos 4:6-11), causes death. Thus talion is frequently but a literary figure for the purpose of vividly emphasizing that God's justice is uncompromisingly inexorable.

[24:19] "so it shall be done to him." It may be that literal talion is intended. Doron claims that this phrase occurs in the story of Samson (Judg 15:11), where literal talion was not enacted—Samson burned the Philistines' grain stacks because they had deprived him of his wife.[26] The loose wording of the narrative, however, should not be taken as a legal pronouncement. All it may mean is that Samson is boasting: "I gave it right back to them."

---

[23] *ANET,* 540, §95.
[24] Milgrom 1991:254–61.
[25] 1999:207.
[26] Doron 1969. See also Ibn Ezra.

[24:21] The verse is here for stylistic reasons: to complete the giant introversion of this pericope. Furthermore, it provides the seventh law of this pericope, thereby artfully perfecting its structure (see the Theme below).

"but one who kills a human being shall be put to death." Another reason for this repetition (cf. v. 17) is to emphasize the basic legal postulate: no compensation for homicide—a leniency allowed in ancient Near Eastern law (and practice) to those of a higher social status. Note this Hittite example: "they seize the killer of such a person and hand him over to the brothers of the murdered man. His brothers take the monetary compensation for the murdered man and they perform the expiatory ritual on the murderers, through whose act a life was taken. But if the brothers do not want to accept monetary compensation, they execute that man who has taken a life."[27]

[24:22] H insists that both religious, or cultic, and civil law are binding on the alien (Num 15:16); the former, however, is qualified by being limited to prohibitions (chap. 17, Theme A). That the observance of both religious and civil law is incumbent on the alien is vividly expressed in this pericope, which expressly mentions the alien in regard to both the law of blasphemy (v. 16) and the talion laws for injuries (v. 22).[28]

The egalitarian treatment of the alien stems from H's theology. Since YHWH is the owner of the land (see 25:23), all who settle on it—provided they obey his laws mutatis mutandis—are entitled to his protection (chap. 17, THEME A). "The stranger was to be protected, although he was not a member of one's family, clan, religion, community or people, simply because he was a human being. In the stranger, therefore, man discovered the idea of humanity."[29]

Selected Theme: The Structure of 24:13-23 and Its Significance

A   And YHWH spoke to Moses, saying: (v. 13)

    B   Take the blasphemer outside the camp, and have all who were within hearing lean their hands on his head; then have the whole community *stone* him. (v. 14)

      C And to the Israelites speak thus: (v. 15a)

1.   D Anyone who curses *his God* shall bear his punishment (v. 15b)   3.   E If anyone kills any human being, he must be put to death. (v. 17)

---

[27] Oppenheim 1967:144.
[28] Knohl 1995:175.
[29] Hermann Cohen, cited in Telushkin 1997:467.

2. a but if he (also) pronounces the name of *YHWH,* he must be put to death. (v. 16aα)

    x The whole community shall *stone* him; alien as well as citizen, (v. 16aβ, bα) if he has (thus) pronounced the Name,

    a' he must be put to death.

F But anyone who kills an animal shall make restitution for it, life for life. (v. 18)

G If anyone maims another, as he has done so shall it be done to him: (v. 19)

X fracture for fracture, eye for eye, tooth for tooth. (v. 20a)

4. G' The injury he has inflicted on the person shall be inflicted on him. (v. 20b)

5. F' One who kills an animal shall make restitution for it; (v. 21a)

6. E' but one who kills a human being shall be put to death. (v. 21b)

7. D' *You* shall have one law for the alien and the citizen alike; for

I, YHWH your God (have spoken). (v. 22)

C' Moses spoke (thus) to the Israelites. (v. 23aα)

B' And they took the blasphemer outside the camp and *pelted* him with stones. (v. 23aβ)

A' The Israelites did as YHWH had commanded Moses. (v. 23b)

Lund's *Chiasmus in the New Testament,*[30] with examples from the Hebrew Bible, was the first major work that treated seriously Scripture's large, widely attested chiastic structures, alternately called introversions[31] or palistrophes,[32] as one of the preeminent organizational devices employed by the biblical authors. They have proved to be more than literary artifices. By the use of repeated words and inner chiasms, and, above all, by the choice of the center or fulcrum around which the introversion is structured, the ideological thrust of each author is revealed. In a word, structure is theology.

The heart of H's message must be contained within the talion laws, particularly in law no. 5 (GXG'), the heart of the structure. It states that any injury inflicted (presumably, maliciously) on another is subject to talion. Here the priestly author (H) pur-

---

[30] 1942.

[31] Kikawada 1974.

[32] McEvenue 1971:29 n. 18.

posely uses the word "blemish" to describe the effect of the injury.[33] It is hardly coincidental that the same term, the physical defects of persons and animals, disqualifies them from entering the service of, and to, God (21:16-23; 22:19-25). A theological message emerges here: He who injures a person has disfigured "the image of God" (Gen 1:27; 9:6b). For the priestly legist, this is blasphemy, and so he applies the law of talion to the case of the blasphemer. Thus the law of talion is operative because, in effect, the crime was committed not only against the person and hence was adjudicable in the human court, but also against God and hence subject to his law of talion (e.g., Deut 32:21; Isa 5:8-9; Jer 32:19; Prov 26:27; and see the curses, Lev 26:14-39, which largely reverse the blessings of vv. 3-13). In the talion laws of Leviticus (and Deuteronomy), literal talion is intended.

I was justifiably asked by B.-Z. Horowitz, a seminar student, why talion is at the center of the structure (GXG') rather than the law about the blasphemy of the alien (DD'), which, after all, is the subject of the story. We must keep in mind that H is obsessed with the problem of the alien both legally and theologically. Since H has expanded P's horizons from the sanctuary to the promised land, it must ipso facto be concerned with the alien, because, as a resident of the land, he is capable of polluting it. Thus the alien must heed all the prohibitions incumbent on the Israelite (but not the nonpollutable permissive commandments; see chap. 17, Theme A) against blasphemy. This prohibition, however, lies in a marginal area. Since a resident alien is not bound by a covenant to worship YHWH, is it truly a crime if the alien cursed him, pronouncing his name? The structure provides the answer in the juxtaposition of D and E and of E' and D'. Blasphemy is equivalent to murder; both are capital crimes requiring the death penalty. This equation in D E is completed in E' D', which adds the alien to the equation. Since blasphemy is the novel law in biblical jurisprudence, it is only logical that it, rather than the case about murder, be cited.

It should also be added, parenthetically, that in the theology of H, the alien simulates the life of holiness demanded of the Israelite. This theological postulate perhaps justifies and motivates H's general ruling that for violations of all prohibitions, civil and religious alike, the alien is subject to the same penalty as the Israelite.

To recapitulate: on one level, the structure emphasizes that the blasphemy prohibition applies to the alien. But on a deeper level, indicated by the true center of the structure (X), H makes the point that talion for permanent injuries is justified theologically because just as blasphemy is an offense against God, so are injuries that disfigure God's image—the human being. Thus we see that the episode of the blasphemer bears a secondary role. The talion laws for blemishes are H's primary objective; it attaches the case of blasphemy only to provide a *Sitz im Leben* for the legislation.

---

[33] Contrast the classic statements of the talion laws, Exod 21:23b-25; Deut 19:21b.

Jubilee, the Priestly Response
to Economic Injustice

The basic postulate of the Jubilee is:

> (25:23) Furthermore, the land must not be sold beyond reclaim, for the land is mine; you are but resident aliens under my authority. (24) Therefore, throughout the land you hold, you must provide redemption for the land.

"Land" here is Canaan, the promised land, and "you" refers to the people of Israel. They are to keep in mind that the owner of the land is YHWH and that they are only resident aliens; that is, YHWH is the landlord and the Israelites are tenants. The Deity-Landlord has decreed that "the land must not be sold beyond reclaim."

Each Israelite clan has been assigned a plot of land (Numbers 26) that must always remain in its possession.[1] Even when it is sold it can be reclaimed, a process called "redemption," and every fiftieth year (Jubilee) it must be restored to its original owner. Cancellation of debts and return of forfeited land was also known in other civilizations of the ancient Near East.[2] It usually occurred when a king acceded to the throne. Its purpose was to "prevent the collapse of the economy under too great a weight of private indebtedness."[3] However, it was generally limited to the king's retainers[4] and subject to his whim. The biblical Jubilee, in contrast, was inexorably periodic and incumbent on every Israelite.

The chapter, as is, flows logically and coherently. Even if the redactor had different sources before him, he welded them together in such an artistic and cogent sequence that it suffices to determine what he had in mind. This view is echoed in rabbinic literature:

> R. Samuel the son of Gedaliah said: There is no unit in the Torah whose opening subject is not followed by its substantiation. How does it [chap. 25] begin? "The Lord spoke to

---

[1] Milgrom 1990:219, 480–82.
[2] Weinfeld 1990.
[3] Edzard 1965:225.
[4] Bar-Maoz 1980.

Moses . . . the land shall rest . . ." (vv. 1-7). It is followed by the subject of the Jubilee, "You shall count for yourself seven weeks of years . . ." (vv. 8-13). If he has not observed the sabbaticals and Jubilees, he will ultimately sell his moveables, "when you sell [i.e., lease] your property . . ." (vv. 14-23). If he repents [i.e., changes his ways], fine; if not, he will ultimately sell his land, "When your brother [Israelite] becomes impoverished and has to sell part of his holding . . ." (vv. 25-28). If he repents, fine; if not, he will ultimately sell his house, "If a man sells a dwelling house . . ." (vv. 29-34). If he repents, fine; if not, he will ultimately go begging, "If your brother, being (further) impoverished, falls under your authority . . ." (vv. 35-38). If he repents, fine; if not, he will ultimately sell himself to you, "If your brother, being (further) impoverished under your authority, is sold to you . . ." (vv. 39-46). If he repents, fine; if not, he will ultimately sell himself to the gentile, "If the resident alien under your authority has prospered, and your brother, being (further) impoverished, comes under his authority and is sold to the resident alien . . ." (vv. 47-55), not only he himself but (ultimately) all of Israel.[5]

What makes this sequence so compelling is that it reveals both the logic of the chapter's order and its underlying theology. With one stroke, it solves the problem of why the passage on houses was placed in its spot (vv. 29-34), and it settles the question of why the series of successive impoverishments (vv. 25-55) follows the Jubilee law (vv. 8-24), which is applied in case a landowner is forced to sell his property. Indeed, this midrash perceptively recognizes that the selling here is in fact leasing, since he is selling only his moveables—that is, his usufruct.

Selected Themes

A. Destitution and Redemption

What are the circumstances that necessitate the sale of the land? The key verses are 25-28, 35-38, and 39-43. They represent three stages of destitution.

Verses 25-28. Stage One: Sold Land and Its Redemption

(25) When your brother becomes impoverished and has to sell part of his holding, his closest redeemer shall come and redeem the sold property of his brother. (26) If a man has no redeemer but prospers and acquires enough for this redemption, (27) he shall compute the years since its sale, refund the difference to the man to whom he sold it, and return to his holding. (28) If he does not acquire sufficient means to recover it, his sold property shall remain with its buyer until the Jubilee Year; it shall be released in the Jubilee, and he shall return to his holding.

The assumed background to the directive is that an impoverished farmer takes out a loan for the purchase of seed. In the event of crop failure, he is forced to sell part of his land to cover the previous loan and purchase new seed. Then his closest kinsman

---

[5] *Midr. Tanḥuma* B2.

(the redeemer) is required to intervene. The buyer must allow the redeemer to repurchase the land. The buyer is paid the value of the crop years remaining until the next Jubilee. In effect, the buyer has never even purchased the property; he has only leased it until the Jubilee (or earlier, if it is redeemed).

I must emphasize that the redeemer does not return the land to the original owner but keeps the land until the Jubilee. In this way he gets back his redemption costs and will not incur a loss. One might ask: What purpose does redemption serve if, whether the land remains sold or is redeemed, the original owner does not get his property back until the Jubilee? The answer lies in the basic principle: The land should not be alienated from the clan to whom it was assigned by God.

Verses 35-38. Stage Two: Lost Land

(35) If your brother, being (further) impoverished, falls under your authority, and you hold him (as though he were) a resident alien, let him subsist under your authority. (36) Do not exact from him advance or accrued interest. Fear your God, and let your brother subsist under your authority. (37) Do not lend him money at advance interest, or lend him food at accrued interest. (38) I, YHWH, am your God, who freed you from the land of Egypt, to give you the land of Canaan, to be your God.

For this section, the underlying assumption is that the sold land was not redeemed. The owner incurs a crop failure on his now reduced property and is forced to take out a new loan, and again he defaults. This time he forfeits all of his land, and he becomes a "tenant farmer" for the creditor ("falls under your authority," v. 35). Technically, he has lost all his land, but the creditor must allow the farmer to try again: "let him subsist under your authority" (v. 35), which means: lend him his required funds (increasing his indebtedness) but "do not exact from him . . . interest" (v. 36). He may not be treated as a foreigner on whom interest may be charged. Since he pays no interest, the produce from the land can amortize his loan. Assumed is that if he cannot repay the loan, the land will return to him (or his heirs) at the Jubilee. The redeemer is not obligated to intervene in this case (nor the following one), since his redemptive duties fall only on sold land (and persons) but not on indebtedness (see below).

Still, the problem remains. Because of his indebtedness, the farmer has been forced to sell his remaining land, reducing him to the status of a "tenant farmer" on his own land. Why then isn't the redeemer obligated to redeem his lost property? The only possible answer is that this case assumes all the conditions of the prior one (stage one): the obligation of redemption falls on the redeemer (v. 25). If the debtor acquires enough funds, that is, if he redeems himself (v. 26), he computes the amount owed to the buyer (v. 27) according to the years until the Jubilee (v. 28). There is no need to repeat these conditions; all of them are presumed in stage two. Thus the obligation upon the redeemer persists. The case in stage three (vv. 39-43), however, is entirely different (see below).

300

Verses 39-43. Stage Three: "Slavery"

(39) If your brother, being (further) impoverished under your authority, is sold to you, do not make him work as a slave. (40) He shall remain under you as a resident hireling: he shall work under you until the Jubilee Year. (41) Then he and his children with him shall be released from your authority; he shall return to his kin group and return to his ancestral holding. (42) For they are my slaves, whom I freed from the land of Egypt; they shall not be sold as slaves are sold. (43) You shall not rule over him with harshness; you shall fear your God.

If, as a tenant (stage two), the debtor still cannot repay his loan and otherwise cannot support himself and his family, he and they enter the household of the creditor. He no longer enjoys the usufruct of his forfeited land. Nonetheless, his status is not that of a slave but that of a resident hireling; he receives wages, all of which pay off his debt. They may even provide him with a surplus with which to free himself of his debt and status. Thus, for Israel, slavery is unequivocally abolished. As far as we know, these antislavery laws remained utopian; there is no hard evidence they were ever enacted.

At stage three, as well as stage two, the absence of the provision for redemption is startlingly conspicuous, a fact that the rabbis confirm when they declare that relatives are under no obligation to redeem their indentured kinsman.[6] Furthermore, it would not be true redemption. The redeemer might give him a free loan, an act of charity, but he may not hold him and his land until the Jubilee, which he could do were it a case of redemption.

The superior status of the hireling over the slave is manifest not only in his economic advantages but also in his working conditions. This is implied by the repeated admonition: "You shall not rule over him with harshness" (vv. 43, 46). After all, the terms of the hireling's labor are stipulated in advance; the slave, in contrast, is subject to the whims of the master. Considering that the hireling is a free person, it may well be that if he finds the creditor's conditions too harsh or his wages too low, he can seek another employer.

Note that he returns "to his ancestral holding" (v. 41b). The significance of this clause rests on the supposition that the Jubilee cancels his entire debt. His restored land can now provide him with subsistence so that he need not fall immediately into debt and ultimately have to be sold once more into servitude.

It is striking that there is no mention of the wife in the discussion of the Israelite hireling. I submit that one has to consider seriously the possibility that Leviticus deliberately omits any mention of the Israelite's wife in order to make a legal statement: She does not exit the creditor's service because she does not enter it. Here Leviticus is conducting a tacit polemic against Exod 21:7-11 (and Deut 15:12, 17): the wife may not be indentured. What then is the meaning of the emphasis

---

[6] *t. Qid.* 15b.

provided by the repeated mention of the release of the children (vv. 41, 54)? There again Leviticus is waging a polemic against the earlier slave law, but this time verbally. Exod 21:4 states that if the master provides the slave with a wife, "the wife and her children belong to the master and he is released alone. No, says Leviticus. Even if the master provides him with a wife, she is entirely free of the master's control, but her children, who are temporarily indentured, are released with her hireling husband at the Jubilee.

Many more postulates undergird the Jubilee. I would only add one more: the statement in the last verse (v. 42), which forms an inclusion with the first (vv. 23-24): "For they are my slaves whom I freed from the land of Egypt." YHWH owns Israel because he is their redeemer. Freedom means simply a transfer of masters; henceforth the Israelites are servants of YHWH, and of no one else. Thus just as the nearest relative (the redeemer) is obligated to redeem the land of his kinsman sold (or forfeited) to another, so he is obligated to redeem the person of his kinsman sold to (i.e., enslaved by) another. The debtor falling into the hands of a non-Israelite creditor is considered a captive. The obligation to redeem captive Israelites is traceable back to Abraham and Lot (Genesis 14), and it persists in biblical and rabbinic tradition. Indeed, when King Herod wanted to sell abroad, to a foreign nation, Jewish criminals who had been punished with slavery, he was warned that the people's hatred of him would only increase.[7] The hatred thus incurred indicates that the repugnance of selling Jews—even criminals—to Gentiles was not a theoretical desideratum but a tradition practiced by the people at large.

To recapitulate: YHWH is Israel's landlord and redeemer. Thus, as YHWH's tenants and servants, Israel is doubly obligated to follow the Deity's laws. These include redemption and the Jubilee. If inherited land is alienated, the nearest kinsman (the redeemer) is required to buy it back; if he fails, the land automatically returns to the owner at the Jubilee; simultaneously his debt is cancelled, and he begins his life anew. Redemption is not charity. The redeemer keeps the land until the Jubilee. His purchase price is thus covered by the land's usufruct, and he will be induced to redeem.

Descent into poverty can never terminate in slavery. Even at his nadir, the hireling's status is that of a wage-earning resident worker. His loan is interest free, which allows his wages to amortize it, possibly allowing him to be released from the creditor even before the advent of the Jubilee. Redemption is not prescribed, however, since it applies only to sold land and persons, but not to loans.

Thus the Jubilee is a socioeconomic mechanism to prevent latifundia (the loss of the debtors' land to the creditor-rich) and the ever widening gap between the rich and the poor—which Israel's prophets can only condemn, but which Israel's priests attempt to rectify in law and practice in this chapter of Leviticus.

---

[7] Josephus, *Ant.* 16.1-4.

Indeed, this is the problem that faced the outstanding spiritual authority of the first century CE, Rabbi Hillel. He found that loans were not being made because of their automatic cancellation at the Sabbatical Year (Deut 15:1-2). As a solution, he issued an edict of Prosbul,[8] a Greek legal term meaning "before an assembly." It circumvented the Sabbatical by empowering the court, in place of the creditor, to collect the debt from the real property of the debtor if the bond were delivered to it in advance of the Sabbatical Year.[9]

Perhaps the invention of Prosbul could serve as a model for us in our relations to the third world today, not necessarily in its particulars but in the rabbis' willingness to find creative mechanisms to ensure simultaneously (economic) justice in the laws even as they cultivated a viable economic framework.

B. Slavery

If, as a tenant (vv. 35-38), the debtor still cannot repay his loan and otherwise cannot support himself and his family, he and his children enter the household of the creditor (vv. 41a, 54b). He no longer enjoys the usufruct of his forfeited land. Nonetheless, his status is not that of a slave, but of a resident hireling; he receives wages, all of which pay off his debt. However, non-Israelites may become bona fide slaves.

Slavery was widespread in the ancient Near East, including Israel: "The basic supply source for slaves was the freeborn native defaulting debtor. Mesopotamian law[10] recognizes the right of the creditor to seize the defaulting debtor and force him to perform compulsory service."[11] "To stave off his own enslavement, the debtor handed over to the creditor as hostages his slave, concubine, wife, and children. Theoretically, they were kept in bondage until the debt has been worked off. In practice, however, unless they were redeemed, they remained in the possession of the creditor as long as they lived."[12] In Rome, according to the Twelve Tables (fifth century BCE), the praetor could ultimately assign the debtor to the creditor, who was authorized to seize him and keep him bound with rope or fetters. If at the end of sixty days the debt could still not be repaid, the debtor could be sold abroad as a permanent slave to a foreigner.[13]

In Israel slaves were supplied by war captives (Num 31:7-12; Deut 21:10-14; 2 Chr 28:8) and by the native population: by sale of minors (2 Kgs 4:1; Neh 5:5); by self-sale due to hunger or debt (Exod 21:5-6; Lev 25:39-43; Deut 15:16-17); or by enslavement of defaulting debtors, including the thief who could not pay his fines

---

[8] *m. Šebi.* 10:3.
[9] *m Šebi.* 10:2, 4, 6.
[10] CH §§114-19; MAL A §48.
[11] I. Mendelsohn 1962:385.
[12] I. Mendelsohn 1949:7, 14.
[13] Aulus Gellius, *Attic Nights* 20.1.41–46, cited in Jackson 1988:89.

Leviticus 17–27: The Holiness Source (H)

(Exod 21:37—22:3), the widow who could not pay her late husband's debts (2 Kgs 4:1), and, in general, impoverished Israelites who were unable to repay their loans (Neh 5:1-13; cf. 1 Sam 22:2; Isa 50:1; Amos 2:6; 8:6). That Israel knew from past (and exilic?) experience the meaning of slavery is attested by the terminology employed by Second Isaiah.[14] "A borrower is a slave of the lender" (Prov 22:7) was most often the bitter reality.[15] If the historical references (or lack thereof) are reliable, however, certain self-imposed limits on the extent of slave practice seem to have existed. No captive during Israel's internecine wars was ever forced into slavery; the one ostensible exception, Israel's treatment of Judean prisoners, was terminated by the prophet Obed (2 Chr 28:7-15). Jeremiah, who relies on the debt-slave law of Deut 15:12, nonetheless adds that "no one should keep his fellow Judean enslaved" (Jer 34:9b), a clause probably based on Lev 25:40.

Indirect evidence that H abolished the slavery of Israelites can be derived from the prohibition against tattooing. The other pentateuchal law codes, which accede to the institution of slavery, allow a permanent slave to be marked (i.e., tattooed; Exod 21:6 [JE]; Deut 15:17 [D]), a practice attested in Babylonia and in Elephantine.[16] If H had accepted the slavery of Israelites, it would have allowed the indentured servant to remain in the servitude beyond the Jubilee. Perhaps just as Mesopotamian land and slave contracts could stipulate that the king's edict of release would have no effect on the sale, so Israelite contracts might have stipulated that the slave willingly waived his Jubilee rights if his debt had not been repaid. Thus tattooing may be a discrete prohibition aimed at preventing the (permanent) enslavement of Israelites.

Prophetic remonstrances and Israelite law against the excesses of slavery and especially this pericope (Lev 25:39-43), which virtually abolishes the institution of slavery, may, however, never have been put into practice. Exodus 21, followed by Deuteronomy 15, demands the release of the Israelite slaves after six years of service. However, Jeremiah 34 testifies that this law was not observed. In Mesopotamia Hammurabi's Code §117 proclaims that three years of enslavement suffice to work off any debt. But not a single Mesopotamian document, whose number is legion, testifies that this law was ever enforced.[17] On the contrary, Hammurabi's son Samsuiluna and his successors effectively circumvented Hammurabi's Code §117 by limiting release from debt slavery to the first year of the king's reign and special occasions.[18] The same, of course, holds true for Israel. The Jubilee laws remain utopian; there is no hard evidence that they were ever enacted. Although never put into practice, the Israelite laws on slavery do bear some significant theoretical differences from the laws of surrounding nations. For example, as mentioned above, Israel alone does not

---

[14] Baltzer 1987:47-82.
[15] Cf. Lang 1983:114-27.
[16] See, respectively, CH §§226–27; Crowley 1923:28.
[17] Cf. Finkelstein 1961; Leemans 1991:414-20.
[18] Hallo 1995.

distinguish between chattel-slaves and debt-slaves. Moreover, H abolishes both kinds of slavery for Israelites.

The pernicious hold of slavery in modern societies, even democratic ones, is best illustrated in the case of India (c. 1992):

> Bonded labor—the practice of engaging laborers without wages to pay off real or imagined debts—is against the law. But it persists despite court rulings [and] occasional police intervention. . . . We estimate, a very conservative estimate, that there are five million adults and ten million children in bonded labor in India. . . . Virtually all of India's bonded laborers are untouchables, who are on the bottom of the caste hierarchy. Some were born into this condition because their parents or grandparents were sold long before they were born. Others were lured into servitude by agents for quarry owners or brick kiln managers with promises of higher paying jobs than those they had. Still others fell into their position from the need to repay loans that were already given, but that can never be fully repaid. Once indentured, it is almost impossible to escape. (*New York Times,* 4 June 1992)

If, in a democracy, despite its laws and enforcement agencies, slavery of the most invidious kind—not of the few, but of millions—exists in the twenty-first century, how can we expect the slave laws of the Torah to have taken root in Israelite society except in the minds of idealists and prophets?

According to "iAbolish—the anti-slavery portal" (http://www.iabolish.com), slavery occurs in every continent except Antarctica. It is estimated that there were 27 million slaves in the world in the year 2001, more than any other time in history. A few selected sites include:

Albania:	Teenage girls are tricked into sex slavery and trafficked by organized crime rings
Brazil:	Lured into the rainforest, families burn trees into charcoal at gunpoint
Burma:	The ruling military junta enslaves its own people to build infrastructure projects, some benefiting U.S. corporations
Dominican Republic:	Haitians are rounded up at random, taken across the border, and forced to cut cane in sugar plantations
Ghana:	Families repent for sins by giving daughters as slaves to fetish priests
India:	Children trapped in debt bondage roll beedi cigarettes 14 hours a day
Ivory Coast:	Child slaves forced to work on cocoa plantations
Mauritania:	Arab-Berbers buy and sell black Africans as inheritable property

Leviticus 17–27: The Holiness Source (H)

Pakistan:	Children with nimble fingers are forced to weave carpets in looms
Sudan:	Arab militias from the north take southern Sudanese women and children in slave raids
Thailand:	Women and children become sex slaves for tourists
United Arab Emirates:	Bangladeshi boys are transported and exploited as jockeys for camel racing
United States:	The CIA estimates that 50,000 people are trafficked as sex slaves, domestics, garment, and agricultural slaves

Scant few passages in Scripture attest to an antislavery idealism, but they indicate its existence. The prophets, for example, rail against the brutalities of slavery, but they do not advocate its abolition. Yet "I will even pour out my spirit on male and female slaves" (Joel 3:2 [Eng. 2:29]) surely evinces an egalitarian tendency, and "Did not he who made me in my mother's belly make him" (Job 31:15) argues for it. That these were not isolated voices in the wilderness but represent an entire branch of Israel's spiritual leadership will be demonstrated in this pericope, which openly, univocally, and unambiguously looks forward to the dissolution of slavery. How else can we explain the sharp contrast between the intellectual leaders of Israel and those of the Hellenistic world except by the legacy provided by prophecy and law? As noted by Kalisch, Philo admits that "the law does permit the acquisition of slaves from other nations . . . that most indispensable possession, domestic service, should not be absolutely excluded from his commonwealth."[19] But Philo adds, "For servants are free by nature, no man being naturally a slave."[20] Contrast Aristotle's view that "a slave is an animated tool, and a tool is an inanimate slave, whence there is nothing in common" between master and slave,[21] and Plato's advice to the master "to treat his slaves well, not for their sake but for his own; but it would be foolish to treat them as free men for it would make them arrogant,"[22] with a contemporary Israelite statement: "If you have one slave treat him like yourself . . . deal with him as a brother" (Sir 33:31). Philo also testifies, "Not a single slave is to be found among them [the Essenes], but all are free . . . and they denounce the owners of slaves, not merely for their injustice in outraging the law of equality, but also for their impiety in annulling the statute of Nature, who mother-like has born and reared all men alike, and created them genuine brothers."[23]

---

[19] Kalisch 1867–72:2.573 referring to Philo, *Spec. Laws* 2.123.

[20] *Laws* 2.69; cf. also Colson 1968:624–25, refuting the contention that Stoics harbored a similar doctrine.

[21] *Eth. nic.* 8.11; cf. *Pol.* 1.3-6.

[22] *Spec. Laws* 6.19.

[23] *Good Person* 79; cf. *Mos.* 2:70.

The redemption of debt-slaves prevails in Mesopotamia. Why, then, is it missing in Israel? There is also, surprisingly, no allowance for self-redemption (contrast vv. 26, 48-49). The answer is that the Israelite slave is not a slave; he is a "hireling," whose work amortizes the principal. The wages he earns may even provide him a surplus with which to free himself of his debt and status. His family has no obligation to redeem him. Only if neither he nor his family can supply the means for his redemption will the Jubilee free him, cancel his debt, and give him back his land. Thus he (or his inheritor) will be able to start out afresh as a debt-free landowner who will be independent of his family.

C. The Sabbatical and Jubilee: Their Observance

Based on all available evidence, the land Sabbatical ritual was observed widely and regularly. From earliest times, farmers realized that fertility was a coefficient of periodic fallowness,[24] and that there was an economic advantage to accumulating a surplus during the first six years to be consumed in the seventh, thereby obviating the need to engage in a money economy.[25] And, as demonstrated by M. Hildenbrand and Hopkins, leaving the entire land fallow for the seventh year, provided there had been judicious rotation during the previous six, need not have resulted in economic stress.[26]

The absence of data regarding the Sabbatical for the preexilic period stands in sharp contrast to the plethora of data for the Second Temple period[27] and to the era after the destruction of the temple. During the Sabbatical Year, Jews were supported by gentile enclaves and diaspora Jews, on whom the prohibition did not fall. Concessions were made by the rabbis to work the land in order to pay the Roman taxes.[28] There also exists evidence that pious Jews would tear down the fences of their farms and vineyards in order to fulfill literally the command to "abandon it" (Exod 23:11a).

In contrast to the land Sabbatical, there is no evidence at all that the Jubilee was ever observed. There is no doubt that the obligation of land redemption existed. Certainly, Jeremiah observed it (Jer 32:6-12), but Naomi's required redeemer opted to ignore it (Ruth 4:6). As pointed out by Amit,[29] Nehemiah's written pledge mentions the Sabbatical (Neh 10:32b), but not the Jubilee. Indeed, on the basis of the text that the Jubilee is proclaimed "for all its inhabitants" (v. 10), the rabbis conclude that the

---

[24] Cf. Philo, *Laws* 2.97-98.

[25] Soss 1973.

[26] Hopkins 1985: 201; for Hildenbrand see Theme D below.

[27] Neh 10:32; 1 Macc 6:49, 53; Philo, cited in Eusebius, *Praep. ev.* 8.7; Josephus, *Ant.* 12.378; 23.234; 14.202-6, 475; 15.7; *War* 1.60; Tacitus, *Hist.* 5.4.

[28] Cf. R. Yanni's proclamation, *b. Sanh.* 26a. The exemption of taxes during the Sabbatical Year since the days of Caesar (Josephus, *Ant.* 14.202-6) was abrogated in 261 CE.

[29] 1992:58.

Leviticus 17–27: The Holiness Source (H)

Jubilee was suspended after the first recorded exile at the fall of Samaria.[30] Was it, then, "a utopian law [that] remained a dead letter"?[31]

To be sure, the main postulate of the Jubilee, that ancestral land is inalienable, or cannot be given away, is attested in many societies contemporary with and prior to Israel. Such is the case in old village communities.[32] The evidence is particularly abundant for ancient Greece. For example, in the foundation of a new community at Kerkyra Melaina, it was decreed that a portion of the original allotments to the first settlers belonged permanently to them and their descendants. In 228/227 BCE, Miletus gave land to some Cretan refugees, specifying that it was inalienable. The Gortyn Code distinguished between property acquired by inheritance and that obtained in other ways.[33] The decree of the Arcadian league mandated that "none of those receiving a *kleros* [land allotment] or house . . . may alienate them for twenty years."[34]

The Bible itself hints that the Jubilee law was enacted, even if attempts at its enforcement may have failed. Patrick observes correctly that one must distinguish between moral law, governed by social mores, and judicial law, which is enforceable by the use of sanctions.[35] Since the Jubilee legislation is devoid of sanctions, "obedience must be elicited by appeal to the theological and moral sensibilities of the community."[36]

That the Jubilee was not completely utopian is, in my opinion, proved by the insertion into the law of the section on houses in walled cities (vv. 29-34); had the Jubilee been a utopian statute, there would have been no need to alter or add to it.[37] Moreover, Ezek 46:17 takes the concept of release for granted—that is, when allotted or inherited property returned to its original owner.[38]

Finally, I would like to cite a modern, if exotic, example where some of the Jubilee provisions, mutatis mutandis, are operative and effective. As reported by Dommen,[39] in the kingdom of Tonga, an island in the South Pacific, some ninety thousand people live under laws reminiscent of those in Leviticus 25.

"All the land of the Kingdom is the property of the Crown." Every Tongan male, on reaching the age of sixteen (law of 1839), is entitled to a farm plot sufficient to support himself and his family. The payment of an annual tax guarantees tenure on the land and the right to bequeath it to his heir. Sales (even most leases) between

---

[30] *Sipra Behar* 2:3; *b. ʿArak.* 32b; *y. Šebi.* 10:3.
[31] De Vaux 1961:177; and Driver and White 1898.
[32] Maine 1890:81–88.
[33] 6:2-12.
[34] Details in Finley 1968.
[35] 1985:5–6.
[36] Fager 1993:106.
[37] Elliger 1966; Loewenstamm 1958.
[38] Eerdmans 1912:123–28.
[39] 1972.

Tongans are forbidden. On the approval of the cabinet, foreigners may lease land, provided that they keep it productive (and pay their taxes), but, even after renewals, they may hold it for a maximum of only ninety-nine years. Otherwise, foreigners are restricted to trading.

Note the parallels:

1. Land belongs to the Crown/YHWH.

2. The Crown/YHWH has granted the land to his (chosen) people and divided equitably among them.

3. Each landowner is subject to an annual tax/tithe.

4. Sales of land, whether to citizens or foreigners, are forbidden. Land may be leased to foreigners, but only for a number of years.

These laws were passed in the nineteenth century. They have prevented the development of latifundia among the Tongans and takeovers by foreigners. The kingdom of Tonga has for more than a century succeeded in preserving its independence and has guaranteed, until recently, economic security for its citizens.

Differences should not be overlooked, but they are readily explicable. There is no necessity to sell (or lease) land, because destitution is nonexistent. The land is perpetually fertile. Copra and other coconut products, the main export, never fail. The land's produce is always self-sustaining. The termination of a lease is not at a fixed year.

Overpopulation has forced many Tongans off the land. Today, the landless amount to about 25 percent of the population. But they do not lack for employment. The slack is filled by jobs in government, tourism, handicrafts, church, and commerce related to agriculture.

To be sure, this island paradise is so far unaffected by racial or religious conflict or by global economics. Yet, at the least, it shows that the Jubilee laws were, for their time, practical and workable. And as more and more third world countries have discovered, they provide a model for solving their own economic distress (see THEME E).

D. The Sabbatical and Jubilee: Can They Be Consecutive?

How can a farmer afford to leave his entire land fallow for an entire year,[40] much less two successive years (if the Sabbatical is followed by the Jubilee)? First, this question must be put into the perspective of the ancient Israelite farmer, not his modern counterpart. My student M. Hildenbrand contributes (privately) from his ample farming background the following observation:

> There is often expressed objection to the practice demanded in chapter 25 of leaving the land fallow for one, and even two years (assuming a separate, consecutive Jubilee). One

---

[40] Elliger 1966, among others, claims that the fixed year is utopian.

might think that the land would be left a jumbled mess of weeds by leaving it fallow, and that farmers would face great difficulty, and even hardship, preparing the soil for planting following the fallow year(s) with only oxen and plow to do the job. In reality, these objections have no basis in the reality of agriculture. Soil, under the duress of modern farming practice, becomes so difficult to work after remaining fallow for any length of time because of the heavy machinery used to work the land. This heavy machinery causes the soil only a few inches below the surface to compact and become very hard. Any weeds and aftergrowth make it necessary to reuse the same heavy machinery to again work the land. Additionally, as the subsurface soil hardens, erosion of the topsoil begins, eventually rendering the land nearly useless for agricultural purposes. On the other hand, ground which is worked by single plowing with animals never develops this hard-packed subsurface soil, leaving the ground quite soft and useable, even after being allowed to lie fallow. It is true that the ground would need to be ploughed twice (or even three times) to eliminate any weed-seeds that would have dropped during the fallow year, but ground that has only been plowed by single plows with animals will remain quite soft for the first plowing after a fallow year and a second plowing of ground is never very difficult. Additionally, after completing his final harvesting before the fallow year a wise farmer could spread a leguminous ground cover like beans, or somesuch, which would benefit the soil by restoring its nitrogen content and cut[ting] down on weed growth.

Moreover, according to Hopkins,[41] the Israelite farmer probably fallowed his land more frequently than one year out of seven, most likely biennially, on a rotation basis. Such an arrangement could be incorporated into a Sabbatical system. In the year before the Sabbatical, the farmer could increase production by eliminating fallow (F) of half the farmland (P) just cropped (C). In order to compensate for this heavy use, this area would then be rested not only for the Sabbatical Year (S), but also for the subsequent year as the other half of the farmland (Q) continued in its regular biennial rotation.[42]

Thus the Jubilee law existed, was intended to be implemented, and would have been implemented, were it not for the typical and expected resistance from those who might be adversely affected: the rich and the political leaders in control, who, unless

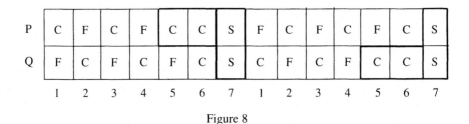

Figure 8

---

[41] Hopkins 1985:201; Borowski 1987:8, 15–18, 143–48.
[42] UN Human Development Report 1993, 37.

religiously motivated to observe the Jubilee, would have been overjoyed to confiscate indebted lands permanently.

E. Jubilee: A Rallying Cry for Today's Oppressed

I was invited to participate in a "Jewish-Christian Symposium on the Jubilee," sponsored by the World Council of Churches at the Ecumenical Institute, Bossey, Switzerland, May 19–23, 1996. Present were thirty-two representatives from fifteen countries, including India, Uganda, Brazil, the Philippines, and Indonesia. I single out the third world nations because, first, I was able to feel, even vicariously, their people's pain and suffering, and, second, I was witness to a vivid demonstration that their hopes for remedial action are expressed in the biblical Jubilee.

The Jubilee has become the rallying cry for oppressed peoples today, as was the exodus theme for their counterparts in previous decades. This time, however, they are not enslaved politically (except when colonial rulers have been replaced by corrupt rulers of their own), but shackled economically. The global market economy has generated unprecedented growth and prosperity, but not for them. Twenty percent of the world's people possess 83 percent of the wealth.[43] Moreover, "three quarters of adjusting countries in Sub-Sahara Africa have suffered declining per capita incomes and in Latin America the declines were at least as bad."[44]

The impoverishment of the third world has brought attendant injustices. Relevant to the Jubilee (and Sabbatical) theme is the issue of global pollution, especially in the developing nations. The depletion of the rain forests in the interest of the timber and mining industries, for example, has caused irremedial losses to Costa Rica. Although it, singularly among Latin American countries, experienced significant economic growth between 1970 and 1990, the concomitant environmental decay of its soils and forests produced the loss of natural capital totaling six percent of the gross domestic product of that period; in Indonesia, the loss was nine percent.[45]

As a result, the debtor world has issued the following demands to the creditor nations (which operate through the International Monetary Fund and similar agencies): (1) cancellation of their debts; (2) restitution of land and resources to their original owners; (3) cessation from pilfering natural resources and polluting them (one paper cited Gen 2:15b: God leased us the earth "to fill it and tend it," but not to despoil it); and (4) termination of economic slavery (e.g., the atrocious case in democratic India, cited in THEME B) by universally raising wages to a subsistence level.

The Jubilee, by prescribing remissions of debts, restoration of land, Sabbath rest for land and people, and release from economic servitude, corresponds to all four demands. Obviously, their implementation would be met by large-scale resistance. Some demands would have to be modified. For example, as one symposium paper

---

[44] Ibid., 45.
[45] Ibid., 30.

pointedly asked: Wouldn't the simultaneous remission of all debts inhibit creditors from lending at all? Yet evidence can be adduced that countries employing some of the Jubilee provisions have experienced spectacular economic growth rather than precipitous decline. For example, in just the two years from 1952 to 1954, the percent of South Korean farmers who owned their land instead of working as tenants jumped from 50 to 94 percent. Something similar happened in Taiwan, another Asian tiger. Thus the Jubilee laws, mutatis mutandis, offer a realistic blueprint for bridging the economic gap between the have and have-not nations, a gap that, if unattended, portends political uprisings that can engulf the entire world.

In May 1996, in Bossey, Switzerland, I witnessed the unfurling of the flag of the Jubilee. Who will carry it forward remains to be seen.

Selected Texts

[25:6-7] These verses ostensibly contradict v. 5a, which forbids the landowner to harvest his field and vineyard.[46] The solution is that the landowner is not free to harvest as in normal years, when he can do with his produce as he wills: to store and sell in addition to eat. Its point is that the harvest may satisfy only the hunger of those listed. Presumably just as one may pluck standing grain from a neighbor's field to satisfy one's hunger (Deut 23:26), so a landowner may gather his aftergrowth to satisfy the hunger of his family and wards. Also, as pointed out by Lowery,[47] that the aftergrowth of the Jubilee Year could be eaten (v. 12b) implies the same concession for the Sabbatical Year. Indeed, the verb "to eat" is repeated in v. 6b in order to emphasize the point.

Verses 6-7 are based on Exod 23:10-11, but are altered it to allow the landowner and his entire household, including his animals; however, the poor are excluded. Thus Leviticus 25 does not supplement Exodus 23 but patently opposes it. Leviticus is thus a corrective to Exodus, which, in depriving the landowner and his household of the aftergrowth, is harsh and, indeed, utopian. It is Leviticus that makes the Sabbatical law workable.[48] This realistic aspect of Leviticus 25 will again be demonstrated by its adjustment for urban centers (vv. 29-34) and its extension of the Sabbatical from seven to fifty years, thereby providing greater inducement for creditors to lend (see "and each of you shall return to his kin group," v. 10).

The exclusion of the poor is not that they are "not their [P and H's] primary concern,"[49] but that, on the contrary, H has provided for them elsewhere (19:9-10; 23:22), laws that apply to the Sabbatical as well as all other years.

---

[46] Contra Ginzberg 1932:353.
[47] 2000:60.
[48] Cf. Ginzberg 1932:355–56.
[49] Van Houten 1991:121.

The plural verb "who live" applies to all the previously listed: family, slaves, and hirelings, provided that they live with and are under the authority of the landowner. Thus the married daughter (cf. 22:12), the divorced wife, or the married son, not to speak of brothers and sisters, who live independently or who live under someone else's authority, are not eligible for the aftergrowth. This condition also explains the otherwise inexplicable absence of the resident alien from the list. The alien does not live on the landowner's property. For that reason, he is grouped with the poor (19:10; 23:22) as recipients of charity. Both are outsiders, and their support is not one of patriarchal obligation, but of individual generosity.

[25:9] Why did the Jubilee Year begin on the tenth day of the seventh month, the Day of Purgation, rather than at the beginning of the agricultural year, the first day of the month? One can suggest a number of reasons:

1. The shofar call would not be confused with that on the first day (23:24b).

2. A "holy" year would be initiated only after the sanctuary and, symbolically, the people and land have been purged of their impurities (see chap. 16, esp. v. 33 [H]).

3. Philo, as usual, adopts a more allegorical view: Yom Kippur celebrates the liberation of the body and soul.[50]

Safren suggests that New Year's Day could simultaneously fall on the first and tenth of the month.[51] He points to prolonged New Year festivals in ancient Mesopotamia. He might have added that these festivals are bound up in temple purgations.[52] This correspondence with Yom Kippur has led me to conclude:

> if the tenth of Tishri can be seen as the culmination of Israel's New Year festival, then it was the tenth and climatic day of Israel's ten-day New Year festival. The first ten days of Tishri are, in Jewish tradition, its penitential period during which man, through his repentance, can alter the divine decree.[53] Its roots could then be traced back to a putative ten-day New Year festival, ending in the joyous celebration of the sanctuary's purgation on the tenth and last day.[54]

[25:20-22] As seen in the table below, Ramban's system is most plausible; it presumes a spring calendar, except for the Sabbatical and Jubilee. The harvest of the sixth year lasts for three years (v. 21); what is sown in the eighth year is reaped in the

---

[50] *Prelim. Studies* 107–8.

[51] 1999.

[52] Milgrom 1991:1067–70.

[53] *b. Roš Haš.* 18a.

[54] Milgrom 1991:1069; cf. *b. Roš Haš.* 8b.

ninth; and vv. 10-22 are in place, as part of the Jubilee pericope. There is one defect, however. The years should not read 6, 7, 8, and 9, but 48, 49, 50, and 51. Perhaps the latter notation was considered too cumbersome. (Also, there is no year 51 in the pentecontad system.) Alternatively, the possibility must be considered that originally vv. 20-22 were attached to v. 7 as part of the Sabbatical pericope and subsequently were reformulated and moved into its present place as an appendix to the Jubilee pericope. Hartley prefers the latter solution because "the text says that they will sow in the eighth year, which would be forbidden in the year of the Jubilee if it is the fiftieth year, but not if it was the eighth year of a sabbatical-year cycle."[55] Ramban, however, avoids this pitfall by positing that the Sabbatical and Jubilee Years are fixed according to the agricultural, or fall, calendar.

Fall		Spring
5. Sow		6. Reap
6. ----	Sabbatical	7. ----
7. ----	Jubilee	8. ----
8. Sow		9. Reap

Figure 9. Sabbatical and Jubilee according to Rambam

Is it possible that Scripture actually ordains that for two successive years the farmer is barred from working the fields? Does this not throw the Sabbatical cycle out of kilter, since eight years will elapse between the last Sabbatical of one cycle (the forty-ninth) and the first Sabbatical of the next cycle? If, however, one should posit that the seven-year count should be maintained, then the first Sabbatical will fall on the sixth year of the new cycle, allowing only five years for farming the fields. This possibility must be ruled out because Scripture specifically demands, "Six years you may sow . . . and you may prune" (v. 3). Thus the Jubilee cannot enter into the Sabbatical count.[56] Does this not prove that the Jubilee system is sheer utopia? The questions of the feasibility of two successive fallow years as well as the historical evidence for the observation of the Sabbatical and Jubilee are discussed in THEMES B and D.

[25:42] As shown by Daube,[57] the legal aspect of redemption operates in the exodus: God owns Israel because he is their redeemer. Freedom means solely a change of

---

[55] 1992:437.
[56] M. H. Segal 1946:53
[57] 1963:27–29, 42–45.

master; henceforth, the Israelites are slaves of God. Daube, however, was long anticipated by the rabbis: "My deed (of ownership) has first priority"[58] because God
redeemed them from the "house of slaves" (Exod 20:2),[59] and the redeemer becomes
the new owner.

Israel's enslavement to God is not an innovation of Leviticus; it is found in the
earliest levels of Scripture: "For YHWH will vindicate his people, and take revenge
for his servants/slaves" (Deut 32:36).[60] Moreover, since a slave's children are the
master's property, which he also bequeaths to his children (v. 46), so the Israelites are
God's slaves throughout their generations. Furthermore, since the same word means
"servant" as well as "slave," Israel is obligated to serve YHWH by worshiping him;
he becomes not only their master but also their God.[61]

Implied is that Israel owes no obligations to any other power but God. This
concept also prevailed in the ancient Near East. The caretakers of a Hittite mau-
soleum are exempt from villeinage or compulsory labor,[62] and residents of sacred
cities are considered servants of the gods. They have been freed from all outside jurisdictions and impositions (e.g., taxes) so they may serve their respective gods.[63] Each
sacred city, not just its sanctuary, belongs to the resident god.[64] As Joosten independently deduces: "the underlying idea of H seems to be much the same: if YHWH took
the Israelites for his slaves so that they might serve him, he must also provide them
with a dwelling-place; he therefore settles them on this land around the sanctuary."[65]
However, a fundamental difference should not be overlooked: Israel serves its God by
obeying God's commandments; in the ancient Near East, the gods are served just in
their sanctuaries.[66]

[25:47-55] The underlying theology needs to be underscored. YHWH redeems on
both a national and an individual scale. YHWH is the redeemer of the people of Israel
whenever it is subjected to (i.e., enslaved by) a foreign nation. This was the case in
the Egyptian bondage (Exod 6:6; 15:13; cf. Isa 63:9; Ps 106:10). According to Second Isaiah, such will be the case in the Babylonian exile (Isa 35:4, 9; 43:1; 44:22, 23;
48:20; 51:10; 52:3; 63:9; cf. Mic 4:10). Thus the example of divine intervention
whenever any part of God's land is lost (i.e., the Jubilee) is to be duplicated whenever
any of God's people is lost (i.e., enslaved). Just as the nearest relative is obligated to

---

[58] *Sipra Behar,* par. 6:1.
[59] Ibn Ezra; cf. Exod 6:6.
[60] Hurowitz 1992:66.
[61] Joosten 1994:137–38; 1996:98.
[62] Otten 1956:102–5.
[63] Weinfeld 1995:133–39.
[64] Cf. Weinberg 1992:103.
[65] 1994:140; 1996:99.
[66] Weinfeld 1995:16.

redeem the land of his kinsperson sold (or forfeited) to another, so he is obligated to redeem the person of his kinsperson sold to (i.e., enslaved by) a non-Israelite. As explained earlier (see THEME B), no such obligation rests on the redeemer if his kinsperson is sold to an Israelite, since such a sale does not constitute enslavement. The principle of *imitatio Dei* applies only when the loss of land or person stands in jeopardy, but not in situations where, in addition, the repayment of a loan is required, which can be accomplished by using the debtor's wages.

Blessings, Curses, and the
Recall of the Covenant

Selected Texts

Verses 1-2. The Essence of God's Commandments

The H legist sums up in a condensed form the divine laws determinative for Israel's continuous presence on its land by selecting three commandments of the Decalogue: the worship of one God, but not with images, and the observance of the Sabbath. He adds reverence for the sanctuary as a generic encompassing all the duties incumbent on the Israelites for the maintenance of the cult. Since he is interested in only those national factors that decide Israel's destiny, he cites 19:30 as his proof text for the Sabbath because it contains an additional national factor: reverence for the sanctuary (i.e., the cult).

Verses 3-39. The Blessings and Curses

The number and length of curses generally exceed those of blessings in the law codes. Ramban's sharp observation deserves to be mentioned: "the empty-headed who remarked (in puzzlement) that the curses are more numerous than the blessings, have not told the truth. The blessings are stated as generalizations whereas the curses are stated in detail in order to frighten the hearers."

The first set of curses is marked by the measure-for-measure principle: "I in turn will do this to you" (v. 16). The following sets utilize the refrain "sevenfold for your sins" (a metaphoric number) in crescendo intensity. There are clear echoes of the blessing in the curses: "covenant" (vv. 9, 15, 25, 42, 44); "commandments" (vv. 3, 14-15); "become their (your) God" (vv. 12, 45); "brought you out of the land of Egypt" (vv. 13, 45); "loathe" (vv. 11, 15, 30, 43); "and I shall give" (vv. 4, 6, 11, 17, 19, 30-31).[1]

---

[1] Wenham 1979.

Leviticus 17–27: The Holiness Source (H)

Levine aptly refers to the distinctions between the rewards and punishments as an "asymmetry of contrasts":[2] the fertile land (vv. 4-5, 10) will become unproductive (vv. 16, 19-20, 26); God will turn with favor toward his people (v. 8) or will set his face against them (v. 17); Israel will repulse its enemies (v. 9) or be battered by them (vv. 17, 25); wild beasts will disappear from the land (v. 6) or devour the people (v. 22); the sword will not traverse the land (v. 6) or will bring destruction (v. 25); obedience brings secure settlement (v. 5), whereas disobedience brings exile (v. 33a).

Verses 3-13. The Blessings: Obedience Is Rewarded

Verses 4-5. The First Blessing: Plenty
Verse 6. The Second Blessing: Peace inside the Land

Economic security (vv. 4-5) is followed by political security (vv. 6-8); the former is worthless without the latter.[3]

Verses 9-10. The Fourth Blessing: Abundant Life and the Fulfillment of the Covenant

The covenant promised Israel progeny and land. The progeny, however, cannot survive unless the land, too, is fruitful.

Verses 11-12. The Fifth Blessing: God's Presence in Israel

[26:11] "my presence." The usual translation of *miškani,* "my tabernacle," cannot be correct. To be sure, this is its meaning elsewhere, but not here. H has here transformed P's tabernacle into an expression connoting the divine presence.[4] Manifestly, Ezekiel, the earliest interpreter of this verse, understood it this way (37:27-28).

The clear implication is that YHWH is not confined to a sanctuary but is present everywhere in the land. Perhaps this theology betrays the influence of the eighth-century prophets, who also posit that YHWH is dissociated from any sanctuary (e.g., Hos 5:6, 15; 9:15) and, moreover, that his sanctuary is actually located in the heavens (Isa 6:1; Mic 1:2-3). However, the theology of the P school also postulated that though YHWH is to be sought in the sanctuary, he was at any time capable of leaving it.[5]

[26:12] "I will walk about in your midst." God will walk with his people, as he walked with Adam and Eve in the garden of Eden (Gen 3:8; cf. Deut 23:15 [Eng. 14]).[6] That is, God's blessings can bring a return of paradisal conditions.[7]

---

[2] 1989:276.

[3] *Sipra Beḥuqqotay* 1:8; Rashi; Bekhor Shor.

[4] Wessely 1846; Hoffmann 1953; Levine 1989; Sun 1990:476; Haran 1978:14 n. 3.

[5] Milgrom 1991:258–61.

[6] *Sipra Beḥuqqotay* 3:3; Wenham 1979.

[7] For the tradition that the garden of Eden was a sanctuary, see *Jub.* 3:8-14; *Pesiq. Rab Kah.* 1:1.

[26:13] "I YHWH am your God." This is the self-declaration formula of the Decalogue, but addressed to the people of Israel (hence, the plural). It is not a blessing in itself. It is the Deity's assurance that the blessings will take place if Israel deserves them, a fitting closure to the blessings pericope.

"who freed you from the land of Egypt." This is a continuation of the Decalogue self-declaration (see Exod 20:2). There, however, its purpose is to claim God's ownership of Israel (so too in Lev 25:42, 55). Here it assures Israel that the one who performed the miraculous exodus from Egypt is therefore capable of performing all the enumerated blessings.[8]

"I broke the bars of your yoke." This clause is repeated in Ezek 34:27b. "The ancient 'yoke' was a pole of wood, resting horizontally on the neck of an animal, or on the necks of a pair of animals; and the . . . 'bars' consisted of pieces of wood passing perpendicularly through the yoke, and fixed on each side of the neck by 'thongs' (Jer 2:20; 27:2)."[9] Resting on the hump of the animal, the yoke appears to hold the animal down. Israel is here pictured as a beast of burden (cf. Isa 9:3 [Eng. 4]; 10:27; 14:25).Therefore, when the yoke is removed, Israel can stand upright.

Verses 14-39. The Curses: Disobedience Is Punished

Five sets of curses (vv. 16-17, 18-20, 21-22, 23-26, 27-39) match the five sets of blessing. The increasing severity of the punishments can be seen in the introduction to each curse.

Verses 16-17. The First Set of Curses: Illness, Famine, and Defeat

[26:16] "I in turn."[10] The divine response to Israel's defection follows the principle of talion, which is a recurring motif in H. As pointed out by Douglas,[11] righteousness that should prevail in the human realm, both positively (chap. 19, esp. vv. 11-18, 35-36) and negatively (24:17-22), is modeled on righteousness in the divine realm: If Israel will fulfill its covenantal obligations, God will bless it (26:3-13); but if it violates them, God will punish it commensurately (vv. 14-39).

"you shall be routed by your enemies." Reversing the blessing of v. 7a.

"you shall flee though nobody pursues." In contrast to the blessing of v. 8. This theme returns in more poignant detail in vv. 36-37.

Verses 18-20. The Second Set of Curses: Drought and Poor Harvests

[26:19] "I will break the pride of your strength." This contrasts with to "I broke the bars of your yoke" (v. 13bα), referring to Israel's resistance, stubbornness, in its

---

[8] *Sipra Beḥuqqotay* 3:4.
[9] Driver and White 1898:101.
[10] With NJPS.
[11] 1995:252.

refusal to heed the punishment. God will break Israel's strength and resistance through the new punishment, famine.[12]

"I will make your skies like iron and your earth like copper." In contrast to the blessing of v. 4a.[13] The entire statement occurs once more in Deut 28:23, but in reverse order: "The skies above your head shall be copper and the earth under you iron." It occurs again in expanded form in an ancient Near Eastern treaty curse (the parallel in italics): "May all the gods who are named in this treaty tablet reduce your soil in size to be narrow as a brick, *turn your soil into iron,* so that no one may cut a furrow in it. Just as *rain does not fall from a copper sky,* so may there come neither rain nor dew upon your fields and meadows, but let it rain burning coals in your land instead of dew."[14]

[26:20] "Your land shall not yield its produce." Reversing the blessing "the earth will yield its produce" (v. 4bα).[15]

"nor shall the trees of your land yield their fruit." Reversing the blessing "the trees of the field will yield their fruit" (v. 4bβ).

Verses 21-22. The Third Set of Curses: Harmful Beasts

[26:22] "I will let loose wild beasts against you." Reversing "I will eliminate vicious beasts from the land" (v. 6bα).[16]

"they shall bereave you." Reversing "and (I) shall make you fruitful" (v. 9aβ).

"make you few." This statement is not redundant in view of the previous "they shall bereave you," since its purpose is to reverse the blessing "multiply you" (v. 9aγ).[17]

Verses 23-26. The Fourth Set of Curses: War, Pestilence, and Famine

[26:25] "I will bring a sword against you." Reversing "no sword shall traverse your land" (v. 6bβ).

"vengeance for the covenant." This refers to the Sinaitic covenant (Exod 24:8), which Israel has broken (Lev 26:15b). Elements of rewards and punishments are absent from the patriarchal covenant (Genesis 17).[18]

[26:26] "staff of bread." That is, "your supply of food."[19]

---

12 Mendelssohn 1846.
13 Bekhor Shor.
14 *VTE,* vii, 526-33; *ANET,* 539.
15 Bekhor Shor; cf. Deut 11:17.
16 Bekhor Shor.
17 Hazzequni.
18 Cf. Knohl 1995:141–45.
19 *Tg. Onq.;* cf. *Tg. Ps.-J.*

"in a single oven." For lack of wood[20] or for lack of bread dough,[21] one oven can suffice. The simple oven was a pit about 2.5 feet in diameter. The dough was slapped against its sides or placed in a vessel. Branches, rape, or dung (Mal 3:15) served as fuel. To prevent fires or smoke, ovens were sometimes built not in private courtyards but in public places.

Verses 27-39. The Fifth Set of Curses: God Abandons His Cult Places and Land and Pursues Israel in Exile

[26:29] Cannibalism is a frequent theme in ancient Near Eastern curses.

[26:30] "I will expel you." This is a negation, expressed in the first person, of God's blessing (v. 11b).

[26:31] "your sanctuaries." In contrast to v. 30, which speaks of idolatrous cult sites, this verse focuses on the legitimate cult. "I will not smell your pleasant odors" (v. 31b) implies that if Israel were obedient, God would indeed look with favor on his people's sacrifices at their "sanctuaries." H acknowledges the existence and legitimacy of multiple sanctuaries.

[26:33] "and I will unsheathe the sword after you." That is, in exile,[22] in order to prevent anyone from returning. Contrast the blessing "no sword shall traverse your land" (v. 6b).

"When your land will be a desolation and your cities a ruin."[23] If v. 33b is translated as a separate punishment (in all translations, to my knowledge), it is a redundancy (see vv. 31a, 32a); it is out of place—the action has moved into exile (v. 33a). Moreover, it breaks the thought; Israel is being punished in exile, and there is no reason to mention again the condition of its land.

[26:36-39] The continuation of v. 33a in v. 36 (vv. 34-35 are parenthetical) describes the final stage of punishment: psychological disintegration and total demoralization.

[26:36] "As for those of you who survive." That is, those who have not been cut down by the pursuing sword (v. 33a).[24] The change from second- to third-person suffixes is necessitated by this subject. But there is a subtler reason: God is distancing himself from the remnant.

---

[20] Rashi; Ehrlich 1899–1900:242 (H).
[21] Rashbam.
[22] NEB, correctly.
[23] With Ibn Ezra and Abravanel.
[24] Ibn Ezra.

"they shall fall though nobody is pursing." This accelerated punishment of "You shall flee though nobody pursues you" (v. 17b) totally reverses the blessing of v. 7, "they shall fall before you by the sword."

[26:37] As a result of their panic, they not only will flee with none pursuing, but also will stumble on one another.

"to stand (your ground)." This word reverses the blessing "upright" (v. 13).[25] Not coincidentally, both occur at the end of each series of blessings and curses, respectively.

[26:38] "You shall be lost." Others render "perish." The difference between the two renderings is not inconsequential. Rendering "perish" would contradict the following verses, which speak of survivors.

"devour." Reversing the blessing of vv. 5, 10: not only will you not eat, but you will be eaten. The remnant in exile will be "eaten" by wars and conquest, as attested in Num 13:32; Jer 2:3; 30:16, among others.

[26:39] "because of the iniquities of their ancestors." This is in keeping with the "visiting the sins of the fathers on the children" theology (cf. Exod 34:7b; Num 14:18b), exemplified in the lament of the generation of the destruction: "Our fathers sinned and are no more; and we must bear their guilt" (Lam 5:7).[26]

Verses 40-45. Remorse and the Recall of the Covenant: Return from Exile Implied

This appendix to the section of curses functions much like Deut 30:1-10 for the curses of Deut 28:15-68. Verses 40-41a constitute Israel's confession that it committed sacrilege and stubbornly resisted God, and consequently God brought them into exile. Verses 41b-45 constitute God's response: if Israel truly humbles itself and accepts (the justice of) its punishment, then God will remember the covenant and, as soon as the land has made up its neglected sabbaticals, will restore Israel to the land.

The importance of this concession should not be underestimated. It approximates and perhaps influences the prophetic doctrine of repentance, which not only suspends the sacrificial requirements but eliminates them entirely.

[26:40] "iniquity of their ancestors." Herewith H sets a precedent for all subsequent confessions: "We have sinned with our ancestors" (Ps 106:6); "for because of our sins and the iniquities of our fathers, Jerusalem and your people have become a mockery among all who are around us" (Dan 9:16b; cf. vv. 8, 11, 20). This view, an offshoot

---

[25] Levine 1989:276.
[26] Ibn Ezra.

of the doctrine of collective responsibility—a cardinal plank in the structure of priestly theology—is vehemently rejected by Jeremiah for the future (Jer 31:29) and by Ezekiel for the present (Ezekiel 18, esp. vv. 2-3, 30-33). Thus Ezekiel, following the lead of Jeremiah, doffs his priestly vestments to drape himself in the prophetic mantle of repentance, which denies both sacrifices and collective responsibility as requisites for divine expiation.

"in that they committed sacrilege against me." Which group committed the sacrilege, and what precisely did it do? Ibn Ezra simply states "the ancestors" without further specification. Presumably, he means that all past violations were responsible for the destruction of the land and temple.

[26:41] The implication is that Israel, in a state of remorse, must wait passively until its punishment is paid in full[27]—that is, until its land has been paid back its neglected sabbaticals (vv. 34-35)—and then God will act by virtue of his commitment to the covenant. This thought, I submit, is fully echoed by Second Isaiah, using the same vocabulary: "Speak tenderly to Jerusalem and declare to her that her term of service [i.e., the exile] is completed, that her punishment is accepted" (Isa 40:2).

[26:42] There was only one covenant with Abraham, renewed with Isaac and presumably renewed with Jacob (the term "Abraham's blessing" is used, Gen 28:4). There is a cogent reason for particularizing the patriarchal covenant: it alone specifies the promise of *land* and *seed.* The Sinaitic covenant bound Israel and God together— Israel became his people—but even if the Sinaitic covenant implied the eternity of Israel and its inheritance of the land, it derived these doctrines from the earlier patriarchal covenant, in which they were made explicit.

The concept of forgiveness is absent. One has to keep in mind at all times that this is a priestly document, the product of a theology, one of whose dogmas is that there is no full expiation—without the requisite sacrifices. Thus total reconciliation with God will occur only after Israel returns and rebuilds its sanctuary. Another omission already alluded to (v. 41) is the requirement of repentance, for which confession and remorse (vv. 40-41) are only the initial steps. Again, we must keep in mind that this is a priestly, not a prophetic, document, and as I have argued in explicating Lev 5:20-26, the priestly doctrine, as exemplified here, laid the foundation for prophetic repentance.

[26:43-44] Not only does Israel have to repent of its sins and thereby motivate God to recall his covenant, but it also has to atone to the land for neglecting its sabbaticals. It is almost as if there are two independent agencies requiring reparation—God and the

---

[27] With Driver and White (on vv. 21, 25) 1898:201.

land. The theological postulate underlying this doctrine needs to be underscored. It recalls the primeval flood, which was not a punishment but a necessary consequence, to cleanse the earth, which had become polluted by human corruption (Gen l6:11-12 [P]).[28]

Once again, the land (of Israel) is polluted by its residents, by depriving it of its sabbatical rest to recoup its depleted energies. The remedy is identical. The land must be rid of its inhabitants. This time, however, the purifying agency is not the flood—nor can it be, since God swore never again to flood the earth (Gen 9:15; Isa 54:9)—but exile. Moreover, in the priestly view, the flood was the only way to purify the earth (and hence had to entail the almost total loss of human and animal life), since the cleansing of pollution in every case (for P) requires ablution. The sin of working the land on the Sabbath, however, does not generate pollution. The earth has been violated nonetheless, and since it is God's land (Lev 25:23) and the Sabbath is his time (25:2, 4), they are sanctums and their violation constitutes desecration (26:40). Desecrated sanctums must be compensated and a fine exacted (5:14-16)—neglected sabbaticals repaid by exile.

In either case, flood or exile, the result is the same: the restoration of the status quo. Noah's earth is returned to the days of creation so that the human race may be constituted afresh, and Israel's earth is returned to its pristine status so that it may be repopulated by a repentant Israel.

[26:45] "the covenant with the ancients." H was telling his audience (and us) that God will restore Israel to its land both on the basis of the patriarchal covenant, the promise of progeny and land (v. 42), and on the basis of the Sinaitic covenant, Israel's observance of the revealed commandments (vv. 3, 14-15). The tacit assumption derivable from the conclusion is that with the Sinaitic covenant continuing in force, the gruesome consequences detailed in this chapter also remain in force. As explicated in vv. 40-41, the divine willingness to fulfill the covenant is dependent on Israel's penitence. Moreover, even the Abrahamic covenant is contingent on the behavior of his progeny "in order that YHWH may bring about for Abraham what he has promised him" (Gen 18:19b). YHWH need not change; his promise remains unbroken. But for it to be realized, Israel must change. Otherwise, Israel remains in exile (the ultimate national punishment) forever.

The prophets maintain that God purges the wicked, but not the entire people. Yet his fidelity to Israel is always contingent on the existence of a righteous remnant (e.g., in the eighth century, Isa 1:18-20; 10:20-22; 17:4-6). Thus God's covenant with Israel is conditional. To be sure, this view changes in the exile. As indicated in the exilic additions to Leviticus 26 (vv. 33b-35, 43), the return to the land will take place only after the barren land makes up the number of its violated Sabbatical Years. Isaiah

---

[28] Cf. Frymer-Kensky 1977.

of the exile transfers the determining factor from the land to the people: Israel must pine sufficiently in the exile (Isa 40:2). However, H and the other preexilic sources maintain that God's fidelity to his covenant is *conditional* on the observance of the covenant.

In sum, P does not know the Sinaitic revelation and covenant; it relates only to YHWH's cloud (presence) condescended into the completed tabernacle (Exod 40:34-35) and, by means of incinerating the altar's sacrifices with the divine fire emanating from the adytum (indicating his presence there; Lev 9:24), YHWH indicates his acceptance of the priestly service. That is, he demonstrates his willingness to abide among Israel. But H is as much aware of the Sinaitic narrative as it is of P. Therefore H can and does absorb the Sinaitic revelation and covenant. And as exemplified by this chapter, H has incorporated both of JE's covenants (patriarchal and Sinaitic) and both revelations (P's tabernacle and the Sinaitic narrative).

Consecrations and Their Redemption

Introduction

This chapter concerns gifts to the sanctuary: vows of persons and animals (vv. 1-13), consecrations of houses and fields (vv. 14-25), firstlings, proscriptions, and tithes (vv. 26-33). The laws of redemption fit into the following graded systems:

1. Proscriptions are "most sacred" and irredeemable

2. Offerable animals—be they firstborn, tithes, or consecrations—are irredeemable

3. Nonofferable consecrations—such as impure animals, land, houses, and crops except when they are proscriptions—are redeemable.

One postulate explains the gradations: offerable animals are irredeemable because they must be sacrificed on the altar, and nonofferable animals and other consecrations are always redeemable unless they are proscriptions.

Verses 1-13. Vows of Persons and Animals

Philo sums up the import of this pericope succinctly and accurately:

> the law laid down a scale of valuation in which no regard is paid to beauty or stature or anything of the kind, but all are assessed equally, the sole distinctions made being between men and women and between children and adults . . . that all males and all females should be assessed equally at every age was made for three cogent reasons. First, because the worth of one person's vow is equal and similar to that of another, whether it is made by a person of great importance or one of mean estate; secondly, because it was not seemly that the votaries should be subject to the vicissitudes of slaves who are valued at high price or on the other hand are rated low accordingly as they have or have not a time condition of body and comeliness; thirdly, and this is the most convincing of all, that in the sight of men inequality, in the sight of God equality, is held in honor.[1]

---

[1] *Spec. Laws* 2.32-34.

When male and female valuations are compared, the results show that women, as a class, must have been considered an indispensable and powerful element in the Israelite labor force (Fig. 10). Meyers cogently argues that the variation in the female percentage of the combined value of a male and a female in each group reflects realistically the value of the woman's productivity relative to the male's.[2] Obviously, children below the age of five would contribute little to the labor force; and especially in view of their high mortality rate, their valuations would be low. In the next age group, five to twenty years, the percentage of the woman's value is at its lowest, which one would expect since it coincides with her highest childbearing years,[3] with their attendant mortality risks. In the following years, the woman's relative worth increases, reaching its maximum in the senior years when male efficiency declines, whereas the female is able to continue her domestic responsibilities and register a minimal decrease in productivity. Above all, the high relative percentage of women, at or near 40 percent, demonstrates without a doubt that they achieved a high status in Israelite society.

Age (in years)	Male (in shekels)	Female (in shekels)	Combined Value	Female Percentage of Combined Value
0-5	5	3	8	38
5-20	20	10	30	33
20-60	50	30	80	38
60+	15	10	25	40

Figure 10. Valuation for Vows

[27:20] "But if he is too poor." The ethical and theological significance of this concession needs to be emphasized. Concessions to the indigent are also granted in the sacrificial system (e.g., for the burnt offering, 1:14-17; the graduated purification offering, 5:1-13; the parturient, 12:6-8; the scale-diseased person, 14:21-32). Here, however, although a vow is made in the name of God, and a specific person, whose worth is fixed in the holy writ, is stipulated in the vow, the priest is allowed to lower the valuation of the vowed person according to the financial ability of the vower (v. 8).

---

[2] 1983:584–87.
[3] Cf. de Vaux 1961:29.

Verses 9-33. Redemptions

Leviticus 27 discloses a consistent criterion for all consecrations: offerable animals must be consumed on the altar; all other sanctums, being unofferable, are therefore redeemable.

This criterion can now be demonstrated as the postulate underlying all the redemption rules of Leviticus 27:

1. The redemption of consecrated animals (vv. 9-13) is informed by this postulate: only impure (unofferable) animals may be redeemed, whereas offerable ones must be sacrificed on the altar.

2. Consecrated land may be redeemed (vv. 14-19, 22-25) because land is unofferable. Only proscriptions (human, animal, or land, vv. 20-21, 28-29) may not be redeemed. However, one who objects that proscribed land is a nonofferable category and should therefore be redeemable should note the explanatory clause: every "proscription may neither be sold nor redeemed because it is totally consecrated to YHWH" (v. 28). In other words proscribed land is distinguished from all other consecrated land in that it remains the permanent property of the sanctuary.

3. It clearly holds true for firstborn animals. They must be sacrificed on the altar unless they are unofferable (i.e., impure), in which case they are redeemed or sold (v. 27; cf. Num 18:17).

4. Finally, it is the shamir stone that cleaves the two tithe laws (vv. 30-33) into logically differentiated categories: the unofferable crop tithe is redeemable, but the animal tithe, being offerable, is therefore irredeemable.

The underlying postulate of Leviticus 27 is also its organizing principle. The laws of redemption in Leviticus 27 fit into a graded system that is simple, logical, and clear:

1. Proscriptions are "most sacred" and irredeemable.

2. Offerable animals, be they firstborn, tithes, or consecrations are also irredeemable.

3. Nonofferable consecrations, such as impure animals, land, houses, and crops (except when they are proscriptions), are redeemable.

Only one postulate has been needed to explain the gradations: offerable animals are irredeemable because they must be sacrificed on the altar, and nonofferable animals and other consecrations are always redeemable unless they are proscriptions.

[27:10] "One may not exchange it or substitute for it." Some claim that the two verbs are synonymous.[4] However, on the principle that synonymity is eschewed in law, these two consecutive verbs must differ from each other. Their most likely meaning is that "exchange" refers to another kind (cf. Isa 9:9 [Eng. 10]), while "substitute" refers to the same kind (cf. Jer 2:1).

Verses 14-25. Consecrations of Houses and Fields

The Jubilee institution is mentioned and its laws (chap. 25) are assumed (cf. 27:17, 21a). Vows (vv. 1-13) are, in the main, for animate things; consecrations, for inanimate things (vv. 14-25). Presumably one can also vow inanimate things (e.g., Jacob's vow to pay crop tithes to a temple that he will build, Gen 28:22), and animate things, such as impure animals for temple maintenance (e.g., Num 7:3-8); but one cannot, in the priestly view, consecrate animate things such as persons. Consecrations differ from vows in that they take effect the moment they are verbalized.

[27:14] "consecrates." Consecration can be defined as a transfer from the realm of the profane to the realm of the holy.[5] Examples include sacrifices (22:2-3), dedications to the sanctuary (Exod 28:38), and the firstborn (Num 3:13). God, too, is "sanctified" when he is treated as holy (Num 20:12; 27:14).

[27:20] The inherited land must revert to its owner at the Jubilee. He consecrates (or sells) its usufruct, that is, he only leases the land until the Jubilee. However, if he consecrates the land after selling it, he thereby indicates that he does not want the land back, and the land becomes sanctuary property after the Jubilee, as if it had not been consecrated but proscribed. The basic postulate behind this law is that the sanctuary takes no priority over the landowner. The priestly legists have made an amendment to the "the land is mine" principle. Inherited land always reverts to the owner, except when by word (v. 28) or act (vv. 20-21) he consecrates his land (and not just its usufruct) to the sanctuary. Why this alteration of the divine (i.e., the sanctuary) principle of ownership? Perhaps it is the priests' response to the condemnation by the eighth-century prophets of the growing latifundia of their time: indentured land being swallowed up by avaricious creditors (e.g., Isa 5:8-10; Mic 2:12). On the one hand, they devised the Jubilee system whereby the status quo would be restored and indentured Israelites would be released (Lev 25:8-43). On the other hand, they insisted that consecrated land was also subject to the Jubilee (vv. 20-21) so that the priests could not participate in the land-grabbing practices that prevailed all about them. We must remember that in the neighbouring high civilizations of Egypt and Mesopotamia, the temples acquired vast tracts of land. This example as well as the temptation always lay before Israel's priesthood.

---

[4] LXX, *Tg. Neof.*, *m. Tem.* 5:5; Maimonides, *Sacrifices* 1:1.
[5] Milgrom 1976c:782.

[27:21] "as a proscribed field." The field belongs to the priesthood, as does any other proscribed object (Num 18:14). This entitlement does not contradict the basic rule that priests (and Levites) may not possess inherited land (Num 18:20, 23). This rule must be properly understood: Israel's priesthood may not be *allotted* any land, but is permitted land that has been *voluntarily* proscribed—that is, intended by the owner to be transferred to the sanctuary.

Proscribed property is unsalable and irredeemable (v. 28a); it is not transferable. The consecration or sale of tenured land is never final; the land returns to its owner at the Jubilee. This verse continues and spells out the apodosis "it shall no longer be redeemable" (v. 20b). Consecrated land that had been sold does not revert to the owner at the Jubilee. The implication is clear: land that is consecrated while in its owner's possession does revert to him at the Jubilee, even if he does not redeem it.

Verses 26-27. Firstlings

The conflicting laws on the firstling reflect historical development. Originally, sacrificeable firstlings were entirely incinerated on the altar as burnt offerings. "Therefore I sacrifice to YHWH every first male issue of the womb" (Exod 13:15). The priestly laws, however, prescribe that the meat of the sacrificed firstling is a priestly perquisite: "but their meat shall be yours" (Num 18:18a [P]). Finally, Deuteronomy revokes both laws by declaring that the meat of the sacrificed firstling belongs to its owner: "You and your household shall eat it annually before YHWH your God" (Deut 15:20a).

"Ransom" refers to the price set by the sanctuary, a price that others, but not the owner, pay; "redeem" refers to the price paid by the owner, which includes the one-fifth surtax. What is the rationale for the surtax? One is readily understandable for consecrated property: to prevent a cycle of consecration and redemption by an owner who regrets losing his field or animal. But the firstling is not his to begin with; it belongs to God from birth. Since there can be no suspicion of fickleness on the part of the owner, why not let him ransom the firstling by paying its valuation price as may any other purchaser? Perhaps the priestly legist insisted on consistency in the five redemptive procedures of Leviticus 27: for the impure vowed animal (v. 13), the consecrated house (v. 15), the consecrated tenured field (v. 19), the impure firstling (v. 27), and the crop tithe (v. 31).

Verses 28-29. Proscriptions

"Proscription" is succinctly and accurately defined by P. D. Stern as "consecration through destruction."[6] This definition defies its usual understanding as a form of taboo. The proscription attested in the Bible is exercised by Israel against other nations as the result of either a vow (Num 21:2-3) or God's command (Num 25:16-

---

[6] 1991:226.

18; 31:1-12), or against its own rebels (Exod 22:19 [Eng. 20]; Deut 13:13-19 [Eng. 12-18]; Judg 20:48; 21:10-11). The antiquity of the word and the concept is confirmed by the ninth-century BCE Mesha inscription: "I seized it (Nebo) and I slew everybody in it—seven thousand m[e]n, b[oy]s, women, gi[rl]s and maidens—for to the warrior Kemosh I proscribed them."[7]

The biblical proscription manifests different degrees: (1) death of all persons and animals, and burning of all property on the site itself (Deut 13:16-17 [Eng. 15-16]); (2) death of all persons and animals, and consecration of all precious metals to the sanctuary (Josh 6:16-19); (3) death of all persons, but animals and goods are kept as booty (Deut 2:34-35; 3:6-7; 20:16; Josh 8:2, 26-27); (4) death of all persons, with the exception of virgins (Num 31:9-11, 17-18); and (5) death of all men and married women (Judg 21:11-12).[8]

Apparently, a curse pronounced against those who would settle a sacked enemy city takes effect because the city is consecrated to the Deity. Thus Joshua's proscription on Jericho implies that not only have its people and property been consigned to God, but also their very land—all are "most holy." Therefore, a curse against resettlement (Josh 6:26, fulfilled according to 1 Kgs 16:34) can be pronounced.[9]

Thus far, the war proscription. What of the "peace proscription" of Leviticus 27? Its only biblical example is the proscription imposed by Ezra on the property of those who deliberately would absent themselves from the national assembly (Ezra 10:8). Coevally with the war proscription, there must have been a "peace proscription," whereby a person's property could, voluntarily or forcibly, be irredeemably consecrated to the Deity.

[27:29] "has been proscribed." The death sentence is imposed by an authorized body after due process of law. This interpretation is bolstered by the absence of the object "to YHWH"[10] and by the fact that this passive is once again attested in "He who sacrifices to any god shall be proscribed" (Exod 22:19a [Eng. 20a]; see also Deut 13:13-19 [Eng. 12-18]), a law that again implies a judicial sentence.[11] My student S. Nikaido adds the argument that whereas "a man" in Lev 27:28 testifies that an individual is proscribing, the unstated subject in v. 29 indicates that the subject is no longer an individual but a collective body.

What would motivate an authorized body to impose the extreme proscription, the death penalty, on a human being? R. Akiba avers that the king of the Sanhedrin (i.e., the highest court) might impose the death penalty on Israel's enemies, citing the

---

[7] Lines 16-17, following P. D. Stern 1991:23–38, 55.
[8] Dillman and Ryssel 1897.
[9] my student D. Stewart.
[10] Shadal; Dillmann and Ryssel 1897; Heinisch 1935.
[11] Ramban; Wessely 1846.

example of the oath taken by the Israelite tribes against the people of Jabesh-gilead (Judg 21:5).[12] In other words, this law reflects the war proscription—for example, Achan (Josh 7:25),[13] Arad (Num 21:2), Mesha—which would bespeak its antiquity.

Verses 28-29 speak of two different fates that await a proscribed person: consigned as a slave to the sanctuary by his owner (v. 28), and sentenced to death by a judicial body (v. 29). The proscription imposed voluntarily by the owner on his property, whether it is his slaves, animals, or tenured fields, transfers it to permanent sanctuary ownership where it may be neither sold nor redeemed because of its most sacred status. But persons who are proscribed by some outside body (presumably, an authorized court) must be put to death.

Verses 30-33. Tithes

The tithe was not assigned only to temples. As may be learned from 1 Sam 8:15, 17, and from Ugarit, it could also be a royal tax that the king might exact and give to his officials.[14] This ambiguity of the tithe, as a royal due on the one hand, and as a sacred donation on the other, is to be explained by the fact that the temples to which the tithe was assigned were royal temples (see esp. Amos 7:13). As such, the property and treasures in them were at the king's disposal. This can best be exemplified by the two instances of tithe mentioned in older sources of the Pentateuch. In Gen 14:20 Abraham gives a tithe (after his battle with the four kings of the north) to Melchizedek, the king-priest of Shalem (= Jerusalem); and in Gen 28:22 (cf. Amos 4:4), Jacob vows to pay a tithe at Bethel, the "royal chapel" of the northern kingdom (Amos 7:13).

The specific mention of these two "royal temples" in connection with the tithe is not a coincidence. It seems that these two traditions have an etiological slant. The institution of collecting tithes in the royal chapel at Bethel is linked to Jacob, the ancestor hero par excellence of the northern tribes, whereas the institution of the tithe in the royal sanctuary of Jerusalem is traced back to Abraham, whose traditions are mainly attached to the south. As is well known, the kings controlled the treasure of palace and temple alike (1 Kgs 15:18; 2 Kgs 12:19; 18:15), which is understandable since they were responsible for the maintenance of the sanctuary and its service not less than for the service of the court (cf. Ezek 45:17). It stands to reason that the tithe, which originally was a religious tribute, came to be channelled to the court and was therefore supervised by royal authorities. This is actually attested in 2 Chr 31:4-21, where Hezekiah is said to organize the collection and the storage of the tribute, including the tithe.

The property that was subject to the tithe in Israel was grain, new wine, and new oil (e.g., Deut 14:23), as well as cattle and sheep (Lev 27:32). In a general con-

---

[12] *Yal.* Judges 76. Cf. Ramban; Wessely 1846; Dillmann and Ryssel 1897.

[13] Bekhor Shor.

[14] Anderson 1987:86.

text, however, the tithe appears to have embraced all kinds of property. Abraham gives Melchizedek one-tenth of everything, which seems to refer to the booty of the war, and Jacob vows that "of all that you give me, I will set aside a tithe for you" (Gen 28:22).

Verse 34. Summary

The author of Lev 27:34 was keenly aware of 26:46. Perhaps he wrote "commandments" precisely because this term was not in 26:46, and hence he regarded both verses as a combined subscript to the book of Leviticus. He could not, however, have had in mind only chapters 17–26, since "rituals" clearly refers to the sacrifice and impurity laws of chapters 1–16.

The repetition of "Mount Sinai" shows that the editor is deliberately completing 26:46. The purpose of the second subscript (27:34) is, indeed, to provide a separate ending for chapter 27. However, it also supplements and completes the previous subscript (26:46) so that both effect a proper closure for the entire book, the "priestly manual," in distinction to the laws (not the narrative) in the book of Numbers, which, in the main, could be called "the levitic manual."

Glossary

Abravanel	1437–1508. Spain and Italy. Statesman, philosopher, exegete
adytum	the holy of holies, the innermost room in the tabernacle and temple
ʾašam	sacrifice of reparation
Arad	site of a sanctuary of YHWH during the time of the First Temple
Azazel	the name of the demon residing in the wilderness
Bel	another name of Marduk, the god of Babylon
cubit	an ancient measure of length approx. 1 1/2 feet
Esarhaddon	emperor of Assyria during the seventh century BCE
First Temple	approx. tenth century till 586 BCE
H	The Holiness Code in Leviticus. It refers to chaps. 17–27; also found in Genesis, Exodus, and Numbers
H_R	the redactor of H
Hammurabi	Babylonian ruler, eighteenth century BCE
Hittites	(or Hattians) ancient people of Anatolia (Turkey)
Horus	the hawk-headed god of Egypt
Ibn Ezra	1089–1164. Spain. Poet, grammarian, exegete, philosopher, astronomer, physician, and itinerant scholar
JE	the epic (mainly narrative) tradition in the Pentateuch (absent from Leviticus)
Josephus	Jewish historian of the first century CE
Ka	in Egyptian religion the double residing in a person or statue
kapporet	golden slab atop the ark bearing two cherubim
karet	the punishment of excision from this world and exclusion from the afterworld
kavod	YHWH's earthly presence as a cloud-encased fire

335

Glossary

Masoretes	authors of vocalizations and cantillations on the words of the Pentateuch
Mesopotamia	lit. "between two rivers"; name for ancient Iraq
Molek	god of the underworld who demands child sacrifices for access to the ancestors
P	The Priestly Code in Leviticus. It refers to chaps. 1–16; also found in Genesis, Exodus, and Numbers
pe³ah	the crops at the end of the field left for the poor
Philo	Alexandrian Jewish philosopher, c. 20 BCE–50 CE
Qumran	site of the authors of the Dead Sea Scrolls
R. Akiba	Palestinian rabbi, second century CE
Ramban	1194–1270. Spain. Philosopher, kabbalist, exegete, talmudist, poet, physician
R. Eleazar (ben Arakh)	Palestinian (Tannaitic) rabbi, end of first century CE
R. Hillel	Palestinian rabbi, first century BCE to first century CE
R. Ishmael	Palestinian rabbi, second century CE
R. Jose the Galilean	Palestinian rabbi, beginning of the second century CE
R. Meir	Palestinian rabbi, second century CE
R. Shammai	colleague of R. Hillel, c. 50 BCE–30 CE
R. Yannai	Palestinian rabbi, early third century CE
R. Yohanan ben Zakkai	rabbinic leader during the period of the destruction of the temple, 70 CE
R. Yose bar Hanina	Palestinian rabbi, end of the third century CE
Second Temple	516 BCE–70 CE
ṭame³	"impure," defiling on contact
Tannaites	rabbis referred to in rabbinic literature before the third century CE
Tell el-Amarna	Egyptian site where royal international correspondence of the fifteenth century BCE was unearthed
Topheth	cult place in valley below the temple where Molek was worshiped
torot	the title to the priestly ritual documents in Leviticus
Trisagion	the word *qadoš*, "holy," uttered three times by the divine cherubim (Isa 6:3)
Yom Kippur	the Day of Purgation, the tenth of Tishri

Bibliography

Abravenel (Isaac ben Jehuda)
    1964   *Commentary on the Torah*. [Hebrew.] 3 vols. Jerusalem: Bnai Arbel.
Ackerman, S.
    1992   *Under Every Green Tree: Popular Religion in Sixth-Century Judah*. HSM 46. Atlanta: Scholars.
Albeck, H
    1952   *Seder Moʾed*. Jerusalem: Bialik Institute [Hebrew].
Albright, W. F.
    1949   *The Archaeology of Palestine*. Harmondsworth: Penguin.
Alfrink, B.
    1948   L'expression *neʾĕsap ʾel-ʿammāyw*. *OTS* 5:118–31.
Almagro-Gorbea, M.
    1980   Les reliefs orientalists de Pozo Moro. Pp. 123–36 in *Mythe et personification: Travaux et memoires. Actes du colloque du Grande Palais (Paris)*. Paris: Société d'Edition "Les Belles Lettres."
Amit, Y.
    1992   The Jubilee Law—An Attempt at Instituting Social Justice. Pp. 47–59 in *Justice and Righteousness* [Fest. B. Uffenheimer]. Ed. H. G. Reventlow and Y. Hoffman. JSOTSup 137. Sheffield: JSOT Press.
Anderson, G. A.
    1987   *Sacrifices and Offerings in Ancient Israel: Studies in Their Social and Political Importance*. Atlanta: Scholars Press.
Aubrey, J.
    1881   *Remains of Gentilisme and Judaisme*. London: W. Satchess, Peyton.
Audet, J.-P.
    1952   La Sagesse de Ménandre l'Egyptien. *RB* 59:55–81.
Baentsch, B
    1903   *Exodus, Leviticus und Numeri*. Göttingen: Vandenhoeck & Ruprecht.
Baltzer, K.
    1987   Liberation from Debt Slavery After the Exile in Second Isaiah and

Bibliography

Nehemiah. Pp. 477–84 in *Ancient Israelite Religion* [Fest. F. M. Cross]. Ed. P. D. Miller Jr. et al. Philadelphia: Fortress Press.

Bar-Maoz, Y.
  1980   The "Misharum" Reform of King Ammisaduqa. [Hebrew.] Pp. 40–74 in *Researches in Hebrew and Semitic Languages*. Tel Aviv: Bar Ilan.

Barr, J.
  1963   Sacrifices and Offerings. Pp. 868–76 in *Dictionary of the Bible*. Ed. J. Hastings. Rev. ed. F. C. Grant and H. H. Rowley. New York: Scribner.

Bayliss, M.
  1973   The Cult of the Dead Kin in Assyria and Babylonia. *Iraq* 35:115–25.

Beck, P.
  1990   A Note on the "Schematic Statues" from the Stelae Temple at Hazor. *Tel Aviv* 17:91–95.

Beek, G. W. van
  1960   Frankincense and Myrrh. *BA* 23:70–95.

Ben-Tuvia, A.
  1966   Red Sea Fishes Recently Found in the Mediterranean. *Copeia* 2:255–75.

Bergman, J., H. Ringgren, and W. Dommershausen
  1995   *kōhēn*, priest. In *TDOT* 7:60–75.

Blackman, A. M.
  1918–19 The Sequence of the Episodes in the Egyptian Daily Temple Liturgy. *Journal of the Manchester Egyptian and Oriental Society* 27–53.

Blome, F.
  1934   *Die Opfermaterie in Babylonien und Israel*. Rome: Biblical Institute Press.

Boehmer, R. M.
  1975   Hörnerkrone. *RLA* 4:431–34.

Boleh, M.
  1991–92 *The Book of Leviticus*. [Hebrew.] 2 vols. Jerusalem: Mosad Harav Kook.

Borger, R.
  1973   Die Weihe eines Enlil-Priesters. *BO* 30:163–76.

Borowski, O.
  1987   *Agriculture in Iron Age Israel: The Evidence from Archaeology and the Bible*. Winona Lake, Ind.: Eisenbrauns.

Bottéro, J., and H. Petschow
  1975   Homosexualität. In *RLA* 4:459–68.

Breasted, J. H.
  1906   *Ancient Records of Egypt*. Vol. 4. Chicago: Univ. of Chicago Press.

338

Brichto, H. C.
1976   On Slaughter and Sacrifice, Blood and Atonement. *HUCA* 47:19–56.
Buber, M.
1964   *The Way of the Bible*. [Hebrew.] Jerusalem: Mosad Bialik. [Abridged as *On the Bible*, by N. M. Glatzer (New York: Schocken, 1982)].
Burton, J.W.
1974   Some Nuer Notions of Puity and Danger. *Anthropos* 69:517–36.
Caloz, M.
1968   Exode XIII, 3-16 et son rapport au Deutéronome (Planches 1–11). *RB* 75:5–62.
Caplice, R.
1965–71 Namburbi Texts in the British Museum I, II, III. *Or* 34:105–31; 36:1–38, 273–98; 39:118–51; 40:133–83.
Carmichael, C. M.
1982   Forbidden Mixtures. *VT* 32:394–415.
1995   Forbidden Mixtures in Deuteronomy XXII 9-11 and Leviticus XIX 19. *VT* 45:433–48.
1997   *Law, Legend, and Incest in the Bible*. Ithaca: Cornell Univ. Press.
Černy, J.
1954   Consanguineous Marriages in Pharaonic Egypt. *Journal of Egyptian Archaeology* 40:23–29.
Childs, B. S.
1974   *Exodus*. OTL. Philadelphia: Westminster.
Cholewiński, A.
1976   *Heiligkeitsgesetz und Deuteronomium: Eine vergleichende Studie*. AnBib 66. Rome: Pontifical Biblical Institute Press.
Cohen, M.
1993   The Terms "Purity" and "Impurity" in Biblical Hebrew and Their Relation to the Concept of Prohibition and Permission in Rabbinic Hebrew. *BM* 38:289–306.
Cohen, S. J. D.
1983   From the Bible to the Talmud: The Prohibition of Intermarriage. *HAR* 7:23–40.
Cohen, Y. A.
1969   Ends and Means in Political Control: State Organization and the Punishment of Adultery, Incest, and the Violation of Celibacy. *American Anthropologist* 71:658–87.
Colson, M. A.
1968   *Philo,* 10 vols. LCL. Cambridge, Mass.: Heineman.

Bibliography

Cooper, J. S.
1983   *The Curse of Agade*. Johns Hopkins Near Eastern Studies. Baltimore: Johns Hopkins University Press.

Coulanges, F. de
1956   *The Ancient City: A Study on the Religion, Laws and Institutions of Greece and Rome*. Garden City, N.Y.: Doubleday.

Cowley, A. E.
1923   *The Aramaic Papyri of the Fifth Century B.C.E.* Oxford: Clarendon.

Cross, F. M.
1998   *From Epic to Canon: History and Literature in Ancient Israel*. Baltimore: Johns Hopkins Univ. Press.

Dalman, G.
1928–39 *Arbeit und Sitte in Palästina*. 6 vols. Gütersloh: Bertelsmann.

Dandamaev, M. A.
1984   *Slavery in Babylonia (626–331BC)*. Ed. M. Powell. Trans. V. A. Powell. Dekalb: Northern Illinois Univ. Press.
1993   The Sick Temple Slaves' Rations in Babylonia in the Sixth Century BCE. *ErIsr* 24:19–21.

Daube, D.
1947   *Studies in Biblical Law*. Cambridge: Cambridge Univ. Press.
1963   *The Exodus Pattern in the Bible*. Westport, Conn.: Greenwood.

Davis, S.
1985   The Large Animal Bones. In *Excavations at Tell Qasile*, part two. Ed. A. Mazar. *Qedem* 20:148–50.

Derrett, J. D. M.
1971   Love Thy Neighbor as a Man Like Thyself? *ExpTim* 83:55–56.

Dillmann, A., and V. Ryssel
1897   *Die Bücher Exodus und Leviticus*. 3d ed. Leipzig: Hirzel. 1st ed. 1880.

Dommen, E. C.
1972   Social Justice and Economic Development. *Rural Life* 17:13–20.

Dommershausen, W., and H.-J. Fabry
1995   *leḥem*, bread. In *TDOT* 7:521–29.

Doron, P.
1969   A New Look at an Old Lex. *JNES* 1:21–27.

Douglas, M.
1966   *Purity and Danger*. London: Routledge & Kegan Paul.
1995   Poetic Structure in Leviticus. Pp. 239–56 in *Pomegranates and Golden Bells* [Fest. J. Milgrom]. Ed. D. P. Wright et al. Winona Lake, Ind.: Eisenbrauns.
1999   *Leviticus as Literature*. Oxford: Oxford Univ. Press.

Driver, S. R.
    1895   *Deuteronomy*. ICC. New York: Scribner.
    1900   Offer, Offering, Obligation. Pp. 587–89 in vol. 3 of *Dictionary of the Bible*. Ed. J. Hastings. New York: Scribner.

Driver, S. R., and M. A. White
    1898   *The Book of Leviticus*. New York: Dodd, Mead, and Co.

Durkheim, E.
    1965   *The Elementary Forms of the Religious Life*. Trans. J. W. Swain. Repr.
    (1915) New York: Free Press.

Ebeling, E.
    1949   Beschwörungen gegen den Feind und den bösen Blick aus dem Zweistromlande. *Archív Orientální* 17:203–6.
    1954   Beiträge zur Kenntnis der Beschwörungsserie Namburbi. *RA* 48:178–91.

Edzard, D. O.
    1965   *The Near East: The Early Civilisations*. Ed. J. Bottéro et al., chaps. 2, 4, 5. Trans. R. F. Tannenbaum. London: Weidenfeld and Nicolson.

Eerdmans, B. D.
    1912   *Das Buch Leviticus*. Alttestamentliche Studien 4. Giessen: Töpelmann.

Ehrlich, A.
    1899–
    1900   *Hamiqra kifshuto*. [Hebrew.] 3 vols. Berlin: Poppelauer.
    1908–14 *Randglossen zur hebräischen Bibel*. 7 vols. Leipzig: Hinrichs.

Eichrodt, W.
    1961–67 *Theology of the Old Testament*. Trans. J. A. Baker. 2 vols. OTL. Philadelphia: Westminster.

Eilberg-Schwartz, H.
    1990   *The Savage in Judaism: An Anthropology of Israelite Religion and Ancient Judaism*. Bloomington: Indiana Univ. Press.

Eisenman, R. H., and M. Wise
    1992   *The Dead Sea Scrolls Uncovered*. New York: Penguin.

Eitam, D., and H. Shomroni
    1987   Research of the Oil Industry During the Iron Age at Tel Miqne. Pp. 37–56 in *Olive Oil in Antiquity*. Ed. M. Heltzer and D. Eitam. Haifa: Univ. of Haifa Press.

Elliger, K.
    1966   *Leviticus*. HAT 4. Tübingen: Mohr (Siebeck).

Erman, A.
    1907   *A Handbook of Egyptian Religion*. Trans. A. S. Griffith. London: Constable.

Bibliography

Fager, J. A.
1993   *Land Tenure and the Biblical Jubilee: Uncovering Hebrew Ethics through the Sociology of Knowledge.* JSOTSup 155. Sheffield: JSOT Press.

Feldman, E.
1977   *Biblical and Post-Biblical Defilement and Mourning: Law as Theology.* New York: Ktav.

Fensham, F. C.
1977   The Numeral Seventy in the Old Testament. *PEQ* 109:113–15.

Finkelstein, L.
1961   Ammisaduqa's Edict and the Babylonian Law codes. *JCS* 15:91–104.
1962   *The Pharisees.* 3d ed. 2 vols. Philadelphia: Jewish Publication Society.
1966   The Genealogy of the Hammurapi Dynasty. *JCS* 20:95–118.

Finley, M. I.
1968   The Alienability of Land in Ancient Greece: A Point of View. *Eirene* 7:25–32.

Fitzmyer, J. A.
1981   *The Gospel according to Luke (I–IX).* AB 28. New York: Doubleday.

Frankel, D.
1994   The Stories of Murmuring in the Desert in the Priestly School. Ph.D. diss., Hebrew University [Hebrew].

Frankel, E.
1998   *Five Books of Miriam: A Woman's Commentary on the Torah.* San Francisco: Harper SanFrancisco.

Freedman, D. N., and M. O'Connor
1995   *kĕrûb,* cherub. In *TDOT* 7:307–19.

Friedman, R. E.
1980   Sacred History and Theology: The Redaction of the Torah. Pp. 25–34 in *The Creation of Sacred Literature.* Ed. R. E. Friedman. Berkeley: Univ. of California Press.
1987   *Who Wrote The Bible?* New York: Summit.

Fröhlich, J.
1994   Themes, Structure and Genre of Pesher Genesis. *JQR* 85:83–90.

Frymer-Kensky, T.
1977   The Atrahasis Epic and Its Significance for Our Understanding of Genesis 1–9. *BA* 40:147–55.
1979   Israel and the Ancient Near East: New Perspectives on the Flood. *Proceedings of the Rabbinical Assembly* 41:213–25.

Galling, K.
1925   *Der Altar in den Kulturen des alten Orients: Ein archäologische Studie.* Berlin: K. Curtius.

Gaster, T. H.
   1962a   Demon, Demonology. In *IDB* 1:817–24.
   1962b   Sacrifices and Offerings in the OT. In *IDB* 4:147–59.
Gennep, A. van
   1960   *The Rites of Passage.* Chicago: Univ. of Chicago Press.
Gerstenberger, E. S.
   1996   *Leviticus.* Trans. D. W. Stott. OTL. Louisville: Westminster John Knox
           Press.
Ginsberg, H. L.
   1982   *The Israelian Heritage of Judaism.* New York: Jewish Theological
           Seminary.
Ginsburg, C. D.
   1966   *Introduction to the Massoretico-Critical Edition of the Hebrew Bible.*
           Repr. New York: Ktav.
Ginzberg, E.
   1932   Studies in the Economics of the Bible. *JQR* 22:343–408.
Goldstein, J. A.
   1976   *I Maccabees.* AB 41. Garden City, N.Y.: Doubleday.
Goodfriend, E. A.
   1992   Prostitution: Cultic Prostitution. In *ABD* 5:510–13.
Goodman, L. E.
   1986   The Biblical Laws of Diet and Sex. Pp. 17–57 in *Jewish Law Associa-*
           tion Studies II. Ed. B. S. Jackson. Atlanta: Scholars.
Gorman, F. H.
   1990   *The Ideology of Ritual: Space, Time and Status in the Priestly Theol-*
           ogy. Sheffield: JSOT Press.
Greenberg, M.
   1962   Crimes and Punishments. In *IDB* 1:733–44.
   1971   Sabbath. In *EncJud* 14:558–62.
   1983   *Biblical Prose Prayer.* Berkeley: Univ. of California Press.
   1985   *On the Bible and Judaism: A Collection of Writings.* [Hebrew.] Tel
           Aviv: Am Oved.
   1996   The Value of Controversy. Pp. 4–9 in *Judaism and Humanism.* Ed. N.
           Gruber et al. Jerusalem [Hebrew].
Grintz, Y. M.
   1966   Do Not Eat over the Blood. [Hebrew.] *Zion* 31:1–17.
Gruber, M. I.
   1983a   The *qādēš* in the Book of Kings and in Other Sources. [Hebrew.] *Tar-*
           biz 52:167–76.
   1983b   The Many Faces of Hebrew *ns' pnm* "Lift up the Face." *ZAW*
           95:252–60.

1986   Hebrew *qĕdēšâh* and Her Canaanite and Akkadian Cognates. *UF* 18:133–48.

Gurney, O. R.
1935   Babylonian Prophylactic Figures and Their Rituals. *AAA* 22:31–95.

Haag, H.
1980   *chāmās*. In *TDOT* 4:478–86.

Halivni, D. W.
1989   On Man's Role in Revelation. Pp. 29–49 in *From Ancient Israel to Modern Judaism*, vol. 2 [Fest. M. Fox]. Ed. J. Neusner et al. BJS 173.. Atlanta: Scholars.

Hallo, W. W.
1986   The Origins of the Sacrifical Cult: New Evidence from Mesopotamia and Israel. Pp. 3–13 in *Ancient Israelite Religion* (Fest. F. M. Cross). Ed. P. D. Miller et al. Philadelphia: Fortress Press.

1995   Slave Release in the Biblical World in Light of a New Yext. Pp. 79–83 in *Solving Riddles and Untying Knots* [Fest. J. C. Greenfield]. Ed. Z. Zevit et al. Winona Lake, Ind.: Eisenbrauns.

1996   *Origins: The Ancient Near Eastern Background of Some Modern Western Institutions*. SHANE 6. Leiden: Brill.

Haran, M.
1955   The Ephod According to the Biblical Sources. [Hebrew.] *Tarbiz* 24:380–91.

1978   *Temples and Temple Service in Ancient Israel*. Oxford: Clarendon.

Hartley, J. E.
1992   *Leviticus*. WBC 4. Dallas: Word.

Hass, G.
1953   On the Occurrence of Hippopotamus in the Iron Age of the Coastal Area of Israel (Tell Qasileh). *BASOR* 132:30–34.

Hayley, A.
1980   A Common Relationship with God: The Nature of Offering in Assamese Vaishnavism. Pp. 107–25 in *Sacrifice*. Ed. M. F. C. Bourdillon and M. Fortes. London: Academic.

Hazzequni, H. (Hezekiah ben Manoah)
1981   *The Torah Commentaries of R. Hizqiah b. Manoah*. [Hebrew.] Ed. H. D. Chavel. Jerusalem: Mosad Harav Kook.

Heimpel, W.
1981   The Nanshe Hymn. *JCS* 33:65–139.

Heinisch, P.
1935   *Das Buch Leviticus*. Bonn: Hanstein.

Hertz, J. H.
1941   *The Pentateuch and Haftorahs*. 2 vols. New York: Metzudah.

Hoffmann, D. Z.
    1953   *Leviticus.* [Hebrew.] Trans. Z. Har-Shafer and A. Lieberman. 2 vols. Jerusalem: Mosad Harav Kook. [Trans. of *Das Buch Leviticus*, I-II (Berlin: Poppelauer, 1905–6)].

Hoffner, H. A.
    1973   Incest, Sodomy and Bestiality in the Ancient Near East. Pp. 81–90 in *Orient and Occident* [Fest. C. H. Gordon]. Ed. H. Hoffner et al. AOAT 22. Kevelaer: Butzon & Bercker.
    1974   *Alimenta Hethaeorum: Food Production in Hittite Asia Minor.* AOS 55. New Haven: American Oriental Society.

Hooks, S. M.
    1985   Sacred Prostitution in the Bible and Near East. Ph.D. diss., Hebrew Union College.

Hopkins, D. C.
    1985   *The Highlands of Canaan: Agricultural Life in the Early Iron Age.* SWBA 3. Sheffield: Almond.

Houten, C. van
    1991   *The Alien in Israelite Law.* JSOTSup 107. Sheffield: JSOT Press.

Houtman, C.
    1984   Another Look at Forbidden Mixtures. *VT* 34:226–28.

Hulse, E. V.
    1975   The Nature of Biblical "Leprosy" and the Use of Alternative Medical Terms in Modern Translations of the Bible. *PEQ* 107:87–105.

Hurowitz, A.
    1974   Building Consecration Ceremonies in the Bible. [Hebrew.] M.A. thesis, Hebrew University, Jerusalem.

Hurowitz, V.
    1992   "His Master Shall Pierce His Ear with an Awl" (Exodus 21:6)—Marking Slaves in the Bible in Light of Akkadian Sources. *PAAJR* 58:47–77.

Ibn Ezra, Abraham
    1961   *Leviticus with Ibn Ezra's Commentary.* [Hebrew.] Mehoeqeqe Yehudah. Ed. J. L. Krinsky. Horeb: Bnai Brak.

Jackson, B. S.
    1988   Biblical Laws of Slavery: A Comparative Approach. Pp. 86–101 in *Slavery and Other Forms of Unfree Labor.* Ed. L. J. Archer. History Workshop Series. New York: Routledge.

Jacobsen, T.
    1961   Toward the Image of Tammuz. *History of Religions* 1:189–213. (= Pp. 73–103 in *Toward the Image of Tammuz.* Ed. W. L. Moran. Harvard Semitic Series 21. Cambridge: Harvard Univ. Press, 1970).

Bibliography

Japhet, S.
1977   *The Ideology of the Book of Chronicles and Its Place in Biblical Thought.* [Hebrew.] Jerusalem: Mosad Bialik. Eng. Trans. New York: Lang. 1989.

Johnson, A.
1947   Aspects of the Use of the Term *pānîm* in the Old Testament. Pp. 155–59 in *Festschrift Otto Eissfeldt.* Ed. J. Fück. Halle an der Saale: Niemeyer.

Johnson, L. T.
1982   The Use of Leviticus 19 in the Letter of James. *JBL* 101:391–401.

Joosten, J.
1994   The People and Land in the Holiness Code. Ph.D. diss., Universitaire Protestante Godgeleerdheid to Brussel.

Junker, H.
1959   Vorschriften für den Tempelkult in Philä. *Analecta Biblica* 12:151–60.

Kalisch, M. M.
1867–72   *Leviticus.* 2 vols. London: Longmans.

Kaufmann, Y.
1937–56   *The History of the Israelite Religion.* [Hebrew.] 4 vols. Tel Aviv: Dvir.
1960   *The Religion of Israel.* Trans. and abridged M. Greenberg. Chicago: Univ. of Chicago Press.

Kedar-Kopfstein, B., and G. J. Botterweck
1980   *ḥag.* In *TDOT* 4:201–13.

Keel, O.
1972   Erwägungen zum Sitz im Leben vormosäischen Pascha und zur Etymologie von *psḥ. ZAW* 84:414–34.

Keil, C. F., and F. Delitzsch
1956   *Biblical Commentary on the Old Testament.* Vol. 2, *The Pentateuch.*
(1874)   Trans. J. Martin. Repr. Grand Rapids: Eerdmans.

Kelso, J. L.
1962   Pottery. In *IDB* 3:846–53.

Kennedy, C. A.
1981   The Mythological Reliefs at Pozo Moro, Spain. In *SBLSP* 20:209–16.

Kikawada, I. M.
1974   The Shape of Genesis 11:1-9. Pp. 18–32 in *Rhetorical Criticism* (Fest. J. Muilenburg). Ed. J. J. Jackson and M. Kessler. Pittsburgh Theological Monograph Series 1. Pittsburgh: Pickwick.

Kimche, D. (Radak)
1847   *The Book of Roots.* Ed. H. R. Bresenthal and H. Lebricht. Berlin: Friedlander [Hebrew].

Kiuchi, N.
1987   *The Purification Offering in the Priestly Literature: Its Meaning and Function.* Sheffield: JSOT Press.
Klein, J.
1992   Akitu. In *ABD* 1:138–39.
Knohl, I.
1987   The Priestly Torah versus the Holiness School: Sabbath and the Festivals. *HUCA* 58:65–117. [Originally published in 1983–84. *Shnaton* 7-8:109–46].
1991   Between Cult and Morality. *S'vara* 2:29–34.
1995   *The Sanctuary of Silence: The Priestly Torah and the Holiness School.* Trans. E. Feldman and P. Rodman. Minneapolis: Fortress Press.
Koch, K.
1959   *Die Priesterschrift von Exodus 25 bis Leviticus 16: Eine überlieferungs-geschichtliche und literarische Untersuchung.* FRLANT 71. Göttingen: Vandenhoeck & Ruprecht.
Kugel, J. L.
1996   The Holiness of Israel and the Land in Second Temple Times. Pp. 21–32 in *Texts, Temples and Traditions* [Fest. M. Haran]. Ed. M. V. Fox et al. Winona Lake, Ind.: Eisenbrauns.
1997   *The Bible as It Was.* Cambridge: Harvard Univ. Press.
Kugler, R. A.
1997   Holiness, Purity, the Body, and Society: The Evidence for Theological Conflict in Leviticus. *JSOT* 76:3–27.
Lambert, W. G.
1959   Three Literary Prophets of the Babylonians: Prayer to Marduk, No 1. *AfO* 19:55–60.
1960   *Babylonian Wisdom Literature.* Oxford: Clarendon.
1967   Enmeduranki and Related Matters. *JCS* 21:126–33.
1980   The Theology of Death. Pp. 53–68 in *Death and Mesopotamia.* Ed. B. Alster. Copenhagen: Akademisk.
Lang, B.
1983   *Monotheism and the Prophetic Minority.* Sheffield: Almond Press.
Langlamet, F.
1969   Israel et "l'habitant du pays": Vocabulaire et formules d'Ex xxxiv, 11-16. *RB* 76:321–50, 481–507.
Leach, E.
1976   *Culture and Communication.* Cambridge: Cambridge Univ. Press.
Leemans, W. F.
1991   Quelques considerations à propos d'une étude récente du doit du Proche-Orient ancien. *BO* 48:409–37.

Bibliography

Levenson, J. D.
   1985   *Sinai and Zion.* Minneapolis: Winston.
Levine, B. A.
   1989   *Leviticus.* JPSTC. Philadelphia: Jewish Publication Society.
   1992   Leviticus, Book of. In *ABD* 4:311–21.
Licht, J.
   1968   *Sukkôt.* [Hebrew.] *EM* 6:1037–43.
Licht, J., and Y. Leibowitz
   1962   *mûm.* [Hebrew.] *EM* 4:724–28.
Lieberman, S.
   1950   *Hellenism in Jewish Palestine.* New York: Jewish Theological Seminary.
   1967   *Tosefta Kiofeshutah,* vol.5, *Seder Nashim.* New York: Jewish Theological Seminary.
Loewenstamm, S. E.
   1958   Jubilee. [Hebrew.] In *EM* 3:578–82.
   1968   Law, Biblical. [Hebrew.] In *EM* 5:614–37.
Lohse, E.
   1951   *Die Ordination in Spätjudentum und im Neuen Testament.* Göttingen: Vandenhoeck & Ruprecht.
Lowery, R. H.
   2000   *Sabbath and Jubilee.* Understanding Biblical Themes. St. Louis: Chalice.
Lund, N. W.
   1942   *Chiasmus in the New Testament.* Chapel Hill: Univ. of North Carolina Press.
Magonet, J.
   1983   The Structure and Meaning of Leviticus 19. *HAR* 7:151–67.
Maine, H. J. S.
   1890   *Village Communities in the East and West.* London: Murray.
Malamat, A.
   1962   Mari and the Bible: Some Patterns of Tribal Organization and Institutions. *JAOS* 82:143–50.
   1990   "You Shall Love Your Neighbor as Yourself": A Case of Misinterpretation. Pp.111–16 in *Die Hebräische Bibel und ihre zweifache Nachgeschichte* [Fest. R. Rendtorff]. Ed. E. Blum et al. Neukirchen-Vluyn: Neukirchener Verlag.
Manor, D. W., and G. A. Herion
   1992   Arad. In *ABD* 1.331–36.
Marcus, J. M., and J. J. Francis, eds.
   1975   *Masturbation: From Infancy to Senesence.* New York: International Univ. Press.

Matthiae, P.
1979   Princely Cemetery and Ancestor Cult at Ebla During Middle Bronze II: A Proposal of Interpretation. *UF* 11:563–69.

Mazar, A.
1990   *Archaeology of the Land of the Bible.* Garden City, N.Y.: Doubleday.

Mazar, B.
1954   Canaan on the Threshold of the Age of the Patriarchs. [Hebrew.] *ErIsr* 3:18–32.

McEvenue, S. E.
1971   *The Narrative Style of the Priestly Writer.* AnBib 50. Rome: Biblical Institute Press.

McKeating, H.
1979   Sanctions against Adultery in Ancient Israelite Society, with Some Reflections on Methodology in the Study of Old Testament Ethics. *JSOT* 11:57–72.

Meier, G.
1937   *Die assyrische Beschwörungssammlung Maqlû.* AfO Beiheft 2. Osnabrück: Biblio.

Mendelsohn, I.
1949   *Slavery in the Ancient Near East.* New York: Oxford Univ. Press.
1962   Slavery in the OT. In *IDB* 4:383–91.

Mendelssohn, M.. Ed.
1846   *Netivot Ha-shalom.* [Hebrew.] Vol. 3. Vienna: Von Schmid und Busch.

Meyers, C. L.
1983   Procreation, Production and Protection: Male-Female Balance in Early Israel. *JAAR* 51:569–93.

Meyers, C. L., and E. M. Meyers
1993   *Zechariah 9–14.* AB 25C. New York: Doubleday.

Milgrom, J.
1964   Did Isaiah Prophesy During the Reign of Uzziah? *VT* 14:164–82.
1970   *Studies in Levitical Terminology.* University of California Publications. Near Eastern Studies 14. Berkeley: Univ. of California Press.
1976a   *Cult and Conscience: The Asham and Priestly Doctrine of Repentance.* SJLA 18. Leiden: Brill.
1976b   Encroachment. In *IDBSup.* 264–65.
1976c   Sanctification. In *IDBSup.* 782–84.
1976d   The Legal Terms *šlm* and *brʾšw* in the Bible. *JNES* 35:236–47.
1976e   *qĕtōret.* [Hebrew.] In *EM* 7:112–20.
1977   The Betrothed Slave-Girl. *ZAW* 86:43–50.
1978   Priestly Terminology and the Political and Social Structure of Pre-Monarchic Israel. *JQR* 69:65–81.

Bibliography

1979	The Offering of Incense in Second Temple Times. [Hebrew.] Pp. 330–34 in *Sefer Ben-Zion Luria*. Jerusalem: Kiryat Sefer.

1979   The Offering of Incense in Second Temple Times. [Hebrew.] Pp. 330–34 in *Sefer Ben-Zion Luria*. Jerusalem: Kiryat Sefer.

1981   The Case of the Suspected Adulteress, Num. 5:11-31: Redaction and Meaning. Pp. 69–75 in *The Creation of Sacred Literature*. Ed. R. E. Friedman. Berkeley: Univ. of California Press.

1982   Religious Conversion and the Revolt Model for the Formation of Israel. *JBL* 101:169–76.

1983a   Of Hems and Tassels. *BAR* 9/3:61–65.

1983b   *Studies in Cultic Theology and Terminology*. SJLA 36. Leiden: Brill.

1983c   The Tassels Pericope, Num. 15:37-41. [Hebrew.] *BM* 92:14–22.

1990   *Numbers*. JPSTC. Philadelphia: Jewish Publication Society.

1991   *Leviticus 1–16*. AB 3. New York: Doubleday.

1992a   Two Biblical Priestly Terms: *šeqeṣ* and *ṭāmēʾ*. *Maarav* 8:107–16.

1992b   Two Biblical Priestly Terms: *šeqeṣ* and *ṭāmēʾ*. *Tarbiz* 60:423–28. [Hebrew].

1994   Sex and Wisdom: What the Garden of Eden Story Is Saying. *BR* 10:21.

1996   Law and Narrative and the Exegesis of Leviticus XIX. *VT* 46:544–48.

2000   *Leviticus 17–22*. AB 3A. New York: Doubleday.

2001   *Leviticus 23–27*. AB 3B. New York: Doubleday.

Monkhouse, W.

1989   Consanguineous Marriage in the Ancient Near East. B.A. Honors thesis.

Moore, S. F., and B. G. Meyerhoff

1977   Introduction: Secular Ritual: Forms and Meanings. Pp. 3–24 in *Secular Ritual*. Ed. S. F. Moore and B. G. Meyerhoff. Amsterdam: Van Gorcum.

Moran, W. L.

1962   A Kingdom of Priests. Pp. 7–20 in *The Bible in Current Catholic Thought*. Ed. J. L. McKenzie. New York: Herder and Herder.

1963   The Ancient Near Eastern Background of the Love of God in Deuteronomy. *CBQ* 25:77–87.

Mowinckel, S.

1921   ʿAwan und die individuelle Klagepsalmen. *Psalmenstudien I*. Skrifter utgitt av det Norske Videnskaps-Akademie in Oslo. Hist.-Filos. Kl. Kristiana: Dybwad.

Moyer, J. C.

1969   The Concept of Ritual Purity Among the Hittites. Ph.D. diss., Brandeis.

Muffs, Y.

1965   Covenantal Traditions in Deuteronomy. Pp. 1–9 in vol. 3 of *Readings in the History of Biblical Thought*. Lectures at the Jewish Theological Seminary. New York: Jewish Theological Seminary.

Muraoka, T.
1985   *Emphatic Words and Structures in Biblical Hebrew*. Leiden: Brill.
Murray, M. A.
1927   Notes on Some Genealogies of the Middle Kingdom. *Ancient Egypt* 13:45–51.
Noth, M.
1977   *Leviticus*. Trans. J. E. Anderson. Rev. ed. OTL. Philadelphia: Westminster.
Nussbaum, D.
1974   The Priestly Explanation of Exile and Its Bearing upon the Portrayal of the Canaanites in the Bible. Master's thesis, Univ. of Pennsylvania.
Obbink, H. T.
1937   The Horns of the Altar in the Semitic World, Especially in Jahwism. *JBL* 56:43–49.
Olyan, S. M.
1997   Cult. Pp. 79–86 in vol. 2 of *Archaeology in the Near East*. Ed. E. M. Meyers. Oxford: Oxford Univ. Press.
Oppenheim, A. L.
1964   *Ancient Mesopotamia: Portrait of a Dead Civilization*. Chicago: Univ. of Chicago Press.
1967   *Letters from Mesopotamia*. Chicago: Univ. of Chicago Press.
Otten, H.
1956   Ein Text zum Neujahrfest aus Bogazköy. *Orientalistiche Literaturzeitung* 51:102–5.
Otto, E.
1960   Das ägyptische Mundöffnungsritual, I-II. *Ägyptologische Abhandlungen*, vol. 3. Wiesbaden: Harrassowitz.
Paran, M.
1989   *Forms of the Priestly Style in the Pentateuch*. Jerusalem: Magnes. [Hebrew].
Pardee, D.
1979   A New Ugaritic Letter. *BO* 34:3–20.
Paschen, W.
1970   *Rein and Unrein*. SANT 24. Munich: Kosel.
Paton, L. B.
1897   The Original Form of Leviticus XVII–XIX. *JBL* 16:31–77.
Patrick, D.
1985   *Old Testament Law*. Atlanta: John Knox Press.
Pedersen, J.
1940   *Israel: Its Life and Culture*. Vols. 3 and 4. London: Oxford Univ. Press.

Bibliography

Péter, R.
    1977   L'Imposition des mains dans l'Ancien Testament. *VT* 27:48–55.
Pope, M. H.
    1976   Homosexuality. In *IDBSup.* 415–17.
Por, F. D.
    1971   One Hundred Years of Suez Canal—A Century of Lessepian Migration: Retrospect and Viewpoints. *Systematic Zoology* 20:138–59.
Porter, J. R.
    1976   *Leviticus.* CBC. Cambridge: Cambridge Univ. Press.
Preuss, J.
    1971   *Biblisch-talmüdische Medizin.* Trans. F. Rosner. New York: Ktav. Reprinted New York: Sanhedrin, 1978. Original ed. Berlin: S. Karger, 1911.
Radday, Y. T.
    1981   Chiasmus in Hebrew Biblical Narrative. Pp. 50–117 in *Chiasmus in Antiquity.* Ed. J. W. Welch. Hildesheim: Gerstenberg.
Rambam (Moses ben Maimon, also called Maimonides)
    1963   *Mishnei Torah—The Book of Commandments.* Rambam L'Am. Jerusalem: Mosad Harav Kook. [Hebrew].
Ramban (Moses ben Nahman, also called Nahmanides)
    1960   *Comments of the Ramban on the Torah.* [Hebrew.] Ed. H. D. Chavel. 2 vols. Jerusalem: Mosad Harav Kook.
Rashbam (Samuel ben Meir)
    1969   *Commentary of the Rashbam on the Torah.* [Hebrew.] Ed. A. I. Bromberg. Jerusalem: Privately printed.
Rashi (Solomon ben Isaac)
    1946   *Pentateuch with Rashi's Commentary.* Trans. and annotated by A. H. Silbermann and M. Rosenbaum. 2 vols. London: Shapiro, Valentine.
Rattray, S.
    1987   Marriage Rules, Kinship Terms and Family Structure in the Bible. In *SBLSP* 26:537–44.
Reichart, A.
    1972   Der Jehowist und die sogenannten deuteronomistischen Erweiterungen im Buch Exodus. Ph.D. diss., Univ. of Tübingen.
Reiner, E.
    1956   *Lipšur* Litanies. *JNES* 15:129–49.
    1958   *Šurpu: A Collection of Sumerian and Akkadian Incantations.* AfO 11. Osnabrück: Biblio.
Rendtorff, R.
    1967   *Studien zur Geschichte des Opfers im Alten Israel.* WMANT 24. Neukirchen: Neukirchener Verlag.

Ridderbos, N. H.
1948   ʿāpār als "Staub des Totenortes." *OTS* 5:174–78.
Ringgren, H.
1966   *Israelite Religion*. Trans. D. E. Green. Philadelphia: Fortress Press.
Ritter, E. K.
1965   Magical-Expert and Physician. *Assyriological Studies* 16:299–321.
Robinson, H. W.
1942   Hebrew Sacrifice and Prophetic Symbolism. *JTS* 43:129–39.
Safrai, S.
1965   *Pilgrimage at the Time of the Second Temple*. [Hebrew.] Tel Aviv: Am Hassefer.
Safren, J. D.
1999   Jubilee and the Day of Atonement. Pp. 107–14 in *Proceedings of the Twelfth World Congress of Jewish Studies*. Jerusalem: World Union of Jewish Studies.
Saggs, H. W. F.
1962   *The Greatness That Was Babylon*. New York: Hawthorne.
Sansom, M. C.
1982–83 Laying on of Hands in the Old Testament. *ExpTim* 94:323–26.
Sauneron, S.
1960   *The Priests in Ancient Egypt*. New York: Grove.
Schiffman, L. H.
1983   *Sectarian Law in the Dead Sea Scrolls*. BJS 33. Chico, Calif.: Scholars Press.
Schmidt, B. B.
1996   *Israel's Beneficent Dead: Ancestor Cult and Necromancy in Ancient Israelite Religion and Tradition*. Winona Lake, Ind.: Eisenbrauns.
Schwartz, B. J.
1978a   Selected Chapters of the Holiness Code—A Literary Study of Leviticus 17–19. Ph.D. diss., Hebrew University [Hebrew].
1987b   Selected Chapters of the Holiness Code—A Literary Study of Leviticus 19:20-22. *Scripta* 31:341–55.
1991   The Prohibitions Concerning the "Eating" of Blood in Leviticus 17. Pp. 34–66 in *Priesthood and Cult in Ancient Israel*. Ed. G. A. Anderson and S. M. Olyan. JSOTSup 125. Sheffield: Sheffield Academic Press.
1999   *The Holiness Legislation*. [Hebrew.] Jerusalem: Magnes.
Seeligmann, J. L.
1954   Ger. In *EM* 2:546–50 [Hebrew].
Segal, M. H.
1964   *Introduction to the Bible*. 4 vols. Jerusalem: Kiryat Sefer [Hebrew].

Bibliography

Seidel, M.
1978 Parallels Between Isaiah and Psalms. [Hebrew.] Pp. 1–97 in *Studies in Scripture*. Jerusalem: Mosad Harav Kook.

Selms, A. van
1954 *Marriage and Family Life in Ugaritic Literature*. London: Luzac.

Shadal (Luzzato, Samuel David)
1965 *Commentary on the Pentateuch and the Hamishtadel*. [Hebrew.] Ed. P. Schlesinger. Tel Aviv: Dvir.

Shaughnessy, J. D., ed.
1973 *The Roots of Ritual*. Grand Rapids: Eerdmans.

Smith, M.
1971 *Palestianian Parties and Politics That Shaped the Old Testament*. New York: Columbia Univ. Press.

Smith, W. Robertson
1927 *Lectures on the Religion of the Semites*. 3d ed. Annotated by S. A. Cook. New York: Macmillan.

Snaith, N. H.
1967 *Leviticus and Numbers*. NCBC. London: Nelson.

Soss, N. M.
1973 Old Testament Law and Economic Society. *Journal of the History of Ideas* 34:323–44.

Stager, L. E., and S. R. Wolff
1984 Child Sacrifice at Carthage—Religious Rite or Population Control? *BAR* 101:30–51.

Stern, E.
1991 Phoenicians, Sikils and Israelites in the Light of Recent Excavations at Tel Dor. Pp. 85–94 in *Phoenicia and the Bible*. Ed. E. Lipiński. Studia Phoenicia 11. Leuven: Peeters.

Stern, P. D.
1991 *The Biblical ḥerem: A Window on Israel's Religious Experience*. BJS 211. Atlanta: Scholars.

Sun, H. T. C.
1990 An Investigation into the Compositional Integrity of the So-Called Holiness Code (Leviticus 17–26). Ph.D. diss., Claremont Graduate School.

Tadmor, H.
1962 Chronology. [Hebrew.] In *EM* 4:245–310.

Telushkin, J.
1997 *Biblical Literacy*. New York: Morrow.

Thompson, R. C.
1903–14 *The Devils and Evil Spirits of Babylonia*. 2 vols. London: Luzac.

1971
(1908)   *Semitic Magic*. Repr. New York: Ktav.

Tigay, J. H.
1996   *Deuteronomy*. JPSTC. Philadelephia: Jewish Publication Society.

Toorn, K. van der
1985   *Sin and Sanction in Israel and Mesopotamia*. Studia Semitica Neerlandica 22. Assen: Van Gorcum.

1989   Female Prostitution in Payment of Vows in Ancient Israel. *JBL* 108:193–205.

1991a   The Babylonian New Year Festival: New Insights from the Cuneiform Texts and Their Bearing on Old Testament Study. Pp. 331–44 in *Congress Volume: Leuven 1989*. Ed. J. A. Emerton. VTSup 43. Leiden: Brill.

1991b   Funerary Rituals and Beatific Afterlife in Ugaritic Texts and in the Bible. *BO* 48:40–66.

1992   Prostitution (Cultic). In *ABD* 5:510–13.

1996a   Ancestors and Anthroponyms: Kinship Terms as Theophoric Elements in Hebrew Names. *ZAW* 108:1–11.

1996b   *Family Religion in Babylonia, Syria and Israel*. SHANE 7. Leiden: Brill.

Tov, E.
1982   *TaNaK*: Greek Translations. [Hebrew.] In *EM* 8:774–803.

Turner, V. W.
1967   *The Forest of Symbols*. Ithaca: Cornell Univ. Press.

1969   *The Ritual Process*. Chicago: Aldine.

1979   The Anthropology of Performance. Pp. 60–93 in *Process, Performance, and Pilgrimage. A Study on Comparative Symbology*. New Delhi: Concept.

Vaux, R. de
1961   *Ancient Israel*. Trans. J. McHugh. New York: McGraw-Hill.

1964   *Studies in Old Testament Sacrifice*. Cardiff: Univ. of Wales Press.

1968   Le Pays de Canaan. *JAOS* 88:23–29.

Veenhof, K. E.
1966   Review of E. Kutsh, *Salberig als Rechtsakt im Alten Testament und im Alten Orient. BO* 23:308–13.

Vermes, G.
1981   Leviticus 18:21 in Ancient Jewish Bible Exegesis. Pp. 108–24 in *Studies in Aggadah, Targum and Jewish Liturgy in Memory of Joseph Heinemann*. Ed. J. J. Petuchowski and E. Fleischer. Jerusalem: Magnes.

1987   *The Dead Sea Scrolls*. 3d ed. London: Penguin.

Bibliography

Volz, P.
 1901   Die Handauflegen beim Opfer. *ZAW* 21:93–100.
Wacholder, B. Z., and M. Abegg
 1992   *A Preliminary Edition of the Unpublished Dead Sea Scrolls.* 2 vols. Washington, D.C.: Biblical Archaeology Society.
Weinberg, J. P.
 1992   *The Citizen-Temple Community.* Trans. D. L. Smith-Christopher. JSOTSup 151. Sheffield: Sheffield Academic.
Weinfeld, M.
 1972   *Deuteronomy and the Deuteronomic School.* Oxford: Claredon.
 1982   Instructions for Temple Visitors in the Bible and Ancient Egypt. In *Egyptological Studies. Scripta Hierosolymitana* 28:223–50.
 1990   Traces of a Hittite Cult in Shilo and Jerusalem. [Hebrew.] *Shnaton* 10:107–14.
 1993   *The Promise of the Land: The Inheritance of the Land of Canaan by the Israelites.* Berkeley: Univ. of California Press.
 1995   *Social Justice in Israel and in the Ancient Near East.* Jerusalem: Magnes; Minneapolis: Fortress Press.
Weiss, M.
 1984   *The Bible from Within—The Method of Total Interpretation.* Jerusalem: Magnes.
Wellhausen, J.
 1963   *Die Composition des Hexateuchs und die historischen Bücher des*
 (1885)   *Alten Testaments.* 4th ed. Repr. Berlin: de Gruyter.
Wenham, G. J.
 1979   *The Book of Leviticus.* NICOT. Grand Rapids: Eerdmans.
Wessely, N. H.
 1846   *Netivot Ha-shalom.* Vol. 3, *Leviticus.* Ed. M. Mendelssohn. Vienna: Von Schmid und Busch.
Westerndorf, W.
 1972   Homosexualität. Pp. 1272–74 of vol. 2 in *Lexikon der Ägyptologie.* Ed. H. W. Helck. Wiesbaden: Harrassowitz.
Wiseman, D. J.
 1958   *The Vassal-Treaties of Esarhaddon. Iraq* 20, Part 1. London: British School of Archaeology in Iraq.
Wold, D. J.
 1978   The Biblical Penalty of *Kareth.* Ph.D. diss., Univ. of California, Berkeley.
Wouk, H.
 1955   *Marjorie Morningstar.* New York: Doubleday.

Wright, D. P.
  1987   *The Disposal of Impurity: Elimination Rites in the Bible and in Hittite and Mesopotamian Literature.* SBLDS 101. Atlanta: Scholars.
  1991   The Spectrum of Priestly Impurity. Pp. 150–82 in *Priesthood and Cult in Ancient Israel.* Ed. G. A. Anderson and S. M. Olyan. JSOTSup 125. Sheffield: Sheffield Academic.

Wright, D. P., and R. N. Jones
  1986   The Gesture of Hand Placement in the Hebrew Bible and Hittite Literature. *JAOS* 106:433–46.

Yerkes, R. K.
  1952   *Sacrifice in Greek and Roman Religions and Early Judaism.* New York: Scribner's.

Zevit, Z.
  1996   The Eastern Altar Laws of Exodus 20:24-26 and Related Sacrificial Restrictions in Their Cultural Context. Pp. 53–62 in *Texts, Temples and Traditions* [Fest. M. Haran]. Ed. M. V. Fox et al. Winona Lake, Ind.: Eisenbrauns.

Zias, J.
  1991   Death and Disease in Ancient Israel. *BA* 54:146–59.

Zimmern, H. and H. Wincklen, eds.
  1905   *Die Keilinschriften und das Alte Testament.* 3rd ed. Berlin: Reuter and Reichard.

Ziskind, J. R.
  1988   Legal Rules on Incest in the Ancient Near East. *RIDA* 35:79–107.
  1996   The Missing Daughter in Leviticus xviii. *VT* 46:125–30.

Biblical Index

Note: Verse numbers in [brackets] indicate English verses. Leviticus references in **bold** indicate the location of the primary discussion.

Biblical Index

Biblical Index

Biblical Index

Biblical Index

Biblical Index

Biblical Index

Biblical Index

Biblical Index

Biblical Index

Index of Ancient
and Medieval Sources

Index of Ancient and Medieval Sources

Index of Ancient and Medieval Sources

Index of Authors

385

Index of Authors

Index of Authors

CPSIA information can be obtained
at www.ICGtesting.com
Printed in the USA
LVOW01*2039250516

489782LV00004B/5/P